PHILOSOPHERS ON FREUD

PHILOSOPHERS ON FREUD

New Evaluations

EDITED BY

RICHARD WOLLHEIM

Jason Aronson, Inc.

New York

CONTENTS

viii   *Contents*

INTRODUCTION

It is frequently asserted that in our thinking we all nowadays lie in the shadow of Freud: so powerful, indeed, has his influence been that it is all but impossible for us to imagine ourselves out from under it and to reconstruct the mental habits or attitudes of a pre-Freudian age. If this is true, it is so only subject to two heavy qualifications. In the first place, the Freud who has so successfully entered general consciousness bears little resemblance, except in gross outline, to the Freud of reality. In the course of transmission most of his leading ideas have been distorted, in some cases beyond recognition. And, secondly, if Freud's ideas have, in one form or another, overrun the awareness of our age, if they have deeply influenced the minds of intellectuals of various kinds, of artists, of common people, they have barely impinged upon philosophers. The progress of those ideas has been halted at the very point where their arrival might naturally have been expected to be received with most interest and concern. Twentieth-century philosophy has, by and large, gone on as if Freud were a figure of only peripheral significance. And these two qualifications connect. For one of the reasons—though barely a good reason—why philosophers have exhibited such little curiosity about Freud, or why they have found so little in him to take seriously, is that they have accepted the prevailing travesty.

Of course, there are further reasons why in the middle years of this century Freud should have been neglected by philosophers: reasons internal to philosophy, or that revolve upon current philosophical preoccupations. And here a distinction needs to be made. For, if what I have so far said generally about the indifference to, and ignorance of, Freud is true across the total range of philosophical tradition in America, Great Britain and Europe, the more specific reasons that I want to go on to adduce for the philosophical neglect of Freud are more local in application. They relate to academic philosophy as this developed in British and North American universities under the broad title of logical empiricism.

But, first, a reservation. The greatest thinkers are often exceptions to any generalization about their age, and it is interesting that the three philosophers who can make a good claim to be the most distinguished of the mid-century—Russell, Sartre and Wittgenstein— have all given Freud some consideration. It is totally in keeping with Russell's elevated conception of a philosopher that he should have found it intellectually inconceivable to ignore or show disrespect for Freud's innovatory thinking. Any major contribution to scientific culture had to be mirrored in philosophy, and in *The Analysis of Mind* Russell accepts as a specific constraint upon his reconstruction of the concept of desire that it should be able to accommodate the findings of "depth-psychology," as he referred to psycho-analysis. In his social thought, from 1916 onwards, the influence of Freud is even more marked. When we turn to Sartre and Wittgenstein—and I have included in this anthology crucial passages from each—we encounter a relationship to Freud of much greater complexity. I do not simply refer to the fact that both are more overtly critical of psycho-analysis, but both would appear to treat Freud more as a rival than as an intellectual colleague. A rival, we might ask, in what? The relationship between Wittgenstein and Freud, so far inadequately examined, would seem to have been especially ambiguous, and there is evidence, of both a textual and a contextual kind, to suggest that its significance for Wittgenstein was greater than is generally appreciated. There is, however, little reason to believe that any of these three philosophers had an extensive knowledge of the detail of Freudian theory.

Nevertheless, there is a very real difference when we set beside their work the general body of philosophical literature that issued from British and North American universities under the influence of logical empiricism in the period from, say, 1920 to 1965. Russell, Sartre and Wittgenstein all paid attention to Freud, and they paid attention to him specifically for what he had to say about the nature of the mind. By contrast, the philosophy of mind that is associated with logical empiricism was written virtually without reference to Freud; and, in so far as reference is made to him within this whole tradition, it is likely to occur in the philosophy of science. That this is so is the consequence of two heuristic principles powerful in, indeed largely definitive of, that tradition. The first assumption is that philosophy can have nothing to say on any substantive, as opposed to formal or methodological, issue, whether about nature or knowledge. The second assumption is that the scientific status of any form of inquiry can be determined in a totally *a priori* fashion.

It can be determined by considering whether the assertions in which the inquiry issues are or are not deductively related to observation statements: where observation statements are fully specifiable in terms of "sensory" or "experiential" predicates whose instantiation these observation statements express. For—the argument goes—if science were not in this way grounded in observation, and if observation were not in this way a primitive notion, how could science be what it supremely is—an object of knowledge? The more specific consequences of these two assumptions is that virtually the only issue raised about Freudian theory within logical empiricism is the question whether the theory contains, in the technical sense, verifiable assertions.

Representative of this sort of discussion is the collection of papers, all originally contributed to a conference of philosophers and psychoanalysts held in New York in the spring of 1958, which appeared under the title *Psychoanalysis, Scientific Method and Philosophy*, edited by Sidney Hook. Most of these papers are highly critical of Freudian theory as failing to satisfy the demands of verificationism, and I regret that I was unable to include in this anthology the most distinguished of them: I have in mind Ernest Nagel's "Methodological Issues in Psychoanalytic Theory." Unfortunately the piece is too firmly embedded in the discussion that surrounds it to be successfully extracted. The only piece I have included from this anthology, the article of Wesley Salmon, adheres to a more flexible view of scientific testing than was current at the time.

In the last fifteen years or so a number of views have been advanced which have at once led to a more complicated philosophy of science and also attenuated the claim of philosophy to adjudicate issues of scientific respectability. The unitary character of a scientific theory, or the importance of not judging a theory by its parts taken in isolation, has been stressed. The clear-cut distinction between theoretical and observation statements has been disputed, and the claim has been made that all observation is theory-laden. The difference between the truth-conditions of a given assertion—on which, indeed, its sense depends—and the evidence that we might seek to obtain for it or that we might be able to amass on its behalf—matters which are more historically specific—has been argued for, and verificationism has been criticised precisely for confusing the two. And as an extension of this it has been suggested that the question of what is to count as evidence for an empirical assertion, or how we are to test it, may itself be an empirical issue: and this, of course, runs directly counter to the tenet of logical empiricism that the connection between non-observation-statements and the relevant observation-statements is deductive. The conjoint effect of this whole revisionary exercise has been to dispel somewhat the epistemological preoccupations of a narrowly empiricist philosophy of science. It would be premature to say what is the bearing of these views upon the status of Freudian theory, but there is no doubt that the issue will be reconsidered in their light. We can see their influence at work in the articles of J. O. Wisdom and Clark Glymour.

But alongside the more sympathetic consideration that Freudian theory has come to receive within the philosophy of science, an equally interesting development is that it has come to be considered at all within the philosophy of mind. These two developments are not unconnected, and one of the most significant links between them is the gradual decline of philosophical behaviourism. The thesis that mental notions, if meaningful, are of necessity analysable in terms of behaviour or external criteria is a natural application of verificationism to the field of psychology, and in the heyday of behaviourism philosophers could be found who claimed that Freudian theory was after all scientifically respectable because it, or its leading concepts, could be interpreted behaviouristically. Indeed, from this point of view Freudian theory was regarded as superior to old-fashioned "introspectionist" psychology. And it was behaviourism that precluded any recognition within the philosophy of mind of the new complexity that Freudian theory assigned to a significant range of mental phenomena. Errors, dreams, defence, symptom-formation— all these involve or presuppose structurally intricate mechanisms of which philosophy should take note but on which it was likely to say little so long as it was held that they could be fully analysed in terms of their outward manifestations.

It is then precisely to this newly discovered complexity that the contributions by Hampshire, Fingarette, Pears, Thalberg, O'Shaughnessy, Sachs, Weiss and Wollheim address themselves. And it is a fair comment on the state of the existing literature that the majority of these essays were specially commissioned for this anthology. Nevertheless, in one very important respect all depend upon the philosophy of mind of the immediate past. For it was Wittgenstein and Ryle who claimed back for philosophy many problems about the nature or detail of the mind which had been treated by their

more positivistically minded predecessors as irreducibly substantive
and therefore to be left to "the psychologist"—a kind of Unknown
Soldier in the army of science. Without their example it is not easy
to see how many of the essays in this volume could have come to
be written.

One paramount attraction of behaviourism is that it offered a firm
connection between the mind and the body. It is, therefore, a significant aspect of its fall from favour that of recent years philosophers have taken an increasing interest in the other important
philosophical doctrine that effects this connection: materialism. Materialism also, though very differently, links the mind and the body.
And one of the differences between the ways in which the two doctrines link mind and body is that materialism seems to allow some
space—though clearly not of a self-subsistent kind—to the mental.
For, unlike behaviourism, materialism is not a reductionist doctrine.
This is so for two reasons: First, the identities that at any rate contemporary materialism postulates are contingent in character. Second,
though there may be identities that hold between type entities or
events, materialism is satisfied if there are identities between token
or particular entities or events. Materialism has, however, more than
a general relevance for Freud's theory of the mind. Ever since the
original publication in 1950 of Freud's early unfinished manuscript which is now commonly known as the *Scientific Project,* students of Freud have been conscious of the fact that he was and
remained all his life a materialist. At any rate for the founder of depth
psychology the mind's depths were reconcilable with materialism.
And in the last ten or fifteen years the conjunction of complex internal mechanisms and an overall materialism has reappeared in
another theory which both in its general presuppositions and in its
tendency to provoke violent controversy has much in common with
psychoanalytic theory: that is, the theory of transformational grammar. In this volume Robert C. Solomon writes of the *Project* in the
light of contemporary materialism, and Thomas Nagel draws the
parallel between the theories of Freud and Chomsky.

If revisions within the philosophy of science have revitalised the
philosophy of mind, there has also been an influence in the other
direction. Psychology and sociology are, amongst other things, instruments of explanation. But any discussion of the kind of explanation that these sciences provide—an issue that certainly falls within
the philosophy of science—must appeal explicitly or implicitly to a

theory of human nature. For it would seem unlikely that whether a theory provides a good explanation of, say, human actions or human institutions depends uniquely on whether the regularities that it presupposes obtain. Other factors—for instance, rationality—would seem to be involved. Does the theory explain human action only at the expense of rationality, or, alternatively, does it require us to postulate rationality even where this clearly does not hold in reality? To these and related issues the contributions of Alexander, Mischel and Neu refer. Into any such discussion the relations of fact and norm, and the idea of a value-free science, are bound to enter. In a wide-ranging essay, De Sousa argues that Freudian theory at once presupposes certain normative considerations about man and also allows others to be drawn from it. He claims that this is so sometimes to the detriment, sometimes to the credit, of Freudian theory.

It has become increasingly evident that language, man's most distinctive attribute, plays a very special role in Freud's conception of man, and it is safe to predict that in the near future this is a subject that will increasingly gain attention. In this volume Marshall provides the historical background to Freud's view of language—his psycho-linguistics—and he shows how there are not merely structural but also substantive similarities between Freud's views on these matters and Chomsky's.

As I have already said, many of these essays were specially commissioned for this volume. In part this was due to necessity, but I was glad of the opportunity offered since it seemed to me that the time was ripe to initiate philosophical discussion of Freud's many and varied ideas. In having done so I may be charged by some with undue partisanship. I doubt if the justice of such charges can ever be objectively decided, but I would plead guilty to this extent: that I have seen it as my primary task to exhibit the range and wealth of philosophical discussion to which Freud's ideas can give rise. At the moment, at any rate, this is only likely to be gleaned from those who find themselves in general sympathy with Freud's position. I am pleased that in two cases a line of discussion links different pieces into a continuing debate. The pieces by Sartre, Fingarette and Pears, and again by Alexander and Mischel, are in suit.

An incalculable advantage for the present-day student of Freud is *The Standard Edition of the Complete Psychological Works of Sigmund Freud,* ed. James Strachey, in collaboration with Anna Freud, assisted by Alix Strachey and Alan Tyson (Hogarth, London

1953–). So far twenty-three volumes of text have appeared, and the final volume, the Index, is imminent. The student must also feel grateful for Sigmund Freud, *The Origins of Psychoanalysis,* ed. Marie Bonaparte, Anna Freud, Ernst Kris (Imago, London, and Basic Bks., New York, 1954), in which the *Scientific Project* was first published in English. (The original German publication of the text was in 1950.) *The Origins of Psychoanalysis* includes a selection of Freud's letters to Wilhelm Fliess, the recipient of the *Project.* Much of this material is also reproduced in Volume I of the Standard Edition.

In this anthology, all references (except some to the *Project,* which may be to *The Origins of Psychoanalysis*) are to the Standard Edition and they are of the form: 1910c, XI, 133. The second item in any such reference is to the volume number, and the third is to the page, while the first, which is based on a convention borrowed from the Standard Edition, identifies each work by the year in which it was published and its place within that year. For ease of reference I have appended at the back of this volume a list of all such identifications cited in the various essays. I am grateful to Mr. Ronald de Sousa for this suggestion. In compiling the bibliography I have been aware that the distinction between the philosophical and the non-philosophical literature on Freud is somewhat arbitrary.

I should like to thank Katherine Backhouse and Dinah Perry for their work on the text. I have received much encouragement from the general editor of the series.

INTRODUCTION

by Simon A. Grolnick, M.D.

This volume reflects the growing congenial dialogue between philosophers and psychoanalysts. While these disciplines had long reacted to each other as two positive magnetic poles, they now seem attracted by common affective as well as intellectual interests. That the issues of philosophy mesh seamlessly with those arising in the psychotherapeutic situation has become clearer; validation, causality, values, consciousness, space, time, language, symbolism, the mind-body and subject-object relationships, determinism and free will, and the hierarchical levels of knowledge are problems crucial to both.

However, for many psychotherapists these issues exist in covert form. For instance, a patient may ask a therapist, simply, openly, or implicitly, "Can I change?" (Presumably he should not be answered with a philosophical argument.) A philosophical issue, that of free will, haunts the two participants. Eventually each therapist develops a stance toward this question, but one that often cannot be articulated. Reading these valuable papers should provide a more explicit understanding of the methodological and ontological issues which underlie the psychotherapeutic situation. A more sophisticated and wiser therapist will emerge. The more extensive the background with which he can order and test his methods and ideas, the more he can develop the courage and intuition that arise from expanded awareness.

The philosopher authors represented here demonstrate an unusual knowledge of psychoanalytic theory. They are people outside our field, trained in rational argument and methodology, and can conveniently provide us with a "crow's nest view" of psychoanalysis. Interestingly enough, they regard the therapist more as a fellow traveler than as a dangerous enemy seeking to reduce philosophy itself to an obsessional system or infantile complex. American psychoanalysis has missed the active, beneficial cross-pollination that has occurred between various intellectual disciplines in Europe, especially in France. Some of this exciting atmosphere and mutuality is reflected in these papers, enabling them to serve perhaps as catalysts for two important American intellectual disciplines—psychoanalysis and philosophy.

Because of these special qualities these essays may help provide the groundwork for the ultimate creation of a philosophy of psychoanalysis, a field that should take its legitimate place alongside the philosophies of art, history, language, education, mathematics, science, religion, law, and politics. The unique qualities of psychoanalysis, including the fact it bridges so many disciplines and methodologies, point to the real possibility of its own departmental philosophy.

Some of the essays date back two or three decades, but most were written more recently. Actually, the book should be viewed in the context of the publication in 1959 of the proceedings of the New York University Sidney Hook Symposium, a colloquium comprising leaders in the fields of psychoanalysis and the philosophy of science. When *Psychoanalysis, Scientific Method and Philosophy* appeared, as Richard Wollheim explains in his introduction to the present volume, philosophy of science in England and this country was more behavioristically and empirically oriented. Also, it should be added, psychoanalysis was only beginning to emerge as a general ego psychology. The psychoanalysts felt it necessary to defend a scientific, observational methodology and a rather rigid psychic determinism. The result was interesting and stimulating, but the discussion often became a bitter, unconstructive interchange that helped set an alienated tone for some time. When in 1970 the collection *Psychoanalysis and Philosophy* appeared, psychoanalyst Charles Brenner, in a contribution entitled "Psychoanalysis: Philosophy or Science?," was still attempting to distinguish rather sharply between psychoanalysis and philosophy. At another level, he tried to separate psychoanalysis as an observational science and philosophy as an introspective discipline. Brenner cited the problem of the error-producing "personal equation," as it has been termed by astronomers, and associated it with the more complex "countertransference" of psychoanalysis. With the analyst's own psychoanalysis, the "adverse influence of personal bias and incapacity on the use of the psychoanalytic method can be kept to a minimum." This analogy seems forced, for it tends to imply that an analyzed psychoanalytic observer can correct for error *exactly* as the astronomer does when he observes the data of his field. However, the data, or "facts," of the psychoanalytic universe are symbols (verbal and nonverbal), meanings, and intentions. As such, a psychoanalytic "personal equation" is not simply a bias; rather, it comprises the *essence* of the interpretive or hermeneutic act.

The present volume represents a significant widening of perspective on the part of the philosopher of science. And, though not reflected directly here, the median position of the psychoanalytic movement has shifted from the primarily defensive. This defensiveness is perhaps less necessary now, and these responsive essays are a testimony to the increased respectability that psychoanalysis has earned in current philosophical circles. All this is fine, but now, with the philosopher of science reaching out, what will be the response of psychoanalysis? More specifically, how will this affect its accumulated body of theory and practice? As in any discipline, background principles with their elucidating models are at different methodological levels than their pragmatic applications. To reduce confusion, the therapist often suppresses the issues and relies on intuitively acquired guidelines. When this happens, theory too often merges with and seems to dictate technique, resulting sometimes in the typical caricature of the cold, noninvolved analyst, sometimes in equally unfortunate reactions in the opposite direction.

The fact is, there has always been a developmental lag between psychoanalytic theory and psychoanalytic technique. When the issue is raised, we sometimes try to take up the slack by citing passages from Freud which show him acting in a human manner toward his patients in spite of his theoretical blank screen model. The therapist must somehow practice a constant methodological sorting out that keeps theory and application working together, yet does not permit them to be concretely equated. This task is becoming even more complex as psychoanalysis widens its scope, both as a general psychology and in terms of the larger patient population now considered treatable with psychoanalytic methods. Moreover, distinct internal movements have arisen. Those oriented toward a developmental, object relations, preoedipal, preverbal viewpoint—often child analysts—seem to vie with a more conservative group who feel the workable, operative arena for psychoanalysis remains the oedipal level of the personality. The latter espouse the conflict model of neurosis and underplay developmental factors. The developmental framework tends to imply that change results from experience with a new developmental figure, while the conflict model implies that the interpretation of meaning is the essential act. Hopefully a synthesis is ultimately possible here. There have already been attempts (by Gedo and Goldberg) to construct a hierarchical model of the mind using object relations theory to take into account early, preoedipal development, and an interweaving conflict, structural model for issues at an oedipal and, hence, higher symbolic level.

In addition to these trends, psychoanalytic researchers attempting to meet the issue of mind-body dualism are creating new models: computer, cybernetic, classificatory, even molecular. The interest in mind-body identity inevitably takes them back to Freud's "Project for a Scientific Psychology." (In this volume this interest is reflected in Robert C. Solomon's tightly reasoned paper, "Freud's Neurological Theory of Mind," in which he tries to show how the basic psychophysical monism of the Project persisted in Freud's later models.) The Project was Freud's early, materialistic explanation of mental processes. Its recent, seemingly anachronistic revival is hardly welcomed by the conflict theory group. They tend to view psychoanalytic structure basically as a bundle of psychic functions, which seems rather close to a radical idealism. Here the psychic apparatus becomes metaphorical, with no ontological status. Emmett Wilson has written of the ironically empiricist implications of this position. It would seem that many psychoanalytic hands are thrown up in the face of the mind-body issue, and a Cartesian split, implying psychophysical parallelism, is accepted. Possibly the psychoanalyst must function as if the mind-body gap were not only mysterious, but reminiscent of the abyss Emily Dickinson wrote about: "To fill a Gap/ Insert the Thing that caused it—/ Block it up/ with Other—and 'twill yawn the more—/ You cannot solder an Abyss/ with Air."

The picture for the involved therapist is even more complicated by the mounting mass of information from observers of infant states. They are studying the vital interface between sensorimotor gropings and the earliest beachheads of internalized psychic structure. This is the world of Spitz, Piaget, Mahler, and Winnicott. It involves a time when the "body" and the "mind" are as close as they will ever be. This period, extrapolated into the later developing mind, offers us an opportunity for new discovery and conceptualization. It has, for example, led to Piaget's exciting "genetic epistemology." Not surprisingly, Piaget believes that the formation of intellectual thought, and of epistemology, will parallel (but be irreducible to) the stages of development of psychic structure and function.

As the various yet related developments touched on here might suggest, psychoanalysis is now gradually finding its own uniqueness, in interplay with other disciplines. Time is necessary to develop fully a philosophy of psychoanalysis. But certainly such contributions as those bound into this volume will be important steps in this direction.

PHILOSOPHERS
ON FREUD

Conversations on Freud

LUDWIG WITTGENSTEIN

Notes by Rush Rhees after a Conversation: Summer 1942*

When we are studying psychology we may feel there is something unsatisfactory, some difficulty about the whole subject or study—because we are taking physics as our ideal science. We think of formulating laws as in physics. And then we find we cannot use the same sort of "metric," the same ideas of measurement as in physics. This is especially clear when we try to describe appearances: the least noticeable differences of colours; the least noticeable differences of length, and so on. Here it seems that we cannot say: "If A=B, and B=C, then A=C," for instance. And this sort of trouble goes all through the subject.

Or suppose you want to speak of causality in the operation of feelings. "Determinism applies to the mind as truly as to physical things." This is obscure because when we think of causal laws in physical things we think of *experiments*. We have nothing like this in connexion with feelings and motivation. And yet psychologists want to say: "There *must* be some law"—although no law has been found. (Freud: "Do you want to say, gentlemen, that changes in mental phenomena are guided by *chance?*") Whereas to me the fact that there *aren't* actually any such laws seems important.

Freud's theory of dreams. He wants to say that whatever happens in a dream will be found to be connected with some wish which analysis can bring to light. But this procedure of free association and so on is queer, because Freud never shows how we know where to stop—where is the right solution. Sometimes he says that the right solution, or the right analysis, is the one which satisfies the patient. Sometimes he says that the doctor knows what the right solution or analysis of the dream is whereas the patient doesn't: the doctor can say that the patient is wrong.

The reason why he calls one sort of analysis the right one, does

* Reprinted from Ludwig Wittgenstein, *Wittgenstein: Lectures and Conversations,* ed. Cyril Barrett (Basil Blackwell & Mott, Oxford; and University of California Press, Berkeley, 1966), pp. 42–52, by kind permission of the publishers.

not seem to be a matter of evidence. Neither is the proposition that hallucinations, and so dreams, are wish fulfilments. Suppose a starving man has an hallucination of food. Freud wants to say the hallucination of anything requires tremendous energy: it is not something that could normally happen, but the energy is provided in the exceptional circumstances where a man's wish for food is overpowering. This is a *speculation*. It is the sort of explanation we are inclined to accept. It is not put forward as a result of detailed examination of varieties of hallucinations.

Freud in his analysis provides explanations which many people are inclined to accept. He emphasizes that people are *dis*-inclined to accept them. But if the explanation is one which people are disinclined to accept, it is highly probable that it is also one which they are *inclined* to accept. And this is what Freud had actually brought out. Take Freud's view that anxiety is always a repetition in some way of the anxiety we felt at birth. He does not establish this by reference to evidence—for he could not do so. But it is an idea which has a marked attraction. It has the attraction which mythological explanations have, explanations which say that this is all a repetition of something that has happened before. And when people do accept or adopt this, then certain things seem much clearer and easier for them. So it is with the notion of the unconscious also. Freud does claim to find evidence in memories brought to light in analysis. But at a certain stage it is not clear how far such memories are due to the analyst. In any case, do they show that the anxiety was necessarily a repetition of the original anxiety?

Symbolizing in dreams. The idea of a dream language. Think of recognizing a painting as a dream. I (L.W.) was once looking at an exhibition of paintings by a young woman artist in Vienna. There was one painting of a bare room, like a cellar. Two men in top hats were sitting on chairs. Nothing else. And the title: "Besuch" (Visit). When I saw this I said at once, "This is a dream." (My sister described the picture to Freud, and he said, "Oh yes, that is quite a common dream"—connected with virginity.) Note that the title is what clinches it as a dream—by which I do not mean that anything like this was dreamt by the painter while asleep. You would not say of *every* painting, "This is a dream." And this does show that there is something like a dream language.

Freud mentions various symbols: top hats are regularly phallic symbols, wooden things like tables are women, etc. His historical explanation of these symbols is absurd. We might say it is not needed anyway: it is the most natural thing in the world that a table should be that sort of symbol.

But dreaming—using this sort of language—although it *may* be used to refer to a woman or to a phallus, may *also* be used not to refer to that at all. If some activity is shown to be carried out often for a certain purpose—striking someone to inflict pain—then a hundred to one it is also carried out under other circumstances *not* for that purpose. He may just want to strike him without thinking of inflicting pain at all. The fact that we are inclined to recognize the hat as a phallic symbol does not mean that the artist was necessarily referring to a phallus in any way when she painted it.

Consider the difficulty that if a symbol in a dream is not understood, it does not seem to be a symbol at all. So why call it one? But suppose I have a dream and accept a certain interpretation of it. *Then*—when I superimpose the interpretation on the dream—I can say, "Oh yes, the table obviously corresponds to the woman, this to that, etc."

I might be making scratches on the wall. It seems in a way like writing, but it is not a writing which either I or anyone else would recognize or understand. So we say I'm doodling. Then an analyst begins to ask me questions, trace associations and so on; and we come to an explanation of why I'm doing this. We may then correlate various scratches which I make with various elements in the interpretation. And we may then refer to the doodling as a kind of writing, as using a kind of language, although it was not understood by anyone.

Freud is constantly claiming to be scientific. But what he gives is *speculation*—something prior even to the formation of an hypothesis.

He speaks of overcoming resistance. One "instance" is deluded by another "instance." (In the sense in which we speak of "a court of higher instance" with authority to overrule the judgment of the lower court. R.R.) The analyst is supposed to be stronger, able to combat and overcome the delusion of the instance. But there is no way of showing that the whole result of analysis may not be "delusion." It is something which people are inclined to accept and which makes it easier for them to go certain ways: it makes certain ways of behaving and thinking natural for them. They have given up one way of thinking and adopted another.

Can we say we have laid bare the essential nature of mind? "Concept formation." Couldn't the whole thing have been differently treated?

NOTES FOLLOWING CONVERSATIONS IN 1943; RUSH RHEES

DREAMS.   The interpretation of dreams. Symbolism.

When Freud speaks of certain images—say the image of a hat—as symbols, or when he says the image "means" so and so, he is speaking of interpretation; and of what the dreamer can be brought to accept as an interpretation.

It is characteristic of dreams that often they seem to the dreamer to call for an interpretation. One is hardly ever inclined to write down a day dream, or recount it to someone else, or to ask, "What does it mean?" But dreams do seem to have something puzzling and in a special way interesting about them—so that we want an interpretation of them. (They were often regarded as messages.)

There seems to be something in dream images that has a certain resemblance to the signs of a language. As a series of marks on paper or on sand might have. There might be no mark which we recognized as a conventional sign in any alphabet we knew, and yet we might have a strong feeling that they must be a language of some sort: that they mean something. There is a cathedral in Moscow with five spires. On each of these there is a different sort of curving configuration. One gets the strong impression that these different shapes and arrangements must mean something.

When a dream is interpreted we might say that it is fitted into a context in which it ceases to be puzzling. In a sense the dreamer re-dreams his dream in surroundings such that its aspect changes. It is as though we were presented with a bit of canvas on which were painted a hand and a part of a face and certain other shapes, arranged in a puzzling and incongruous manner. Suppose this bit is surrounded by considerable stretches of blank canvas, and that we now paint in forms—say an arm, a trunk, etc.—leading up to and fitting on to the shapes on the original bit; and that the result is that we say: "Ah, now I see why it is like that, how it all comes to be arranged in that way, and what these various bits are . . ." and so on.

Mixed up with the shapes on the original bit of canvas there might be certain forms of which we should say that they do not join on to further figures in the wider canvas; they are not parts of bodies or trees, etc., but bits of writing. We might say this of a snake, perhaps, or a hat or some such. (These would be like the configurations of the Moscow cathedral.)

What is done in interpreting dreams is not all of one sort. There is a work of interpretation which, so to speak, still belongs to the dream itself. In considering what a dream is, it is important to consider what happens to it, the way its aspect changes when it is brought into relation with other things remembered, for instance. On first awaking a dream may impress one in various ways. One may be terrified and anxious; or when one has written the dream down one may have a certain sort of thrill, feel a very lively interest in it, feel intrigued by it. If one now remembers certain events in the previous day and connects what was dreamed with these, this already makes a difference, changes the aspect of the dream. If reflecting on the dream then leads one to remember certain things in early childhood, this will give it a different aspect still. And so on. (All this is connected with what was said about dreaming the dream over again. It still belongs to the dream, in a way.)

On the other hand, one might form an hypothesis. On reading the report of the dream, one might predict that the dreamer can be brought to recall such and such memories. And this hypothesis might or might not be verified. This might be called a scientific treatment of the dream.

Freier Einfall and wish fulfilments. There are various criteria for the right interpretation: e.g., (1) what the analyst says or predicts, on the basis of his previous experience; (2) what the dreamer is led to by *freier Einfall*. It would be interesting and important if these two generally coincided. But it would be queer to claim (as Freud seems to) that they *must always* coincide.

What goes on in *freier Einfall* is probably conditioned by a whole host of circumstances. There seems to be no reason for saying that it must be conditioned only by the sort of wish in which the analyst is interested and of which he has reason to say that it must have been playing a part. If you want to complete what seems to be a fragment of a picture, you might be advised to give up trying to think hard about what is the most likely way the picture went, and instead simply to stare at the picture and make whatever dash first comes into your mind, without thinking. This might in many cases be very fruitful advice to give. But it would be astonishing if it *always* produced the best results. What dashes you make, is likely to be conditioned by everything that is going on about you and within you. And if I knew one of the factors present, this could not tell me with certainty what dash you were going to make.

To say that dreams are wish fulfilments is very important chiefly because it points to the sort of interpretation that is wanted—the sort of thing that would be an interpretation of a dream. As contrasted with an interpretation which said that dreams were simply memories of what had happened, for instance. (We don't feel that memories call for an interpretation in the same way as we feel this about dreams.) And some dreams obviously are wish fulfilments; such as the sexual dreams of adults, for instance. But it seems muddled to say that *all* dreams are hallucinated wish fulfilments. (Freud very commonly gives what we might call a sexual interpretation. But it is interesting that among all the reports of dreams which he gives, there is not a single example of a straightforward sexual dream. Yet these are common as rain.) Partly because this doesn't seem to fit with dreams that spring from fear rather than from longing. Partly because the majority of dreams Freud considers have to be regarded as *camouflaged* wish fulfilments; and in this case they simply don't fulfil the wish. Ex hypothesi the wish is not allowed to be fulfilled, and something else is hallucinated instead. If the wish is cheated in this way, then the dream can hardly be called a fulfilment of it. Also it becomes impossible to say whether it is the wish or the censor that is cheated. Apparently both are, and the result is that neither is satisfied. So that the dream is not an hallucinated satisfaction of anything.

It is probable that there are many different sorts of dreams, and that there is no single line of explanation for all of them. Just as there are many different sorts of jokes. Or just as there are many different sorts of language.

Freud was influenced by the 19th century idea of dynamics—an idea which has influenced the whole treatment of psychology. He wanted to find some one explanation which would show what dreaming is. He wanted to find the *essence* of dreaming. And he would have rejected any suggestion that he might be partly right but not altogether so. If he was partly wrong, that would have meant for him that he was wrong altogether—that he had not really found the essence of dreaming.

NOTES FOLLOWING CONVERSATIONS, 1943; R.R.

Whether a dream is a thought. Whether dreaming is thinking about something.

Suppose you look on a dream as a kind of language. A way of saying something, or a way of symbolizing something. There might be a regular symbolism, not necessarily alphabetical—it might be like Chinese, say. We might then find a way of translating this symbolism into the language of ordinary speech, ordinary thoughts. But then the translation ought to be possible both ways. It ought to be possible by employing the same technique to translate ordinary thoughts into dream language. As Freud recognizes, this never is done and cannot be done. So we might question whether dreaming is a way of thinking something, whether it is a language at all.

Obviously there are certain similarities with language.

Suppose there were a picture in a comic paper, dated shortly after the last war. It might contain one figure of which you would say it was obviously a caricature of Churchill, another figure marked somehow with a hammer and sickle so that you would say it was obviously supposed to be Russia. Suppose the title of the picture was lacking. Still you might be sure that, in view of the two figures mentioned, the whole picture was obviously trying to make some point about the political situation at that time.

The question is whether you would always be justified in assuming that there is some one joke or some one point which is *the* point which the cartoon is making. Perhaps even the picture as a whole has no "right interpretation" at all. You might say: "There are indications—such as the two figures mentioned—which suggest that it has." And I might answer that perhaps these indications are all that there is. Once you have got an interpretation of these two figures, there may be no ground for saying that there *must* be an interpretation of the whole thing or of every detail of it on similar lines.

The situation may be similar in dreams.

Freud would ask: "What made you hallucinate that situation at all?" One might answer that there need not have been anything that *made* me hallucinate it.

Freud seems to have certain prejudices about when an interpretation could be regarded as complete—and so about when it still requires completion, when further interpretation is needed. Suppose someone were ignorant of the tradition among sculptors of making busts. If he then came upon the finished bust of some man, he might say that obviously this is a fragment and that there must have been other parts belonging to it, making it a whole body.

Suppose you recognized certain things in the dream which can be interpreted in the Freudian manner. Is there any ground at all for assuming that there must be an interpretation for everything else in the dream as well? that it makes any sense to ask what is the right interpretation of the other things there?

Freud asks, "Are you asking me to believe that there is anything which happens without a cause?" But this means nothing. If under "cause" you include things like physiological causes, then we know nothing about these, and in any case they are not relevant to the question of interpretation. Certainly you can't argue from Freud's question to the proposition that everything in the dream must have a cause in the sense of some past event with which it is connected by association in that way.

Suppose we were to regard a dream as a kind of game which the dreamer played. (And by the way, there is no one cause or one reason why children always play. This is where theories of play generally go wrong.) There might be a game in which paper figures were put together to form a story, or at any rate were somehow assembled. The materials might be collected and stored in a scrap-book, full of pictures and anecdotes. The child might then take various bits from the scrap-book to put into the construction; and he might take a considerable picture because it had something in it which he wanted and he might just include the rest because it was there.

Compare the question of why we dream and why we write stories. Not everything in the story is allegorical. What would be meant by trying to explain why he has written just that story in just that way?

There is no one reason why people talk. A small child babbles often just for the pleasure of making noises. This is also one reason why adults talk. And there are countless others.

Freud seems constantly to be influenced by the thought that a hallucination is something requiring a tremendous mental force—*seelische Kraft. "Ein Traum findet sich niemals mit Halbheiten ab."* And he thinks that the only force strong enough to produce the hallucinations of dreams is to be found in the deep wishes of early childhood. One might question this. Supposing it is true that hal-

lucinations in waking state require an extraordinary mental force—
why should not dream hallucinations be the perfectly normal thing
in sleep, not requiring any extraordinary force at all?

(Compare the question: "Why do we punish criminals? Is it from
a desire for revenge? Is it in order to prevent a repetition of the
crime?" And so on. The truth is that there is no one reason. There
is the institution of punishing criminals. Different people support
this for different reasons, and for different reasons in different cases
and at different times. Some people support it out of a desire for
revenge, some perhaps out of a desire for justice, some out of a wish
to prevent a repetition of the crime, and so on. And so punishments
are carried out.)

NOTES FOLLOWING CONVERSATION, 1946; R.R.

I have been going through Freud's *Interpretation of Dreams* with H.
And it has made me feel how much this whole way of thinking wants
combatting.

If I take any one of the dream reports (reports of his own dreams)
which Freud gives, I can by the use of free association arrive at the
same results as those he reaches in his analysis—although it was not
my dream. And the association will proceed through my own experiences and so on.

The fact is that whenever you are preoccupied with something,
with some trouble or with some problem which is a big thing in your
life—as sex is, for instance—then no matter what you start from, the
association will lead finally and inevitably back to that same theme.
Freud remarks on how, after the analysis of it, the dream appears
so very logical. And of course it does.

You could start with any of the objects on this table—which certainly are not put there through your dream activity—and you could
find that they all could be connected in a pattern like that; and the
pattern would be logical in the same way.

One may be able to discover certain things about oneself by this
sort of free association, but it does not explain why the dream occurred.

Freud refers to various ancient myths in these connexions, and
claims that his researches have now explained how it came about
that anybody should think or propound a myth of that sort.

Whereas in fact Freud has done something different. He has not given a scientific explanation of the ancient myth. What he has done is to propound a new myth. The attractiveness of the suggestion, for instance, that all anxiety is a repetition of the anxiety of the birth trauma, is just the attractiveness of a mythology. "It is all the outcome of something that happened long ago." Almost like referring to a totem.

Much the same could be said of the notion of an "Urszene." This often has the attractiveness of giving a sort of tragic pattern to one's life. It is all the repetition of the same pattern which was settled long ago. Like a tragic figure carrying out the decrees under which the fates had placed him at birth. Many people have, at some period, serious trouble in their lives—so serious as to lead to thoughts of suicide. This is likely to appear to one as something nasty, as a situation which is too foul to be a subject of a tragedy. And it may then be an immense relief if it can be shown that one's life has the pattern rather of a tragedy—the tragic working out and repetition of a pattern which was determined by the primal scene.

There is of course the difficulty of determining what scene is the primal scene—whether it is the scene which the patient recognizes as such, or whether it is the one whose recollection effects the cure. In practice these criteria are mingled together.

Analysis is likely to do harm. Because although one may discover in the course of it various things about oneself, one must have a very strong and keen and persistent criticism in order to recognize and see through the mythology that is offered or imposed on one. There is an inducement to say, "Yes, of course, it must be like that." A powerful mythology.

Freud's Anthropomorphism

THOMAS NAGEL

Freud was a materialist, and at an early stage of his psychological inquiries attempted to construct an explicitly physiological psychology based on the interaction of neurons. This attempt, by now well known under the title "Project for a Scientific Psychology," was abandoned shortly after Freud sent the draft to Fliess in October 1895. And when he learned in 1937 that Marie Bonaparte had unearthed the manuscript, he sought to have it destroyed.

His subsequent theories were of an entirely different character, for they contained only psychological terminology and did not refer explicitly to neuron interaction. Nevertheless, there is a good deal of structural continuity between the earlier and later views, and Freud continued to be convinced that the psychic apparatus which he was investigating and describing in mentalistic terms was in its true nature a physical system—though too little was known about neurophysiology to permit anyone to think about psychology in physical terms. That is why Freud felt it necessary to abandon the line of investigation represented by the *Project*.

The question therefore arises in what sense it is possible to think about a physical system in mentalistic terms, taken from the vocabulary of experience, perception, desire, etc., without having any idea of the physical significance of those descriptions. This question bears not only on psychoanalytic theory, but also on current disputes about the status of mentalistic hypotheses in linguistics, and in other areas where it is maintained that a mentalistically or anthropomorphically described process or function can be assumed to have a physical realization. What is the meaning of such claims?

Freud was not silent on the subject, and his explanations of how it is possible to think anthropomorphically about a physical system when one lacks an explicitly physical understanding of that system are among the most philosophical passages in his writings.[1] They

[1] Freud often gives the impression of being hostile to philosophy, but in a letter to Fliess of January 1, 1896, he says, "I see that you are using the circuitous route of medicine to attain your first ideal, the physiological understanding of man, while I secretly nurse the hope of arriving by the same route at my

also contain a contribution to discussion of the mind-body problem, which deserves examination.

The remarks which will occupy us form part of Freud's general defense of the existence of unconscious mental states. There are four main locations: *The Interpretation of Dreams*[2], "The Unconscious,"[3] *An Outline of Psychoanalysis*[4] and "Some Elementary Lessons in Psychoanalysis."[5] It will be useful to quote one typical passage at length.

> The hypothesis we have adopted of a psychical apparatus extended in space, expediently put together, developed by the exigencies of life, which gives rise to the phenomena of consciousness only at one particular point and under certain conditions—this hypothesis has put us in a position to establish psychology on foundations similar to those of any other science, such, for instance, as physics. In our science as in the others the problem is the same: behind the attributes (qualities) of the object under examination which are presented directly to our perception, we have to discover something else which is more independent of the particular receptive capacity of our sense organs and which approximates more closely to what may be supposed to be the real state of affairs. We have no hope of being able to reach the latter itself, since it is evident that everything new that we have inferred must nevertheless be translated back into the language of our perceptions, from which it is simply impossible for us to free ourselves. But herein lies the very nature and limitation of our science. It is as though we were to say in physics: 'If we could see clearly enough we should find that what appears to be a solid body is made up of particles of such and such a shape and size and occupying such and such relative positions.' In the meantime we try to increase the efficiency of our sense organs to the furthest possible extent by artificial aids; but it may be expected that all such efforts will fail to affect the ultimate outcome. Reality will always remain 'unknowable.' The yield brought to light by scientific work from our primary sense perceptions will consist in an insight into connections and dependent relations which are present in the external world, which can somehow be reliably reproduced or reflected in the internal world of our thought and a

own original objective, philosophy. For that was my original ambition, before I knew what I was intended to do in the world" (Letter 39 in *The Origins of Psychoanalysis*, p. 141).

2 1900a, V, esp. 612–13, 615–16.
3 1915e, XIV, esp. 166–71.
4 1940a, XXIII, Chapters 4 to 8, esp. 157–60 and 196–97.
5 1940b, XXIII, esp. 282–83 and 285–86.

knowledge of which enables us to 'understand' something in the external world, to foresee it and possibly to alter it. Our procedure in psycho-analysis is quite similar. We have discovered technical methods of filling up the gaps in the phenomena of our consciousness, and we make use of those methods just as a physicist makes use of experiment. In this manner we infer a number of processes which are in themselves 'unknowable' and interpolate them in those that are conscious to us. And if, for instance, we say: 'At this point an unconscious memory intervened,' what that means is: 'At this point something occurred of which we are totally unable to form a conception, but which, if it had entered our consciousness, could only have been described in such and such a way.'[6]

Freud appears to have arrived at this position by the following process of reasoning. If one tries to construct a science of psychology dealing only with conscious processes, the task seems hopeless, for there are too many evident causal gaps. The conscious material is fragmentary and unsystematic, and therefore unlikely to be theoretically understandable in terms that do not go beyond it. It is natural to suppose these gaps filled in by neurophysiological processes, which give rise from time to time to conscious states. And the purposes of theoretical unity are served by supposing that, instead of an alternation and interaction between unconscious physical processes and conscious mental ones, there is a causally complete physical system, some of whose processes, however, have the property of consciousness in addition, or have conscious concomitants. The mental then appears as the effect of a certain kind of physical process.[7]

Further reflection, however, suggests that it may be wrong to identify the mental with these conscious effects, and that it should be identified with the physical processes themselves. These can appear to consciousness but are in themselves unconscious, as all physiological processes are. And since the true nature of the mental processes that appear to consciousness is physical, with consciousness

---

[6] 1940a, XXIII, 196–97.

[7] This is the view expressed in Freud's monograph *On Aphasia:*
It is probable that the chain of physiological events in the nervous system does not stand in a causal connection with the psychical events. The physiological events do not cease as soon as the psychical ones begin; on the contrary, the physiological chain continues. What happens is simply that, after a certain point of time, each (or some) of its links has a psychical phenomenon corresponding to it. Accordingly, the psychical is a process parallel to the physiological—'a dependent concomitant.' (1891b, XIV, 207)

being just one added quality of them, there can be no objection to also describing as mental those intermediate processes, occurring in the same physical system, which do not appear to consciousness even though they may be in many respects physically and functionally similar to those that do. Moreover, as we do not have the requisite physical understanding of the nervous system to be able to think about these processes in physical terms (perhaps we will never be able to reduce them to *cellular* terms), our best hope of progress in understanding the physical system is to think about it in terms of the conscious aspects under which some mental processes appear to us. This is analogous to our use of visualization in thinking about physics—even about physical phenomena that are not actually visible. By thinking about mental processes in terms of the appearances of consciousness, we do not imply that their intrinsic nature is conscious. In fact, the intrinsic nature of both conscious and unconscious mental processes is unknown to us, and both types are merely represented, and not exhausted, by conscious imagery. Thus all of the psychical, and not only the unconscious, is *in itself* unconscious.

> Just as Kant warned us not to overlook the fact that our perceptions are subjectively conditioned and must not be regarded as identical with what is perceived though unknowable, so psycho-analysis warns us not to equate perceptions by means of consciousness with the unconscious mental processes which are their object. Like the physical, the psychical is not necessarily in reality what it appears to us to be.[8]

I want to consider three questions about this view. First, is the analogy with the use of visual imagery in physics accurate? Second, does the view imply a particular position on the mind-body problem (e.g., materialism), or is it compatible with several alternatives? Third, does the view supply a rationale for the employment of mentalistic concepts, taken from the psychology of consciousness, in theorizing about processes of whose physiological or chemical nature we are unable to form a conception?

It is certainly true that we find visual imagery helpful in thinking about structures that are invisible, invisible either because they are too small or because they do not reflect light. Thus we can imagine the DNA molecule as a double helix. Does this mean that we believe that if our vision were acute enough, that is how it would look to us?

---

[8] 1915e, XIV, 171.

Perhaps so; but for some objects, such as atomic nuclei, the supposition that our vision should become acute enough to enable us to *see* their structure makes doubtful sense. It is more plausible to suppose that *if* we believe the hypothetical proposition, it is because we believe something else: namely that there is a similarity in structure between the invisible thing we are talking about and other, visible things that look a certain way; and that this structural feature is responsible for their looking that way. If the structural feature is what we see in the case of the visible objects, then we can use this kind of visual image to represent the same structural feature in invisible objects. Hence our image of the DNA molecule.

An important aspect of such cases is that the structure being imagined can be independently characterized. A double helix can be described in purely geometrical terms, without reference to its visual appearance, and it is the former, not the latter, that the DNA molecule and a visible model have in common.[9] But if the significance of the hypothetical, "If we could see it, it would look like this," depends on the availability of an independent characterization in nonvisual terms, then the usefulness of this example as an analogy for the relation between conscious and unconscious mental processes is problematic. For in the latter case we have no independent way to characterize the unconscious mental process "which, if it had entered our consciousness, could only have been described in such and such a way."

However, we can still make sense of the supposition in terms of the *possibility* of an independent characterization of the unconscious process. We may be supposing that, although we are at present totally unable to form a conception of it, nevertheless it shares features with a corresponding conscious mental process, and that these features are partly responsible for the latter process appearing to consciousness in the form it does. This supposition seems to legitimate the peculiar counter-factual conditional, even if we do not now possess the vocabulary or concepts for describing the common features. They need not, for example, be features describable in the terms of current neurophysiology. They may be describable only in the terms of a future psychology whose form will be in part determined by the development of psychoanalytic theory. And there may be no reduction of the general terms of that theory to the terms of current neuro-

---

[9] Similarly, it is possible to speak of sounds so faint or so high that they cannot be heard by any organism, because we have a physical theory of sound.

physiology (though it is possible that Freud himself thought there would be). I believe that this interpretation makes Freud's mentalistic discourse about what he regards as a physical system comprehensible, and makes the analogy with visualization in physics acceptable, though not so close as might initially appear. Instead of inferring specific similar causes from similar effects, he infers *similarity* of causes in unknown respects from observed similarity of effects.

Our knowledge of the unconscious, he says, is very like our knowledge of another person's mind, for it rests on circumstantial and behavioral grounds.[10] Since we have standard reasons of this kind for believing that certain features of our own and others' behavior have a psychical explanation, and further reasons to deny that these psychic phenomena are conscious,[11] the natural conclusion is that they are unconscious but otherwise similar to the potentially or actually conscious mental processes to which our ordinary explanations refer. Since they do not appear similarly to consciousness, the resemblance must be found in other, presumably physical, characteristics.

Since consciousness does not exhaust the nature of, for example, conscious hostility, it is possible to employ the imagery of consciousness to think about that which is common to both the conscious and the unconscious forms, as we use visual imagery in thinking about the structure of both visible and invisible double helices.

The main difficulty with this view is that it may assume too much, even though what it assumes is less specific than in the case of visual

[10] In neither case does he believe these grounds have to operate as the premises of a conscious *inference,* however:
(It would no doubt be psychologically more correct to put it in this way: that without any special reflection we attribute to everyone else our own constitution and therefore our consciousness as well, and that this identification is a sine qua non of our understanding.) (1915e, XIV, 169)
[11] He may be overhasty in this assumption. His main reason for refusing to extend the analogy with other minds to the attribution of consciousness to the Unconscious is that
a consciousness of which its own possessor knows nothing is something very different from a consciousness belonging to another person, and it is questionable whether such a consciousness, lacking, as it does, its most important characteristic, deserves any discussion at all. (1915e, XIV, 170)
But of course if the Unconscious were conscious of *itself,* then it would have a "possessor" distinct from the subject of ordinary consciousness in the same person, and it would be only the latter who was unconscious of these conscious states of the Unconscious. However, Freud also offers other reasons against their consciousness, namely problems of inconsistency, peculiarity and incoherence, as well as indeterminateness in the number of subjects required to accommodate all other states consciously in more or less unified fashion.

images of submicroscopic or invisible entities. It assumes that there *is* some definite objective character or disjunctive set of characters common to the states that are ordinarily grouped together by their similarity of appearance to consciousness (and their contextual and behavioral connections and significance.) Only if that is true can we pick out a type of state of the nervous system by a mentalistic concept without implying anything about its conscious manifestations. But it is by no means obviously true, at least for many of the examples important to Freud, like beliefs, wishes, identifications.

It is most implausible, of course, that there is a general *neurological* character or set of characters common to all instances of the desire to kill one's father; but that is not the problem. A defender of the Freudian view need not claim that the objective character of these states can be accounted for in terms of any existing physical concepts. Perhaps it is only a developed psychology, not reducible to current neurophysiology, that can accommodate them.[12] But even to assume this, i.e., to assume that an objective psychology, whose concepts refer to physical phenomena, will roughly preserve the distinctions and categories embodied in common-sense mental concepts, is to assume a great deal. (It is perhaps less implausible in the case of sensations than in the case of thought-related mental states.) If this criticism should be correct, and the assumptions of Freud's account too strong, there may be other accounts of the significance of the attribution of unconscious mental states which would involve weaker theoretical assumptions: dispositional accounts referring only to the behavioral and circumstantial similarities, perhaps with an added condition that the unconscious state can reach consciousness under certain conditions. Certainly such accounts have been offered by philosophers. But they are different from Freud's, and in this case

---

12 See, however, *Beyond the Pleasure Principle:*
We need not feel greatly disturbed in judging our speculation upon the life and death instincts by the fact that so many bewildering and obscure processes occur in it—such as one instinct being driven out by another or an instinct turning from the ego to an object, and so on. This is merely due to our being obliged to operate with the scientific terms, that is to say with the figurative language, peculiar to psychology (or, more precisely, to depth psychology). We could not otherwise describe the processes in question at all, and indeed we could not have become aware of them. The deficiencies in our description would probably vanish if we were already in a position to replace the psychological terms by physiological or chemical ones. It is true that they too are only part of a figurative language; but it is one with which we have long been familiar and which is perhaps a simpler one as well. (1920g, XVIII, 60)

his remarks about what he means are not so easily dismissed as the philosophical *obiter dicta* of a scientist commenting on the nature of his primary professional activity.

Let us now turn to the second of the three questions we have posed: since Freud's view is that both conscious and unconscious mental processes are *in themselves* physical—though we can think of them at present only in mentalistic terms—it might appear that he is committed to a materialistic position on the mind-body problem. However, I believe that this is not the case. Freud apparently *accepted* a materialist position, but it is not *entailed* by the views we are now considering. Everything depends on what is said about consciousness itself. Only if it, too, is a physical phenomenon or a physical feature of those brain processes which are conscious mental processes, would Freud's account be materialistic.

In the *Project* this is in fact his position, for he posits a special class of neurons, the ω-neurons, whose activation is in some sense identified with conscious experience. His most careful statement of the view is as follows:

> A word on the relation of this theory of consciousness to others. According to an advanced mechanistic theory, consciousness is a mere appendage to physiologico-psychical processes and its omission would make no alteration in the psychical passage (of events). According to another theory, consciousness is the subjective side of all psychical events and is thus inseparable from the physiological mental process. The theory developed here lies between these two. Here consciousness is the subjective side of one part of the physical processes in the nervous system, namely of the ω processes; and the omission of consciousness does not leave psychical events unaltered but involves the omission of the contribution from ω.[13]

To say that consciousness is the *subjective side* of a certain kind of neurophysiological process is not compatible with dualism, although it may also be a mistake to call it materialism. The view appears to combine the following points. (1) Every conscious mental process is[14] a physical process, of which consciousness is an aspect.

---

[13] 1950a, I, 311.

[14] The identification is made explicitly in the following passage:
Thus we summon up courage to assume that there is a third system of neurones—ω perhaps (we might call it)—which is excited along with perception, but not along with reproduction, and whose states of excitation give rise to the various qualities—are, that is to say, *conscious sensations*. (1950a, I, 309)

(2) The consciousness is not an *effect* of the physical process; its existence is not compatible with the nonoccurrence of that physical process, nor is its absence compatible with the occurrence of the physical process. This view, though not developed, is subtle and interesting. His later views on the subject are probably contained in the lost metapsychological paper on Consciousness, written in the same year as "The Unconscious."[15] Unfortunately it was never published, and appears to have been destroyed.

Freud might have retained the double-aspect view (if that is what it can be called), in which case the other doctrines we are considering could provide a justification for thinking about physical phenomena in mentalistic terms, without implying the existence of any nonphysical processes. It would also be possible, however, to hold that consciousness makes us aware of psychic processes that are in themselves physical and can exist unconsciously, *without* allowing that the events of consciousness are themselves physical. In either case the rationale for thinking about the unconscious psychical in terms of conscious appearances is the same, and the analogy with physics can be appealed to.

But the position that consciousness too is a physical process, or the "subjective side" of certain physical processes, while obscure, is more interesting philosophically. It is worth saying a few words about how such a view may be construed, since it may bear on current discussion of the mind-body problem. Ordinarily, when the phenomenal appearance of something is contrasted with its objective nature, the former is explained as an *effect* of the latter on human observers. Thus ice feels cold in virtue of its effect on our sense of touch, and the physical property which we identify with its coldness—viz., low average kinetic energy—is something distinct from this sensory effect. If a corresponding view were taken about the relation between consciousness and the brain processes of which it is an appearance, then the conscious state would have to be described as an *effect* of the brain process on the subject's awareness, the brain process being something distinct.[16]

The view suggested by Freud, however, is that the brain process corresponding to a conscious state is *not* something distinct from

---

15 See the editor's introduction to the papers on metapsychology, XIV, 105–7.
16 See Saul A. Kripke, "Naming & Necessity," in *Semantics of Natural Language,* ed. G. Harman and D. Davidson (Reidel, Dordrecht, Holland, 1972), esp. pp. 334–42.

the consciousness which is the awareness of it. The conscious qualities do not supply a complete description of the process, since its
objective nature is physical, and consciousness is only its "subjective
side." But consciousness is not an *effect* of this physical process any
more than the surface of an object is an effect of *it*. Nor is it a detachable part. Philosophers of mind do not at present have much to
say about the hypothesis that a neural process could appear to its
subject as a conscious process, without producing subjective *effects,*
simply in virtue of its own subjective qualities. This seems to me a
question worth pursuing.

Let me turn to the last of the three questions posed above. Does
Freud's view provide a justification for *theorizing* about the central
nervous system in mentalistic terms? This question is not, I think,
settled in the affirmative by the discussion so far. We have argued
that Freud's account explains how mentalistic terms, with or without
the implication of consciousness, may in principle *refer* to physical
processes of which no explicitly physical conception can be formed
at present. This does not mean, however, that a useful theory of these
matters can be constructed using the mentalistic concepts, as may be
seen if we return to the analogy with the role of visual imagery in
physics.

Visualization is useful in thinking about molecular or atomic
structure, but most of the important quantitative concepts used in
physical or chemical theory are not represented visually, but more
formally. Even our understanding of the visible world depends on
concepts such as weight, energy, and momentum, that can be represented in visual terms only crudely. Physical theory depends on the
development of non-phenomenal concepts.

Why then should it be expected that our understanding of the
brain can be advanced by theorizing with phenomenal concepts of a
mentalistic type? Desires and aversions, pleasures and pains, intentions, beliefs, and thoughts certainly provide very useful explanations of what people do. But is there any reason to expect that further
refinement and systematization of these explanations will yield a theory of how the central nervous system operates? Freud argues persuasively that a complete theory is not to be expected if we restrict
ourselves to describing the connections among states that are actually
conscious. But is it enough to expand our field of investigation to
include unconscious psychical states, i.e., those that are analogous, in
structure and causes and effects, to conscious psychical states? That

would be like trying to do physics entirely in terms of visible substances and phenomena plus invisible substances and phenomena structurally and causally analogous to them. The result would be some kind of mechanism. Is not psychologism a correspondingly narrow view about the brain?

The idea that we may expect to discover something about the brain by developing mentalistic theories in psychology and linguistics has been revived recently in connection with the mentalism of Noam Chomsky.[17] It is not necessary to offer this as one of the justifications for mentalistic linguistics, which is after all the only promising method currently available for investigating how natural languages function. We can at least try to discover phonetic, syntactic and semantic rules that people talk as if they were following. Linguists have had considerable success with this mode of description of grammar. But it is important to recognize that if people do not *consciously* follow certain statable rules in some area of activity, there is no *guarantee* that rules can be discovered which they may be said to be *unconsciously* following—rules which they behave *as if* they were following, and to which their judgments of correct and incorrect usage conform.

This should be evident to anyone who reflects on the failures of conceptual analysis in philosophy, for conceptual analysis is a type of mentalistic theory that tries to formulate rules for the application of concepts, which users of those concepts speak *as if* they were following. Wittgenstein's *Philosophical Investigations* devotes much energy to combatting the assumption that such statable rules must always be discoverable behind our intuitions of correctness and incorrectness in the use of language.

Moreover, even if a mentalistic theory of the *as if* type succeeds reasonably well in accounting for human abilities or competence in some domain, as has been true of grammar, there remains a further question: what significance is to be attached to the claim that people don't merely talk *as if* they were following certain rules, but that they actually *are* (unconsciously) following them? The grounds for this further assertion are unclear.

Chomsky suggests, without making it a central part of his view, that when a mentalistic theory of some domain like grammar is successful, it may come to have physical significance. His cautious but

[17] See Noam Chomsky, *Aspects of the Theory of Syntax* (MIT Press, Cambridge, Mass., 1965), p. 193.

interesting comment on this possibility, at the end of *Language and Mind,* is as follows:

> I have been using mentalistic terminology quite freely, but entirely without prejudice as to the question of what may be the physical realization of the abstract mechanisms postulated to account for the phenomena of behavior or the acquisition of knowledge. We are not constrained, as was Descartes, to postulate a second substance when we deal with phenomena that are not expressible in terms of matter in motion, in his sense. Nor is there much point in pursuing the question of psycho-physical parallelism, in this connection. It is an interesting question whether the functioning and evolution of human mentality can be accommodated within the framework of physical explanation, as presently conceived, or whether there are new principles, now unknown, that must be invoked, perhaps principles that emerge only at higher levels of organization than can now be submitted to physical investigation. We can, however, be fairly sure that there will be a physical explanation for the phenomena in question, if they can be explained at all, for an uninteresting terminological reason, namely that the concept of "physical explanation" will no doubt be extended to incorporate whatever is discovered in this domain, exactly as it was extended to accommodate gravitational and electromagnetic force, massless particles, and numerous other entities and processes that would have offended the common sense of earlier generations.[18]

This is consonant with the outlook we have found in Freud, but it raises the question how a mentalistic theory would have to develop before its subject matter was admitted to the physical world in its own right. A theory from which the mentalistic character can be removed without explanatory loss is not essentially mentalistic. One might, for example, construct a mentalistic version of Newtonian mechanics, describing the attractions of bodies to one another and their stubbornness in moving in a straight line unless acted upon by an external force (all these psychic states being unconscious, of course). But the explanatory content of such a theory could be given in clearer, more formal, quantitative and non-mentalistic terms.

If, on the other hand, a theory is essentially mentalistic in that its explanatory value cannot be recaptured by a non-anthropomorphic version, then it may be doubted whether the things it describes will

[18] Noam Chomsky, *Language and Mind* (Harcourt, New York, 1968), pp. 83–84.

be admitted to the domain of physics. This is because mentalistic descriptions, connections, and explanations have to be understood by taking up, so far as is possible, the point of view of the subject of the mental states and processes referred to. Even where the mental states are unconscious, the understanding such a theory gives us requires that we take up the subject's point of view, since the form of explanatory connection between unconscious mental states and their circumstantial and behavioral surroundings is understood only through the image of conscious mental processes, with all the appeals to meaning, intention, and perception of aspects that this involves.

Since it appears to be part of our idea of the physical world that what goes on in it can be apprehended not just from one point of view but from indefinitely many, because its objective nature is external to any point of view taken toward it, there is reason to believe that until these subjective features are left behind, the hypotheses of a mentalistic psychology will not be accepted as physical explanations. The prospects for such an objectification of psychology are obscure, as is the form it might conceivably take. But this is a difficult topic which cannot be pursued here.

It should be mentioned that some psychoanalysts have maintained that Freud's theories are already far advanced toward objectivity—that his psychodynamics are impersonal and scientific, that the anthropomorphic terminology is only metaphorical and plays no essential theoretical role.[19] But these claims have been very persuasively challenged in a paper by William I. Grossman and Bennett Simon,[20] which is also an excellent guide to the psychoanalytic literature on this subject. Subjective anthropomorphic thinking seems indispensable to the understanding of such statements as this:

[19] For example, H. Hartmann, E. Kris, and R. M. Loewenstein, "Comments on the Formation of Psychic Structure," in *The Psychoanalytic Study of the Child* 2 (1946), pp. 11–38. Also in *Psychological Issues* 14 (Inter. Univ. Press, New York, 1964), pp. 27–55. The claim that Freud's theories are essentially mechanistic is sometimes also offered as a criticism. See for example A. C. MacIntyre, *The Unconscious* (Routledge, London, 1958), p. 22: "Although Freud abandoned finally and decisively the attempt at neurophysiological explanation . . . it is my contention and the most important contention in this part of my argument that Freud preserved the view of the mind as a piece of machinery and merely wrote up in psychological terms what had been originally intended as a neurological theory."

[20] "Anthropomorphism: Motive, Meaning, and Causality in Psychoanalytic Theory," in *The Psychoanalytic Study of the Child* 24 (1969), pp. 78–111.

The analytic physician and the patient's weakened ego, basing themselves on the real external world, have to band themselves together into a party against the enemies, the instinctual demands of
the id and the conscientious demands of the super-ego.[21]

Psychoanalytic theory will have to change a great deal before it
comes to be regarded as part of the physical description of reality.
And perhaps it, and other mentalistic theories, will never achieve the
kind of objectivity necessary for this end. Perhaps finally the physical
explanations of the phenomena in question will not be reached by
progressive refinement and exactness in our mentalistic understanding, but will come only in a form whose relation to mentalistic theories cannot be perceived by us.[22] Now, as in 1896, it is too early to
tell.

[21] 1940a, XXIII, 173.
[22] A similar view is found in Donald Davidson, "Mental Events," in *Experience and Theory*, ed. Lawrence Foster and J. W. Swanson (Univ. of Mass.
Press, Amherst, Mass., 1970), pp. 79–101.

Freud's Neurological Theory of Mind*

ROBERT C. SOLOMON

Sigmund Freud began his medical career as a neurologist. But this familiar fact is too often treated either as an irrelevancy or as a threat to Freudian theory. It is argued that Freud's genius lay in his acute and even brilliant clinical observations and that these observations were obscured and even subverted by his dangerous tendency to return to speculative neurology. Freud's materialist presumptions, his dedication to the "unity of science," and his desire for a systematic theory of both mind and brain are dismissed as disruptions to psychoanalytic theory. The consequence of this mixture of psychology and neurology is presumed to be a series of confusions and category mistakes. And so, in defense of Freud, psychoanalytic theory is typically separated from neurology, and Freud himself is quoted from those appropriate passages in the later works where he does appear to separate psychology and neurology and endorse a type of psychophysical dualism. This causes some problematic discontinuities, for example, the severing of the quasi-physicalistic notion of "energy" from its materialist moorings. But such conceptual incoherence is even welcomed by analysts who insist upon isolating concepts original to psychoanalysis from similar notions derived from other fields. Accordingly, Freud's lapses into neurological theory and his neurological background are treated as unimportant digressions and influences which can be eliminated without loss of comprehension or theoretical completeness.

Against such objections and interpretations, I want to argue that Freud's "speculative" neurological theory is central to his work from the very first studies to the last summaries and that the basic claims of his entire theory are dependent upon his neurological observations and speculations. Furthermore, I want to argue, with reference to current philosophical theories of mind and body, that Freud's theory does not thereby become a series of category mistakes. Freud is often criticized for his philosophical naïveté, largely on the basis of his "confusing" mentalistic and biological categories and remaining

* Research for this study was supported by The Research Foundation of the City University of New York, faculty grant number 1477. My thanks to Bernard Gendron for his helpful comments.

ignorant of the complexities of psychophysical dualism. I will argue that Freud was not only aware of these problems, but that he was one of the very few psychologists or philosophers of his times (another being William James)[1] who began to see the serious problems in the linguistic and metaphysical conservativism that provided the inertia of Cartesian dualism in psychology. Accordingly, I want to use this occasion not only to explicate an interpretation of Freud's work, but to show how I believe that some ideas which are still rejected in that work can be used to answer a number of long-standing and currently pressing problems in philosophy.

Freud's theory of mind, which he was already formulating in systematic form in 1895, begins with an explicit acceptance of a neurophysiological and partially neuroanatomical model. (This distinction is often ignored by philosophers and psychologists. I shall argue that Freud never gives up his neurophysiological model, but he does give up the neuroanatomical commitments of that model.) In an unpublished, untitled "pre-psychoanalytic" project,[2] Freud writes a "psychology for neurologists."[3] One might begin by claiming that Freud presents a "theory of mind" which is based on the form of, or is isomorphic with, a neurological theory. But the *Project* is more than this. Psychophysical isomorphism, as we find it, for example, in the Gestalt psychology of Wolfgang Köhler,[4] is essentially dualistic. It is of the essence of Freud's theory, I shall argue, that it is not dualistic, and does not even depend upon what is now glibly referred to as the "correlation" of mental and bodily processes.[5]

I have said that Freud's neurology is "speculative." This is not to say that it is unrelated to evidence or that it is wild or unconfirmable. Rather, it is to say that there was little knowledge of the nervous system and its physiology, and consequently most of the hypotheses and theories advanced by Freud were to be investigated and confirmed

---

[1] "Our first conclusion, then, is that a certain amount of brain physiology must be presupposed or included in psychology . . . the psychologist is forced to be something of a nerve physiologist." William James, *The Principles of Psychology* (Dover, New York, 1950), Vol. 1, p. 5.

[2] All page references to the *Project* will be to the Standard Edition and these will be included in brackets in the text.

[3] Letter to Wilhelm Fliess, April 27, 1895.

[4] See, for example, W. Köhler, *Gestalt Psychology* (Liveright, New York, 1947), and his *Dynamics in Psychology* (Liveright, New York, 1940).

[5] Cf. The "psycho-physical parallelist theorem" attacked by Sandor Ferenczi in his *Further Contributions to the Theory and Technique in Psychoanalysis,* (Hogarth, London, 1926), pp. 16 f.

in dissection and experiment only years later. Karl Pribram, a contemporary psychophysiologist who is one of the few scholars to write a serious study of Freud's *Project,* says of the work, "I found that the *Project* contains a detailed neurological model which is, by today's standards, sophisticated . . . The *Project* is very much alive and not just of historical importance."[6] The neurone as the basic unit of the nervous system had just been discovered and named (W. Waldeyer, 1891). The locus of interaction between neurones (Freud's "contact barriers," now known as "synapses" since Sherrington) was just becoming known anatomically and remained a complete mystery physiologically. Most importantly, the nature of the impulses was not known (although Helmholtz had established their approximate speed of transmission), and the relations between anatomical arrangement, physiological processes, conscious occurrences, and behavior were, apart from a few crude correlations, a matter of speculation. It was known, for example, that the "higher levels" of human intelligence were "located" in the cerebral hemispheres, but the neurological theory of mind for Freud (and, we might add, for James) was based more upon an enthusiastic confidence in the rapid development of these new sciences and upon the ultimate heuristic principle of the "unity of science" than upon concrete discoveries of neurological functions.

The absence of nearly all information regarding the mechanisms of stimulation and conduction, and the localization of physiological or psychological processes in the central nervous system left huge gaps which, in Freud's time, could only be filled by sophisticated guesswork, as often as not supported by theories borrowed wholesale from physics, chemistry, and biology as well as common-sense notions of psychology. The rapid advance of neurology fed Freud's speculative enthusiasm. But as the complexity of the problems became more apparent, Freud recognized the deficiencies in his early *Project* and saw that neurology would not provide the sought-after details in his lifetime. For these reasons, Freud discouraged psychoanalytic theorists from guessing prematurely at neuroanatomical functions. He did not publish and rarely referred to the *Project,* and he apparently attempted to destroy it.[7]

[6] K. Pribram, "The Neuropsychology of Sigmund Freud" in *Experimental Foundations of Clinical Psychology,* ed. Arthur J. Bachrach (Basic Bks., New York, 1962), p. 443.

[7] Ernest Jones, *The Life and Work of Sigmund Freud* (Basic Bks., New York, 1953), Vol. 1, chap. 13, pp. 316–18.

Yet the neurological theory remains as what Thomas Kuhn has called a *paradigm* of psychoanalytic theory.[8] Even where it is not mentioned as such, it provides the model of explanation, it circumscribes the data and their interpretation, and it gives form to the psychoanalytic model which is typically but wrongly supposed to be derived from clinical observation and description. As the editors of the Standard Edition tell us,

> But in fact the *Project*, or rather its invisible ghost, haunts the whole series of Freud's theoretical writings to the very end. [290]

THE "PSYCHOLOGY FOR NEUROLOGISTS"

What defines the temperament of the *Project* is its Newtonian demand that "psychology shall be a natural science,"

> that is, to represent psychical processes as quantitatively determinate states of specifiable material particles . . . [295]

The "specifiable material particles" are the neurones; the theory is explicitly a neuroanatomical model. Then, "what distinguishes activity from rest is to be regarded as Q, subject to the general laws of motion" (295).[9] The theory is a working out of the relationship between the neurones and Q. But the emphasis on the newly discovered neurone must not mislead us. The subject matter of the study is ultimately not the neurone but the (central) nervous *system* (*Nervensystem*, not *Neuronensystem*). Freud says, "a single neurone is thus a model of the whole nervous system . . ." (298). But this is misleading, since it is transmission of Q between neurones which is

---

[8] See Thomas S. Kuhn, *The Structure of Scientific Revolutions*, 2d ed. (Univ. of Chicago Press, Chicago, 1962), pp. 10 ff. A paradigm need not itself be explicitly stated as theory. More typically, it is presupposed by the theory. Often the paradigm is openly expressed only in an author's early writings and then remains implicit in his later works. One might compare the relationship between Freud's *Project* and his later work to the relationship between some of Hegel's early manuscripts and his later philosophy. Hegel never published these, and considered them a source of embarrassment. Yet they provide one of the best available clues to the intentions and origins of his mature philosophy.

[9] Q is "quantity of excitation in flow" or, occasionally, "current" or "impulse" or "stimulation." Freud distinguishes, but we need not, Q and Qή, the latter being of an "intercellular" and "lesser order of magnitude," not measurable (at that time). It might be noted that Freud's talk of "activity and rest" and "motion" here represent deliberate and perhaps gratuitous appeals to Newtonian science. Cf. also ". . . only matter in motion" (327).

central to Freud's theory, it is always systems of neurones and not individual neurones which are the subject matter. We shall see that there are important' properties of the system which could not be properties of the single neurone.

The first "theorem" is what Freud calls the "principle of *neuronal* inertia,"[10] "that neurones tend to divest themselves of Q. On this basis the structure and development as well as the functions [of neurones] are to be understood" (296). The cell's divesting itself of Q is "discharge"; "this discharge [of Q*ή*] represents the primary function of the nervous system" (296). Reflex movement is the primary mode of discharge; "the principle [of inertia] provides the *motive* [my italics] for reflex movement" (296). The principle of inertia is a form of what biologists refer to as *homeostasis,* the maintenance of steady physiological states of a system through self-regulating mechanisms. On the one hand, Freud traces the law of inertia to the general irritability of protoplasm of any living cell. But, more importantly, he stresses that the tendency to discharge Q manifests itself in *"flight from the stimulus"* (296). Notice that the neurological model thus rests from the start on a behavioral model. Notice also that the model incorporates from the start purposive or teleological explanations in terms of "tendency," "motive," "flight." These notions, like the "principle of inertia" itself, are ambiguous between mechanistic and purposive models: we shall see that Freud's "hydraulic model" of mind deliberately persists in this ambiguity.

But the principle of inertia requires serious modification. The human nervous system is so complex that it is stimulated not only by "external stimuli," but by "internal" or "endogenous stimuli" (later, "instincts"), from which the organism cannot flee. Accordingly, "the nervous system is obliged to abandon its original trend to inertia . . ." (297). "It must put up with a store of Q*ή* sufficient to meet the demand for a specific action . . ." (297) and "endeavor at least to keep the Q*ή* as low as possible . . . and keep it constant" (297). Freud refers to the tendency to reduce the level of Q*ή* to zero as the "primary function," the maintenance of a low and constant level of Q to cope with the "exigencies of life" (hunger, respiration, sexuality) as the "secondary process."[11]

---

10 Attributed by Freud to Fechner, later called "the Constancy Principle."
11 Perhaps it would be wise to caution the reader against confusing the primary and secondary processes that appear in the *Project* with the processes that carry the same names in the later works. The secondary processes of the

It is noteworthy that Freud first distinguishes the primary and secondary processes on the basis of the behavioral distinction between those stimuli that one can flee from and those that one cannot. In fact, his definitive reason for making this distinction is also psychological, but with a physiological basis. It is one of the peculiarities of the nervous system, Freud tells us, that it can both retain and remain capable of receiving stimuli (302). In psychological terms, we might say that the reflex model so far introduced as the primary process cannot account for memory and learning. In neurological terms, it was already known that excitation might increase or decrease in nerve tissue without discharge. Freud refers to this retention of non-discharged Q as *cathexis*.[12] To account for the psychological data of learning and memory, Freud incorporates the neurological discovery. He distinguishes between two systems of neurones, ϕ and ψ, the former entirely "permeable" (allowing free flow of Q), the latter to some degree "impermeable" (restricting or resisting the free flow of Q). Freud notes with some concern that there is no histological basis for this psychologically based distinction. But he does not maintain, as his language and his interpreters suggest, the existence of two types of neurones in addition to two types of neurone systems. (He attacks, for example, the then current distinction between "perceptual cells" and "mnemic cells"—"a distinction . . . which fits into no other context and cannot itself appeal to anything in its support" [299].) Rather, the difference between neurones is a *functional* difference depending upon their location in one of the two systems. Furthermore, the distinction between ϕ and ψ systems does have neurological support—the distinction between the gray matter of the spinal cord (with its sensory and motor attachments to the "external world") and the gray matter of the brain ("to which the development of the nervous system and the psychical functions are attached" [303]).

The distinction between two systems of neurones can be used to explain learning, memory, and coping with instincts by appeal to the two central activities of the nervous system discharge and cathexis.

Project encompass *both* primary and secondary processes in the later theory of the instincts and their "vicissitudes."

[12] Concerning Freud's notion of "cathexis" (*Besetzung*), Pribram comments, "This emphasis on cathexis is one of those strokes of luck or genius which in retrospect appears uncanny, for only in the past decade have neurophysiologists recognized the importance of the graded nonimpulsive activities of neural tissue . . ." (op. cit., p. 445).

Cathexis is the unique ability of the ψ, or impermeable, neurones. The source of the resistance to discharge which allows for cathexis, Freud tells us, is the "contact barrier" (or "synapse"). The contact barriers of the ϕ neurones offer no resistance: the contact barriers of the ψ neurones resist discharge and allow buildup or cathexis of Qη. Again, Freud warns that this distinction has "an unfortunate tinge of arbitrariness" (303), but that it does explain how "the secondary function . . . is made possible by the *assumption* [my italics] of resistances which oppose discharge" (298). Learning and memory can thus be explained by appeal to the distinction between the ϕ and ψ systems. The resistance of the ψ neurones to discharge varies according to both the amount of Q passed to them from the ϕ system and the number of previous stimulations. The result is facilitation of certain neurone pathways (James's *habit,* the neurological analogue of learning). Through differentiated facilitation of different pathways, Q can follow different courses to discharge. Learning is the development of such differentiation of the ψ neurones, but always leaving the ϕ neurones free of Q and ready for new stimulation.

The notion of "neurones" seems clear enough—the neurone is, as Freud insisted, a "specifiable material particle." But what is Q (Qη)? What is it that "flows" through the neurones? Today we know that the nerve impulse within the neurone is an electrochemical charge at the nerve-cell membrane which results from the movement of ions across the membrane, while the nerve impulse which is transmitted across the synaptic space (between the axon of the transmitting neurone and the dendrite of the receiving neurone) is a release of a chemical "transmitter substance" upon impulse within the first neurone, which stimulates the second neurone. But Freud had no way of knowing any of this. For him, the evidence pointed to the transmission of an unknown substance which could be stored in a cell or passed between cells. Were he the thoroughgoing materialist he is sometimes claimed to be (as he poses in the opening paragraph of the *Project*), he might have pursued his suggestion that what flows is a quantity (thus "Q") of material particles in undetectably tiny amounts within and between neurones. But Freud's thought aims in a different direction with a notion of "energy," and this is clearly borne out in the later theoretical works where "psychic energy" becomes the central variable of the theory. Accordingly, Q is the energy utilized and released by the neurones. Of course, Freud could have no way of specifying what *kind* of energy this would be (i.e., electrical or chemical or mechanical or some peculiarly "psychic" energy). In *Studies on Hysteria,* Breuer had commented that the potential energy of the cell was known to us as chemical but was unknown to us in its state of discharge and in the "tonic excitement of the nervous system."[13] It is, according to Freud, "a quantity—although we possess no means of measuring it—a something which is capable of increase, decrease, displacement and discharge, and which extends itself over the memory traces of an idea like an electric charge over the surface of the body. We can apply this hypothesis in the same sense as the physicist employs the concept of a fluid electric current."[14] Accordingly, Freud's Q has been typically interpreted as electrical current. (Pribram [op. cit.], explicitly interprets it so.) But the editors of the Standard Edition reject any such interpretation:

> nowhere in the Project is there a word to suggest that any such idea was present in Freud's mind. On the contrary, he repeatedly emphasizes the fact that the nature of 'neuronal motion' is unknown to us. [393]

The editors are surely correct in reminding us that the notion of Q is speculative. Yet there is no point in overstressing its unknown quality. While Freud did not narrowly intend "Q" to signify "electrical energy," it must not be supposed that his notion of Q is to be interpreted differently from notions of energy in the physical sciences. The notion is essentially a borrowed notion, and to divorce the Freudian notion of "Q," and, later, "psychic energy," from its physicalistic origins is to rob the concept of its substantial meaning. Freud did not have evidence that Q was distinctively electrical energy; but he did have evidence that Q was some combination of energies (electrical plus chemical), as we now know it to be. So long as the notion of "Q" (or "energy") is tied up to the neurophysiological model, there is ample evidence for the existence of Q. But if the model of the "psychic apparatus" is divorced from the neurophysiological model, the central notion of "energy" becomes little more than a metaphor.[15] It has been argued that the concept of "energy"

13 1895d, II, 193.
14 1894a, III, 60.
15 It is on this basis that K. Colby attacks what I shall be calling "the hydraulic model," of "the psychic apparatus as a series of pipes or passageways in and out of which energy flows like a fluid." But, because he separates the model of the psychic apparatus ("PA") from the neurological model, his central concept of energy begins to look exactly like this metaphorical fluid flowing

cannot be more than a metaphorical and ultimately unjustifiable attempt to construct psychoanalytic theory on a physicalistic basis.[16] In defense, the psychoanalytic concept of "energy" has been often distinguished as an autonomous explanatory concept which does not require conceptual ties to other sciences.[17] Both these objections to and defenses of the concept of "energy" ignore the intentionally ambiguous status it holds in Freud's theories. It is the neurophysiological model that gives conceptual anchorage to the concept. The evidence for calling Q "energy" is exactly identical with the justification for identifying any form of energy, discovery of detectable electric current, and detectable change in activity with addition of chemical substance or electric charge. What Freud could not know was only what kind(s) of energy were involved in the cathexis and transmission of the nervous impulse. This does not mean—cannot be allowed to mean—that Q or "psychic energy" was a form of energy different (or different in "level of abstraction" [Colby, op. cit., pp. 25 f]) from "physical energy." The mistake is to think that "physical" restricts us to Newtonian physics and mechanical energy.[18] The concept of "energy" in Freud's theories comes directly from the biological sciences (specifically neurology) and only indirectly from physics. Since Q, or "energy," is clearly not mechanical energy, it may be admitted from the first that there are serious dissimilarities with the quantitative concept of "energy" in Newtonian physics. (Here the "hydraulic model," taken literally, breaks down.)

Freud knew of the physical existence of neurones and postulated, with ample evidence shared by many scientists of that period, that these neurones collected together as nerves provided pathways for impulses to and from the "higher centers" in the brain. The nature of these impulses was unknown, but not completely unknown. The no-

through a "cyclic-circular" structure that looks not unlike the heating system of a New York tenement building. K. Colby, *Energy and Structure in Psychoanalysis* (Ronald, New York, 1955), pp. 18, 79 ff.

[16] E.g., by L. Kubie, "The Fallacious Use of Quantitative Concepts in Dynamic Psychology," *Psychoanalytic Quarterly* 16 (1947), pp. 507–8, and, more recently, by R. K. Shope, "Physical and Psychic Energy," *Philosophy of Science*, 38 (1971), pp. 1–11.

[17] E.g., K. Colby, op. cit.; and D. Rapaport, "On the Psychoanalytic Theory of Motivation," *Nebraska Symposium on Motivation*, 1960, ed. M. Jones (Univ. of Neb. Press, Lincoln, 1960), and "The Conceptual Model of Psychoanalysis" in *Theoretical Models and Personality Theory* (Duke Univ. Press, Durham, N.C., 1952).

[18] Cf. Shope's argument that "the concepts of *energy, work* and *force*" in psychoanalysis and physics are "quite dissimilar" (op. cit., p. 2).

tion of Q, or "energy," is a theoretical construct borrowed from other sciences to explain both these impulses and their similarities with processes in other sciences.[19]

In a later section, we shall analyze the notion of Q in the *Project* and "energy" in the later works in more detail. Even at this stage, however, we may appreciate how ingeniously these notions bridge the conceptual-theoretical gap between teleological theories of psychology and mechanistic theories of neurology. "Energy" holds a respectable role in Newtonian science while holding at the same time a tradition-honored role in the philosophy of the mind.[20] It is thus that Freud will be able to transcend the crude distinction between the human body as mere "mechanism" and the human person as goal-directed and conscious.

THE PSYCHOLOGICAL MODEL

Where in this apparently neurological model are we to find *consciousness?* It is with this question that Freud's psychological monism fails him just when he needs it most. On the one hand, Freud realizes that the value of his theory is that it does not limit us to a mere description of consciousness in the style of the old empirical psychologists, and that it allows us to treat psychic phenomena as "natural" phenomena and not as mysterious Cartesian substances.

> We at once become clear about a postulate which has been guiding us up till now. We have been treating psychical processes as something that could dispense with this awareness through consciousness, as something that exists independently of such awareness. We are prepared to find that some of our assumptions are not confirmed

[19] Freud was well aware of the problematic status of these theoretical concepts. So in "Instincts and their Vicissitudes," he begins with the recognition that no science, not even the most exact, begins with "clear and sharply defined basic concepts. . . . Even at the stage of description it is not possible to avoid applying certain abstract ideas to the material in hand, ideas derived from somewhere or other but certainly not from the new observations alone" (1915c, XIV, 117). This recognition surely places Freud far ahead of his interpreters and critics alike, who wrongly suppose that the distinction between theoretical and observation concepts is clear, exact and valid independently of a concept's role in a particular theory. Freud's anticipation of the Kuhnian thesis is evident here: we need only repeat that the "abstract ideas" of central importance here are of biological (neurological) origin.

[20] We recall, for example, a dispute between Plato and Aristotle concerning the relationship between tragedy and catharsis some 2,000 years before Freud.

through consciousness. If we do not allow ourselves to be confused on that account, it follows, from the postulate of consciousness providing neither complete nor trustworthy knowledge of the neuronal processes, that these are in the first instance to be regarded to their whole extent as unconscious [*unbewusst*] and are to be inferred like other natural things. [308]

What appears above is not only the germ of the concept of "unconscious psychic processes" which will form the radical foundation of Freud's later theory. We can also see in the *Project* the recognition of a crucial philosophical or methodological point—the separation of a scientific and "naturalistic" account of psychological functions and the very different sort of account that emerges from introspection or phenomenological description. It is only the first that interests Freud. Emphatically, this is not to deny that people "have" feelings and sensations, but only to deny that these have any role as data in a causal theory of psychology. As Freud often stresses, (e.g., in "The Unconscious"), the model of the psychic apparatus is essentially a theory of the *Other*. Accordingly, psychological predicates are not first person observation reports but rather theoretical terms that serve a function in an overall theory of human behavior and psychology. This is not to reject all dualism, but rather to replace the troublesome metaphysical dualism of mind and body with a methodological dualism between science and empirical phenomenology.

But Freud is not satisfied with methodological dualism, and he consequently makes himself vulnerable to the plague of metaphysical dualism throughout his career. Early in the *Project,* he tells us:

> Hitherto, nothing whatever has been said of the fact that every psychological theory, apart from what it achieves from the point of view of natural science, must fulfill yet another major requirement. It should explain to us what we are aware of, in the most puzzling fashion, through our 'consciousness'; since this consciousness knows nothing of what we have so far been assuming—quantities and neurones—it should explain this lack of knowledge to us as well. [307–8]

He insists that his theory find "a place for the content of consciousness in our quantitative psychic processes." The *"quality"*[21] (of

---

[21] This notion of "quality" (of sensations) is common in German thought since at least Kant (see, e.g., his *Critique of Pure Reason,* 2d ed. ("B"), trans. N. Kemp-Smith, [Macmillan, London, 1929], pp. 182 ff.), and it is still evident in the works of recent phenomenologists (see, notably, E. Husserl, *Ideas,* Vol. 1, trans. W. R. Boyce Gibson [Macmillan, New York, 1931], sections 12, 15).

sensations) must be accounted for. But how? In the neurones, there is only quantity. And so it must be that "quality" is not "in" the nervous system but yet determined by it. And here, of course, we return at once to Cartesian dualism.

The "problem of quality" never gives Freud satisfaction. From the beginning, he recognizes that consciousness cannot be accounted for as an effect of either the ϕ or the ψ system of neurones, and so, he insists,

> We summon up the courage to assume that there is a third system of neurones—ω perhaps—which is excited along with perception [ϕ] but not along with reproduction [ψ], and whose states of excitation give rise to the various qualities—that is to say, are—*conscious sensations*. [309][22]

Freud is never sure whether $Q\acute{\eta}$ *is* consciousness, or whether $Q\acute{\eta}$ rather "generates" consciousness. Nor is it clear to Freud *where* in this neurological model the ω-neuronal system is to be located. In desperation, he is forced to abandon any attempt to solve the dualistic "problem of quality" in the context of his monistic model:

> No attempt, of course, can be made to explain how it is that excitatory processes in the ω neurones bring consciousness *along with them* [my italics]. [311]

But if Freud had remained faithful to his own philosophical demands, he might have seen that there was no need to "explain consciousness," and consequently no need for an ω system of neurones.

Yet Freud is not, and need not be, a behaviorist. Motives, memories, pains, and pleasures play an essential role in his theory. They cannot be eliminated or "reduced" to behavioral formulae of any complexity. The remainder of the *Project* consists of a sketch of a general theory of mind, not behavior. It includes a theory of the ego, an analysis of cognition and thought, a dream psychology that remains intact in *The Interpretation of Dreams,* an analysis of hysteria,[23] and attempts to analyze sensation, judgment, motivation, and

---

[22] The use of ω involves a slight pun; it resembles a small *w* for *Wahrnehmung* (Perception). Cf. "Perception-system" in later works.

[23] *Studies on Hysteria* had just been published that year. The main theoretical study in that work, however, was by Breuer, not by Freud. While Breuer concerned himself with a primitive "excitation theory" not unlike the *Project,* and also introduced (before Freud, at least in writing) a notion of "the unconscious," Freud restricted his attention to problems of psychotherapy. See 1895d, II, chaps. 3 and 4.

rationality in neurological terms. It may seem as if there are two separate psychological models operating in the *Project* (and later works) which are confused together and with the third neurological model. The first is what contemporary psychologists call a "drive-reduction model,"[24] a neo-behaviorist non-teleological Stimulus-Response theory which takes "drive"—a state of "arousal"—as an intervening variable and attempts to explain "goal-oriented behavior" according to Thorndike's "Law of Effect" (Hull's "Law of Reinforcement"); i.e., a reaction followed closely by diminution of need or drive will increase the tendency or similar stimuli to evoke a similar reaction. Insofar as Freud's *Project* stresses learning as facilitation of neural pathways following previous discharge and reduction of tension, it parallels such theories. Thus even the editors of the Standard Edition comment,

> it may be an alluring possibility to see him as a precursor of latter-day behaviorism. [293]

Freud also employs a purposive or *teleological* model of explanation in which intentionalistic notions such as "goal," "wish," and "expectation" play a central role. But the definitive conceptions of the teleological model are identical to those of the "drive-reduction model," such as the concepts of "tension" or "urgency to discharge." The notions of perception and memory correspond to the ϕ and ψ systems respectively. From his teacher Brentano, Freud takes the notion of an "intentional object," and the operations of the psychic apparatus are explained in terms of satisfaction and frustration of wishes by such objects. A wish is a motive or urgency directed towards a particular object or type of object. Satisfaction is the congruence of perception and wish. Thinking emerges from an "incongruity" between memory and perception. Dreams are distorted wish fulfillments. A defense mechanism is a memory disconnected from its associated wishes. In primary processes, the object is simply the stimulus, and the wish is either for continuation or cessation. In the more sophisticated secondary processes, the object is an intentional object in a more literal sense, an object in "the outside world."

This synthesis of teleology, cybernetics, and neurology has often

---

[24] See, e.g., Clark Hull, *The Principles of Behavior* (Appleton, New York, 1943); and J. W. Atkinson, *Introduction to Motivation* (Princeton Univ. Press, Princeton, 1964). For a devastating critique of all such theories, see Charles Taylor, *The Explanation of Behavior* (Routledge, London, 1965), pp. 236 ff.

been reproached as "naïve." Critics have delighted in pointing out inconsistencies and "category mistakes." Those who would "save" Freud's theory have accordingly attempted to squeeze it into one of the three models. For example, R. S. Peters and A. MacIntyre have attempted to argue that Freud has only extended the teleological model and not provided alternative (causal) explanations at all; B. F. Skinner has argued that Freud should be purged of all "psychological concepts" in favor of terms of the "explicit shaping of behavioral repertories."[25] And Pribram often appears to be interpreting at least the early Freud as a primarily neurological theory. But Freud is none of these, or is rather all of these, and the charge of "naïveté" presupposes the incompatibility of the three models. Before Freud's early theory is dismissed, it must be demonstrated that there cannot be a single psychological model which is both "drive-reductionist" and teleological as well as neurological, a model which can provide us with what Pribram appropriately calls a "psychobiological Rosetta stone."[26]

THE PERSISTENCE OF THE PARADIGM

At first appearance, it might seem that Freud abandoned the *Project* and its neurological model. He never published it, rarely referred to it, tried to destroy it, and evidently turned increasingly towards psychophysical dualism. Thus we find the editors of the Standard Edition writing,

> And after all, we must remember that Freud himself ultimately threw over the whole neurological framework. Nor is it hard to guess why. For he found that his neuronal machinery had no means of accounting for what, in *The Ego and the Id* he described as being 'in the last resort our one beacon-light in the darkness of depth-psychology'—namely, 'the property of being conscious or not.' [293]

25 See R. S. Peters, *The Concept of Motivation* (Routledge, London, 1958); A. MacIntyre, *The Unconscious* (Routledge, London, 1958); B. F. Skinner, "Critique of Psychoanalytic Concepts and Theories" in *Minnesota Studies in the Philosophy of Science*, Vol. I, ed. Herbert Feigl and Michael Scriven (Univ. of Minn. Press, Minneapolis, 1956).

26 On these issues, see Charles Taylor, op. cit.; Alvin Goldman, "The Compatibility of Mechanism and Purpose," *Philosophical Review*, 78, no. 4 (October 1969), pp. 468–82, and *A Theory of Human Action* (Prentice-Hall, Englewood Cliffs, N.J., 1970).

Again,

> He believed it should be possible to state the facts of psychology in neurological terms and his efforts to do so culminated in the *Project*. The attempt failed: the *Project* was abandoned and in the years that followed little more was heard of a neurological basis of psychological events. . . . Nevertheless, this repulse did not involve any wholesale revolution. The fact was, no doubt, that the formulations and hypotheses which Freud put forward in neurological terms had actually been constituted with more than half an eye to psychological events; and when the time came for dropping the neurology, it turned out that the greater part of the theoretical material could be understood as applying, and indeed applying more cogently, to purely mental phenomena. [1894a, III, 64]

The editors, it appears, are not unsympathetic to dualism themselves. Of course Freud did construct his theory with "more than half an eye to psychological events," and of course it is much easier to formulate a theory of psychology which simply neglects the difficult questions concerning the relationship of psychology to neurology. What Freud attempted in the *Project* was monumental effort, an attempt to overcome the dualism that plagued and still plagues psychology and neurology. But the idea that Freud abandoned the *Project* because of a return to dualism is common. Pribram, for example, tells us that,

> . . . the results of behavioral observations as well as the inferences drawn from them were often couched in neurological terms. These confusions between the behavioral and neurological levels of discourse made these early attempts so 'difficult' that Freud finally abandoned the explicit neuropsychological approach. [Op. cit., p. 443]

Again, we have to appreciate the "difficulty" of such attempts, but we are not willing to admit that they are "confusions." It is true that Freud abandoned the "explicit" neuropsychological approach. But it is also true that he retained an "implicit" one. Or rather, he retains the neurophysiological "hydraulic" model of energy, resistance, discharge, inertia, storing, urgency, and primary and secondary processes. What he abandons is only the neuroanatomical model, the attempt to locate these physiological processes in specifiable anatomical positions in the central nervous system. It is only the "specifiable material particles" that are given up. This is not to say, of course, that Freud supposed that he could apply neurological predicates to anything other than a nervous system. But it is to the nervous system in general, viewed not as an isolated system within a person but as equivalent to something slightly less than a person (e.g., a "patient"), that these predicates apply. Freud no longer hopes that neurology will progress sufficiently in his lifetime for completion of the neuroanatomical model. As his youthful hopefulness gives way to the urgency of advancing age, Freud replaces the anatomy-dependent model of the *Project* with a noncommittal quasi-spatial "psychic apparatus" which provides us with—in contemporary terms—a functional localization of psychic processes without committing us to a mapping of this apparatus onto the brain.[27]

Yet Freud's metaphors are persistently spatial—and these are not, as he sometimes claims, "only pictorial" or "merely expository." The *paradigm* of his theory remains, from the *Project* to the final *Outline,* a neurophysiological model which makes sense only if understood on the basis of a neuroanatomical system, whether or not the "spatial arrangement" of its components has the same spatial (as opposed to functional) localizability in the brain. Freud remains aware of this peculiar modeling procedure. For example, in *The Interpretation of Dreams,* he writes,

> I shall entirely disregard the fact that the mental apparatus with which we are here concerned is also known to us in the form of an anatomical preparation, and I shall carefully avoid the temptation to determine psychical locality in any anatomical fashion. . . . Accordingly, we will picture the mental apparatus as a compound instrument, to the components of which we will give the name of 'agencies,' or (for the sake of greater clarity) 'systems.' It is to be anticipated, in the next place, that these systems may perhaps stand in a regular spatial relation to one another . . . Strictly speaking, there is no need for the hypothesis that the psychical systems are actually arranged in a *spatial* order. It would be sufficient if a fixed order were established by the fact that in a given psychical process the excitation passes through the systems in a particular *temporal* sequence . . .
>
> The first thing that strikes us is that this apparatus compounded of ψ-systems, has a sense or direction. All our psychic activity starts from stimuli (whether internal or external) and ends in inner-

---

27 Cf. James, ". . . in *some* way, it is true, our diagram [of the association of ideas] must be realized in the brain; but surely in no such visible and palpable way as we first suppose" (op. cit., p. 81).

vations . . . The psychical apparatus must be constructed like a reflex apparatus. Reflex processes remain the model of every psychical function.[28]

This sort of noncommittal spatial modeling is familiar to us. "Flow charts," for example, showing functional relations within a computer, a business or political organization, a complex biological process (e.g., photosynthesis, Krebs cycle), are spatially committed in the abstract (to the physical components of the computer, to the individuals and/or offices of the organization, to the biological organism). Yet there need be no mapping onto the physical structure. (The computer circuits need not be arranged in the same physical-spatial order as the flow chart; the president's office might be on the ground floor; the arrangement of structures in the cell or the organism need not correspond to the mapping of the biosynthetic cycle.) Thus Freud retains the crude functional mapping of the *Project,* but gives up hope of locating the components of this map in the physical structure of the brain.

The "theoretical" seventh chapter of *The Interpretation of Dreams* retains virtually every feature of the *Project* except for the commitment to specific neuronal pathways. The distinction between ϕ and ψ neurone-systems is reintroduced as two psychic systems:

> But, as already has been pointed out elsewhere, there are obvious difficulties involved in supposing that one and the same system can accurately retain modifications of its elements and yet remain perpetually open to the reception of fresh occasions for modification. . . . We shall distribute these two functions on to different systems.[29]

In this work, Freud distinguishes between the system *Pcpt* (perception), which is "at the front of the apparatus [and] receives the perceptual stimuli," and the system *Pcs* (Preconscious), which is "the last of the systems at the motor end" which allows "the excitatory processes occurring in it [to] enter consciousness without further impediment. . . ." There is no clear analogue to the ω system of the *Project*. Freud's work from 1895 until 1915 is generally acknowledged to retain some hope of neurological support. But I want to argue that the "change" so often pointed out that then appears is not an abandonment of the neurological model but only an abandonment of that hope for neuroanatomical support. When, for example,

28 1900a, V, 536–38.
29 1900a, V, 538.

he later refers to his entire *Jokes and their Relation to the Unconscious* as "economic" (as when, e.g., "one laughs away, as it were, this amount of psychic energy"), it is clear that the hydraulic model was still with him. After 1915, there is a nominal change, most often pointed out in Freud's own claim in his metapsychological essay "The Unconscious" that "our mental topography has nothing to do with anatomy." But the complete statement in this essay simply bears out our interpretation, that Freud held on to the neurological model (or "paradigm") and gave up, and only *"for the present,"* the hope that the systems of his psychic apparatus could be localized in the brain. A precise conception of psychic topography, he writes,

> touches on the relations of the mental apparatus to anatomy. We know that in the roughest sense such relations exist. Research has given irrefutable proof that mental activity is bound up with the function of the brain as it is with no other organ . . . But every attempt to go on from there to discover a localization of mental processes, every endeavour to think of ideas as stored up in nerve-cells and of excitations as travelling along nerve-fibres, has miscarried completely. The same fate would await any theory which attempted to recognize, let us say, the anatomical position of the system *Cs*—conscious mental activity—as being in the cortex, and to localize the unconscious processes in the subcortical parts of the brain. There is a hiatus here which at present cannot be filled, nor is it one of the tasks of psychology to fill it. Our psychical topography has *for the present* nothing to do with anatomy; it has references not to anatomical localities, but to regions in the mental apparatus, wherever they may be situated in the body.[30]

About the same time he writes, in "Instincts and their Vicissitudes" that his postulate is

> of a biological nature, and makes use of the concept of 'purpose' . . . and runs as follows: the nervous system is an apparatus which has the function of getting rid of the stimuli that reach it, or of reducing them to the lowest possible level.[31]

It has been pointed out (e.g., by K. Colby, op. cit., p. 12) that Freud summarizes his own work as a dualism in his final *An Outline of Psychoanalysis.* But what Freud there denies is, once again, only the *present* knowledge of localization and the idea that *understand-*

[30] 1915e, XIV, 174–75 (my italics).
[31] 1915c, XIV, 120.

ing of psychic processes can be afforded by knowledge of anatomical localization:

> Psychoanalysis makes a basic assumption, the discussion of which is reserved to philosophical thought, but the justification for which lies in its results. We know two kinds of things about what we call our psyche (or mental life): firstly, its bodily organ and scene of action, the brain (or nervous system), and, on the other hand, our acts of consciousness, which are immediate data and cannot be further explained by any kind of description. Everything that lies between is unknown to us and the data do not include any direct relation between these two terminal points of our knowledge. If it existed, it would at the most afford an exact localization of the processes of consciousness and would give us no help towards understanding them.[32]

On the same page Freud restates his theory again in spatial terms without apology or justification:

> We assume that mental life is the function of an apparatus to which we ascribe the characteristics of being extended in space and of being made up of several portions.

And towards the end of the same work, he talks of

> The hypothesis we have adopted of a psychical apparatus, extended in space, expediently put together, developed by the exigencies of life, which gives rise to the phenomena of consciousness only at one particular point and under certain conditions.[33]

Now, why does Freud so persistently pursue these spatial notions? They are not confined to the *Project,* but continue and proliferate into his later work. In, for example, *The Ego and the Id* we again find clearly spatial notions, "interior of the apparatus," "advance toward the surface," "displacement" (of mental energy). If Freud occasionally protests that these are metaphorical and not spatial, it is perhaps only to avoid having his functional localizations confused with anatomical commitments. Otherwise, how can we explain why a gifted writer and brilliant theoretician should have been plagued for forty years by a metaphor, a *façon de parler?*

What persists, I suggest, is the neurophysiological model as the

[32] 1940a, XXIII, 144–45.
[33] 1940a, XXIII, 196.

foundation of the so-called "psychic apparatus" with its essential connection to the brain even in the absence of specific localizations. As Freud increasingly despairs of confirmation of his structural model by neuroanatomical research, he separates his models from neurology, but only in a formal gesture (like the apologetic and humble comments in the preface of a book) which he never really accepts.

THE STRUCTURE OF THE MODEL

What persists throughout Freud's work is a neurophysiological model of mind with its neuroanatomical commitments suspended. This is not to say, of course, that there could be neurophysiological processes without a brain and nervous system. It is rather to admit ignorance—along with Freud—of the exact localizability of those physiological processes in the brain and nervous system. What can be maintained with some certainty is that psychological processes are functionally equivalent to some physiological processes without assuming that the arrangement of such processes corresponds in any specifiable way to the anatomical structure of the central nervous system.

The key to this physiological model is the notion of energy, its sources, aims, objects, and obstacles in "the hydraulic model." While the notion of energy cannot be further specified as electrical, chemical, mechanical, and so on, it is clear that this notion can only make sense when still grounded in the neurophysiological model. It might be noted that this conceptual demand has not changed with the dramatic advances in neurology since Freud's work. We can now specify the nature of neural transmission, cathexis, and resistance in terms of the properties of an ion-sensitive polarized cell membrane and a chemical substance released in transmission. But an adequate description of the nervous system as a whole, whether in terms of "energy" or not, in specifiable anatomical terms is still not available to us. Whether or not such an adequate description could or will be available is a question which a wise neuropsychologist—like Freud —will abstain from answering. Sufficient changes in our knowledge of the nervous system may very well change the concepts and models we will use to describe and account for both the workings of that system and human behavior and thought in general. With Freud, I want to maintain that, for the present, our understanding of the "psychic apparatus" can neither rely upon nor rule out a correlative neuro-anatomical model.

The problem facing Freud is to bridge the conceptual-theoretical abyss between the concepts and principles of psychology and those of neurophysiology. Several problems are involved, not the least of which are those dilemmas which surround the traditional dualism of mind and body. But, before we tackle those dilemmas, there is another set of problems which we have already encountered. I argued that Freud combines teleological, drive-reduction, and neurological models of his "psychic apparatus." The first model is straightforwardly purposive, as defined by Charles Taylor (op. cit., p. 6), and "invokes the goal for the sake of which the explicandum occurs." The last model is mechanistic or causal, explaining its occurrences by appeal to antecedent conditions and general laws according to a (more-or-less) Hempelian-type model. The drive-reduction model holds a somewhat debatable position, and when regarded as successful (e.g., by Clark Hull or Edward C. Tolman), is taken to be an example of the latter model, but, when rejected (e.g., by Taylor), is taken as a disguised version of the former model. Because Freud repeatedly points to the "mechanistic" nature of his model (e.g., 295, 308, 322, 360) it might appear that his model shares the controversies of the drive-reduction model. It is not unreasonable, however, to view Freud's appeal to "mechanism" as little more than verbal appeal, once again, to a Newtonian paradigm of science. But, at this point, it is necessary for us briefly to examine this appeal, for Freud's prejudice that only the "mechanical" is truly scientific is a prejudice shared to this day.

I have several times mentioned the "unity of science" as Freud's working hypothesis. If this precise phrase has come into prominence only in recent philosophy, Freud had a similar if not identical hypothesis in mind. In his *New Introductory Lectures,* Freud says of psychoanalysis,

> As a specialist science . . . it is quite unfit to construct a *Weltanschauung* of its own; it must accept the scientific one . . . the *uniformity* of the explanation of the universe . . . the intellect and the mind are objects for scientific research in exactly the way as any non-human things.[34]

This scientific *Weltanschauung,* Freud insists, requires "objective"

---

[34] 1933a, XXII, 158–59.

explanation of phenomena by subsumption under general (causal) law. But then, as now, this Hempelian claim has been augmented with the demand that all entities, concepts, laws, and theories of every science be *reducible* to basic physicalist or materialist entities, concepts, laws, and theories. Psychological explanation is thus thought to be a threat to the unity of science hypothesis because its entities, concepts, laws, and theories are thought not to be so reducible. But, without argument, I want to stress only the first part of this requirement, not the second. Freud's model of mind must explain public phenomena by subsuming them under general law. The "bogey of mechanism" (as Ryle and others have attacked it) is not sufficiently clear, nor is the need for reduction to materialism or mechanism sufficiently sharp, to trouble our account at this stage. Freud's scientific outlook does *not* commit him, despite his frequent nominal appeals to Newtonian science, to a mechanistic or materialist outlook.

To fill the gap between teleological and causal models of mind, Freud ingeniously employs the concept of "energy." "Energy" serves this purpose in at least two vital ways. First, "energy" is an accepted concept in causal explanations in the natural sciences, yet it does not consist solely of "specifiable material particles" and need not itself be spatially extended or precisely localizable in space. As it is one of the obvious (not to say essential) attributes of mental events that they are, as Descartes characterized them, "not extended in space," it is the energy of a neurological system—and not the anatomical system—to which psychic processes are directly related or identical. Our picture of "nervous energy" has changed, of course, but the principle remains the same. Over and above the specifiable anatomical components of the nervous system, there is nervous activity, the system and its properties, and this activity can be sensibly interpreted as psychic activity. Secondly, "energy" plays more than a causal role in neurological theory. It also manifests a direction, has tendencies, and serves functions in the system as a whole.[35] Thus the notion of energy fits well in teleological explanations. What is essential to this idea of teleological explanation is the idea of function. An event is explained by appeal to its function in a system. What is not essential,

[35] Cf. R. R. Holt, "Beyond Vitalism and Mechanism: Freud's Concept of Psychic Energy" in *The Historical Roots of Contemporary Psychology*, ed. E. Wolman, (Harper, New York, 1968), pp. 196–226. One can also say of a charged particle that it has a direction, tendencies, and serves systematic functions.

but is typically confused with or even the paradigm of such explanation, is reference to consciousness. It is here that Freud's separation of the psychic from the conscious is most important. To say that energy fits into teleological explanations and thereby functions in laws which are isomorphic with psychological laws is not to say that energy—or psychological functions—are essentially conscious. (Cf. Kant's *Zweckmässigkeit ohne Zweck.*)

In Freud's *Project,* the activities of the nervous system, e.g., are accounted for in terms of a teleological or functional model, e.g., "The *function* of the system is to discharge Q." In psychological explanations, Freud offers the same sort of account, e.g., in terms of the function of a desire, of a hysterical attack, or repression and défense. Of key importance is the fact that consciousness need play no role whatever in this account. Moreover, this stress on teleological explanation in no way supposes that teleological explanations are opposed to causal explanations. In psychology as well as neurology, any teleological explanation can be replaced (but not strictly reduced to) a causal explanation. (On this thesis, see Goldman, *passim.*)

We are now in a position to see how Freud's model in the *Project* can be both a teleological and a "mechanistic" neurological model of mind. One and the same set of concepts can be used to signify both the functions of the "psychic apparatus" and the nervous system. This set of concepts will be the concepts of the "hydraulic model," "discharge," "cathexis," "hypercathexis," "repression," "resistance," and so on. It is the always quasi-material notion of energy that allows Freud the theoretical freedom to draw this equivalence. It is the neurophysiological hydraulic model that defines the concepts of his psychic apparatus throughout his works, even after he had given up hope of neuroanatomical localizations of physiological-psychic processes. It should not surprise us, then, as it does most commentators, that Freud's emphasis upon the notion of "energy" increases in his later work just as his confidence in the ability of neurology to localize processes decreases.

MIND AND BODY

I have already indicated that I believe that Freud's theory can best be interpreted as a psychophysical *monism*. Of course, traditional dualist tendencies threaten him throughout, from the problem of

48   ROBERT C. SOLOMON

"quality" in the *Project* to the apparent dualism in the *Outline of Psychoanalysis*. But the thrust of Freud's theory is essentially to deny the distinction between a concept of the mental which is essentially conscious and a concept of the brain and nervous processes which are "correlated" with mental events and states. Where he loses hold of this radical monism, his theory suffers as well, as in the treatment of consciousness in the *Project* and in his perennial struggles to defend the notion of "unconscious mental process" as more than a mere *façon de parler*. It is ironic that most of Freud's critics attack his "philosophical naïveté" in his attempted monism, but not his dualism. The *identity* of mind and body is his most radical and problematic insight.

We have seen in some detail how Freud attempts to derive a theory of the mind and a neurophysiological theory which are identical in *form*. This is not yet to say, however, that mind and the nervous system themselves are identical. What is the relation between the body—or the brain and nervous system—and the mind—i.e., certain primitive or basic mental events, e.g., sensations? The metaphysical dispute surrounding this question since Descartes appears formidable, but there really are a small number of proposed solutions and variations, only one of which seems to be the subject of raging controversy at the present time.

Either mind and body (sensations and brain processes) are ontologically distinct, or they are not. If they are distinct, there is the question of whether they *merely* parallel each other—an intolerable proposal which dismisses the unity of science hypothesis from the outset—or whether there is causal interaction between them. But causal interactionism raises its problems also, since the nature of such causal connections is at best obscure. Moreover, there is the traditional Cartesian problem of how such different "substances" could possibly causally interact with each other. For those materialists who are not yet willing to abandon dualism, there is epiphenomenalism, the suggestion that bodily processes cause mental events but not the converse. But this leaves those entities or laws to which J. J. C. Smart and Herbert Feigl have respectively referred as "nomological danglers," entities or laws which are impervious to further scientific explanation. Thus epiphenomenalism, although it reduces the importance of mental entities to a minimum within the context of dualism, still remains an obstacle to the unity of science. This leaves the (non-empirical) hypothesis that mind and body (sensations and brain processes) are not merely correlated but *identical*. And "identical," in this context, usually means identical to brain processes (since the idea that certain brain processes are nothing but mental events, though this follows from the thesis, would appeal only to an overzealous idealist). It is the identity theory which is the center of the current mind-body controversy, whether it be thought that mind and body (sensations and brain processes) are but different aspects or modes of one and the same *x*, or different features of one and the same *x*, or *x* described from two different standpoints in two different languages. In one sense, Freud agrees with the monism of the identity theory. But in another, philosophically more important sense, he rejects it. Traditional mind-body monism has always been an awkward affair. The nagging presence of pains and sensations haunted those materialists who denied their independent existence. And there were awkward questions, "Does losing an arm entail losing a part of your mind?" Moreover, most mental events were recognized to be—following Brentano—intentional: that is, ideas which are true or false and which might refer to objects which do not exist. Surely there could be no comparable events or states in the body. Consequently, the current dispute over the identity theory does not concern mind and body as such, but carefully restricts itself to the possible identity of certain brain processes on the one hand and sensations (non-intentional mental events) on the other.

We cannot possibly do justice to the intricacies of argument that now populate philosophical journals, but we can localize the two primary points of dispute. First, if the identity thesis is correct, then every property of sensations must also be a property of brain processes and vice versa. According to Leibniz's law, if $p=q$ then every property of p must be a property of q, and vice versa. (This is not to say that we now speak this way, or that sentences about sensations are synonymous with sentences about brain processes, only that they are about the same entities.) Second, the defense of the identity thesis rests upon heuristic considerations of simplicity and parsimony, for the sake of the unity of science. It must be pointed out that there is no more *evidence* for the identity thesis than there is for mere psychophysical parallelism or epiphenomenalism; the difference between these "hypotheses" lies in their ontological and heuristic appeal. Yet it is not at all clear that the identity theory is any more "simple" than its rivals. It only replaces a duality of entities with a duality of aspects, features, or descriptions.[36]

We cannot enter into these disputes as such, but we can enter the problem at a level where these disputes have not yet begun. The particulars to be identified in the current controversy are sensations and brain processes. But here is where Freud can be forced into the mind-body problem. Freud's *Project* is always a *systematic* analysis (as are his later theoretical writings). It is not individual brain processes that concern him, but the nervous *system*. Similarly, he is not concerned with individual psychic processes, but processes of the psychic apparatus. Particular processes, either neurological or peculiarly psychological, always play a systematic role. Using Freud's model, we make what at first appears to be an innocent modification of the identity thesis.[37]

Rather than take sensations as isolated particulars, we will take sensations as a function of Freud's "psychic apparatus." And rather than presumptuously suppose that we have identified specifiable brain processes (which we surely have not) we shall take brain processes to be a condition of the nervous system. But now the identity thesis is not the identity of sensations and brain processes any longer, but the identity of the psychic apparatus and the nervous system and their respective functions. This is, of course, exactly what Freud has argued. But what sort of identity is this? At first, we might say that both the psychic apparatus and the nervous system are nothing less than a *person*, that persons are the particulars that have both minds and nervous systems, sensations and brain processes. But this will not quite do. A nervous system is not a person, nor is a psyche a person. We need something less than a person for our locus of identity. Wilfrid Sellars has suggested a slightly grotesque model of a "core person," "a person defleshed and deboned, but whose nervous system is alive, intact and in functioning order."[38]

---

[36] See, e.g., J. Kim "On the Psycho-Physical Identity Theory," *Amer. Phil. Quart.* 3, no. 3 (July 1966), pp. 227–35, reprinted in *Modern Materialism: Readings on Mind-Body Identity,* ed. John O'Connor (Harcourt, New York, 1969).

[37] One anticipated by T. Nagel, "Physicalism," *Philosophical Review* 74, no. 3 (July 1965), pp. 339–56, reprinted in *Modern Materialism: Readings on Mind-Body Identity.*

[38] Wilfrid Sellars, "The Identity Approach to the Mind-Body Problem," *Review of Metaphysics* 18, no. 3 (March 1965), pp. 430–51, reprinted in *Philosophy of Mind,* ed. Stuart Hampshire (Harper, New York, 1966), and in *Modern Materialism: Readings on Mind-Body Identity.*

I wish to adopt a less gruesome but similar conception, what I shall call a *neuroid*—the person as viewed through the theory of a neurologist. He need not be defleshed and deboned, but the flesh has only the function of protecting the nervous system, the bones of holding it up, the sense organs of providing it with stimuli, the heart and blood of giving it nutrition and oxygen and so on. Now, while the neuroid is something less than a person, we can see that it is precisely the unspecified organism which is the subject of Freud's *Project*. It is at once the subject of both neurological and psychological predicates. In other words, it is both a nervous system and the psychic apparatus. Now, it might be argued that we have only replaced a dualism of entities, features and descriptions with a new dualism of properties and descriptions of the neuroid. But it is at this point that the substance of Freud's *Project* becomes crucial. The properties of the neuroid can be referred to with the concepts of the *Project* without distinguishing—in sense or reference—neurological from psychological predicates. The basic concepts of the *Project*—"discharge," "cathexis," "tension," "hypercathexis," "resistance," "quantity," or "psychic energy" and the like provide the beginnings of the "topic neutral language" demanded by J. J. C. Smart and others. Freud's descriptions in terms of "tension" and "facilitation" refer indiscriminately to psychological and neurological processes; or, more accurately, they refer to one set of processes as functions of the psychic apparatus which are neither peculiarly psychological nor neurological. The Cartesian distinction between the mental and the mechanical can find no expression in such a language.

Freud's monism differs from current versions of the "mind-body identity thesis" in its insistence that both psychological and neurological processes are *essentially* functions of the overall *system* and cannot be treated—even in theory—as isolated processes. Notice that this is in part an empirical hypothesis, but one that has been well confirmed in recent neurological studies. There is no "one-one correlation" between mental events and physical events, for it is now understood that there is no satisfactory way to individuate such events in any way that makes such a correlation intelligible. But such a correlation thesis is not necessary to defend either psychological monism or the unity of science hypothesis. For such purposes, the *functional equivalence* of Freud's precocious model is sufficient;

psychophysiological monism and the unity of science do not need *specific* neuroanatomical correlations.

Karl Pribram has praised Freud's *Project* for its sophistication even by today's standards in neurology. I would like to add that it is sophisticated by today's standards in philosophy as well. As in so many other instances, a work of this outstanding genius of our century has been abused for "naïveté" only because it was too radical to be appreciated in its own time.

Meaning and Dream Interpretation

FREDRIC WEISS

I

A hill, on which there was something like an open-air closet: a very long seat with a large hole at the end of it. Its back edge was thickly covered with small heaps of faeces of all sizes and degrees of freshness . . . I micturated on the seat; a long stream of urine washed everything clean; the lumps of faeces came away easily and fell into the opening . . .

Taking the terms or elements of the dream-report one by one, Freud wrote down what each in turn led him to think of: what he called the "associations" to each part of the dream.[1] Some of Freud's "associations" to this dream-report were as follows: washing away excrement made him think of Hercules' task in the Augean stables. "Urinating over" called to his mind Gulliver in Lilliput, putting out the palace fire with his urine, and Gargantua urinating over Paris. He thought, in connection with the rapid disappearance of the feces, of a motto, *"Afflavit et dissipati sunt* [he blew and they—a fleet— were dissipated]," which he had considered using as an epigraph in an elucidation of hysteria. Human excrement led him to think of the "dirt" he spent his time grubbing about in—whether usefully or not, he had not lately been sure—that is, neurosis. (Someone had recently compared Freud's accomplishments with Hercules'. When he was a student in Paris, his favorite haunt was Gargantua's—the platform of Notre Dame. Aside from the hole, the bench was like a piece of furniture that had been given him by a grateful patient.)

Freud's "associations" each led to some unstated *y* and provided a point of correlation or comparison (Freud said in the *Introductory Lectures,* a *"tertium comparationis"*) between the given element in the dream-report, and the unstated *y*.

For instance, Freud's "association" to the element "I urinate over" —the urinary feats of Gulliver and Gargantua—leads to the notion of a demonstration of towering stature in relation to other people,

[1] 1900a, V, 468-70.

for the relative hugeness of Gulliver and Gargantua was epito-
mized in their "urinating over." The "association," providing a point
of correlation between the given element and the unstated y "I demonstrate towering stature," indicates the meaning which is to be
assigned to the manifest element.

In a similar way, a reader of figurative poetry or prose, or an
observer of films, may be said to think of certain connections upon
noting the given terms, and to apply the connections to the terms
to determine their meaning. For instance, as Freud's "association,"
Gulliver and Gargantua, is a middle term connecting the given x, "I
urinate over," with a meaning, "I demonstrate towering stature [in
relation to others]," similarly, observing in a film the given x, "The
hero, cornered by the panicked mob, stands calmly and raises his
arms, outstretched, at shoulder height," a moviegoer applies to it
the obvious "association" or connection, Christ. This is a middle
term relating the given element to what has to be considered (given
the context in which the element appears), to be its meaning, i.e.,
"the hero shows his forgiving, propitiatory, scapegoat nature."

Again, Freud's "association" to human excrement—the muck of
neurosis, which he spends his time dealing with—allows a reading
of the element "I [easily] clear away excrement," by relating the
given x to the unstated y, "I clear away neurotic muck [with ease]."
To this series compare another from a more familiar field. Given the
element "I am a camera," a reader may think, camera, a mechanism
for recording, an impersonal recorder; this connection allows a reading of the given proposition by relating it to an unstated y, "I record
what I see without becoming involved in it."

When all the "associations" that are immediately forthcoming, and
all the unstated y's, are collected, the second step is to put them
together to assign a meaning to the dream-report as a whole. The
various "associations," and the y's to which they severally lead, operate in a qualifying manner upon one another; and although the
dreamer isolates the elements from one another and "associates"
to each in turn, the final conclusion or interpretation is not a string-
ing together of separate meanings. Given the "associations" to
Freud's dream-report and the part-meanings to which they lead: "I
easily clear away neurotic muck," "I have only to blow and it is
dissipated," "I demonstrate my towering stature," "I show my
heroic nature" (Hercules), and so on, the conclusion that the meaning to be assigned to the dream-report is "I am [shown to be] an

exceedingly great man" is, as Freud once said about another conclusion, virtually "inevitable."

II

What sort of conclusion is it which is (in the above instance)
virtually inevitable? What type of meaning is Freud establishing for
a dream-report? What are the relationships between a dream-report,
the subject's "associations," and the meaning assigned to the report?
The example I used suggests directions in which answers to these
questions may be sought. One of these leads has been brought out,
to some extent, in my re-presentation of Freud's example: Freud's
dream interpretation has similarities to the interpretation of aesthetic objects, such as poems or films. On the basis of these similarities, one can form a conception of Freud's method of establishing
a meaning through "associations" as analogous to the way in which
the meaning of an object like a poem is established, and of his aim as
the same as a literary analyst's: i.e., to find in a dream-report the type
of meaning that a literary analyst finds in a poem. This conception of
dream interpretation seems consistent with Freud's own central tenets: that a "manifest dream" (that is, dream-report, regarded as
equivalent to dream-dreamt) contains, represents, or expresses a
meaning of the dreamer's which is not in general evident in it, but
"latent"; and that, through the dreamer's "free associations," the
psychoanalyst can interpret or decode the "manifest dream": i.e.,
determine the meaning which it contains.

Freud certainly encouraged the view of dream interpretation as
analogous to art interpretation by talking about dreams as if they
were in the same category as things like poems, plays, jokes, or
rebuses—word and picture puzzles—and by talking about the method
of establishing a meaning in such a way as to bring out its similarities
to the interpretation of aesthetic objects. But as soon as the view of
dream interpretation as activity analogous to art interpretation is
expanded, it begins to run into difficulties. That someone connects
a given element with some middle term which relates the element
to an unstated y does not in itself establish that the meaning, y, is
conveyed by or implicit in the element. It is possible—for instance,
in reading poetry—to arrive at a meaning for oneself which is not
the or a meaning borne by the piece. One may do so by glancing at

a poem and slapping a meaning on it, or one may do so by a parody of the procedure by which the meaning of the poem may be correctly determined.

There are no doubt various criteria which allow one to judge that the meaning of a piece of literature is or is not being discovered, or to distinguish between a correct or allowable interpretation and a case of reading in or donating meaning. Even authors are not exempt from donating meaning to works of their own; and even authors, though privileged above others in some aspects of interpretation, can be counted right or wrong in supplying connections to the terms of a work (whether as support for a reading or as a step toward formulating one).

The essential and minimal criterion which would allow one to argue that the meaning-of a thing like a film or poem was being determined, through anyone's connections, would seem to be that the connections and the part-meanings, and the meaning-of-the-whole that they lead to, should be consistent with the context constituted by the piece: with its discernible sense, point, direction, tendency, thesis, "tone," whatever content of direct or non-figurative statement it had, whatever part-meanings were evident or readily discernible in it, and so on.

Obviously, this criterion cannot be applied in the case of dreams. In general, a dream-report has no appearance of constituting a context against which "associations" could be measured for consistency. Freud points out, in effect, that most dream-reports have no discernible sense, point, or direction, no thesis, no content that is clear or direct, no discernible part-meanings, no other ingredients of a context. He claims as exceptions to the rule of no context, reports of many children's dreams and certain "dreams of convenience," which, he holds, have evident sense and tendency. On the obviousness or discernibility of their meaning, not to speak of the frequency of their occurrence, Freud might be questioned. But the most important question in regard to them is this: supposing that the dreamer offered "associations" to such a report, which nothing in the context it constituted or seemed to constitute could support, and which did not fit its apparent sense, would Freud count the "associations" wrong, or reject a meaning they established?

Freud would never have counted wrong his "associations" to the report I quoted earlier on the ground that their tone was cheerful and self-assertive, whereas the dream-report, while devoid of tone and of sense or point, included no elements compatible with cheer or self-assertion, and did include some which, if occurring in literature (or for that matter in life) would be expected to call for feelings incompatible with those expressed in the "associations." Freud would never say, as one reader of literature may say to another, "How do you think the text justifies that reading? There is nothing there even to suggest it." Or, for instance, "Go back; you are making some mistake: the text is quite straightforward and you are making something odd and mysterious of it."

Freud does not apply to "associations" the criterion of consistency with context which is used to judge an interpretation of a poem as correct or incorrect. Moreover, he makes no attempt to measure a person's "associations" against *any* criterion, to judge them right or wrong, allowable or not allowable. On the contrary, what is not allowable in dream interpretation is that the subject should try to discriminate among the thoughts which his dream-report suggests to him, or withhold anything that occurs to him in connection with it. Anything goes, so long as it is a complete and sincere account of what the report leads the subject to think of (or, indeed, whatever comes into his head: e.g., what the "associations" he has already uttered lead him to think of). If Freud ever said anything like, "No, you're not giving the right associations," it was to accuse the subject of withholding something that occurred to him, stalling, or substituting a second for a first thought; but second thoughts are not counted wrong. And when the subject has done "associating," the analyst does not try to sort out the "associations" on any such ground as plausibility in relation to the dream-report: he weeds out nothing. "Right," "wrong," "allowable," "not allowable," "plausible," "far-fetched," "relevant," "extraneous," and any other such characterizations do not apply to "associations." If the subject's "associations" do lead to a meaning, that is the meaning which the psychoanalyst assigns to the dream-report: it cannot be rejected on any such ground as incompatibility with the dream-report, and the analyst makes no attempt to reject it on any ground.

III

Freud's method of establishing a meaning for a dream-report is not a way in which to determine a meaning that is conveyed, represented, or expressed by an object, which *anyone,* including the author, may interpret correctly or misinterpret. Does this mean that Freud's use of "associations" excludes the attempt to determine any meaning that may be inherent in a dream-report? Not necessarily. Dream-reports may have another sort of intrinsic meaning than that of aesthetic objects: Freud might attempt to determine this other meaning through a person's "associations."

However, in many instances, Freud uses dream-reports and "associations" in such ways that he gives every indication of foregoing the attempt to discover *any* sort of meaning that may be inherent in a dream-report.

The example of Freud's "associations" to his dream-report of the outdoor closet is atypical, especially in the abbreviated form in which I quoted it: the example was chosen precisely because it gave the clearest possible illustration of the way in which "associations" may lead to a meaning which can be assigned to a dream-report. Even in that case, as Freud presents it, there were many "associations" which, while related to the other "associations," were not themselves related to the elements of the dream-report in such a way as to allow the assignment of meaning to them. And of course Freud's presentation was a condensed version of his original "dream-analysis." In psychoanalysis, trains of "associations" may be pursued at considerable length, not only during one session, but for some time, now temporarily dropped, now interrupted for consideration of some other topic, and again resumed. They are evidently pursued for the sake of whatever they may be leading to, providing that what they are leading to is or reveals something about the subject—e.g., his feelings toward his friends. There may be no attempt to assign everything to which the "associations" lead, to the dream-report as its meaning. All reference to the dream-report may be dropped; the question of what meaning is to be assigned to it tends to fade out of consideration.

When meaning is assigned, it is, of course, assigned to the dream-report. But although the meaning established through "associations" is supposed to be inherent in the report, that object, the report, may be of a very tenuous character. What is presented as a dream-report may be, in the subject's estimation, incomplete, vague, fragmentary, and/or uncertain. Freud supposed that many if not most dream-reports were garbled, embellished, truncated, or mutilated; there may be particular reason to suppose that a report has gathered additions or suffered subtractions, e.g., because it is weeks, months, or even years old. Freud accepts all such reports as equal in "interpretability" to any others. He helps patients to "reconstruct" reports from the briefest fragments. He accepts all interpolations and afterthought additions as parts of the object, the report: but if there are no afterthoughts, he accepts a report as complete.

And Freud makes no effort to preserve the identity of the dream-report in distinction from the "associations." There is no line of demarcation between report and "associations" like, for instance, the line between a poem and third terms that are brought forward toward its interpretation: anything pertaining to a dream-report may be regarded as part of the report if a meaning can be assigned to it through the "associations." If there are "associations" to some remark made, apparently outside the report, in presenting it, or to any such thing, the remark is regarded as being an element of the report and is assigned a part-meaning. Freud regards a verbal oddity (which may occur in one, but not another, recital of the report), an apparently accidental hesitation, or the like, as a significant part of the report, if there are "associations" which give significance to it. Once, in writing down a dream-report of his own, Freud made a slip of the pen, repeating a phrase. He let the slip stand, regarding it as a meaningful part of the report, "since," he said, "the analysis showed that it was significant"—i.e., since there were "associations" which connected it with a meaning.[2] If there are "associations" to what might be regarded as qualities of uncertainty or fragmentariness in the report, Freud treats these qualities, or rather the words in which they are mentioned by the subject, as meaningful parts or aspects of the dream-report. Once, in presenting a dream-report, a patient remarked: "Here there are some gaps in the dream; there's something missing." The patient connected this statement of his with a distant fantasy of observing female genitalia. Freud then regarded the remark as part of the report, the meaning of which was revealed by the connection.[3]

What Freud does in dream interpretation, at least in a great many instances, is antithetical to an attempt to discover any meaning that may be inherent in a dream-report—unless, as Freud contends, a person's "associations" to his "manifest dream" *must* be leading, and

[2] 1900a, IV, 210 and note.
[3] 1900a, IV, 332–33.

can only be leading, to the meaning that it contains. In the light of Freud's actions in dream-analysis, the contention that there is such a necessary link between "associations," dream-report, and "latent content" needs strong justification.

But Freud offers no such justification. He does anticipate the possible objection of a skeptical observer, that his claim to be reaching a "pre-existing goal"—i.e., the meaning inherent in the "manifest dream"—by "following the drift" of what may be an "aimless and arbitrary train of thoughts"—i.e., the "associations"—seems unwarranted. And in reply he offers some considerations which he thinks support his view.

These are, that it is implausible that the many, varied, complicated, and often unexpected relationships among the "associations" and between "associations" and elements of a "manifest dream" could exist, were there not "connections already laid down" among these thoughts; that it is highly unlikely that anything which gives such an "exhaustive account of the dream" as the "associations" could be doing anything other than revealing its meaning; and that, in any case, there is no genuinely random, aimless, or arbitrary thinking except in cases of destructive organic cerebral processes; that when thought and utterance are not guided by conscious intention, they are directed by unconscious purposive ideas; and that when the dreamer, giving over conscious control of his thought processes, allows himself to utter whatever occurs to him in connection with his dream-report, what he says must be so directed (toward the meaning inherent in the report).[4]

Indeed, there are many, varied, complicated, and unexpected relationships among the "associations," and between them and elements of the dream-report. (E.g., a theme started in a train of "associations" to one element may be expanded, qualified, and clarified in another train of "associations"; or something which is an element in the dream-report may turn up unexpectedly at the end of a train of "associations" that seemed to be leading nowhere in particular, but which now places this element in a context in which it makes sense in relation to a theme being developed.) Undoubtedly, the "associations" are usually leading somewhere. And, at least sometimes, they are leading to a meaning which can be assigned to the dream-report; and this meaning may be more or less "exhaustive,"

[4] 1900a, V, 527–32.

i.e., elaborate, complex, and/or many-layered. The complexity, multiplicity, and unexpectedness of the relationships among the "associations" may be taken as indicating that these "thoughts" *are* related (e.g., they all have a bearing, directly or indirectly, on some concern of the subject's): that they are not just a random drift of notions, among which *ad hoc* connections happen to arise. That the "associations" do lead to something may be taken as indicating that they are, so to speak, guided by something (e.g., by concerns or emotions of the subject's). All these considerations may be taken, jointly and severally, as indicating that the "associations" are not random, arbitrary, unrelated, aimless chains of thoughts, such as are characteristic of destructive organic cerebral processes. But this is hardly surprising, since the subject who "associates" is not suffering cerebral degeneration.

What Freud offers in place of a justification for his contention that a person's "associations" must be and can only be leading to the "latent content" of his "manifest dream" comes down to a choice between two alternative possibilities—that the "associations" are leading to the meaning contained in the dream-report, and that they are leading nowhere—and an assumption that if a person's "associations" are (unconsciously) guided or directed, they must be guided toward the inherent meaning of his dream or dream-report, and to no other "goal."

But this is not all Freud offers in place of justification for his contention: he also has a framework, within which his considerations are placed, which starts from his choice and his assumption, and allows one to picture the way in which a person's "associations" are directed by an "unconscious purposive idea": that is, precisely the "unconscious purposive idea" which underlies the "pre-existing goal," the meaning contained in the "manifest dream." Freud legislates the legitimacy of his contention that the "associations" are leading to the meaning contained in the dream-report by asserting that they are reproducing a mirror image of themselves, which lies behind them. That is, he holds that a person's "associations" to his dream-report are equivalent to the "dream-thoughts" out of which, through a "process of dream-work," including "condensation and displacement of psychical values," his dream was formed. Freud conceives of the process of interpretation ("manifest dream"→"associations"→

meaning) as an approximate reversal of the process of "dream-formation" (meaning→"dream-thoughts"→"manifest dream").[5]

Freud's picture is of a "manifest dream" as a sort of switchboard, consisting of a few "ideas," in which are stored, in concentrated form, the "psychical values" belonging to a great many "thoughts." These values have been collected by a current—an "unconscious purposive idea" or "wish"—which has added them to itself by moving among the thoughts, laying down lines or circuits of relationship or association among them as pathways for its movement. When a person confronts his "manifest dream" and allows himself to utter whatever may occur to him in connection with it, he is plugging himself into the switchboard. Naturally, what went into it must then issue from it, and no other current can come from it to direct the subject's thoughts than what went in. This current—the "unconscious purposive idea" which brought about the formation of the dream—runs backward along the lines which it had laid down among the "dream-thoughts," thus unfolding and reproducing them or unpacking them from the dream, in the form of the subject's "associations," until it has completed the reversal of the "dream-work."

IV

Freud sometimes helped a person to "reconstruct" a dream-report from "a single remaining fragment." He once remarked that what is reconstructed in such an instance "is not, it is true, the dream —which is in any case a matter of no importance—but all the dream-thoughts."[6]

This statement was, no doubt, based on Freud's faith that the subject's "associations" to his dream-report are equivalent to his "dream-thoughts." But it seems an odd statement in the respect that, theoretically, it was by "associating" to his "manifest dream" that the subject inevitably reproduced his "dream-thoughts"; but in the instances in question, Freud was not willing to say that there was a "manifest dream" for the subject to "associate" to—and he dismissed the dream as a matter of no importance. I think, however, that what Freud was saying was, in a sense, reasonable.

In dream interpretation, the psychoanalyst and the subject are in-

---

[5] 1900a, IV and V, chap. 6 *passim;* see 280–81, 310 ff., 528–32.
[6] 1900a, V, 517.

volved in quite a different sort of activity from that of anyone who wants, in the usual sense of the word, to interpret an object: i.e., to determine the public meaning which the object has. The rules and the criteria which Freud uses allow him to determine a private, not a public, meaning. His immediate aim in dream interpretation is not to establish a meaning that the dream-report may have, but to determine its meaning-for the subject.

To say that a given element of a dream-report, *x,* means *y,* is to say that the subject connects *x* with "associations" which lead to this *y:* that is, that the element suggests to him "thoughts" which, turned back on or connected with or applied to *x,* assign the part-meaning *y* to the element. His "associations" are anything at all which *x* calls to mind or suggests, or which occurs to him in connection with it. What some given element might suggest to anyone other than the subject, or what connections to it would be allowable, or clearly called for, if it appeared in a work of art, is irrelevant to Freud's investigation. If the subject connects the dream-element of a man standing with his arms outstretched with airplanes (and if he is not thought to be *withholding* the "association" Christ) then the *y* to which this "association" leads *is* the meaning assigned to the element.

To say that a dream-report means *Y* is to say that the subject thinks, in connection with its various elements, of "associations" which lead to several or many or innumerable *y*'s, that his connections and the part-meanings they lead to operate in a qualifying and confirmatory as well as cumulative manner upon one another, and that the result is turned back on the dream-report so as to assign the meaning *y* to the whole. The subject's "associations," and the *y*'s they lead to, converge to form a context of their own: as they accumulate, that is, they begin, as a whole, to show a sense, point, tendency, and/or thesis (usually, a group and/or series of tendencies, points, or theses). Further "associations" are placed in this developing context, not to be judged as allowable or not, but to be considered to be leading to just this or that part-meaning, which fits into the context being developed. E.g., Freud judged his "associations" to the element "I urinate over"—the stories of Gulliver and Gargantua—to be leading to the part-meaning "I show my towering stature"—my greatness, not my gigantism—because that *y* fitted into the tendency, point, and sense that was becoming evident in and through the other "associations." And of course he did not consider counting his "associations" wrong on the ground that they were cheerful and self-assertive, whereas the report invited no such connections. The tone of his "associations" did fit other aspects of the context *they* constituted; it was in keeping with the meaning the "associations" were leading to—the proposition "I am [shown to be] an exceedingly great man."

What Freud establishes is a meaning-for the subject. The meaning is not for him (alone) in the sense that it is inaccessible to anyone else, or kept to himself. He makes it available to the psycho-analyst, if to no one else, by revealing it through his "associations." It is a meaning-for him in the respect that *he gives it:* the meaning-for him of something is what it means to him, not what anyone else might or would have to make of it. (Of course, the meaning-for A of object *x could* also be its meaning-for B.)[7] It is a private meaning in the respect that what *x* suggests to him, which he connects with it or overlays it with, is not what the object would be taken to call for, if it could be taken to call for anything: his "associations" may be, and usually in "dream-interpretation" are, idiosyncratic—not such as one could predict from the dream-report, not such as one would expect to occur to anyone; often based on unusual personal experiences. The meaning established through his "associations" is *for* him in the respect that it is something that he means.

When what is in question is the public meaning-of an object, even its author's interpretation of it can be counted wrong as being implausible in relation to, off the point of, or inconsistent with its context. No such criteria apply in the case of "dream-analysis." What is in question is not what the dream-report means or what it might be taken to mean by anyone else, but its significance for the subject; and he cannot be counted wrong in establishing (and revealing) a

---

[7] Freud holds that certain elements commonly appearing in dreams may be regarded as "symbols", i.e., as having a common meaning. He employs "symbolic interpretation" in the event that a subject can produce no "associations" to an element that is thought to be a "symbol." But if a subject does produce "associations" which connect that same element (say, a stovepipe hat) with some other meaning, however distant it may be from the meaning supposed to be general, then the *y* to which his "associations" lead is unequivocally regarded as the meaning of the element in this case. Freud thought "symbolic interpretation" "unscientific" and "arbitrary" if based on nothing other than the interpreter's "intuition" (1900a, V, 350 ff.). Although Freud did not say so, it could be based on nothing better than a finding that subjects A, B, C, etc., have connected element *x* with middle terms which lead to meaning *y;* it could be no better than a guess that the present subject, if he would "associate," would connect *x* with the same *y.*

meaning-for himself. There would be no point in stopping him and telling him that his connections to element x are uncalled for, or bizarre: he is not trying to determine a public meaning for element x; what it means for him may depend on connections which x would not suggest to anyone but himself. To stop him and catch him up or question the validity of his "associations" would not only be nonsensical in this respect, it would also be counter to the purpose of finding out whatever he may mean.

Only the subject can say what his dream-report means for him. But he cannot say, straight off, what significance he gives it: his "associations" construct or reveal its meaning-for him. In principle, whatever the "associations" connect with the dream-report is the meaning established: if the "associations" are leading to meaning Y, that is the meaning established for the dream-report. But it may be the analyst (or possibly someone else) who draws the conclusion from the context constituted by the subject's "associations," as they can be turned back to the report, that the meaning of the report (for the subject) is Y: i.e., that the tendency, sense, and/or point of the "associations," in connection with the report, is Y. And the analyst can be right or wrong in coming to the conclusion that Y is the sense or point or tendency of the "associations." (The conclusion may be more or less inevitable.) The criteria for judging the analyst wrong are the context constituted by the "associations" ("You're wrong: that's not the tendency"), and the subject's word ("No: I'm sure that isn't what I meant/what it means; that doesn't feel right").

Of course, as in other cases where the subject is the arbiter, his first word need not always be accepted as a final dismissal of the analyst's "interpretation"; he too can be wrong in formulating, agreeing to, or rejecting a conclusion as to the meaning that his "associations" are leading to.

Little Hans saw a horse collapse in the street. Later, he became so afraid of going out of doors that he was unwilling or unable to go for the walks which he had greatly enjoyed. It appeared from what he said that at least part of what he was afraid might happen if he went for a walk was that he might again see a horse falling down; he seemed fascinated by this unlikely possibility. Freud wanted to know why Hans was so frightened and so fascinated by the event and the possibility of its recurrence. What did a horse's collapse mean for him? What significance was he giving it?

In Freud's case histories, it becomes clear that a neurotic is living in an idiosyncratic world, surrounded by situations which have a meaning-for him. The Rat Man was unable to work when his fiancée was away, visiting her grandmother; he became despondent, and had gone to get a razor to cut his throat when the "command" occurred to him: "No, you must kill the old woman." On another occasion, when the lady's cousin had been visiting her, he threw himself into a violent regime of diet and exercise, racing up and down mountains in the blazing sun. What did these situations mean for the Rat Man? With what private significance was he investing them?

Freud's psychotherapeutic interest in the meaning-for a person of any object—event, situation—comes under the heading of his interest in what the person means; the meaning-for him of any object is of importance because it is a part of what he means. In other words, Freud is not so much interested in the meaning-for a person of this or that particular object, as in the emotions and desires which are giving significance, for him, to various objects. Freud is interested in the meaning-for the subject of *any* event or situation. Hans might have given a significance such as he gave to the horse's collapse to any event which could have suggested and been overlaid with his ideas concerning something he wanted, and wanted not, to happen. The Rat Man was regarding a great many situations as realizing or epitomizing a set of conflicting emotions, desires, and beliefs. *What the object is* to which the subject gives a meaning is not important for the purpose of discovering what he means. The "object" may be of a tenuous or doubtful character—e.g., an event may not have occurred in just the way he remembers it as having occurred: his report of the event may be a mixture of memory and fantasy. For some purposes it would be of importance to be able to discriminate the elements of fantasy from those of correct memory in his report. But for the purpose of learning something that he means, it is not important to be able to say that an event which occurred has a meaning-for him, as against saying that a fantasized event has this significance.

When Freud is determining a meaning-for, he is not, in general, concerned with meaning-of. That is, he is not concerned to discover what, if any, meaning-of its own the object may have. But he sometimes needs to be concerned with the meaning-of the object, in so far as he must distinguish the meaning it has from the meaning the subject is giving it. If the object in question has no inherent meaning, or no meaning anything like what the subject is giving it, its meaning-for him can be easily distinguished from it and isolated for further analysis. No one would suppose that a horse's collapse had the meaning which it had for Hans. If the object has a public meaning, somewhat similar criteria to those which are used to judge an interpretation of a literary work as correct or incorrect can be applied to distinguish the meaning which object X has for B from the meaning-of X. Clearly, in many instances, it is important for Freud to be able to make such distinctions—not because the meaning-of X is in question, but for the purpose of discovering what the subject means. E.g., the therapeutic use of "transference" depends on the possibility of distinguishing the meaning which a patient gives to the analyst's gestures, actions, remarks, and so on, from a correct apprehension of the meaning-of these things.

A dream-report is a peculiar object, in the respect that it may have a meaning-of its own, but it has no public meaning. If there is a meaning-of a dream-report, it is a meaning-for the subject. He gave it; it is idiosyncratic; it is something that he means. The criteria which are ordinarily used to separate meaning-for from meaning-of do not apply. The meaning-for a person of his dream-report which is established cannot be set apart from the report according to any criteria of congruity, either in the way in which the meaning-for Hans of the horse's collapse could be isolated from the event, or in the way that the meaning-for a patient of an analyst's gestures can be distinguished from the meaning that they have. It could be the meaning-of the dream-report.

This is not to say that the meaning-for which is established *is* the meaning-of the dream-report. To say that if there is a meaning-of X, it is a meaning-for B, is not the same thing as saying that if there is a meaning-for B of X, it is the meaning-of X.

And that no criteria of congruity can be applied either to determine that the meaning-for the subject which is established is the meaning-of his dream-report, or to eliminate it as or distinguish it from the meaning-of the report, does not mean that there can be no way of judging whether or not the subject's "associations" are getting at the meaning which his dream-report may have. There are considerations conducive to the belief that, in some instances, the subject is not getting at any meaning that may be intrinsic to the report. There are considerations conducive to the belief that, in other instances, the subject is getting at a meaning which he had in constructing a dream-report out of dream elements, unuttered "associations," current concerns, and whatever else may have lain to hand; or that he is getting at a meaning which his dream had for him.

Freud's use of "associations" to establish a meaning need not exclude an attempt to discover the meaning-of a dream-report. If what he wanted to do were to determine the meaning-of a dream-report, he could go about accomplishing this aim by eliciting the subject's "associations" to it. But if this were what Freud wanted to do, he would have to observe conditions which could justify a belief that the meaning-for the subject established through his "associations" is approximating the meaning-of the report. I think that such a belief may be justified, for example, in an instance of this type: the subject insists that his dream-report is a correct report of what he dreamt; he wrote it down when he awoke; he woke in a mood which he could not explain; the meaning-for him of his dream-report which is later established through his "associations" offers an explanation of his mood as a response to his dream.

But if, as I have argued, the point of dream interpretation is to discover something that the subject means, if a meaning-for him is something that he means, and if the meaning-of his dream-report is a meaning-for him—if his "associations" reveal his meaning, whether or not they are getting at the meaning which is inherent in his dream-report—then whether or not the meaning-for him which is established through his "associations" is the meaning-for him that is the meaning-of his report is a question that is totally inconsequential in psychoanalysis. The dream *is* a matter of no importance: the analyst need not even be concerned with any meaning it may have in the way that he is concerned with the meaning-of, or the non-meaning-of, other sorts of objects to which the subject may give a meaning-for himself. It is not important, for the purpose of learning what the subject means, to distinguish between meaning-for which is meaning-of, and meaning-for which is not meaning-of; and to try to do so would be counter to that purpose.

In psychoanalysis, Freud treats dream-reports in the same way that he does anything else which the subject may bring up for "interpretation." If in therapy, in the case of dream-reports as in that of other things, Freud is interested in a meaning-for the subject because it is part of what he means, and not because it is the meaning-for him of this or that particular thing, then it is perfectly reasonable of him to treat reports which are garbled, embellished, or truncated, or which are even more than usually uncertain, vague, or unclear as equal in "interpretability" to any others; to make no effort to preserve the identity of a dream-report in distinction from "associations" or remarks upon it; and to think it unimportant whether there is what could be called a dream-report, as against "a single remaining fragment," or a ten-year-old fabrication, for the subject to "associate" to. And if, in the case of dream-reports as in that of other things, Freud's interest in meaning-for the subject is subordinate to his interest in what the subject means, then it is quite understandable that he draws no clear distinction in therapy between establishing a meaning for a dream-report and establishing some other part of the subject's meaning. It does not then greatly matter whether the themes being developed in a train of "association," starting from a dream-report, can only very loosely or perfunctorily be turned back to the report in such a way as to establish a meaning for it, or whether reference to the report is dropped when "associations" starting from it bring up something (e.g., an action of the subject's) which itself becomes the mark for further "associations," or the point of discussion.

But in theory, Freud makes the question central: he makes his claim to be establishing a meaning, which can tell him something about a patient, dependent on the equivalence of the meaning established through "associations" with the meaning-of the "manifest dream"; and he legislates the legitimacy of this equation by taking away the role of "associations," giving it to "latent dream thoughts," and from them reconferring it on the "associations." He is having his cake and eating it too. This is all very well—except that it is confusing, obscures what he is doing in dream interpretation, and invites skepticism, or credulous faith.

Mauvaise Foi and the Unconscious*

JEAN-PAUL SARTRE

The human being is not only the being by whom *négatités* are disclosed in the world; he is also the one who can take negative attitudes with respect to himself. In our Introduction we defined consciousness as "a being such that in its being, its being is in question in so far as this being implies a being other than itself." But now that we have examined the meaning of "the question," we can at present also write the formula thus: "Consciousness is a being, the nature of which is to be conscious of the nothingness of its being." In a prohibition or a veto, for example, the human being denies a future transcendence. But this negation is not explicative. My consciousness is not restricted to *envisioning* a *négatité*. It constitutes itself in its own flesh as the nihilation of a possibility which another human reality projects as *its* possibility. For that reason it must arise in the world as a *Not;* it is as a Not that the slave first apprehends the master, or that the prisoner who is trying to escape sees the guard who is watching him. There are even men (*e.g.*, caretakers, overseers, gaolers) whose social reality is uniquely that of the Not, who will live and die, having forever been only a Not upon the earth. Others so as to make the Not a part of their very subjectivity, establish their human personality as a perpetual negation. This is the meaning and function of what Scheler calls "the man of resentment"—in reality, the Not. But there exist more subtle behaviors, the description of which will lead us further into the inwardness of consciousness. Irony is one of these. In irony a man annihilates what he posits within one and the same act; he leads us to believe in order not to be believed; he affirms to deny and denies to affirm; he creates a positive object but it has no being other than its nothingness. Thus attitudes of negation toward the self permit us to raise a new question: What are we to say is the being of man who has the possibility of denying himself? But it is out of the question to discuss the attitude of "self-negation" in its universality. The kinds of behavior which can be ranked under this heading are too diverse; we risk retaining only the

* This essay is Chapter 2, first section of Jean-Paul Sartre, *Being and Nothingness,* trans. Hazel E. Barnes (Philosophical Library, New York, 1956). Reprinted by kind permission of the publishers.

abstract form of them. It is best to choose and to examine one determined attitude which is essential to human reality and which is such that consciousness instead of directing its negation outward turns it toward itself. This attitude, it seems to me, is *bad faith* (*mauvaise foi*).

Frequently this is identified with falsehood. We say indifferently of a person that he shows signs of bad faith or that he lies to himself. We shall willingly grant that bad faith is a lie to oneself, on condition that we distinguish the lie to oneself from lying in general. Lying is a negative attitude, we will agree to that. But this negation does not bear on consciousness itself; it aims only at the transcendent. The essence of the lie implies in fact that the liar actually is in complete possession of the truth which he is hiding. A man does not lie about what he is ignorant of; he does not lie when he spreads an error of which he himself is the dupe; he does not lie when he is mistaken. The ideal description of the liar would be a cynical consciousness, affirming truth within himself, denying it in his words, and denying that negation as such. Now this doubly negative attitude rests on the transcendent; the fact expressed is transcendent since it does not exist, and the original negation rests on a *truth;* that is, on a particular type of transcendence. As for the inner negation which I effect correlatively with the affirmation for myself of the truth, this rests on *words;* that is, on an event in the world. Furthermore the inner disposition of the liar is positive; it could be the object of an affirmative judgment. The liar intends to deceive and he does not seek to hide this intention from himself nor to disguise the translucency of consciousness; on the contrary, he has recourse to it when there is a question of deciding secondary behavior. It explicitly exercises a regulatory control over all attitudes. As for his flaunted intention of telling the truth ("I'd never want to deceive you! This is true! I swear it!")—all this, of course, is the object of an inner negation, but also it is not recognized by the liar as *his* intention. It is played, imitated, it is the intention of the character which he plays in the eyes of his questioner, but this character, precisely because he *does not exist,* is a transcendent. Thus the lie does not put into the play the inner structure of present consciousness; all the negations which constitute it bear on objects which by this fact are removed from consciousness. The lie then does not require special ontological foundation, and the explanations which the existence of negation in general requires are valid without change in the case of deceit. Of course we have described the ideal lie; doubtless it happens often enough that the liar is more or less the victim of his lie, that he half persuades himself of it. But these common, popular forms of the lie are also degenerate aspects of it; they represent intermediaries between falsehood and bad faith. The lie is a behavior of transcendence.

The lie is also a normal phenomenon of what Heidegger calls the *"Mit-sein."*[1] It presupposes my existence, the existence of the *Other,* my existence *for* the Other, and the existence of the Other *for* me. Thus there is no difficulty in holding that the liar must make the project of the lie in entire clarity and that he must possess a complete comprehension of the lie and of the truth which he is altering. It is sufficient that an over-all opacity hide his intentions from the *Other;* it is sufficient that the Other can take the lie for truth. By the lie consciousness affirms that it exists by nature as *hidden from the Other;* it utilizes for its own profit the ontological duality of myself and myself in the eyes of the Other.

The situation can not be the same for bad faith if this, as we have said, is indeed a lie to oneself. To be sure, the one who practices bad faith is hiding a displeasing truth or presenting as truth a pleasing untruth. Bad faith then has in appearance the structure of falsehood. Only what changes everything is the fact that in bad faith it is from myself that I am hiding the truth. Thus the duality of the deceiver and the deceived does not exist here. Bad faith on the contrary implies in essence the unity of a *single* consciousness. This does not mean that it can not be conditioned by the *Mit-sein* like all other phenomena of human reality, but the *Mit-sein* can call forth bad faith only by presenting itself as a *situation* which bad faith permits surpassing; bad faith does not come from outside to human reality. One does not undergo his bad faith; one is not infected with it; it is not a *state.* But consciousness affects itself with bad faith. There must be an original intention and a project of bad faith; this project implies a comprehension of bad faith as such and a pre-reflective apprehension (of) consciousness as affecting itself with bad faith. It follows first that the one to whom the lie is told and the one who lies are one and the same person, which means that I must know in my capacity as deceiver the truth which is hidden from me in my capacity as the one deceived. Better yet I must know the truth very exactly *in order* to conceal it more carefully—and this not at two

---

[1] A "being-with" others in the world. Tr.

different moments, which at a pinch would allow us to reestablish a semblance of duality—but in the unitary structure of a single project. How then can the lie subsist if the duality which conditions it is suppressed?

To this difficulty is added another which is derived from the total translucency of consciousness. That which affects itself with bad faith must be conscious (of) its bad faith since the being of consciousness is consciousness of being. It appears then that I must be in good faith, at least to the extent that I am conscious of my bad faith. But then this whole psychic system is annihilated. We must agree in fact that if I deliberately and cynically attempt to lie to myself, I fail completely in this undertaking; the lie falls back and collapses beneath my look; it is ruined *from behind* by the very consciousness of lying to myself which pitilessly constitutes itself well within my project as its very condition. We have here an *evanescent* phenomenon which exists only in and through its own differentiation. To be sure, these phenomena are frequent and we shall see that there is in fact an "evanescence" of bad faith, which, it is evident, vacillates continually between good faith and cynicism: Even though the existence of bad faith is very precarious, and though it belongs to the kind of psychic structures which we might call "metastable,"[2] it presents nonetheless an autonomous and durable form. It can even be the normal aspect of life for a very great number of people. A person can *live* in bad faith, which does not mean that he does not have abrupt awakenings to cynicism or to good faith, but which implies a constant and particular style of life. Our embarrassment then appears extreme since we can neither reject nor comprehend bad faith.

To escape from these difficulties people gladly have recourse to the unconscious. In the psychoanalytical interpretation, for example, they use the hypothesis of a censor, conceived as a line of demarcation with customs, passport division, currency control, *etc.,* to reestablish the duality of the deceiver and the deceived. Here instinct or, if you prefer, original drives and complexes of drives constituted by our individual history, make up *reality*. It is neither *true* nor *false* since it does not *exist for itself.* It simply *is,* exactly like this table, which is neither true nor false *in itself* but simply *real.* As for the conscious symbols of the instinct, this interpretation takes them not for appearances but for real psychic facts. Fear, forgetting, dreams

2 Sartre's own word, meaning subject to sudden changes or transitions. Tr.

exist really in the capacity of concrete facts of consciousness in the same way as the words and the attitudes of the liar are concrete, really existing patterns of behavior. The subject has the same relation to these phenomena as the deceived to the behavior of the deceiver. He establishes them in their reality and must interpret them. There is a *truth* in the activities of the deceiver; if the deceived could reattach them to the situation where the deceiver establishes himself and to his project of the lie, they would become integral parts of truth, by virtue of being lying conduct. Similarly there is a truth in the symbolic acts; it is what the psychoanalyst discovers when he reattaches them to the historical situation of the patient, to the unconscious complexes which they express, to the blocking of the censor. Thus the subject deceives himself about the *meaning* of his conduct, he apprehends it in its concrete existence but not in its *truth,* simply because he cannot derive it from an original situation and from a psychic constitution which remain alien to him.

By the distinction between the "id" and the "ego," Freud has cut the psychic whole into two. I *am* the ego but I *am not* the id. I hold no privileged position in relation to my unconscious psyche. I *am* my own psychic phenomena in so far as I establish them in their conscious reality. For example I am the impulse to steal this or that book from this bookstall. I am an integral part of the impulse; I bring it to light and I determine myself hand-in-hand with it to commit the theft. But I *am* not those psychic facts, in so far as I receive them passively and am obliged to resort to hypotheses about their origin and their true meaning, just as the scholar makes conjectures about the nature and essence of an external phenomenon. This theft, for example, which I interpret as an immediate impulse determined by the rarity, the interest, or the price of the volume which I am going to steal—it is in truth a process derived from self-punishment, which is attached more or less directly to an Oedipus complex. The impulse toward the theft contains a truth which can be reached only by more or less probable hypotheses. The criterion of this truth will be the number of conscious psychic facts which it explains; from a more pragmatic point of view it will be also the success of the psychiatric cure which it allows. Finally the discovery of this truth will necessitate the cooperation of the psychoanalyst, who appears as the *mediator* between my unconscious drives and my conscious life. The Other appears as being able to effect the synthesis between the unconscious thesis and the conscious antithesis. I can know myself only through the mediation of the other, which means that I stand in relation to *my* "id," in the position of the *Other*. If I have a little knowledge of psychoanalysis, I can, under circumstances particularly favorable, try to psychoanalyze myself. But this attempt can succeed only if I distrust every kind of intuition, only if I apply to my case *from the outside,* abstract schemes and rules already learned. As for the results, whether they are obtained by my efforts alone or with the cooperation of a technician, they will never have the certainty which intuition confers; they will possess simply the always increasing probability of scientific hypotheses. The hypothesis of the Oedipus complex, like the atomic theory, is nothing but an "experimental idea"; as Pierce said, it is not to be distinguished from the totality of experiences which it allows to be realized and the results which it enables us to foresee. Thus psychoanalysis substitutes for the notion of bad faith, the idea of a lie without a liar; it allows me to understand how it is possible for me to be lied to without lying to myself since it places me in the same relation to myself that the Other is in respect to me; it replaces the duality of the deceiver and the deceived, the essential condition of the lie, by that of the "id" and the "ego." It introduces into my subjectivity the deepest intersubjective structure of the *Mit-sein.* Can this explanation satisfy us?

Considered more closely the psychoanalytic theory is not as simple as it first appears. It is not accurate to hold that the "id" is presented as a thing in relation to the hypothesis of the psychoanalyst, for a thing is indifferent to the conjectures which we make concerning it, while the "id" on the contrary is sensitive to them when we approach the truth. Freud in fact reports resistance when at the end of the first period the doctor is approaching the truth. This resistance is objective behavior apprehended from without: the patient shows defiance, refuses to speak, gives fantastic accounts of his dreams, sometimes even removes himself completely from the psychoanalytic treatment. It is a fair question to ask what part of himself can thus resist. It can not be the "Ego," envisaged as a psychic totality of the facts of consciousness; this could not suspect that the psychiatrist is approaching the end since the ego's relation to the *meaning* of its own reactions is exactly like that of the psychiatrist himself. At the very most it is possible for the ego to appreciate objectively the degree of probability in the hypotheses set forth, as a witness of the psychoanalysis might be able to do, according to the number of subjective facts which they explain. Furthermore, this probability would appear to the ego to border on certainty, which he could not take offence at since most of the time it is he who by a *conscious* decision is in pursuit of the psychoanalytic therapy. Are we to say that the patient is disturbed by the daily revelations which the psychoanalyst makes to him and that he seeks to remove himself, at the same time pretending in his own eyes to wish to continue the treatment? In this case it is no longer possible to resort to the unconscious to explain bad faith; it is there in full consciousness, with all its contradictions. But this is not the way that the psychoanalyst means to explain this resistance; for him it is secret and deep, it comes from afar; it has its roots in the very thing which the psychoanalyst is trying to make clear.

Furthermore it is equally impossible to explain the resistance as emanating from the complex which the psychoanalyst wishes to bring to light. The complex as such is rather the collaborator of the psychoanalyst since it aims at expressing itself in clear consciousness, since it plays tricks on the censor and seeks to elude it. The only level on which we can locate the refusal of the subject is that of the censor. It alone can comprehend the questions or the revelations of the psychoanalyst as approaching more or less near to the real drives which it strives to repress—it alone because it alone *knows* what it is repressing.

If we reject the language and the materialistic mythology of psychoanalysis, we perceive that the censor in order to apply its activity with discernment must know what it is repressing. In fact if we abandon all the metaphors representing the repression as the impact of blind forces, we are compelled to admit that the censor must choose and in order to choose must be aware of so doing. How could it happen otherwise that the censor allows lawful sexual impulses to pass through, that it permits needs (hunger, thirst, sleep) to be expressed in clear consciousness? And how are we to explain that it can relax its surveillance, that it can even be deceived by the disguises of the instinct? But it is not sufficient that it discern the condemned drives; it must also apprehend them *as to be repressed,* which implies in it at the very least an awareness of its activity. In a word, how could the censor discern the impulses needing to be repressed without being conscious of discerning them? How can we conceive of a knowledge which is ignorant of itself? To know is to know that one knows, said Alain. Let us say rather: All knowing is consciousness of knowing. Thus the resistance of the patient implies on the level of the censor an awareness of the thing repressed as such, a comprehension of the end toward which the questions of the psychoanalyst are leading, and an act of synthetic connection by which it compares the *truth* of the repressed complex to the psychoanalytic hypothesis which aims at it. These various operations in their turn imply that the censor is conscious (of) itself. But what type of self-consciousness can the censor have? It must be the consciousness (of) being conscious of the drive to be repressed, but precisely *in order not be conscious of it*. What does this mean if not that the censor is in bad faith?

Psychoanalysis has not gained anything for us since in order to overcome bad faith, it has established between the unconscious and consciousness an autonomous consciousness in bad faith. The effort to establish a veritable duality and even a trinity (*Es, Ich, Ueber-ich* expressing themselves through the censor) has resulted in a mere verbal terminology. The very essence of the reflexive idea of hiding something from oneself implies the unity of one and the same psychic mechanism and consequently a double activity in the heart of unity, tending on the one hand to maintain and locate the thing to be concealed and on the other hand to repress and disguise it. Each of the two aspects of this activity is complementary to the other; that is, it implies the other in its being. By separating consciousness from the unconscious by means of the censor, psychoanalysis has not succeeded in dissociating the two phases of the act, since the libido is a blind conatus toward conscious expression and since the conscious phenomenon is a passive, faked result. Psychoanalysis has merely localized this double activity of repulsion and attraction on the level of the censor.

Furthermore the problem still remains of accounting for the unity of the total phenomenon (repression of the drive which disguises itself and "passes" in symbolic form), to establish comprehensible connections among its different phases. How can the repressed drive "disguise itself" if it does not include. (1) the consciousness of being repressed, (2) the consciousness of having been pushed back because it is what it is, (3) a project of disguise? No mechanistic theory of condensation or of transference can explain these modifications by which the drive itself is affected, for the description of the process of disguise implies a veiled appeal to finality. And similarly how are we to account for the pleasure or the anguish which accompanies the symbolic and conscious satisfaction of the drive if consciousness does not include—beyond the censor—an obscure comprehension of the end to be attained as simultaneously desired and forbidden. By rejecting the conscious unity of the psyche, Freud is obliged to imply everywhere a magic unity linking distant phenomena across obstacles, just as sympathetic magic unites the spellbound person and the wax image fashioned in his likeness. The unconscious drive (*Trieb*) through magic is endowed with the character "repressed" or "condemned," which completely pervades it, colors it, and magically provokes its symbolism. Similarly the conscious phenomenon is entirely colored by its symbolic meaning although it can not apprehend this meaning by itself in clear consciousness.

Aside from its inferiority in principle, the explanation by magic does not avoid the coexistence—on the level of the unconscious, on that of the censor, and on that of consciousness—of two contradictory, complementary structures which reciprocally imply and destroy each other. Proponents of the theory have hypostasized and "reified" bad faith; they have not escaped it. This is what has inspired a Viennese psychiatrist, Steckel, to depart from the psychoanalytical tradition and to write in *La femme frigide:* "Every time that I have been able to carry my investigations far enough, I have established that the crux of the psychosis was conscious." In addition the cases which he reports in his work bear witness to a pathological bad faith which the Freudian doctrine can not account for. There is the question, for example, of women whom marital infidelity has made frigid; that is, they succeed in hiding from themselves not complexes deeply sunk in half physiological darkness, but acts of conduct which are objectively discoverable, which they can not fail to record at the moment when they perform them. Frequently in fact the husband reveals to Steckel that his wife has given objective signs of pleasure, but the woman when questioned will fiercely deny them. Here we find a pattern of *distraction.* Admissions which Steckel was able to draw out inform us that these pathologically frigid women apply themselves to becoming distracted in advance from the pleasure which they dread; many for example at the time of the sexual act, turn their thoughts away toward their daily occupations, make up their household accounts. Will anyone speak of an unconscious here? Yet if the frigid woman thus distracts her consciousness from the pleasure which she experiences, it is by no means cynically and in full agreement with herself; *it is in order to prove to herself* that she is frigid. We have in fact to deal with a phenomenon of bad faith since the efforts taken in order not to be present to the experienced pleasure imply the recognition that the pleasure is experienced; they imply it *in order to deny it.* But we are no longer on the ground of psychoanalysis. Thus on the one hand the explanation by means of the unconscious, due to the fact that it breaks the psychic unity, can not account for the facts which at first sight it appeared to explain. And on the other hand, there exists an infinity of types of behavior in bad faith which explicitly reject this kind of explanation because their essence implies that they can appear only in the translucency of consciousness. We find that the problem which we had attempted to resolve is still untouched.

Self-Deception and the "Splitting of the Ego"*

HERBERT FINGARETTE

I

Who can doubt that we do deceive ourselves? Yet who can explain coherently and explicitly how we do so?

Recent philosophical attempts at such explanation have centered around the assumption that, in essence, the self-deceiver is one who has got himself to believe what he (still) does not believe. So soon as the matter is put thus starkly we are faced with deep paradox, and a good deal of the recent philosophical discussion has been directed toward trying to save the concept while dissolving the paradox.

In the following, I propose a quite different approach to the analysis of self-deception, one which does not center on the co-existence of inconsistent beliefs, and indeed does not center on the understanding of self-deception in terms of belief at all. In consequence, the paradox inherent in the "two-belief" approach does not arise, nor does any other paradox.

The analysis of self-deception which I present here is set beside certain of Freud's doctrines. Setting my own account alongside Freud's work is appropriate inasmuch as his doctrine on defense and the unconscious constitutes the most elaborately worked out, the most extensively applied contemporary doctrine touching self-

---

* This essay consists almost entirely of passages from Herbert Fingarette, *Self-Deception* (Routledge, London, 1969), which appeared in the series entitled Studies in Philosophical Psychology, under the editorship of R. F. Holland. The passages have been selected and reordered in the present form by Professor Fingarette for this anthology. For ease of reading, Professor Fingarette has authorized omission of the usual typographical signs indicating editorial excision or minor editorial alteration. The brief introductory section was specifically prepared for the present text. The locations of the passages in the original text are indicated by the bracketed numerical superscripts at the end of each passage, thus:

    [1.] pp. 66–71
    [2.] pp. 82–85
    [3.] pp. 86–89
    [4.] p. 91
    [5.] pp. 111–12
    [6.] pp. 115–16
    [7.] pp. 125–33
    [8.] p. 142

deception. The juxtaposition of these ways of talking about self-deception results, as I see it, in helping to identify and resolve a central incompleteness in Freud's doctrine, an incompleteness whose centrality Freud himself had just come to appreciate at the very end of his life. In addition, the juxtaposition of Freud's doctrine with my own account in non-psychoanalytic language tends to confirm the validity of the latter, and also makes directly available to it, in the empirical dimension, the depth and illumination afforded by the literature of psychoanalysis.

II

The self-deceiver is one who is in some way engaged in the world but who disavows the engagement, who will not acknowledge it even to himself as his. That is, self-deception turns upon the personal identity one accepts rather than the beliefs one has. It is the hallucinator who speaks, but he will not *acknowledge* the words as his; disowned by him and undetected by others, the voice nevertheless still speaks, and so it is assigned by him to some supernatural being. The paranoid is filled with destructiveness, but he disavows it; since the presence of destructiveness is evident to him, he eventually assigns "ownership" of that destructiveness to others. With this as his unquestionable axiom, and with "conspiracy" as his all-purpose formula, he interprets all that happens accordingly. In general, the self-deceiver is engaged in the world in some way, and yet he refuses to avow the engagement as his. Having disavowed the engagement, the self-deceiver is then forced into protective, defensive tactics to account for the inconsistencies in his engagement in the world as acknowledged by him.

Having afforded ourselves this bird's eye view of the matter, we need now to retrace our steps on foot.

An individual may be born of a certain family, nation, or tradition. Yet it is something else again for that individual to identify himself with that family, nation, and tradition. He may never do so. He may grow up doing so, but then, due to changes in life-circumstances, he may grow out of one or another identity. Even more dramatically, he may as a culminating and decisive act seize a particular occasion to disavow his affiliation, his identity as an American, a Christian, or, merely, a Rotarian. As the individual grows from infancy to adulthood, he identifies himself as a person of certain traits of character, having certain virtues and views, a certain bodily shape, having allegiances, enemies, obligations, rights, a history.

The phrase "identifies himself as," certainly has some reference to discoveries the individual makes; but it refers as well to options adopted. Even with regard to something as "concrete" and "objective" as the body, it is interesting to note that *my* body as I identify it for myself is what the psychiatrist calls a "body image." He calls it my body image just because he sees that it reflects, in effect, my engagement in the world, the way I see things and take them to be, rather than the object the disinterested observer would describe.

A father announces: "You are not my son. From henceforth I disown you." Taken as biological description, the first sentence is false. Taken as the disavowal of identification which the second sentence reveals it to be, the first sentence can be lived up to or not—but it is not false. Although the use of "avow" has in such cases a primary social or legal focus, it is related to the use I propose and is the model for it. The same holds true of typical proclamations such as "I am an American," "I am a union man," "I am no longer a Democrat." Of the existence of such public avowals and disavowals, and of their differences from mere description, there can be no doubt. The further assumption necessary for my thesis is that something significantly analogous can be done—is commonly done—in the privacy of one's own soul. Indeed my assumption is that the analogies between what is done in self-deception (and in undeceiving oneself) and what is done in the examples just cited are so many, so interrelated, and so fundamental that we would do well to talk quite generally of self-deception in the language of avowal and disavowal and in closely related language such as "identify oneself as," and "acknowledge."

The distinction between being a certain individual and avowing one's identity as a certain person is dramatically evident in the case of the amnesiac who admits that the evidence proves he is John Jones, but who does not identify himself to himself as John Jones. Jones does not avow certain memories and commitments. As an individual he has a certain history but he does not avow that history. It is not merely that he will not avow these to us; he does not avow them to himself either. We could express all this by saying that the history in question is no longer his personal history for him.

There is an important element of *authenticity* here: I refer to that respect in which, for the person before us, Jones is indeed alien, someone other. (The person before us is not sure just *who* he is, but he is sure that he does not identify himself to himself as Jones.) It is true that from the standpoint of the observer, Jones is here and is suffering amnesia. But from the standpoint of the person before us, i.e., the subject as reflected in his own consciousness, it is important to say that he is not Jones. It is this latter standpoint which I have in mind when I speak of avowal and disavowal, of identification of oneself to oneself as a certain person or as a certain person being engaged in the world in certain ways.

To avow, then, is to define one's personal identity for oneself, not after the fact, but in that sense where we mean by "defining one's identity" the establishing of one's personal identity in some respect. Moreover, we must include the maintaining of one's personal identity for oneself in the face of occasion for disavowal. Any such establishing or reaffirmation of one's personal identity may come to fruition in a climactic, public act; or it may be so slow and so evenly paced in its development as to seem to be natural evolution, or inherent stability in the face of stress rather than a dramatic act. Nevertheless, avowal and disavowal are always inherently, purposeful self-expression rather than mere happenings suffered by the person. Avowal and disavowal are accomplished by a person; they are responses by him rather than effects upon him.[1]

We must seek now to establish more precisely what are the "materials" which a man uses, what is it for an individual to "possess" these materials *as* material ready for incorporation into, or exclusion from, a unified self; and we must ask what is the significance of such acceptance or rejection. For it is not ignorance or temptation but the authenticity of such exclusion from a self, or inclusion within a self, which is at the core of that spiritual disorder we call self-deception.

The phenomena of self-deception (I include here the phenomena covered by such terms as Sartre's *"mauvaise foi,"* and Freud's "defence") can be consistently interpreted within the framework of the doctrine that the self is a synthesis, an achievement by the individual, something "made." Avowal is the "missing link" which is implicit in the doctrine of the self as synthesis. In order to show how this is so, I do not propose to present a tightly woven theory in a technical language, but to offer a broad and rapid sketch of the familiar course of the emergence of the self, a sketch unified by the view that the self is a synthesis, a creation. Naturally I shall highlight those features I have claimed are essential to self-deception. (The reader who desires to supplement his own observations in reflecting upon the following sketch is referred to such standard descriptive works as Gesell and Ilg's *Infant and Child in the Culture of Today.*)

Before achieving a relatively coherent unity as a self, the child learns relatively specific forms of engagement in the world. First these are quite rudimentary: using a spoon, opening a door, buttoning a coat. Then he learns complexes of interrelated motive, reason, emotion, relevant objectives, appropriate means, and, where relevant, moralistic judgmental tone. We do not normally see the latter sorts of specific engagements, at least not clearly, even at the age of two or three years. For example, the two-year-old does not rise to an insult by adopting a vengeful policy, selecting and using appropriate means to carry out his policy; nor perforce does he feel guilt for this. By the age of three years one has learned, for example, to appreciate both time of day and his own hunger as jointly justifying seating himself at table and eating in certain generally prescribed ways, to the ends of satisfying hunger and pleasing his parents, all the while enjoying the moralistic reaction of feeling "good" (rather than "naughty"). He has also learned that under certain conditions an object is his property, permanent or temporary, and that seizing it without his permission by his peers is occasion for anger on his part, for retaliatory action accompanied by a moralistic reaction which includes quite typically his feeling "naughty" or "bad," as well as feeling "righteously indignant." (The rationality of these moralistic reactions is characteristically not questioned; the pattern as a whole is learned, and only later, when a unified self and its larger perspective can be brought to bear, do moral criticism and personal moral judgment emerge.)

Yet even the four- or five-year-old, capable as he may be of engaging at last in a particular complex activity for childish reasons, with childish aims and methods, and in childish moods, still does not manifest an enduring centre, a personal core whose unity colours and shapes his various particular engagements. He shifts, eccentrically, at the behest of others, or because something in the environment distracts him, or because he is fatigued, from one project to another, each being relatively unaffected by the others; any one of these engagements is not noticeably judged by him with reference to the others, nor is it markedly coloured by them. The overall unity of personal style and attitude, the inwardly governed and relatively smooth transition, are as yet absent. The psychoanalysts tell us that in ways too subtle to be readily apparent, a unified core of personality evolves, at least in nucleus, by age two and a half to four (the oedipal phase); and the careful observer can even then notice certain gross patterns of temperament or style. Yet for the layman the evolution of a noticeable autonomous governing centre does not usually begin to manifest itself until the early school years. Indeed this is a traditional sign of readiness for school beyond the nursery or kindergarten level. At this period the child is able, at least for periods of time and with rudimentary success, to carry on autonomously. One engagement leads into, blends into, another; the child is not *merely* "negative" or else "obedient," but shows a degree of independence in his response to external demands. There begins to emerge a large "plot" determined from within. After a few years, even the immediate moralistic reactions ("nice," "naughty," "shame," "good," "bad") soften—though this is one of the last stages of the process—as one specific form of engagement is related to another, as a coherent self emerges, and as the generality and many-sidedness of judgment which this makes possible nourish more "personal" moral response.[2]

The child learns many particular forms of engagement; he "plays" various roles continually, zestfully, as well as being tutored in some by adults. Some forms of engagement remain merely projects realized and then forgotten, roles learned and then abandoned. However, certain forms of engagement—or even some particular ones—are taken up into the ever forming, ever growing personal self, and they are modified as they become more and more an integral part of this "synthesis." To take some engagement into the personal self is not an act of physical incorporation (though Freud showed how important this image is in this connection). To take something into the self is an "act" which our notion of personal identity presupposes. It is to commit oneself to treat something *as* a part or aspect of oneself, or as something inherent in the engagements which the person avows.

If there were no such thing as a person's *acknowledging* some identity as his and certain engagements as his, and disavowing other identities and engagements, there would be neither persons nor personal identity. Without this, man would be at most a highly coordinated, even highly intelligent animal, engaged in a sequence of pursuits in entire and inevitable unselfconsciousness. Such creatures might be numbered or named, and even referred to as "persons," but they would not have the capacity for the moral or spiritual life.

Generally speaking, with the emergence of the person in the individual, there is a tendency for increasing correlation between what is avowed by the person and the actual engagements of the individual. It is in terms of the tacit ideal of perfect harmony in this respect that we tend to assess the individual. We are less disturbed by the discrepancies we see in the child; children are only "half-formed"; they will "grow up" and "grow out of it"; meanwhile, they go in a hundred directions, and we are patient of this. Yet even for children we do have certain age-level expectations.

It can come about, for child or adult, that our expectations are not met. And, in particular, it happens—witness the self-deceiver—that an individual will be provoked into a kind of engagement which, in part or in whole, the person cannot *avow* as *his* engagement, for to avow it would apparently lead to such intensely disruptive, distressing consequences as to be unmanageably destructive to the person. The crux of the matter here is the *unacceptability* of the engagement to the person. The individual may be powerfully inclined towards a particular engagement, yet this particular engagement may be utterly incompatible with that currently achieved synthesis of engagements which is the person.

The capacity to pursue specific engagements independently, as autonomous projects, without integration into the complex unity of a personal self, is, as we have noted, an early and a fundamental capacity of the human being. We may now add that the phenomena we classify under such headings as "self-deception," "defence," and *"mauvaise foi,"* are "regressions" to this form of engagement; they manifest our capacity for such isolated engagements even after the emergence of a personal self, and in spite of unacceptability to the person. We judge from the totality of the conduct that the individual is engaged in a certain way, and he may even show signs of shame or intense guilt; yet we note what are in fact the characteristic features of disavowal: the person does not speak of the engagement as his, he does not speak *for* it, and he seems sincere; the engagement seems to exist in a certain isolation from the tempering influence of the person's usual reasonableness, his tastes, sensitivities, values; the person accepts no responsibility for being engaged in this way. On occasion we also distinguish the reparative measures being taken in order to minimize the discrepancies.

Let us imagine, for example, an individual who is intensely angered by his employer's attitude towards him. The individual, we shall suppose, is unable to rid himself of this reaction. Yet such anger towards such a person is radically unacceptable to this person. An unprincipled and humiliating subservience in spite of the anger would also be unacceptable, and in any case it would continue to bear the stigma of being his own anger, even if acknowledged to no one but himself. As a least evil, the person disavows the unquenchable anger and aggression: It is not "I" who am angry; from henceforth I disassociate myself from it; it is utterly repugnant to me. By rejecting identity with the anger, the person avoids responsibility, but he also surrenders all authority and direct control.

Nevertheless, the fact remains that the individual is thereafter left to pursue this aggressive relationship as an isolated project. It readily manifests itself in harmful action and hurtful words towards the employer. There may be moralistic guilt reactions associated with it. These, too, are of course disavowed, though the evident manifestations of mood may be rationalized as "depression" or undirected sulkiness.

Because of the moralistic guilt reaction, and also for purposes of protective camouflage against interference, the individual may initiate ameliorating and cover-tactics: he may find or invent some role to play—perhaps the role of the completely respectful and friendly employee. This may, by its practical effect, require a modification of the manner of being aggressive, or it may at least soften the practical impact of the effects of being aggressive. There is no problem, in general, in supposing that an individual can invent congenial explanations or play various roles; what we further assume here is that these activities, too, are disavowed. The individual can speak more or less skillfully the lines which he has learned would in general be appropriate for a friendly and respectful employee. Since this is a generalized role rather than a personal response, and since the self-deceiver may not be a very good actor, we notice a certain artificiality in his friendliness, a tendency to overdo and "ham" it, a certain insensitivity to the subtleties peculiar to the situation, a stereotypy in manner.[3]

In summary, then, I have treated as central the capacity of a person to identify himself to himself as a particular person engaged in the world in specific ways, the capacity of a person to reject such identification and engagement, and the further supposition that an individual can continue to be engaged in the world in a certain way even though he does not avow it as his personal engagement and therefore displays none of the evidences of such avowal.[4]

III

> I find myself for a moment in the interesting position of not knowing whether what I have to say should be regarded as something long familiar and obvious or as something entirely new and puzzling. But I am inclined to think the latter.
>
> I have at last been struck by the fact that . . .[1]

These are the provocative opening words in Freud's last paper, unfinished and posthumously published under the title, "Splitting of the Ego in the Process of Defence." Freud's opening remark is all the more provocative because he had just previously made two attempts, both left incomplete by him, to present a definitive restatement of psychoanalytic theory. With these uncompleted efforts in the immediate background, he turned to the "Splitting of the Ego . . ." and one naturally suspects that the provocative opening words of this last short paper may announce some fundamental new insight which he had been struggling to assimilate.

On its face, this last paper is merely a brief restatement of material quite familiar from discussions in a number of Freud's writings. These discussions go as far back as the early writings; they are found from time to time in later papers; and they constitute an unusually large proportionate part of the highly condensed *An Outline of Psychoanalysis,* on which he had been working only a few months prior.

That the material in "Splitting of the Ego . . ." should look familiar to us is to be expected, since Freud himself introduces it as having a "long familiar and obvious" look. What was there about it, then, that was "entirely new and puzzling"? It must have been a *way* of seeing the familiar "fact" by which he was now "struck" anew.

I believe that what struck Freud was a central insight analogous

[1] 1940e, XXIII, 275.

to that which I have developed in Section II above. He saw a new way of generalizing the role of the ego in defence, a way which for the first time could bring into focus certain fundamental implications of his entire theory, a way which had the potential for resolving certain deep conceptual problems internal to his theory. Freud did not live to develop the potential of this new insight. Some aspects of it have in effect been central to very recent theoretical discussions of defence and the unconscious in the psychoanalytic literature. But these discussions have still failed to expose the central, unifying element in Freud's insight because they are basically cast in the old terms.[5]

Why should the ego aim to keep anything at all unconscious, whether it be defence or impulse? This, which I take to be the fundamental problem at the core of psychoanalytic theory, has so far as I know been raised neither by psychoanalysts nor by contemporary philosophical reinterpreters of Freud such as Sartre or, more recently, Ricoeur. The question bears elaboration.

Let us suppose that the defensive rejection of an impulse is designed not merely to inhibit its expression but characteristically to "hide" its existence. But from whom or what is the impulse to be hidden? Other persons in the environment? If this were all, it would merely be a case of ordinary deception, whereas what is characteristic of defence is that one "hides" something from *oneself*. But where shall we locate the inner "victim" of this secretiveness? Is the impulse to be hidden from the id? This makes no sense, for it is the impulse *of* the id. Is it to be hidden from the superego? No, for it is typically the superego which perceives the emerging id derivatives, and which typically initiates the defence by inducing anxiety in the ego. Is the impulse to be hidden from the ego? Surely not, for the ego is by definition that "agency" which takes into account *both* the impulse and the conflicting superego demands, and which then designs and executes the defensive manoeuvre. Furthermore since the impulse remains active in the id, defence is a continuing process; the ego must therefore remain *continuously* cognizant of all relevant factors if defence is to succeed. However, if nothing relevant is "hidden" from id, ego, or superego, what is the point of keeping anything from being conscious? We can no longer assume it to be—as is usually assumed—some kind of hiding of the impulse from oneself, some kind of ignorance due to successful "disguise." However, in the present case the imputation of knowledge to consciousness, and ignorance to unconsciousness, seems to have lost its justification.

Defence aims to reduce anxiety, of course, and so long as the main outcome of defence was thought to be a form of self-induced ignorance, it made a certain sense to suppose that "what you don't know won't worry you." But once we abandon the notion that defence brings a kind of blissful ignorance to some "agency" of the mind, the question forces itself upon one: why should anxiety be reduced by defence any more than, better than, or differently than would be the case if we merely curbed our impulses and/or deceived others quite consciously?[6]

The question we now face is a surprising question because, after all, one of the earliest and most characteristic insights of psychoanalysis was that the origin of much psychopathology lies in the tactic of defending oneself from threats, inner or outer, by keeping oneself unconscious of them. This distinctive and illuminating insight has suddenly been transformed into a source of puzzlement and obscurity. Recent psychoanalytic theorists have argued, though not always for identical reasons, that the concepts of consciousness, preconsciousness, and unconsciousness play little or no essential role in contemporary theory. I believe they are wrong. However, even if they are right, the problem of the usefulness of defence would remain a central problem unresolved within psychoanalytic theory. The problem is not only unresolved, it is not even recognized by psychoanalytic theorists. Everyone has for long taken it for granted that defence serves a vital purpose; no one has appreciated that the purpose so long taken for granted, the *only* purpose postulated by theory, no longer is adequate to its theoretical burden.

Arlow and Brenner have been among the leading proponents of the thesis that psychoanalytic theory can get along without the use of the "conscious-unconscious" cluster of concepts. They hold that in the work of the analyst, "To characterize a mental element as accessible or inaccessible to consciousness does not tell us what we need to know."[2]

There is much force in their detailed argument. Yet a healthy respect for the oldest and most characteristic of psychoanalytic insights in psychoanalysis might suggest caution. In fact the seeds of

[2] J. A. Arlow and C. Brenner, *Psychoanalytic Concepts and the Structural Theory* (Int. Univ. Press, New York, 1964), p. 112.

inner inconsistency are to be found in Arlow and Brenner's own exposition of their thesis.

For example, Arlow and Brenner present material from two different cases in which, in each instance, it is important to their commentary that certain interpretations, believed to be correct by the analyst, were nevertheless not presented to the patient at a certain time.[3] To have presented these interpretations at that point, say Arlow and Brenner, would have been inappropriate, in one case perhaps dangerous. In thus acknowledging the critical therapeutic role of interpretation, Arlow and Brenner accept in practice what in theory they reject; for, what is interpretation if not the attempt to make explicitly conscious what was not conscious?

It will not help their case to argue that the newer aim of psychoanalysis is not so much "to make the unconscious conscious" but rather to bring it about that "where id was, there shall ego be." We may readily grant the historical shift of emphasis expressed in these familiar slogans. The fact remains that therapeutic interpretation, aimed at dynamic insight, remains a principal analytic tool to achieve this newer aim. As such, interpretation—and thus the making conscious of what was unconscious—must remain of profound interest for both practice and theory. The Arlow and Brenner monograph, however, has little to say about the nature of dynamic insight. This is a predictable oversight in an argument designed to induce us to dispense with the conscious-unconscious distinction.

It seems that, at least in therapeutic practice, we cannot dismiss the question of the consciousness status of a mental content; but neither can we dismiss the more recent, theoretical lines of argument exemplified in the Arlow and Brenner monograph.

I propose, in summary, certain postulates which I believe must be accepted and which in fact are accepted in the solution which I shall present to this dilemma. These postulates derive, respectively, from the traditional psychoanalytic viewpoint, the newer Arlow-Brenner type of emphasis, and my own analysis of self-deception.

(1) *The traditional element:* Defence is not merely the inhibition of discharge, for this in itself would amount only to self-control; defence characteristically has a self-alienating nature as well. Furthermore, this self-alienation in defence is characteristically reflected in an alteration of consciousness.

[3] Ibid., pp. 106–9.

(2) *The Arlow-Brenner thesis:* What primarily counts in defence is the "dynamic" aspect, not the presence or absence of some "mental quality," i.e., some para-perceptual or cognitive element.

(3) *My own thesis:* The alteration of consciousness in defence should not be understood primarily in terms of knowledge and ignorance but, instead, by reference to the "dynamics" of defence— that is, by reference to those features of defence which we would in everyday language refer to in such terms as "purpose," "will," "motive," and, finally, "action."

It is fundamental to the solution I propose that one recalls how, from the very beginning, defence has been conceived psychoanalytically as the establishment of a kind of split in the psyche. Prior to the development of Freud's ego psychology, the split was conceived to be between the Conscious and the Unconscious, each eventually conceived as a system. By the 1920's, when the newer theses concerning anxiety and the ego-id-superego trio were developed, the split was conceived to be essentially between the ego (prodded by the superego) and the id. The two versions, however, retain a remarkable parallelism, a persistent cluster of insights, which is of special interest to us here. In both versions, the conflicting entities are conceived as systems which are quasi-autonomous, indeed incompatible, alienated from one another. One system contains what has been rejected by the other. The former system operates according to the "archaic," "primary process"; logical, temporal, and causal relations are ignored, part stands for whole, isolated similarities establish equivalencies, and so on. The latter system operates according to the more rational "secondary process." The two systems interact by way of conflict rather than co-ordination.

By virtue of the parallelism in these respects of the older and newer versions of the theory, neither system escapes certain problems. For example, unconscious fantasies are assigned in both the earlier and later versions of Freud's theory to the system which contains the repressed, the system which operates according to the primary process. As a matter of clinical fact, however, unconscious fantasies are found to be organized to a good extent according to the (rational) secondary process. Such paradoxes as this arise because both earlier and later versions are parallel in insisting correctly on the fact that there is a split in the psyche, but in failing to define the nature of the split adequately. In both versions, Freud *over*stressed the fact that the element split off from the Ego takes on a markedly "primitive" character, and he fails adequately to stress the great extent to which the element split off still retains fundamental characteristics of the Ego (and superego).

If we correct this one-sidedness, the situation can be stated as follows. The result of defence is to split off from the more rational system (i.e., the system which is defended) a nuclear, dynamic complex. This nuclear entity is a complex of motive, purpose, feeling, perception, and drive towards action. It is, for example, an angry and competitive impulse to damage one's father as object of envy; or it may be an erotic and competitive impulse to arrange matters so as to be the adored son. And in such cases there is typically a sense of guilt as an element in the complex, the guilt being of a kind which is appropriate to a relatively infantile appreciation of the impulse and its expression. Also integral to such impulses is a limited but genuine capacity to adapt the expression of the impulse to varying reality situations.

Of course what we have been describing is a kind of split-off from the highly elaborated *ego*-structure. True, it is only a nucleus of an ego, split off from the highly elaborated Ego. In relation to the Ego it is rudimentary in organization, especially with regard to the way it now fails to reflect the richness of the Ego's learning and many identifications. Isolated as it is from the learning and experimentation constantly engaged in by a healthy Ego, the split-off nucleus remains relatively static (and therefore relatively rudimentary) as compared to the continually maturing Ego. The longer it remains split off, the greater the disparity between split-off nucleus and the Ego—and therefore the greater the tendency for it to remain split off.

Why is such an ego-nucleus split off from the Ego? It is because the incompatibility between the ego-nucleus and the current Ego are so great, relative to the integrative capacities of that Ego, that the latter gives up any attempt to integrate the ego-nucleus itself. The Ego then adopts some more or less sophisticated versions of the *Ur*-defence postulated by Freud: so to speak, the Ego says, This is *not-me*. The Ego treats this unassimilable but still ego-like system as "outside" rather than "inside."

This earliest defence of the infant against stress, as postulated by Freud, is in fact, I maintain, the model of all defence. This proposal is squarely in the spirit of Freud's theory building, in which we find that it is a characteristic conceptual strategy to postulate the earliest form of any category of response as the model upon which later refinements and elaborations of that category of response are built.

The defensive outcome, then, is to establish what we may call a *counter-ego nucleus,* this nucleus being the structural aspect of counter-cathexis. The notion of the counter-ego nucleus is thus a generalization in "structural" terms of the "economic" concept of "counter-cathexis."

What I have said above constitutes, I believe, an account in essentially psychoanalytic language of facts known since Freud, though never before characterized in just this way. I have described these long familiar facts in such a way as to emphasize that the defensive process is a splitting of the ego which is not something that "happens" to the ego but something the ego *does,* a motivated strategy. It is this which I believe at last "struck" Freud and which furnished the central theme of his last paper, "Splitting of the Ego in the Process of Defence." What Freud called the "entirely new" yet "long familiar and obvious" fact was that he was "clearly at fault" to "take for granted the synthetic (i.e., integrative) nature of the processes of the ego."[4] For the ego has another major function which had always had a generic *name,* "defence," but whose *character* as the exact complement of ego-synthesis had never been properly understood or appreciated. "The defence mechanisms" had been the label on a basket into which a categorially mixed collection of items had been stored. It is true that the generic motive for defence—to reduce anxiety—was finally appreciated by Freud in the 1920's. However, the generic mode of operation—the ego's splitting off from itself a counter-ego nucleus—was never appreciated by him until the very last days of his life. At that time, if I am right, he saw this clearly in the course of a final review and restatement of the fundamentals of his theory.

Freud on a number of occasions used language close to that which I have used. He spoke of defence as "disavowal" or a "rejection" in the case of what was "outer" or "inner" respectively.[5] He finally saw, I think, that the generic aim of defence is, in infantile oral terms, to "spit out," or in the more everyday language which Freud used, to "disavow" or "reject." This disavowal or rejection is the generic feature of defence, and it corresponds to what I have called disavowal.

[4] 1940e, XXIII, 276.
[5] 1940a, XXIII, 204.

When this process occurs for the first time there comes into being a nucleus and centre of crystallization for the formation of a psychical group divorced from the ego—a group around which everything which would imply an acceptance of the incompatible idea subsequently collects.[6]

The notion of a "psychical group" was used with some frequency in the earlier writings of Freud,[7] but this notion became assimilated to the word "complex," which in turn came to be associated with certain of Jung's early ideas. The words no longer appear in Freud's writing after his estrangement from Jung; and the Freudian notion they express seems likewise to have dropped below the surface—always implied, as I have argued, but no longer explicit or properly appreciated. (However, a doctrine of "ego-nuclei" has been propounded for many years by the distinguished English psychoanalyst Edward Glover.)

The preceding remarks lead us to see in a new way something of the nature of that resistance which Freud called the resistance of the id. A counter-ego nucleus, however rudimentary, has its own dynamism; it has that thrust towards its own aims which establishes it as ego-like rather than id. Herein is a source of that persistence which Freud ascribed to the id as repository of the repressed. Herein is also a source of what has been called the cathexes from the id which "attract" additional material into the unconscious.

Psychoanalytic therapeutic technique is basically designed to offer to the counter-ego the possibility of some substantial gratification in altered form and harmoniously with the Ego, and to offer to the Ego the possibility of a bearable avowal of the counter-ego. The therapist thus makes possible avowal (removal of counter-cathexis and integration of the counter-ego into the ego).

The most markedly noticeable expression of avowal is usually associated with the new ability to hypercathect, i.e., the readiness of the patient to explicitly avow (not merely to "intellectualize" about) the impulse which had been disavowed. Thus the patient's *explicit* acceptance of a therapeutic interpretation is a distinctive, but not a necessary condition, of the giving up of the defence. Or in still other words, dynamic insight, the becoming conscious of what was unconscious, is not the essence of dissolving the defence, nor is it the ab-

[6] 1895d, II, 123.
[7] 1906c, IX, 100–2.

solute aim of therapy, but it is a distinctive and natural expression of one's having abandoned defence. The "dynamic" essence of defence is what I have called disavowal. This way of putting the matter, which follows from the theoretical critique I have presented, also is consistent with the traditional emphasis by Arlow, Brenner, et al., on the dynamics of defence.

Though I have stressed the ego-like character of what is disavowed, this is by way of corrective compensation for the usual emphasis on its id-character. The rudimentary character of counter-ego nuclei, their isolation from the civilizing influence of the Ego, and the consequent lessening of concern with strict logical, causal, temporal, and other highly rational relationships, makes counter-ego nuclei much cruder, more "primitive," in the form of their expression. They are indeed "closer" to the id insofar as the latter constitutes the uncivilized, highly unspecific basic drives.[7]

IV

Freud eventually appreciated that his therapy had always been oriented primarily to self-acceptance (removal of counter-cathexes) rather than to "knowledge" (consciousness) as curative. Avowal of one's engagements is the optimal goal of classical psychoanalysis. Such avowal is the necessary condition of moral action, but is not itself moral action. It establishes the person as such in a particular respect and thus makes engagement in the moral life possible. As Freud said, the aim of psychoanalysis is not to tell the person what is good or bad, right or wrong in a specific context, but to "give the patient's ego freedom to decide one way or the other."[8] The medical aim is thus in substance a spiritual aim. It is to help the individual become an agent and cease being a patient; it is to liberate, not indoctrinate.[8]

8 1923b, XIX, 50.

Freud, Sartre and Self-Deception

DAVID PEARS

There is an air of paradox about an unconscious desire and an unconscious interpretation of a situation, and especially about an unconscious formulation of a plan. These concepts flout the natural assumption that the contents of a mind all interact freely with one another and can be surveyed from a single vantage point, consciousness. One way of trying to dispel the air of paradox would be to investigate the theory of the unconscious. Another way, which I shall take in this essay,* is to examine some ordinary concepts whose use does not depend on the theory, in order to see if the natural assumption is entirely valid in their case. If it is not, the transition to the theory will not be so sudden and there will not be such a startling break in continuity.

The concept of self-deception seems to be the most suitable object of such an enquiry. It is the most prominent member of a family of pre-theoretical concepts—wishful thinking is another—and it has generated several much discussed paradoxes. For it can hardly combine in one mind everything that in the case of ordinary deception is distributed between two minds. Yet this is what the name "self-deception" seems to imply. In order to avoid this difficulty, some recent accounts[1] have reduced the similarity between the two kinds of deception to a point which deprives the name "self-deception" of its appropriateness. Certainly the thing takes many forms, and perhaps some of them do not quite deserve the name, with its suggestion of deliberateness. But others are more properly so called, and in their case the idea behind the name really does produce the paradoxes.

The paradoxes of self-deception mark dubious similarities between self-deception and ordinary deception. Since ordinary decep-

* This essay was first presented in a slightly different version, to a symposium on "Knowledge and Belief" at the University of Valencia, April 16–18, 1973. The original version will appear in a forthcoming issue of *Teorema*, produced by the Department of Logic and Philosophy of Science of the University of Valencia.

1 E.g., by J. V. Canfield and D. F. Gustafson, "Self-Deception" in *Analysis* 23 (1962); and by T. Penelhum, "Pleasure and Falsity" in *Philosophy of Mind*, ed. Stuart Hampshire (Harper, New York, 1966). Both these accounts are criticized by H. Fingarette, *Self-Deception* (Routledge, London, 1969).

tion is complex, there are several dimensions of possible similarity. They may be pictured as lines radiating from a centre which would represent complete assimilation to ordinary deception. What the paradoxes seem to establish is that on some of these lines self-deception cannot reach the centre. It would follow that no type of self-deception could achieve complete assimilation to ordinary deception. But it would still be possible for certain types to approach very close to the centre along the disputed lines, and even to reach it along others.

I shall enquire whether these possibilities are realized. My strategy will be to resist the conclusions that are commonly drawn from the paradoxes until I have reduced them to an irresistible residue. Self-deception may not be very like ordinary deception, but let us not conclude that it cannot be at all like it until this has been proved. Let us not be stampeded by the paradoxes.

There are four distinct paradoxes which have been discussed in recent accounts of self-deception.

(1) If I have deceived myself that p, I believe p, but at the same time I really know, or believe, or suspect that $not\text{-}p$. These combinations of attitudes seem to be impossible, whatever their cause.

(2) If the cause is a process properly called "self-deception," that process seems to involve another, consequential impossibility: since I am aware that the combination of attitudes is impossible, I cannot intend to produce it in myself.

(3) If it is suggested that my fundamental belief that $not\text{-}p$ is somehow screened from the rest of my thoughts and feelings, the process becomes unintelligible. For awareness of the belief is needed to motivate the process and to guide its strategy: it is, as Sartre says, part of the "unitary structure of a single project."[2]

(4) Perhaps, then, what is screened is the whole plan, together with everything mental that it requires for its existence. But that merely shifts the previous paradox to a different point, where it remains unresolved. If an internally incoherent plan is impossible, it will not be made possible simply by my being unaware of it and not identifying myself with it.

These four paradoxes arise because structures that are subject to the demands of rationality do not meet them fully in cases of self-

2 See J.-P. Sartre, *Being and Nothingness,* trans. Hazel E. Barnes (Philosophical Lib., New York, 1956), pp. 47–54. Most of the relevant passages are included in this volume, pp. 70–79.

deception. The claim made by (1) is that "being self-deceived" is a state which does not conform to the requirements of rational belief. The immediate answer to this is that in fact people do hold incompatible beliefs, and that, when this happens, the requirements are flouted. But this is hardly a sufficient answer, because the explanation of "being self-deceived" is not that the person himself is unaware of the incompatibility—in simple cases he could not be—or that his judgment is equally split between the two alternatives, as might happen if he witnessed an immensely improbable event. Moreover, the name of the state implies an identification of its cause, which runs into the more interesting difficulties raised by (2), (3) and (4). These paradoxes invoke the requirements of rational planning, and their strategy differs from that of (1). (1) claims, in the spirit of Zeno, that the thing cannot happen at all, but the argument of (2), (3) and (4) is that it cannot happen in the way that the name suggests. Here the implied account of the process brings down the requirements of rationality on its own head.

My strategy is to concede to these arguments no more than has to be conceded. So I shall look for ways of evading the requirements of rationality, hoping that they will allow the thing to happen without depriving the name of its appropriateness. Naturally, it is not to be expected that the name will be equally appropriate to every type of the thing. But, if the argument from the paradoxes is valid, there could not be a type to which it would be at all appropriate. It is this conclusion that I shall resist, if it can be resisted.

(1) exploits the fact that a person's beliefs ought to form a system which does not violate the laws of nature or logic. (2), (3) and (4) apply a similar requirement to the contents of the parts of a rational plan: you cannot intend to do what you know that you cannot do, and you cannot execute an intention to eliminate something from consciousness if the intention is partly motivated, and perhaps also guided, by continuing awareness of that very thing. In each case the obstacle is the need for coherence between the elements of a complex structure, and in the second case the obstacle is put there by the implied account of the process of self-deception.

Perhaps we might be able to evade this obstacle if the complexity of the structure of a plan could be reduced a little. This is a possibility worth exploring. But let us first ask how we could make such a large reduction that it would scarcely count as a plan at all. When this question has been answered, we shall have a clearer view of the area within which small reductions might be found.

The phenomenon of wishful thinking offers an instructive example of a large reduction. Suppose that your wish to believe p produces the belief, in spite of the fact that it is not beyond your intellectual powers to realize that your evidence for p is insufficient, and perhaps even points to the conclusion that $not\text{-}p$. Here the idea would be that the wish, by its very nature, tends to produce not only satisfaction that p, when p is believed, but also the belief itself unless it is held in check by the rational assessment of evidence.

There is no need to complicate this theory by supposing that behind some screen the wish is associated with the suspicion that $not\text{-}p$, and that because of this suspicion it develops into the intention to make yourself believe p, and even works out a suitable strategy. All that we have to suppose is that the wish directly produces the ill-founded belief that p, in much the same way that it would have needlessly reinforced it, had it been well-founded. The distinctive mark of wishful thinking is only that the contribution made by the wish to the production of the belief is needed. Naturally, you must be unaware that it is needed, and so there must be some uncharacteristic distortion in your intellectual processes: perhaps you uncharacteristically overestimate the strength of your evidence for p, or—to take a case where your belief is not based on evidence—your memory-impression that p is stronger than it would have been without the wish. But you do not have to be unaware of the wish or of its two general tendencies. For the tendency to produce the belief that p can be held in check, and the tendency to produce satisfaction that p when p is believed is innocent. You can even identify yourself with the wish.

So in a case of wishful thinking only two facts have to be screened: the fact that the contribution made by the wish is needed, and the fact that there is some uncharacteristic distortion in your mental processes.

But what is the screen? In order to determine its nature, various theories would have to be tested against the evidence. But my concern is only with the minimum conditions that have to be met by any explanation of wishful thinking, and it is worth emphasizing how little has to be screened, because it is so easy to exaggerate the amount. We imagine that the wish itself has to be screened, because in fact it often is. And when it is, we have to guard against another exaggeration: we must not suppose that behind the screen the wish is incorporated in a complex structure exactly like a plan. It is naïve to assume that we are bound to explain wishful thinking by reduplicating every detail in the pattern of deliberate agency. We do not even have to suppose that the screen is impervious in both directions. If you are unaware of your wish and do not identify yourself with it, it does not follow that it is no more closely connected with your conscious thoughts and feelings than the altruistic wish of another person who deceives you for your own comfort. To draw that conclusion would be to produce a fifth paradox, sometimes presented in treatments of this topic: wishful thinking and self-deception are interpreted as extraordinary cases of ordinary altruistic deception, but then it is unintelligible how the deceiving agent knows what to do.

But I am still confining the discussion to wishful thinking, and at this point it might be objected that I have reduced its necessary conditions too far. For if you have to be unaware that the contribution made by the wish was needed, will there not necessarily be behind the screen a second associated wish, that your unawareness of the first wish be maintained? And does not that association amount to a plan?

But we do not have to regard even this rudimentary structure as a necessary feature of wishful thinking. For there is another way of explaining your unawareness of the fact that the contribution made by the wish to believe *p* was needed. It might merely be a further intellectual distortion produced directly by that wish. For, if that wish has a natural tendency to produce any distortion in your intellectual processes that is required for the manufacture and maintenance of the belief that *p*, why should the distortions not include the inhibition of any normal mental process that would be incompatible with the belief?

If we choose this explanation of the success of a piece of wishful thinking, we shall be multiplying the effects of a single wish; whereas if we choose the other explanation we shall be multiplying wishes behind the screen.

Neither of the two explanations leads to an infinite regress. For in the second one the extra effect, that you are unaware that the contribution made by the original wish was needed, may well be the last effect to occur in the series. There need not be anything prompting you to ask yourself why you do not believe that it was needed. Perhaps you do not even ask yourself whether it was needed. All that is required is that the original wish should produce the wrong answer to this question, if you ask it, and also to any later question in the series, if, improbably, you persist in your self-examination.

The objection, that the other explanation leads to an infinite regress of associated wishes, may be answered in a parallel way. Instead of multiplying wishes behind the screen, we should put generality into the original wish. We should represent it as the wish to produce the belief that *p,* and to produce unawareness that its contribution to producing the result was needed, and to produce unawareness that its contribution to producing *that* unawareness was needed, and so on for any later unawareness in the series. But since the first unawareness will probably be the only one that actually has to be *produced,* your wish need not reach very far into this potentially infinite series.

It is not clear how we should choose between the two explanations, or even whether there is a real difference between them. But that does not affect the point that I want to make, which is that it is possible to explain the secondary effects of wishful thinking without postulating a plan behind the screen. If it is objected that no such explanation can work, because the complexity of the manoeuvres requires foresight and calculation, it should be remembered that their so-called "complex" pattern has a single principle behind it.

If this is the basic structure of wishful thinking, two questions may now be asked about it. Is it sufficiently complex to count as self-deception? And, if not, can we add enough further elements to transform it into self-deception without falling foul of the paradoxes?

The first question does not deserve a lengthy answer. It will be agreed that, if these minimal cases of wishful thinking do count as self-deception, they certainly do not achieve the maximum possible assimilation to ordinary deception. But it is less important to allocate the name than to discover what these cases lack by seeking an answer to the second question. We should not even assume that the commonest cases of self-deception will be those that come closest to ordinary deception. For it may be that the connotation of the name is not carried over without loss to its most prevalent application. But if that is so, we would expect to find that it has other applications forming a bridge between ordinary deception and minimal wishful thinking.

In fact, there is one very familiar kind of case in which we can add all the elements required for a plan without falling foul of the paradoxes.

Suppose that you begin to suspect that someone whom you had assumed to be honest is defrauding you in some minor way, and then you refuse to take any steps to ascertain whether he is or not, and so you maintain your ailing belief in his honesty. Here paradoxes (1) and (2) hardly make themselves felt. For this kind of belief that *p* is quite compatible with the suspicion that possibly *not-p,* and so there is no incoherence in what you plan. If it is irrational to foster the belief that *p* in such circumstances, that is only because you refrain from using your best available method for reaching the truth, and that kind of irrationality is not incoherence. In any case, truth is not a paramount goal, and so your plan might not even exhibit that kind of irrationality. For your motive might not be merely your own ease of mind, but the sort of visible faith in him that might put a stop to his thefts, if he was thieving.

It is not quite so easy to dispose of (3). The trouble is that your suspicion that possibly *not-p,* is, as Sartre says, "part of the unitary structure of a single plan." But we must not exaggerate the problem in this kind of case. The reason why you need to be aware of your suspicion that possibly *not-p* is not that, in order to neutralize it, you have to work out an elaborate plan. For in this case your plan is a simple one. The reason why it might be held that you need to be aware of your suspicion that possibly *not-p* is only that a typical plan can be reviewed when it is being carried out. But can you in this case reflect that your motive for not seeking more evidence is that you wish to maintain your belief that *p?*

The first step towards answering this question is to realize that in this case the wish does not get between your evidence and your conclusion. There is no intellectual distortion of the sort that occurs in the kind of wishful thinking that has just been described. There does not need to be, because here the wish does not emerge as a deliberate plan to flout the precept: "Accommodate your beliefs to your evidence." It flouts a different precept of reason: "Get all the available evidence that you need." Once this is realized, the paradox vanishes. For there is no incoherence in the structure of the plan, and so no need for any distortion in order to fit its elements together. If the plan is irrational its irrationality is of the other kind.

That disposes of (3) in this kind of case, and (4) does not arise. The case is a simple one, and it is common. Its importance is that it

provides one clear and fairly complete bridge between wishful thinking and the kind of deception of another person that works by depriving him of access to a source of evidence which, you realize, is
likely to lead him to abandon his belief that *p*.

Next let us consider a different kind of case, which raises the
paradoxes in a sharper form. I shall describe this case in extreme
terms which are unlikely to be fully exemplified in real life. The
point of the description will be to show what can happen, even if it
seldom does happen, whereas the previous case was presented exactly
as it frequently occurs.

p is a proposition about yourself which you would like to be true.
But you have sufficient evidence to convince you of *not-p,* if the
proposition were about another person. However, it is about yourself, and you don't like it, and so you set about producing in yourself
the contradictory belief that *p*. Here all the paradoxes are sharper.
For in this case your original attitude to *not-p* is belief, rather than
suspicion, and you have to produce in yourself the belief that *p*
instead of merely maintaining it, and you actually set about producing
it. This is an extreme case, which will seldom be completely exemplified in real life.

Even so, (1) is not too difficult to deal with. In time your belief
that *not-p* will undergo a change, after which, if you are aware of it,
it will be weaker, and if it retains its strength you will not be aware
of it. But *does* it retain its strength behind a screen? One answer to
this question is that it does, if and only if it regains it in front of the
screen when the wish is removed or its operation neutralized, without any new supply of evidence or new instruction in the assessment
of the old evidence. The idea underlying this answer is that new data
which affect the belief in a rational way do not disclose its hidden
strength. There might also be forms of non-rational treatment which
we would prefer to regard as creating a new strong belief rather than
disclosing the old one. Here the precise details depend on theoretical considerations. But all that I need is the outline of a way of dealing with (1) which is used in our everyday judgments about people.

If (1) can be dealt with in this kind of case, so too can (2). For
if the project is feasible, then, as far as this point goes, you can plan
it. But (3) is more difficult and interesting. Two quotations from
Sartre's discussion of this topic will serve to bring out the difficulty.

A. ". . . I must know the truth very exactly *in order* to conceal
it more carefully—and this not at two different moments, which at a

pinch would allow us to reestablish a semblance of duality—but in the unitary structure of a single project. How then can the lie subsist if the duality which conditions it is suppressed?"

B. "To this difficulty is added another which is derived from the total translucency of consciousness. . . . the lie falls back and collapses beneath my look; it is ruined *from behind* by the very consciousness of lying to myself which pitilessly constitutes itself well within my project as its very condition. We have here an *evanescent* phenomenon . . ."[3]

In *B* the word "lie" makes us look in the wrong direction. It is obvious that if you say to yourself something which you believe to be false, that will not persuade you that it is true. But straightforward lying is not the only way of deceiving another person, and so there is no need to suppose that it is the way in which you deceive yourself.

It is, however, an interesting fact that if we do want to find something analogous to lying in your dealings with yourself, it would have to be something of which your mind delivers itself without reflecting on evidence, such as a memory, or an impression of your motivation for an action. But though you receive such items in something like the way in which you receive information from another, you do not issue them, in anything like the way in which he does. In fact, if issuing is an action, you do not issue them at all. For your will cannot attach itself to any part of the project as it could in the previous case, where what you did was to refrain from seeking further evidence. The use of metaphors, such as "spelling out"[4] cannot obliterate this crucial difference. Such deliverances are immediate, and though wishes may influence them directly before they are issued, no such direct influence can be consciously planned.

Perhaps you might plan a course of self-discipline designed to bend your memories in a desired direction, but it is difficult to see what your procedure would be. Getting drunk in order to forget something would involve the wrong kind of causation, because making another person drunk with that end in view does not count as deception. Your treatment of yourself would have to be some kind of intellectual exercise, preferably one which might look as if it could improve your memory. In any case, the causal influence of the exercise would be too indirect for it to be anything like lying, and it would be more like causing another person to lie to a third person.

[3] Sartre, op. cit., p. 49. See page 73 of this volume.
[4] See Fingarette, op. cit., *passim*.

If the type of self-deception now under scrutiny does not have to be assimilated to straightforward lying to another person, (3) does not look so difficult. Self-deception might be a lengthy process somewhat like the process of conditioning another person by a prolonged campaign of subtle deceit. The difference would be that in one's own case the truth-seeking faculty itself has to be held in check. But though this faculty is usually conceded complete sovereignty, it can sometimes be rational to curb it when the object of enquiry is oneself: for a belief about oneself can alter the object (cf. the existentialist paradoxes about sincerity). The real difficulty is the other kind of irrationality, incoherence.

In *A* Sartre goes too far when he argues that we cannot appeal to lapse of time in order to remove the incoherence. True, we cannot if the act is a motivated lie no sooner planned than told. But the type of self-deception which is now being examined usually takes time. The belief in *p* must not only be manufactured but also maintained, and so the plan will be in existence for some time. It is therefore worth asking whether this makes it possible for it to avoid incoherence through some change in its elements or in their relation to one another.

In the discussion of wishful thinking it was pointed out that two facts had to be screened: the fact that the contribution made by the wish was needed, and the fact that there was some consequential uncharacteristic distortion in your mental processes. They also have to be screened in this type of self-deception, because here too the sovereignty of the truth-seeking faculty cannot be manifestly infringed. But *B* draws attention to an unwelcome consequence of supposing that in this kind of case the first fact has to be screened. For this implies that your rational tendency to believe *not-p* has to be screened. But if *this* is progressively screened, the motive behind the execution of the project will gradually lose its force as the project approaches completion.

This is evidently a conclusive argument against interpreting planned self-deception as anything like straightforward lying to another person. For part of the liar's motive for saying *p* has to be that all the time he believes *not-p*. But a more interesting question is whether the argument achieves anything more after the analogy with lying has been dropped.

It tries to exploit the fact that in this kind of planned self-deception you start with strong evidence for *not-p* and when you argue for *not-p* in another person's case you show that you appreciate its strength: for example, *p* is the ascription of a desirable character trait, and the evidence for *not-p* in your own case is your behaviour and the reactions of other people to it. You might even start by believing *not-p*. In some cases it would be an exaggeration to say this, but at least there is a big difference between this kind of case and the case described earlier, in which you only suspected that possibly *not-p,* and so refused to collect any more evidence.

Now, the fact that you have a rational tendency to believe *not-p* is only part of your reason for beginning to do whatever you do to persuade yourself that *p.* The other part is your wish to believe *p.* You are rather like a patient who is aware of his illness and wishes to get well, and begins to take the appropriate medicine. So the first point to be made against the argument from the vanishing motive is that this patient might decrease his dosage as his health improved, and similarly you might reduce your intellectual exercises, as your belief that *p* increased in strength.

But this is only a superficial point because it takes no account of the fact that underneath your increasing belief that *p* there will still be your undiminished rational tendency to believe *not-p.* Naturally, this must be screened from you. But, contrary to Sartre's assumption, the fact that it is screened from you will not necessarily deprive it of its motivating force. Your wish to believe *p* emerges as the plan to deceive yourself that *p* only because you have a rational tendency to believe *not-p.* The fact that you have this tendency may continue to produce its effect even when it has been screened from you.

However, the argument from the vanishing motive does achieve something more than the destruction of the analogy between planned self-deception and straightforward lying. It shows that any plan that there is in this kind of case cannot be fully reviewed when it approaches completion. In the later stages either my original motive must be screened, or it will come through in a version that does not include my rational tendency to believe *not-p.* So if there is a plan here, it cannot contain all the elements of an ordinary plan at every stage in its existence. But if there is no element which it cannot contain at some time, then, contrary to what Sartre implies, its duration is important. For the incoherence indicated by (3) 'can be removed without eliminating any single element for the whole time. No doubt when things have gone a long way you cannot review what you are doing in words such as these: "I am dwelling on certain aspects of my behaviour and relations with other people because I have a rational tendency to believe *not-p*, which I wish to inhibit." At some point in your progress it must become impossible for you to see through what you are doing to your motive for doing it. When this happens, you still have to be able to describe what you are doing in a way that does not mention your motive. For if you could not describe your action in any way at all, it would not be an action under your conscious control. But at the beginning you can include your motive in the formulation of your plan: "I shall dwell on certain aspects . . . etc."

Here there is another important difference between the self-deceiver and the patient taking the medicine. It is unlikely that the patient would continue taking his medicine if he forgot why he had started taking it. But it is not at all unlikely that the self-deceiver would continue his intellectual exercises when his awareness of his motive for starting them began to blur. For in this case all the action is in the mind, and so it is easier for the motive to exert its force stealthily, and perhaps without even being questioned by the agent.

Whether it is at all common for people to embark on self-deception in this candid way is another question. My point is only that it can be done. I want to discover the minimal adjustments that are needed to remove the incoherence from this kind of plan, and, if the self-deceiver's full motivation is screened from him as he proceeds, that is enough to remove the incoherence indicated by (3).

However, this answer to (3) fails to deal with a point which came up in the earlier discussion of wishful thinking. Suppose that you start by formulating your plan to deceive yourself that *p*. Then, as has just been conceded, if this plan is going to succeed, there must come a stage in its execution at which you cannot review it in a way that brings in your motive. Moreover, at the beginning you will know that such a stage is necessary, and so you will have to include it in your plan as an extra task. But in the execution of this task too, there must come a stage at which a review of the plan that brings in your motive is impossible. So the attempt to complete the formulation of your initial plan will lead to an infinite regress. This regress cannot be stopped in the way that the similar regress was stopped in the case of wishful thinking. For in this example you are in the position of a gang leader who is planning an assassination but cannot trust the assassin not to talk; and if he arranges the assassination of the assassin, cannot trust that assassin not to talk . . . etc. It is evident that such a plan would necessarily remain incompletely formulated, and would therefore rely at some point on luck. So too, if someone really did start a course of self-deception, his initial plan could never be completely formulated before he began.

But beneath the similarity between these two plans there are important differences. The gang leader relies on luck, but if at any stage he discovers that he is likely to be unlucky, he can resort to a further assassination. So at the beginning he plans to do whatever he discovers to be needed, hoping that there will come a time when he is lucky and need do no more. But if the self-deceiver plans to do whatever is needed, he has no usable method of discovering at any stage whether further action is needed. For if he investigates his progress with this question in mind, it will follow that further action will be needed. On the other hand, he has an advantage over the gang leader: what he relies on is not luck, but the discreet operation of his own wish to believe p. So though it is true that in the hierarchy of levels there will be one at which he does what happens, it is reasonable for him to expect it to happen.

The main conclusion that I would like to draw from the examination of this type of planned self-deception is that it is possible for it to approximate very closely to one type of ordinary deception. It cannot be at all like straightforward lying to another person, but what it can be like is a carefully planned campaign of deceit, during which you persistently put gentle pressure on him, slightly distorting the evidence or presenting it in a false light. But even this analogy is imperfect, because, when you deliberately set out to deceive yourself in this way, you cannot see every rung of the ladder before you climb it, and at some point you must lose your clear picture of your starting point and of the reason why you have to use this particular ladder to reach your destination. These are important imperfections in an analogy which, nevertheless, remains large.

However, the case, as described, is extreme. In real life it nearly always happens that much more is screened than needs to be. It is rare for anyone who believes *not-p* deliberately to set out to deceive himself that p and to plan the strategy of his campaign in advance. What usually happens is that his project seems to improvise itself as it proceeds. When there is a conscious method, it is more often the negative procedure described in the previous case, in which you deceived yourself about the other person's honesty. It is far easier to avoid looking at what is there than it is to discern what is not there.

If this is done for long enough the buoyancy of the wish may be relied on to support the belief that *p*. So the commonest cases of what we regard as purposive self-deception are mixed cases. Their most conspicuous feature is systematic wishful thinking, but this is punctuated by episodes of deliberate action, which is usually only averting one's gaze, but which is sometimes something more positive.

This brings me to the final, and perhaps the most difficult question that I want to raise. In my comments on the last case of self-deception I did not deal with the whole of (3), or with (4). The argument of the final part of (3) was that, if the self-deceiver's rational tendency to believe *not-p* is screened from him, he will not be able to plan the strategy of his campaign against it. The argument of (4) was that, if our response to this is to say that the whole plan, together with everything mental that it requires for its existence, is screened, we shall merely be shifting the difficulty to a different point where it will remain unsolved. Sartre puts the two points very clearly in his polemic against Freudian theory: ". . . the resistance of the patient implies on the level of the censor an awareness of the thing repressed as such, a comprehension of the end toward which the questions of the psychoanalyst are leading, and an act of synthetic connection by which it [the censor] compares the *truth* of the repressed complex to the psychoanalytic hypothesis which aims at it."[5] From here it seems a short and easy step to the conclusion that all the difficulties described by (3) must now be located in the deliberations of the censor.

These problems are a threat to the thesis that I have been developing. If it is true that any piece of self-deception must contain some mere wishful thinking, and that most pieces will contain a lot, then the case for calling these pieces of self-deception "purposive" will rest very heavily on the fact that the wishful thinking is systematic. But if it is systematic, then it may look as if behind the screen there must be another agency which synthesizes the plan and guides its implementation. If this is so, nothing has been gained.

It would take another paper to answer this objection adequately. I shall merely make three brief points in defence of my treatment of the paradoxes of self-deception.

(1) We ought to distinguish between an ordinary shallow case of self-deception, in which the rational tendency to believe *not-p*

---

[5] Loc. cit. p. 53. See p. 77 of this volume.

is pre-conscious (easily recoverable), and a deep case, in which it is unconscious (too strongly repressed to be recovered easily). In the first kind of case the structure of the so-called "plan" will usually be simple and the wish to believe *p* can do its work without any detailed knowledge of the underlying tendency to believe *not-p*. But the second kind of case is very different, and it may well seem that the patient could not parry the psychoanalyst so effectively unless he had behind the screen much detailed insight into his own case.

(2) However, Sartre's presentation of the Freudian theory about the deep kind of case is excessively intellectualized. Here what has been repressed will not be a single belief but a whole complex of beliefs and feelings. Moreover, the forces stored in this complex will have had a long time to produce other beliefs and feelings of which the patient will be aware. For example, it will produce an elaborate reaction-formation if he is an obsessional neurotic. It would be absurd to describe such a man as simply deceiving himself that *p*, even if *p* were a very complex proposition about himself. His reaction-formation could not be represented as a purely intellectual structure because it would also include feelings, and his resistance to the psychoanalyst would be a natural manifestation of this part of his character. Sartre is quite mistaken when he presents this resistance as a piece of clever acting based on inside information.

(3) Behind this controversy there is a profound question which is hard to formulate correctly. Suppose that we start by considering a shallow case of self-deception. We notice that the process by which the belief that *p* is manufactured and maintained is largely wishful thinking. Then we ask ourselves whether the systematic character of this wishful thinking justifies us in treating the self-deception as purposive. But what does this question mean? If the process is at all complex, it may mean: "What degree of complexity would require unconscious foresight, calculation, feedback and control?" But how are we supposed to answer this question? We have no reliable way of comparing this kind of process where all the action is in the mind, with a skill learned and exercised in the external world. But our difficulty is not merely that we lack a method of answering the question. Its meaning is in doubt. So we try to fill in the disputed part of its meaning by taking all the elements of ordinary agency and imagining that they are screened from the person himself but not from one another. But even if this has a clear meaning, why must it be true? Why must the structure of whatever is behind the screen re-

produce the structure of ordinary agency? Why should it not produce its effects without satisfying the requirements of a coherent plan? The original state of the person might simply cause what follows without that irrelevant constraint. Naturally, no creature's mind could contain a mechanism which eliminated too many of its well-founded factual beliefs. But such a mechanism has a certain survival value for social creatures when its operation is confined to beliefs about themselves and about each other.

Disposition and Memory*

STUART HAMPSHIRE

PREFACE (1973):

This lecture can be attached to a specific text within Freud's works. *Inhibitions, Symptoms and Anxiety* and *New Introductory Lectures* were two works to which I had been paying special attention while I was writing the Ernest Jones lecture. The lecture purposely avoids any mention of repression; the word nowhere occurs in it. Yet Freud's theory of repression was its starting point. The account that I at that time planned to give of mental dispositions, quite independently of Freud, required a theory of inhibition and of repression. At the same time I found an uncertainty, an apparent hesitation between two distinct views, in Freud's theory of repression. On one view repression of libidinal energies is the universal condition of learning and of conscious, rational planning, and even of the power of normal human thought. On another view repression is represented as the necessary cost of that renunciation of instinctual drives which our civilization demands; the implication is that much of the cost in neurosis may be controllable, and that repression need not be so severe and harmful as it has been. Also, there seemed to be in Freud more than one theory of the relation of anxiety to repression: in *Inhibitions, Symptoms and Anxiety* (1926) Freud wrote: "It was anxiety which produced repression and not, as I formerly believed, repression which produced anxiety."[1] I was puzzled by these changes, which have consequences for the philosophy of mind.

I now think that the lecture gives too simple an account of the development of secondary dispositions, and of character traits, and of the inhibition of impulses in the process of growing up. I assume here that the unconscious mind develops only from the inhibition of behaviour and that it has no independent nature. I now think, quite independently of Freud's theories, that our beliefs and prop-

* This essay is a revised version of the paper originally given as the Ernest Jones lecture, delivered before the British Psycho-analytical Association on June 15, 1960. The original version was printed in the *International Journal of Psycho-Analysis* 43, pt. 1 (1962), pp. 59–68. Printed by kind permission of the author and the editor of the journal.

[1] 1926d, XX, 108–9.

ositional attitudes generally can only be explained by reference to a great variety of unconscious thoughts which constitute the background of our conscious reasoning. The development of secondary dispositions, from childhood onwards, has to be interpreted also as the establishment of memories and fantasies which govern conduct directly, even though the thought may be pre-logical and comparatively unstructured and not easily expressed in words. The anxiety that attaches to threatening and painful thoughts, the repression of them, and the defences against them that are elaborated in conscious attitudes and beliefs, have to be acknowledged as psychical realities, which may or may not have a full and detailed expression in behaviour. I would therefore now qualify the argument of the following pages. Certainly there is a range of dispositions formed as residues of inhibited behaviour, and their expressions are legible for this reason. But these dispositions are further differentiated by thoughts and fantasies which do not have an immediate expression in some corresponding pattern of behaviour.

That much of our thought is not conscious thought, and that behaviour by itself cannot reveal the specific detail of the thought from which it issues and which it expresses, are conclusions that are scarcely acceptable within an empiricist theory of knowledge. It now seems to me certain that the theory of knowledge has to accommodate the discovery, and the bringing to consciousness, of thoughts which the subject has not known to be his, and which another person usually can only precariously infer from the most indirect evidence.

It is natural to begin with the assumption that infants, like the higher animals, exhibit for our inspection definitely discriminable patterns of behaviour and that at the very beginning they exhibit no powers that are distinctively mental for our easy discrimination, beyond and behind these patterns of behaviour. As young children learn to communicate, and learn routines of demand and response, and as they finally learn to communicate freely in a language, the notion of the mental states that lie *behind* their behaviour and expression, as something distinguishable from them, becomes more and more definitely applicable to them. Part of the process of becoming more and more adult, and of mental development itself, is the process of learning to inhibit and to control inclinations. There is a primary sense of disposition, disposition in the sense of inclination, typically applied to persons rather than to physical objects:

the sense in which I may report that I was at a certain moment disposed or inclined to laugh or to cry. A disposition in this sense is something that may occur at a particular moment, may be felt, may be disclosed, and may be inhibited or indulged. When children learn in relations with others to control their own behaviour at will, they will sometimes be in the position of being inclined to do something and yet will refrain from doing it. Concurrently, or a little later, they are also learning to express their inclinations in words, and are learning to identify things and persons and actions as having certain names, or as satisfying certain descriptions. They thereby arrive at the position of often knowing what it is they want, or are inclined, to do, in the sense of being able to say and to think what it is that they want or are inclined to do. They are able to identify their wants and inclinations as directed towards this or that object, or kind of object. The power to identify and declare one's wants and inclinations necessarily brings with it an extension of the range of these wants. Not only is the subject able to discriminate specifically the objects of his inclinations, but also his inclinations can be directed towards objects that are not immediately present to him, and that are not even causally connected with anything present to him. Finally, he acquires, together with the power to name and to describe, the power to place the objects of his inclinations in a clearly identified future, and of his wishes also in a clearly identified past. To learn the use of concepts is, among other things, to be able to give a definite ordering to one's experiences in time. A creature who uses language is no longer confined to an undiscriminated present in the direction of his inclinations and in the objects of his desires.

All this happens to a child in a social context, in primitive dealings with other people. From the beginning he is responding to the meaningful gestures of others. He very soon finds himself in a social world: that is to say, he finds himself learning to observe conventions and rules that conflict with his instinctual needs, and to observe the rules *as* rules. He gradually learns, largely by imitation, routines of behaviour, and he learns also the names and proper descriptions of these routines. Thereafter his inhibition of his inclinations is to be distinguished from the inhibition of a trained animal: of a dog trained to restrain its natural inclination to bite something. Because the child may know what it is he is inclined to do, the question of whether he will do it comes up as a question for him to decide. He may *decide* to restrain his inclination to do something, in a sense of "decide" that is not applicable to an animal, which is not a potential language-user. Whether we say that the deliberate and self-conscious inhibition of an inclination by a human being is an inhibition in a different sense, a sense not applicable to animals, is a philosophical issue that need not detain us here. Must we recognize a difference of sense when there is a difference in the method of verification attached to a context transferred from its original context? I think not. But whatever answer philosophers may give to this question, it is obvious that we can give a clear sense to the inclinations that lie *behind* a creature's behaviour, when that creature can report that it is, or was, inclined to do something and that it restrained its inclination. An animal which cannot use a language may be trained not to do that which it would naturally do. But that it was on a particular occasion inclined to bark or to bite, although owing to its training it did not in fact do so, must be shown in its behaviour, if it is to have sense at all. One must see it behaving in a constrained way, just as when it is frightened one must see it behaving in a frightened way. (I oversimplify, but broadly this is so.) The inclinations that lie behind the behaviour, the extra dimension that is gradually added to a human being as he grows up to be a language-user, depend for the possibility of their existence on his ability to recognize them as being what they are. This is not only because his disclosures are in the last resort necessary to the confirmation of the existence of the inclination; but also because the action of inhibiting, as an action of his, requires that he recognize his inclination as an inclination of a certain kind.

It will be evident that I am representing a human being's learning of a language as at the same time the acquisition of inclinations which he may on any occasion choose to realize or to inhibit. His full inner life begins with this power of intentional inhibition. To describe the development of conscious emotion in a very simplified form: a creature attacked becomes frightened or angry in the sense that it perceptibly behaves in the way that we would specify if we were asked for the natural response to attack—that is, by flight or counter-attack. At the next stage of mental development away from the primitive reaction, the behaviour typical of anger—i.e., aggression—may be inhibited, and only the physiognomy, or expression, that normally accompanies the behaviour may remain. The important point is that we know that his expression is an expression of anger because we recognize it as the abstracted residue of aggressive behaviour; it is this aggressive behaviour at its vanishing point. At the third stage of inhibition, even this remaining natural expression of anger may be intentionally controlled; perhaps because it is recognized to be a sign of anger that others can interpret as such. When this stage of interiorization is reached, the natural expression of anger may be used intentionally as a sign in letting others know that one is angry. If there is the power deliberately to inhibit the expression, there is also the power to assume the expression, as a gesture, as a means of communication, and in deceit, mimicry and play; or at least the idea of assuming the expression must be present to a man's mind as a possibility, if the habit of concealing has once been acquired.

Part of that which remains as a residue, when both the behaviour and the physiognomy primitively associated with anger are controlled, is the mere feeling as a state of consciousness, the inner perturbation, the affect by itself. It is "inner" in the sense that nothing of the anger remains to be perceived by an observer. If an observer is ever to know that the subject is angry, he must primarily rely on the subject's avowal of those inclinations, or upon some inference from the situation and from its correlation with these commonly disclosed inclinations. Plainly there will still be many occasions when the inhibition of the natural expression of the anger is incomplete and only partially successful, and when sufficient signs remain as the basis for an inference, or as confirmation of the sincerity of an avowal. On the border line of these two stages of inhibition there will be many impure cases—of angry behaviour half controlled, or of the physiognomy of anger just showing through, in spite of an effort to suppress it. The pure case of mere inclination, as a state of consciousness, with every natural expression of it suppressed, certainly exists; and it is the interesting case, as being part of the pattern of inner, unseen mental states, and of the difficulty, or, as some philosophers have thought, impossibility, of inter-subjective descriptions of them.

A man who feels angry, while concealing every overt sign of his inner perturbation, may not need to exercise his will in the act of concealment. The restraint may already be a habit, natural to him as a civilized man. But the habit of intentional inhibition has been acquired during his lifetime, and acquired gradually as part of the observation of social convention. If he is perturbed in the presence of an attacker, he knows, in a simple case, whether he has the disposition to counter-attack or to escape or both. Therefore he knows, in very simple cases and at a superficial level, whether his excitement is anger or fear, or a mixture of both. He does not have to learn to distinguish anger from fear, as a mere quality of feeling, in the way that he distinguishes one colour from another. He is aware of his own controlled inclination in the situation that confronts him. He feels at once the inclination to flight or to counter-attack and he makes the counter movement of restraint. If his feelings are complex, in the sense that he is, in the normal sense of these words, both frightened and angry at the same time, he has opposing inclinations towards flight and counter-attack; and these inclinations may again not be translated into spasmodic and interrupted actions, but rather remain as mere inclinations. I am not of course denying that a man may experience confused and conflicting inclinations, which he may be unable clearly to distinguish and to describe. Nor am I denying that by some methods of analysis, anger and fear may perhaps be shown to be similar and related strategies in the defence of an organism against danger, the one a variant of the other. But it is enough that simple cases of identification of states of consciousness do occur: for it is on these that the whole psychological vocabulary is ultimately founded. We make a mistake if, as philosophers, we think of the emotions and sentiments as primarily something hidden in a man's consciousness and as linked by a contingent and causal relation to their outcome in behaviour: and this has been at least one prevailing picture in contemporary philosophy. The expression of a sentiment or emotion is not something that is extrinsic to the sentiment or emotion itself, as something that may or may not be added to it. On the contrary, that which we call the natural expression is originally constitutive of the sentiment or emotion itself, and may or may not be subtracted from it. This subtraction is the work of a convention-observing creature who already has an intentional control of his behaviour, and who can recognize his own inclinations while refusing to follow them. So much for the simple concept of primary dispositions, or inclinations, in the conscious mind, as these are identified at the most superficial level.

You will perhaps at this stage want to ask for the justification of this, or for any other, simplified philosophical theory of the emotions in their relation to behaviour: is this *a priori* psychology, and, if not, what is its scientific basis? What is a philosopher's authority for distinguishing phases of human development beginning with primitive behavioural reactions and ending with inner concealed emotion? What is the purpose, and the criterion of success, in such an inquiry as this? It may seem that any such theory must be tested by the observation of children and by careful experiment; and yet this is not the work of philosophers. The answer is that these considerations about the emotions, which I have been putting before you, very dogmatically and in a very simplified form, are part of a more general, and of course disputable, theory of knowledge, a theory of how concepts must be originally acquired and applied in their normal contexts. I am, or I take myself to be, specifying the implications, and the method of confirmation, attached to uncriticized, ordinary statements about human emotions of the most rudimentary kind. And, after all, this must be the starting point in prescribing the use of the vastly complex and derivative concepts of psycho-analysis. They also have been developed through many stages of complication and theory, from a rudimentary base in commonplace usage. We have to retrace the path back to this base if we are to understand how they are made up. We have first to see the rudimentary base clearly before us in some simple form, and then we can make the corrections to the commonplace conceptual scheme which the discoveries of psycho-analysis require.

This is the simplified picture of the concept of disposition, in the sense of inclination, which is, I think, the fundamental mental concept. For the conscious mind has to be conceived—at least in the present state of our knowledge—as, at least in part, a vastly complicated set of dispositions of different orders of complexity. I am speaking only of those dispositions that are simple feelings or affects, interpreted as inclinations to behave in certain more or less determinate ways in certain determinate circumstances. But now doubts arise, doubts that infect the whole study of the philosophy of mind at this time. Let it be admitted that it is characteristic of mental, as opposed to physical, concepts that the conditions of their application can only be understood if they are analyzed genetically: that is, we need to trace the order in which their use is learnt in the history of any individual, beginning with the primitive concepts of sensation, desire and behaviour, concepts that are applicable also to creatures who are not potential language-users, and showing the use of the more distinctively mental concepts as developing from them in successive stages of interiorization. The use of concepts in communication is learnt in parallel with the development of corresponding powers of mind—the power to feel without acting and the power to think without saying. But "in parallel" is an inadequate phrase here; for the one conditions, and makes possible, the other in a complex interaction. A child can have desires and intentions, fears and hopes, directed towards future events, only because he has the means of describing and identifying the remote objects that he desires, fears, or hopes. And the more finely discriminated states of consciousness —embarrassment rather than fear, shame rather than guilt, remorse rather than regret—can be attributed to him, only because his thought about himself in relation to external objects is of a degree of elaboration that allows him to decide which of these words accurately represents his state. The refined vocabulary of intentional states requires disclosures, not only of the inclinations, but also of the beliefs that enter into the definition of these states. A man whose state of mind is remorse must, of logical necessity, believe that he has done wrong, and this belief of his must be in principle expressible. One could summarize this double development—learning the use of mental concepts and simultaneously acquiring the corresponding powers of mind—as the development of intentional states. An intentional state, like an intentional action, is directed towards an object that is identified as the object of the state by the subject's conception of it as having a certain name, or as satisfying a certain description. Neither intentional states, in this sense of the phrase, nor intention in action, can significantly be attributed to creatures that are not language-users or potential language-users. Such creatures may want and fear, pursue and avoid, certain objects, and we may inquire into, and see, the purposes of their behaviour. We may experimentally distinguish the objects of their desires and fears, their rages and their repugnances; and we may also by experiment distinguish those features of the objects that make them objects of desire and fear, of rage and repugnance. But the intentional object is identifiable, apart from the evidence of variations of behaviour, through the subject's expression of his thought of the object as having a certain name or as satisfying a certain description. With imputations and acknowledgements of beliefs and intentions, which are not simple inclinations to behave in certain ways, we therefore enter another phase of the mind's development.

The first difficulty can now be stated. Infants are born into a social world, and they sooner or later learn to inhibit their inclinations in accordance with social conventions. They learn also conventions of communication in responding to, and imitating, the meaningful gestures of adults. They gradually acquire an inner life of unexpressed feeling, which becomes more and more distinct from their overt behaviour; and they acquire intentions that point forward in time, remote from the observed present, and that may be left unrealized. But their earliest behaviour, and particularly their play, already foreshadow the added depth of concealed disposition, and inner emotion, that will come with their own later recognition of this depth. The signs are legible in their play, and in their ordinary behaviour, of that which is beyond and behind them—namely, dispositions and inclinations that are repressed, contained within the child's mind as affects or inner feelings. But the signs of inner feeling can never at this stage be intentional signs, and they still have to be read by someone other than the subjects themselves.

Neither philosophy nor psycho-analysis can be satisfied at this point. How much is included in the child's response to, and imitation of, the meaningful gestures of adults? Is the play of a child revealing of inhibited dispositions, and therefore of a depth of feeling, unrecognizable by the child itself, in a full sense of disposition and of "feeling"? The answer to this last question is "Yes." But how can this be?

One possibility suggests itself. When a man looks back in memory, later intentional expressions of feeling may sometimes be associated with the memories of the earlier play. He finds a continuity from the earlier to the later, the continuity of a familiar pattern repeating itself. The inner inclination, which, as he is now persuaded, was originally expressed in his play, may later, preserved in unconscious memory, be expressed in intentional conduct; or it may at least be recognized as an inclination to behave in a certain way.

The essential problem of the unconscious mind is one of time and of memory. The child's responses to meaningful gestures, and his imitation of them, are the earliest phases of a continuous history, which ends with the use of language, and with those intentions directed towards the future, and those memories of past events, which depend on the use of concepts. The continuity of this history lies in the subject's memory. But the power of memory itself develops from a primitive and pre-conceptual form to an adult's fully articulated dating of his experience in a definite time-order. We may relapse, in dream and fantasy, into the pre-conceptual, childish world, in which past and present are not discriminated by the recognition of memories as memories. But still the power of conscious memory develops alongside these regressions. The word "development," when we speak of the development of a mind or person, implies an order that is held together by manifold links of conscious, half-conscious and unconscious, memory. Looking back in conscious memory, a person can trace a continuity between that which he may with difficulty remember of his early fantasies and play, and his later self-conscious intentional states; and his earliest surviving conscious memories are still memories of a person already carrying a burden of memories, which are no longer available to him. Then, by analogy, it seems that the actions and experiences that he does still remember were originally desirable or repugnant to him partly at least because of memories of earlier experiences now beyond recall. In investigating the development of a man's body, we take it for granted that its earlier states, taken in conjunction with external actors, determine its later states, and its causal properties, in accordance with a great variety of exact and confirmable natural laws. In investigating the development of a man's inclinations, his emotional development, we cannot always, or even generally, in practice apply such a simple scheme of past states determining future dispositions, although the theoretical possibility is always open. It is a fact that the stored, and potentially available, but still unconscious, memories of the past are influencing present inclinations at any time. But what is contained in the word "influencing" here? Is this a familiar causal relationship? I am inclined to think not.

Memory of one's own past may take several very different forms. In the most simple case, we may be aware of our memories as memories, and a memory of something that happened may be the fully conscious ground or reason for a present feeling, or for the behaviour that is the natural expression of this feeling. I am inclined to behave harshly towards him because I remember him harassing me. The word "because" here introduces the reason for, and not only the cause of, my being inclined to behave in this way. But the memory of this same event in the past may have previously existed below the level of consciousness, ready to be evoked as a conscious memory, when the right questions are asked in the right conditions; but the memory is still unrecognized. As soon as the memory is called into consciousness as a memory, the question arises for me—Am I only behaving in this way, and do I only have this inclination, *because of* my memory of this past experience? This might perhaps begin as a causal question, as a matter of objective curiosity about psychology. But it immediately becomes an inquiry into the grounds of my behaviour: are they sufficient grounds or not? I had not realized the fact that I had unconsciously remembered this past experience. This fact—the fact that I had preserved this memory below the level of consciousness—becomes something that I must now take into account in considering my present inclinations. Is it reasonable that this past experience should influence my inclinations and actions in my present situation? Is there a relevant similarity, relevant, that is, to consciously recognized ends, which I can rationally acknowledge, between the past situation and my present situation? Once the question is raised, I may, or may not, consider the past experience relevant to my present situation. This is something that I must now decide for myself.

But at this point any true empiricist will ask—what is the sense of speaking of a memory of a past situation, a memory that exists below the level of consciousness, as a reason for present feeling and behaviour, potentially to be acknowledged as a reason? Is it not clearer, and more economical, in such cases to speak of the past event as the cause of the later feeling or behaviour without the interposition of memory at all? Is it not clearer to speak of memory only as a form of knowledge? And therefore always as conscious memory? I think that the evidence compels us to give the answer "No" to each of these questions. The bringing to the surface of consciousness of an unconscious memory cannot be assimilated to the discovery of a causal connexion. These are discoveries of quite different kinds, and they require quite different methods of inquiry.

The whole issue of dispositions of the mind, contrasted with the causal properties of physical things, turns on this problem of how far the concept of memory is to be extended. Suppose we allow ourselves to speak of early satisfactions and frustrations of instinctual needs as stored in unconscious memory, and as constituting the reasons, or the motives, for varieties of conduct on many later occasions; then we have already begun to substitute a memory-relationship between past and present, peculiar to mental processes, in the place of the normal causal scheme of the natural scientist. This is exactly what Freud did, from the beginning, in his early studies of hysteria. Had he not taken a leap forward in his discoveries of clinical method, he might simply, as a good empiricist, have correlated early alleged sexual experiences, and then, later, the fantasies of such experiences, with subsequent hysterical disorders as causes to effects. He might have adhered to the normal scheme of natural law, without any doctrine of memory traces, interposed as a middle term.

He would thereby have precluded himself from relating his method of treatment to his method of diagnosis within a single theory, each confirming the other. That which is elicited from the unconscious memory is the underlying motive of, or reason for, conduct and inclination; and a motive or reason, unlike a cause, is liable to be immediately acknowledged or repudiated as the real motive, and then judged and criticized by the subject as reasonable or unreasonable. The connexion between the now recalled, unconsciously remembered situation and the later behaviour symptom must be such as to make the behaviour intelligible to him. It is intelligible if it is a variant of behaviour that is normally adapted to the satisfaction of desires, and if this variation is explained as the superimposition of the unconsciously remembered situation on the present situation. Then he understands the motive.

There are specifiable differences between the discovery of a correlation between two classes of events in a person's history, the occurrence of one determining, under statable conditions, the occurrence of the other, and the discovery that a memory of something in the past has been continuously the reason for inclination and conduct, unknown to the subject and without his having been aware of the memory as a memory. In the second case the influence of the past is something that may be recognized by the subject as the explanation of his inclination and conduct when he becomes aware of the memory as a memory; and to say that he recognizes the unconscious memory as the *explanation* of his inclination and conduct is not to attribute to him the discovery of a correlation between two classes of events. He finds that the now consciously remembered experience explains his inclination in the same sense that an observed feature of his present situation might explain his inclination; it is the reason of his being inclined to behave in a certain way. But the reason is not to be identified as an objectively observed feature of a present situation, but rather as a feature of a past situation always superimposed upon the realities of the present. When the repressed memory is revived, there is an instant recognition of the continuity and unbrokenness of the memory discernible in a consistent misreading of situations confronting him. When the memory is recognized as a memory, he recognizes also the consistent superimposition of the past upon the present. Then he finds that the now consciously remembered experience explains his inclination in the same way that an observed feature of his present situation might explain his inclination. The only difference is that, unknown to himself, he has been trying to alter the past instead of acting on the present. It might be shown that there was no universal correlation between the unconsciously remembered event and the later behaviour; and still the subject might be sure that this unconscious memory contains the reason that explains why he, in this particular case, felt and acted as he did. And one of his reasons for being so sure might be that, with his now fully conscious memory of the past event, the inclination to behave and act in the same way returns to him with the same force, even though now, recognizing the past as past and unalterable, he restrains himself. Feeling himself inclined to respond to the fully conscious memory in the same way, he is aware, again by memory, that there is an old cycle repeating itself. Having the memory present to him as a memory, isolated from present realities, he recalls that, at every stage of the repeating cycle, this remembered situation was superimposed upon the present realities, however different, as he now realizes, they were.

The conclusion that, over almost the whole domain of conduct, there are unconscious motives of behaviour to be discovered follows from the hypothesis that there are countless memories below the level of consciousness waiting to be elicited. Where explanations in terms of instinctual needs and rational calculation are inadequate, we can look into the past for explanations of any individual's conduct and inclinations, without recourse to general propositions of natural law, which, in default of experiment, are not generally available. But motives, which explain behaviour and inclination, are one thing and intention is another. "Intention" is the one concept that ought to be preserved free from any taint of the less-than-conscious. Its function, across the whole range of its applications, is to mark that kind of knowledge of what one is doing, and of what one is inclined to do, that is fully conscious and explicit. I have motives for doing things, or for feeling inclined to do things, and I may have purpose in doing things, without recognizing, and without being aware, that these are my motives and my purposes. When I come to recognize what my motives are, or were, or what my purposes are or were, I may certainly be surprised that these were in fact my motives. I may make a discovery. My motives are typically matters for investigation. But I do not investigate, and then discover, my intentions. I may indeed carry out an investigation to see whether my intentions have been consistently related, as they should be, to my actual conduct, externally regarded; and I may then discover, disagreeably, that in fact they have not. And then I need to look for underlying motives and memories, in order to explain this deviation.

If it is once accepted that there are countless unconscious memories of our past satisfactions and frustrations, we see many of our actions and inclinations as, at least in part, directed towards situations in the past, but superimposed on, and confused with, a present situation. When the memory is brought into consciousness, and we retrace the recurring cycle of motive and conduct back to this starting point, our action may appear as motivated by a desire to alter the past, even though the conscious intention was normally directed to the future. If I am convinced that I would not have formed the intention, had I not had the unconscious memory, I may for some purposes re-describe the conduct by reference to its motive rather than to the conscious intention. Then my conduct can be represented as an attempt to change the past, in defiance of the reality principle. For recognition of reality, as it affects behaviour, is recognition of the *present* situation as present, as opposed to the projection into the present situation of the objects of memory and fantasy. Its opposite, loss of the sense of the present, is a partial regression to the childish, pre-conceptual world in which the objects of conduct and feeling are disconnected from an objectively recognized and definite time-order. The ideally rational man would be constantly aware of all his memories as memories, in so far as they influenced his present conduct and inclinations. Correspondingly, his wishes would be attached to definite possibilities in a definite future, and would not be freely floating fantasies, without attachments to possible occasions. He would always distinguish his present situation from unconscious memories of the past projected upon, and obliterating, the present, and would find his motives for action, in satisfying his instinctual needs, within the objectively observed features of the situation, as he sees it now. But this is an ideal of rationality that can never be attained—which is perhaps fortunate, since it would leave us without art, without dream or imagination, without likes and dislikes unconnected with instinctual needs, and indeed without any character at all as individuals. It can never be attained, because our secondary dispositions to behave in certain ways in certain situations, assimilated to unconsciously remembered primitive situations, are being formed, and superimposed upon each other, from the beginning of our life. I speak of "secondary dispositions" here to distinguish dispositions, in the sense of character traits, from dispositions in the sense already mentioned—namely, inclinations to behave in a certain way on a specific occasion. The original formation of secondary dispositions can be traced back to unconscious memories of primitive satisfactions and frustrations of instinctual needs, modified by complicated and continuing processes of repression, projection, displacement, transference, and so on. Ideal rationality, defined as motivation by the recognized features of the present situation alone, together with instinctual drives, would impossibly require that no such dispositions should exist. Every memory of past satisfactions and frustrations would be present to my mind as a conscious memory, and therefore the relevance, for the satisfaction of my instinctual needs, of the past experience to the present situation would be objectively assessed. In fact I necessarily approach situations with already formed dispositions to respond in my conduct principally to those features of them which are easily associated with unconsciously remembered primitive situations. These dispositions, resting on the weight of my earliest memories, constitute my character as an individual. This may be strong or pliable, making me more or less impervious to changing external realities in my feeling and conduct.

It is now possible to see why the genetical method of explanation must lead to apparent paradoxes. In any individual mind, past frustrations and satisfactions, particularly in the earliest phases of the mind's continuous history, foreshadow the direction of later behaviour and inclinations. This foreshadowing is the other face of the fact that experiences that have once aroused strong inclinations are, in one way or another, remembered, if not consciously, then unconsciously. If they are repressed and unconsciously remembered, they remain as unrecognized motives, which explain a recurring inclination to behave in a characteristic way, in comparative independence of the unchanging external realities. A paradox arises when the arrow of historical explanation of a man's secondary dispositions, is thought of as causal determination. If the determination were causal, it should allow prediction. But the determination claimed is only the fact that unconsciously remembered situations in the past supply unconscious motives for present conduct and inclination. This confusion has sometimes led interpreters of Freud to speak of retrospective causal explanation, which is a logical absurdity. Of motives it can indeed be said that they explain retrospectively, and that they do not provide a corresponding basis for prediction of future behaviour. In my stating that it was so-and-so that moved me to laugh or protest, I have not so far committed myself to any general proposition which justifies a prediction of my behaviour on future occasions; and, least of all, is there a basis for prediction when the transition may be made from an unconscious motive to the conscious recognition of it. Once the imposition of the unconsciously remembered past on the present is fully recognized, and the realities of the present situation are no longer consistently misperceived, the foundations of the secondary disposition have been loosened, and therefore the former character trait may be controllable. This character trait was after all something that I found myself to possess, and not something that I had chosen for myself. And now I may be for the first time in a position to choose, within the limits of the other secondary dispositions that constitute my character.

Something is always being added to the weight of motivating memories, both conscious and unconscious, and it is in practice, although not in theory, impossible to isolate the initial conditions on which scientific predictions could be based. It seems that, because of his vastly extended concept of memory, Freud is committed to the reverse of determinism in explaining any individual's emotional development, if determinism is associated with predictability. If we accept the hypothesis of total memory of past satisfactions and frustrations, it certainly follows that we could only approach complete explanations of inclination and behaviour in any individual case through an interminable analysis. The formation of secondary dispositions is a perpetual process, in which recurrent patterns of inclination and behaviour, originally motivated by memories of some primitive situation, are being at all times complicated by displacements and identifications, and by the stress of further frustrations of the dispositions themselves by external realities. And one of the effects and signs of stress, at primitive stages and later, is to make conscious recall more difficult. In any individual case we may be able, by successfully reviving memories, to travel backwards towards the first member of a series, along a series that recalls the recurring motive of inclination and behaviour at every stage. But we cannot infer from this history, or from any finite set of such histories, exactly how the series will be prolonged into the future, if it is prolonged. The vast and continuing accretions of repressed memory provide too many independent variables for any general law of cause and effect to be formulated and tested. We are left only with the recurring pattern itself as a mere tendency; that is, we are left with the old notion of character, of dispositions in the second sense. In extreme cases of illness, a man's character and secondary disposition, which represent attachment, through repressed memory, to the past, will be so strong that patterns of inclination and behaviour will be almost unvarying in changing situations. Selected features of these situations will be read always as changing symbols of emotionally charged features of his primitive past. Then indeed confident prediction may be possible. The cycle of inclination and overt behaviour will simply repeat itself. But when the second dispositions are only of normal (in the sense of "average") strength, and motives for inclination and action can still be found in changing situations, the interaction between present and past, between fate and character, in forming feeling and behaviour becomes, on this hypothesis, too complicated for scientific prediction.

The second difficulty that we confronted was this: that we should not only attribute motives and purposes that have not been previously recognized by the subject himself, but also that we should attribute them to children at a stage of development when they would have been incapable of formulating them, or of recognizing their existence in any way. Searching under guidance through repressed memories, and meeting resistance to their recall, an individual will find one of these recurring patterns of motive, of inclination and of behaviour in his history. The recurrence is itself at every stage an instance of unconscious remembering. If the hypothesis of total memory is correct, the earliest memories of the earliest instinctual needs, and of primitive frustrations of instinctual need, must be the terminus of explanation. This is the hard foundation to which we always return in explaining any individual's secondary dispositions. In order to assert the constancy of the motivation from its starting point in the individual's history, and simultaneously to show the motives for the repression of the relevant memory, the early formation of character traits is assimilated to the problem solving of an adult man. It is characteristic of properly causal explanations of mental processes that highly developed and rational processes are assimilated to the more primitive responses to stimulus; for specifically described behaviour has to be regularly correlated with specifically prescribed initial conditions. It is characteristic of an individual psychology based on the memory relationship that the least developed mental processes are assimilated to the rational or problem-solving kind. We look backwards, from the later to the earlier, in order to understand the present as a lightly or heavily disguised re-enacting of the problems of the past. And in extreme cases of neurotic behaviour, the lapse of time, and the development of rational powers of mind, may be virtually left out of the explanation as an irrelevant superstructure.

For centuries the workings of the mind, in forming inclinations and attachments to objects, have been construed by empiricists on a mechanical model, which the causal scheme of explanation seemed to require: the association of ideas. The laws governing the association of ideas were taken to be strictly analogous to the laws governing the movement of bodies. The separate inclinations formed themselves according to universal causal laws. There was no reason to consider the whole set of a man's secondary dispositions, taken as a whole, as ultimately traceable back to a problem presented to him by some primitive situation or situations. For the simple machinery of the association of ideas, Freud substitutes complex activities of projection, introjection and identification in the solution of conflicts. The importance of this substitution, from the philosophical point of view, is just that these activities are represented as activities; and because they are so represented, the underlying motives of them can be investigated. Within this scheme, the question of "Why?"—the demand for an explanation in any particular case—does not call for a universally valid psychological law and a statement of initial conditions. Since these processes are represented as activities of mind, the question "Why?" asks for a description of the situation or situations, and therefore of the given problem, to which these continuing activities were the solution adopted. The effect of the substitution of the active for the passive mood is that the subject is required to search in his memory for the past situation, as it survives in his mind, and to acknowledge or to disclaim its superimposition on the present. The appeal to his supposed total memory of his unconscious policies in satisfying his instinctual needs, or the needs derived from their frustration, is an appeal to him to understand his own behaviour as a whole, historically: and this form of understanding, the historical and autobiographical form, is taken to be the fundamental form in the explanation of patterns of inclination and conduct. He may resist the appeal and his active exercise of memory may be ineffective. But this failure also will require an explanation in terms of a motive for refusal to remember, and will not be counted as evidence against the hypothesis of total memory itself. If a recurring pattern of feeling and behaviour stands out in an individual's history, and if its first, and only its first, occurrence is explicable by the operation of the instincts against the given resistance of reality, the later instances of the pattern can be traced back, through many complicating stages, to unconscious memories of this primitive occasion.

The whole weight of explaining, and of understanding, human behaviour is placed on the individual subject, as potentially an active, remembering being. Because of this, he can, to some extent, become rather more free and self-determining, through making an active use of memory in disinterring his own unconscious motives, and in acquiring a clearer view of present reality.

On Freud's Doctrine of Emotions

DAVID SACHS

Talk of a summary kind about Freud has for its byword the claim that unconscious items and processes dominate psychic life. Such talk is of course likely to go further: due to the unconscious we are creatures curiously heedless of time, creatures fixed in our early if not earliest ways. The unconscious, to put it dramatically, first maddens us and then keeps us mad. Among its achievements are these: we try to gratify wishes that are opposed to each other, indeed wishes whose descriptions may be paradoxical; we mistake as meaningless what is intelligible, and as trivial the important and even portentous; we confuse the scope and character of our acts and intentions; our denials can often be better understood as affirmations, and often too, the converse obtains; again more or less unbeknownst to us, our lives are largely spent in the quest and avoidance of persons and experiences past, in pursuit of and flight from an array of surrogates *for* those persons and experiences, including even antithetical surrogates. Then, too, prominent if not paramount in any résumé of Freud's thought will be statements about his extensions of commonplace notions of sexuality; that among unconscious entities those which enjoy pride of place and power are dispositions to affects or emotions that derive from early erotic experiences and fantasies. Any adequate abstract of Freud's work will also observe that, according to him, everyone is either neurotic or troubled by neurotic tendencies for some appreciable phase or phases of his life.

No doubt any tolerable summary, however quick or breathless, will seize on other salient points in Freud's thought. Mention will be made of his speculations on the origin and development of mankind, on religion, the occult, and the arts; notice taken of his abiding but flexible differences from the rival schools that arose out of his own, particularly the earlier ones, Adler's individual psychology and the analytical psychology of Jung; emphasis will be placed on Freud's changes of view concerning therapeutic practice and, above all, upon the evolution of his metapsychology. In this last connection, although doubtless in others too, there are likely to be certain omissions, in particular omissions that concern Freud's doctrine of emotions or affects.

One important omission, I shall contend, pertains to the five decades of Freud's psychological investigations: to his persistent adherence, in one form or another, to the idea that, between any person's emotions or affects and the causes or causal objects thereof, there always obtains an actual proportionality or real appropriateness, no matter how discrepant or incongruous those relations may appear to be, and regardless of the person's mental condition, that is, irrespective of whether Freud would deem him psychotic, neurotic, or normal. This claim needs clarification; in what follows I try to clarify it and to show that the attribution to Freud is warranted. At the end I make two observations, the first a suggestion by way of estimating the idea, the second an indication of how, if Freud did hold it, one can thereby be enabled to attain a somewhat novel outlook upon his thought.

I

Among the operative yet unclear expressions that occur in my formulation of the idea I am ascribing to Freud are the phrases "emotions or affects," "causes or causal objects" and "actual proportionality or real appropriateness." First, what is the phrase "emotions or affects" intended to include? Next, what do I mean by "causes or causal objects"? Also, can the relation or relations of proportionality or appropriateness be spelled out? For the moment I leave aside the question about the range of emotions or affects, beginning instead with a set of remarks that I hope will indirectly cast some light on the phrase "causes or causal objects." The words "cause" and "object" have become jargon in the philosophy of mind; nevertheless, they have played important terminological roles in a controversy which it will be helpful to examine.

Some philosophers hold that, for any instance of a person having an emotion, there is some item which is the emotion's object. Assertions to this effect are regularly accompanied by a warning. The warning alerts us that the item, especially in cases of so-called "objectless depression," "free-floating anxiety," and euphoria, is an indefinite collection of more or less randomly hit targets—the objects —of the emotional mood or state. A similar claim is made about certain quite fugitive episodes of emotion or affect: for instance, as when upon waking one just feels—so it is said—good; the claim is that there is no "just" about it, there is still an item, however diffuse or dim, that serves as the object or objects. It is held that if these putatively "objectless" states and episodes did not possess at least such tenuous objects, they would not be correctly called instances of emotions or feelings; they are dependent for their conceptual lives upon their frail object constitutions. Other philosophers, while agreeing that in most if not all putatively "objectless" emotional states and episodes there are the beggarly items to be found hanging about, warn us against regarding them as true or fit objects of emotion. After this divergence, however, there is a joining of forces. Both parties agree that, in Anthony Kenny's words, ". . . the connection between emotions and their objects is not a contingent one."[1] In particular, the connection is not a causal one.

Variations occur upon this theme, variations due to its several possible philosophical motives. The motives are appealed to after making certain assumptions, ones that often hold.[2] Crudely, the assumptions are: when or shortly after a person experiences an emotion, he will be able to say so; he will also be able rightly, even if very roughly, to name or otherwise specify the emotion. At this point one or more of the philosophical motives enters into play. It may be said that, when a person has an emotion and there is some item that is the emotion's object, the person cannot be mistaken as regards at least one identification of it; that is, at least one identification of what is delighting him or making him miserable, what he is feeling hopeful of or fearing, what he is feeling remorseful about or triumphant over, and so on. Or—separately or conjointly—it will be said that the person's identification of the object of his emotion is not a consequence of observation or of any inductive procedure; it is not, as it were, *gathered,* gathered either introspectively or in some other way; it is unmediated. Most commonly the following is said: for a man's identification of the object of his emotion to be an identification of a cause or causal factor of the emotion, he must be able to identify his emotion in a way conceptually independent of—in a man-

[1] Anthony Kenny, *Action, Emotion and Will* (Routledge, London, 1963), p. 62.

[2] Here and in much of this section, I am indebted to David Pears' article "Causes and Objects of Some Feelings and Psychological Reactions," *Ratio* 4, no. 2 (1962), pp. 91–111, reprinted in *Philosophy of Mind,* ed. Stuart Hampshire (Harper, New York, 1966); and to J. R. S. Wilson, *Emotion and Object,* (Cambridge Univ. Press, Cambridge, 1972).

ner only contingently connected with—his identification of its object; and this demand, it is said, cannot be met.

There are three claims, then: a person identifies the object of his emotion without any real possibility of mistake; he identifies it without mediation; and a conceptual link holds between his identification of the emotion and his identification or identifications of its object. Philosophers who hold these views often assert that singly or together they are sufficient to show that a man's identifications of his emotions and their objects are not contingently related; in particular, that they are not related as identifications of items that could possibly be effects of causes. Following Wittgenstein, they make an additional claim: occasionally emotions, although never merely the effects of their objects, manage to enjoy that humble relationship too. Oddly enough, what appears to be a blatant inconsistency, given the additional claim, seems to have been generally overlooked. The position, again, is that alone or together the alleged incorrigibility, immediacy, and conceptual connection *suffice* to make it impossible for an object of an emotion to be its cause; but it is further acknowledged that, in certain instances, the emotions' objects *are* their causes.[3]

It is my belief that repetition has muffled the clang of the counter-intuitive denial that objects of emotions are causally related to those emotions. I believe this notwithstanding the lack of clarity of the term, "object," and the lack of a consensus on the nature of causal relations. A number of refutations of the position have appeared, refutations which have made inroads upon the claim of incorrigibility and which have persuasively argued that the feature of immediacy, insofar as it obtains, is irrelevant to whether the relation may be causal or not; the refutations have also called into question the view that there has to be a conceptual bond between identifications of emotions and of their particular objects.[4] The refutations have not—though this is a rhetorical complaint—re-evoked the loudness of the denial's counter-intuitive clang. It seems one cannot insist enough upon the notable occurrence of ordinary causal locutions in the examples employed by protagonists of both sides of the controversy, indeed in the very examples used to convey some sense of the role or

[3] For one example of the apparent inconsistency see Kenny, op. cit., pp. 73 and 75.

[4] See the works by Pears and Wilson cited above; Wilson usefully refers to a number of other relevant writings.

roles of the term "object"; nor, apparently, is it quite appreciated how easily, when those locutions are absent from the statement of the examples, the examples can be legitimately construed so as to incorporate those locutions. To turn to a few illustrations, I will quote and comment upon a passage from Miss Anscombe's book *Intention*.

She writes:

> . . . in considering feelings, such as fear or anger, it is important to distinguish between mental causes and objects of feeling. To see this, consider the following cases:
> A child saw a bit of red stuff on a turn in a stairway and asked what it was. He thought his nurse told him it was a bit of Satan and felt dreadful fear of it. (No doubt she said it was a bit of satin.) What he was frightened of was the bit of stuff; the cause of his fright was his nurse's remark. The object of fear may be the cause of fear, but, as Wittgenstein remarks, is not *as such* the cause of fear. (A hideous face appearing at the window would of course be both cause and object, and hence the two are easily confused.) Or again, you may be angry *at* someone's action, when what *makes* you angry is some reminder of it, or someone's telling you of it.[5]

The account Miss Anscombe gives of the child seeing the bit of red stuff can, I believe, be usefully glossed. We may assume the child would not have been frightened had the nurse not spoken as she did; once she has, however, it seems undeniable that the bit of red stuff becomes, at a minimum, a causal factor in his fear. For if, after the nurse's words, it were asked, what is making him so afraid, or, indeed, what is causing his fear, a, if not the, natural answer would be: the piece of red stuff. This of course is not to deny that the cause of his being made afraid by it, the cause of its coming to cause him fear, was the nurse's utterance. It may also be useful to take up Miss Anscombe's example of being ". . . angry *at* someone's action, when what *makes* you angry is some reminder of it, or someone's telling you of it." The everyday home for the form of words "what *makes* you angry is some reminder of it, or someone's telling you of it" is where what has caused you to be angry *is* what you are angry about, *is* precisely the reminder or someone's telling you it; but the context shows that Miss Anscombe meant the words to

---

[5] G. E. M. Anscombe, *Intention*, 2d ed. (Cornell Univ. Press, Ithaca, 1963), p. 16.

be lodged elsewhere. Plainly, she meant them this way: the cause of your anger is the reminder, whereas your anger's object is the action the reminder reminds you of. But of course—and I doubt Miss Anscombe would deny it—nothing prevents one's continuing in the following way: the reminder has the effect of your being *made* angry by the action; the reminder causes or occasions your being caused anger by the action—presumably once again.

The passage in Wittgenstein's *Philosophical Investigations* to which Miss Anscombe refers is the *locus classicus* of the controversy: Part I, 476:

> The object of fear should be distinguished from the cause of fear.
> Thus the face that inspires fear or delight in us (the object of fear, of delight) is not thereby its cause but—one could say—its focus.[6]

Neither this passage nor even the pertinent passages in the *Zettel*—488, 489, and 492—establish that Wittgenstein *held* that objects of emotions could not always be causally related to those emotions; the passages seem to me consistent with the view that objects of emotions are often importantly distinguishable causal factors of them: causal factors to which the emotions *also look,* the emotions' foci, or, to put it literally, what the emotions are felt about or are about. For better or for worse, this is the kind of causal factor that I had in mind when, a few pages back, I used the phrase "causal objects."

In the preceding remarks I have wanted to further the clearing away of an obstacle, an obstruction in the path of regarding objects of emotions as causally related to them. For of course Freud thus conceived them. In whatever way Freud would interpret a putative object of an emotion or affect—whether as a more or less straightforward causal factor or as largely symbolic of one or more—he understood himself to be investigating causal relations. (I would guess that, had Freud come across the philosophical claim that objects of emotions are not usually—whether symbolically mediated or not—causes of them, he rightly or wrongly would have reacted with bemusement and scorn, an attitude exemplified by the passage in *An Autobiographical Study* where he says that his avoidance of philosophy was ". . . greatly facilitated by constitutional incapacity.")[7]

[6] I have tinkered with Miss Anscombe's translation.
[7] 1925d, XX, 59.

II

Several points should be made concerning what Freud included under the heading "emotions or affects." First, a cautionary remark: by "*Affekt*" Freud often did not mean merely or only an emotion or feeling. Often, however, he did, and in speaking of Freud on affects I will depend on this latter understanding of "*Affekt*." Secondly, he placed among affects certain instances of lack of affect, that is, affectlessness, and I shall follow him in this. Next, for Freud the range of affects includes anything we would unhesitatingly call emotions, emotional states and moods, whether ostensibly objectless or not, and also emotional aspects of desires and impulses; also boredom, malaise, and amusement; also what Descartes called the false emotions experienced by spectators and readers of fictional works, and of course emotions or feelings experienced in dreams. Then too Freud includes the affective aspects of many thoughts and impressions, and of course such familiar feelings as ordinary objectless nervousness as well as such infrequent feelings as those of strangeness, familiarity, and déjà vu. Next, although at least as early as the mid-nineties Freud spoke of unconscious feelings of guilt and of repressed self-reproach and found it convenient even four decades later to refer repeatedly to an unconscious sense of guilt and to unconscious sexual feelings, he had concluded by 1915 that, strictly speaking, there are no unconscious emotions, no unconscious affects or unconscious affect-laden impulses. Needless to say, he continued to maintain that there are more or less structured unconscious dispositions or "pronenesses" to have feelings; nor did he ever moderate his views on the existence and efficacy of unconscious ideas, motives, intentions, and indeed acts. Yet, for several reasons stated in the third part of his essay "The Unconscious" (1915e, XIV), reasons often controverted in later psychoanalytic literature,[8] he was always inclined thereafter to surround phrases translatable as "repressed affects," "unconscious anxiety, guilt, anger, etc." with scare quotes; or, when they were not thus surrounded, to regard them as fairly harmless, even sometimes useful, but nonetheless *loose* phraseology, loose to a degree incompatible with conscientious or scrupulous

[8] For two recent discussions and references to earlier ones, see the pieces by A. H. Modell and S. E. Pulver in *International Journal of Psycho-Analysis* 52, LII (1971), pp. 337–46 and 347–54.

psychological formulations. This change was no mere terminological shift; it became integral to Freud's metapsychology that emotions and affects should be thought of as "discharges of excitation" of which the subject had to be to some extent aware. Moreover, the change appears to have been effected quite rapidly: two years earlier, in *Totem and Taboo* (1912–13, XIII, 61), Freud had written, and without apparent qualms, about hostility that could be wholly unconscious but distressingly felt; merely a year earlier, in "On the History of the Psycho-Analytic Movement" (1914d, XIV), he wrote of affective internal resistances, unconscious resistances affective in origin. A final point here: though Freud was certainly cognizant of attributions of the vocabulary for emotions and feelings in the absence of any "lively" experience of them, he tended to stress, as it were, felt feelings. Felt, of course, insofar as they involved sensations, sensations however undiscriminated and nonspecific, of the cardiovascular and motoric changes that are so often concomitants of emotions and affects. These sensations include both those that may attend facial and bodily manifestations of emotions, and also some of those that may attend the actions—or inhibition thereof—that we perform to effect the tendentious aims we typically have when subject to certain feelings.

I shall now elaborate—in an impressionistic but schematic way—what I mean by proportionate or appropriate relations between emotions or affects and their causes or causal objects. Suppose, e.g., we learn that something has occurred to an individual, something such that understandably enough we expect it will occasion a certain kind of emotional response on his part; suppose besides that our expectation is not based on any particular psychological information about the individual. What we more or less expect in such a case may well not transpire; relative to our uninformed expectation, the affective response might seem to us quite anomalous. In fact, however, there is a plain enough sense in which it could prove anomalous no matter how predictable it would have been had we possessed and utilized considerable relevant psychological information about the individual; could prove anomalous if we also had made allowances required by cultural or subcultural aspects of his environment or environments; could prove anomalous even if we took into account the stage or phase or special circumstances of his life at the time, and further allowed for constitutional or organic peculiarities, permanent or temporary, of the individual. The anomalous response might be any one or more of the following sorts, sorts by no means sharply differentiable: affectlessness, disproportionately slight affect or, contrariwise, disproportionately great affect, and affect without a causal object. It may well seem that the response could be placed under one or more of these headings, even if we also had discounted the individual's particular temperament, whether it be phlegmatic, excitable, or what have you.

An amplified restatement of the foregoing, one that proceeds in the opposite direction, will be helpful. Suppose that, after any requisite allowances of the kinds mentioned have been made, a person nevertheless could be said to manifest one or another anomaly of affect. My claim is that the anomalies can always be placed under one or more of the following six headings. First, one may experience certain feelings of the type termed "objectless." Thus one may feel and show a quite unfocused chronic or intermittent nervousness; or, one may endure noticeable depression and yet sincerely insist that nothing either in general or in particular is depressing one—*mirabile dictu,* one is content excepting only for one's state of mind; or one may feel and vent a dreadful cheerfulness, dreadful for its invulnerability to whatever befalls one. These types of example are "ideal"; emotional responses, anomalous or not, are usually at least somewhat mixed.

Next, consider anomalies of affect of one or another kind that I shall call "attenuated object feelings." To sketch one extreme example and suggest some others: instead of being purely nervous one may be oddly apprehensive; one can experience a sense of threat or menace but have no notion of what, if anything, is under threat or what threatens it or with what it is threatened. Similarly, feelings of hopefulness may be found loosened from their moorings and, somewhat similarly, feelings of guilt, inferiority, etc.

Next, there are—whether disproportionate or proportionate—affective responses that at the very least are doubtfully appropriate. Indeed, feelings that are both disproportionate and inappropriate are so commonplace that examples are unnecessary. Among roughly proportionate but questionably appropriate affects are the feelings of "counter-phobes"—the fears and exultations that tiger-tamers, aerialists and diverse other daredevils experience distinctively, if not solely, in the pursuit of their vocations and hobbies. Also, while one would want to include among excesses of affect the *horror hominis* and *horror feminae* of some female and male homosexual inverts, more moderate aversive homosexual responses, although doubtfully appropriate, could hardly be termed disproportionate.

Excesses of affect include numerous anomalies of feelings. Perhaps most notable among them are certain feelings of fear and many feelings of sexual excitation; they are alike specified by their causal objects. Conspicuous among such fears, often amounting to terror, are the feelings attached to the large variety of phobias. Other familiar excesses of affect are sexual feelings attendant upon what Freud termed perversions of the sexual aim: narcissistic autoerotism; the couples, sadism and masochism, exhibitionism and voyeurism; and the diverse fetishisms. Then too there are many sexual affects connected with what Freud termed inversions of the sexual object: bestiality, paedophilia, and homosexuality. Accompanying these specialities of sexual aim and object are other excessive affects or lack of affect, e.g., overwhelming disgust or utter lack of response upon proximity to or contact with other persons' persons.

The direction in which I have been proceeding is, I trust, clear: from objectless affects to attenuated object feelings to inappropriate affective responses to excessive feelings about objects; and to these headings there needs to be added disproportionately slight responses to objects, and then, past hebetude, affectlessness. This completes the reversal of the direction I followed all too briefly earlier. Once more, my purpose has been to sketch a schema of anomalies of feeling and emotion, a schema, to use Eugen Bleuler's apt figure of speech, of incongruities of affect. The termini of the path I have traversed back and forth are, again, objectlessness and affectlessness.

For Freud, incongruities of affect were symptomatic. Thus variations of trends toward lack of affect and objectlessness enabled, on his view, differential diagnoses of psychotic tendencies and of the psychoses themselves, psychoses constituting the most marked instances of the loss of or flight from reality, including of course within reality nonanomalous affective responses. (To be sure, there are affects that are part and parcel of total or systematic hallucinatory or delusional confusions; their analogues in the lives of psychologically more or less normal persons are the affects experienced in dreams, dreams that we sometimes explicitly and colloquially call "crazy".)[9] In some advanced forms of melancholia, that is, of psychotic depression, both affectlessness and withdrawal from objects are to be found together. In such cases, so to say, the two termini coincide.

[9] The comparison is often made in Freud's writings; for a very late statement of it, see *An Outline of Psychoanalysis* (1940a, XXIII, 160–61).

Doubtless my schema of anomalies of feeling could be improved in a number of ways; the improvements would require complicating it. Before turning to a few of the complications, I want to take up a likely but misguided objection to the schema. The objection, as I conceive it, will take this form: the schema, whatever other failings it may have, cannot pretend to being an analysis of anomalies of affect. This is patently clear in connection with the third of its six headings: inappropriate—whether proportionate or disproportionate —affects. This heading employs the very notion that, presumably, the schema is meant to analyze, namely, the notion of an affect being anomalous or inappropriate. In answer to this objection it should be enough to observe that the schema is not intended as an analysis— however desirable one might be—of the notion of an affect being anomalous. The schema is intended only to serve as *a* specification— one spelling-out—of the varieties of anomalous emotions and feelings; but it does pretend, and not only trivially, to provide a place or places for every instance of affective incongruity.

One important complication of the schema would be an indication of how persons whose lives are troubled by emotional disorder tend to suffer now from one sort of anomaly of affect and then from another or, indeed, are often subject simultaneously to different sorts. Another important addition would provide for certain feelings people suffer *because* of the incongruities of affect to which they are liable—that is, to sometimes further anomalous feelings whose causal objects are antecedent anomalous ones. Whatever complications might usefully be incorporated in the schema, my claim again is that it specifies, in however general and unrefined a way, all incongruities of affect; and that, consequently, any emotions or feelings which could not arguably be fitted into it would thereby be appropriately related to their causal objects or causes, that is, would be nonanomalous affects.

The notion of an affect arguably or not arguably fitting into the schema may well seem problematic; surely, however, it is implausible to suppose that it is devoid of sense. Consider, for instance, some of the examples I placed under the heading of excessive affects: the gamut of feelings of sexual excitation that, according to Freud, are perverted or inverted. Of some of those feelings it would certainly be reasonable to claim that they are arguably anomalous; and if one concedes this, one concedes that the notion in question does not lack sense. The same gamut of examples is useful in another connection too, indeed in relation to the central concern of this paper: for Freud's discussions of the affective origins and persistence of the inversions and perversions are among the most prominent applications he made of the idea I am ascribing to him: the idea, once again, that between any person's emotions or affects and their causal objects or causes there obtains a real appropriateness or actual proportionality no matter how discrepant or incongruous those relations may seem and regardless of the person's mental condition.

To show convincingly that Freud adhered to this idea in one form or other throughout the five decades of his psychological work would require an appeal to all of his pertinent writings, an appeal, that is to say, to at least a majority of his psychological writings. By way of substitute, I will refer at some length to what I take to be a strategic example of the idea's presence in his work, and then briefly touch upon a number of other examples.

When stating and restating the idea, I have used the disjunctive phrase "causes or causal objects." Indubitably whenever someone experiences an emotion that has a causal object or objects, there are other causal factors involved. I had, however, a special reason for adverting to causes as well as causal objects.[10] I repeatedly singled out causes for mention because of the important role Freud allotted for many years—from at least 1893 until the *New Introductory Lectures* of 1933—to what he called "sexual noxae" in the causality of the emotional aspect of hysterias and in the effecting of the feelings of debility and anxiety characteristic of neurasthenia, anxiety neurosis, and hypochondria—the disorders he termed "actual neuroses," as opposed to psychoneuroses. Only at the end of those forty years did Freud completely abandon the view that lack of sexual fulfillment, whether due to abstinence, masturbation, coitus interruptus, or coitus reservatus, effected "sexual noxae" which in turn effected the marked excitability of many hysterics and the syndromes of feelings which helped enable the differentiation of the actual neuroses both from each other and from the psychoneuroses. He conceived of those noxae as similar to known toxic conditions, and of the feelings they

[10] Perhaps this is a suitable place to emphasize that, in speaking of causal objects of feelings, I am throughout keeping in mind *intentionality,* i.e., that a person's identification of an object of his feelings may contain terms that lack reference; and that, whether or not this is so, he may be able to make few if any substitutions for those terms that would preserve the truth of his identification, assuming it true to begin with; and that, consequently, existential generalization of his identification would be out of order. (See, for a useful account of the matter, J. R. S. Wilson, op. cit., chap. 14.) It may barely be worth remarking that I accept the truism that a person's thoughts or beliefs often have effects upon him, among which effects are affects.

generated as comparable to ones that can be induced by certain drugs or glandular deficiencies. Moreover, he thought the sexual noxae—allowing for constitutional differences—proportionate to the affects they caused. Proportionate, that is, however disproportionate or incongruous those affects appeared to be when viewed against the background of the life circumstances—other than the sexual ones, of course—of the individuals who suffered from those disorders.

When Freud completed the assimilation of the actual neuroses to the psychoneuroses—he had always thought some patients were afflicted with both—he interpreted the relevant incongruities of affect in terms of anxiety responses to repressed tendencies, i.e., to unconscious causal objects, objects in view of which the affects could again be viewed as proportionate.

What then of other anomalous affects? As a matter of theory in regard to the psychoses, and clinically in regard both to psychotic trends and the neuroses, Freud's psychoanalytic interpretations of incongruities of affect *always* try to show that the incongruities are only ostensible. They try, that is, to disclose an actual congruity, a real appropriateness, behind what is taken to be the facade of every apparently discrepant feeling. Thus, on psychoanalytic investigation, the empty spaces of objectless affects are populated: for example, the dejection of depressives is interpreted as self-hatred, and the mania that often alternates with the dejection as relief from the self-hatred. The haze of attenuated object feelings lifts and objects are perceived clearly and forcibly: for example, vague but apprehensive delusions of being observed and watched come to be construed as the workings of a particularly vigilant conscience. Some ostensibly excessive affects, e.g., the ones so noteworthy in compulsive-obsessional neuroses, emerge as fears of ever-tempting transgressions appropriate to those unrelenting feelings. Others, for instance, the *Angst* attached to unrealistic phobic objects, are seen to be symbolic of genuinely terrifying perils; still others, for example, the erotic responses to fetishes, lose their impoverishing extravagance when interpreted as compensatory and reassuring. The counter-phobic objects are seen as furnishing occasion for an enjoyed mastery at least as representative as direct. Feelings of aversion and distaste give way to forbidden longings, to forbidden possibilities of relishing the distasteful. Inadequate affects are supplemented by recourse to understandably—because, for instance, often traumatically—repressed pronenesses to feeling. The apathy of the melancholiac is traced to mourning over one or another unconscious loss of love. And so on for every anomaly of affect.

III

As far as I have been able to discover, the idea I am ascribing to Freud is nowhere stated in his writings; no doubt if he had stated it he would not have expressed it in the cumbersome way I have found unavoidable. Yet neither in ransacking the corpus of his psychological works nor in searching through commentaries and digests have I been able to find any equivalent to it. On the other hand, in the course of that same search I have not encountered any exceptions to it—instead, only confirmations. If I have not lost my way in this, the ironic upshot is that over the half-century of Freud's psychological investigations he was, unbeknownst to himself, steadily faithful to the idea I have attributed to him. What is more, I am inclined to conjecture that it functioned for him as *one* of the criteria for the correctness of psychoanalytic interpretations of affective disorders.

Persons critical of or antagonistic to Freudian doctrines will surely find the foregoing congenial. For if I am right, Freud, although unaware of it, depended—and in a suspiciously *a priori* way—on a crucial and unqualifiedly general view of anomalies of emotion and affect. In fairness, however, it ought to be remarked that if that is the position, it is not without parallel in the origins of other disciplines. In any case, the question of the truth or falsity of the idea is only subject to qualification by its generality and is unaffected by Freud's having failed to formulate it. This is of course obvious and would not be worth mention but for the unspeakable quality of the great majority of criticisms of Freud. The validity of the idea can only be determined in the ways in which the validity of many other Freudian doctrines can be ascertained; and the qualifications required to undertake that task are diverse and rarely found.

To conclude: it is a truism about Freud that he thought that normalcy shades off imperceptibly into neurosis. A prejudice attaches to the way this truism is understood and used. The prejudice shows itself in the contrast between the frequency of claims about the existence of neurotic tendencies in otherwise normal persons and the relative rarity of claims about trends towards normalcy in neurotics and psychotics. That laymen should find this prejudice inviting is, of course, understandable; what is likely to go unnoticed is the deformation of Freud's thought implicit in it. In my belief, the prejudice and consequent deformation tend to be pervasive. For example, people who read Freud know that he regarded dreams as neurotic symptoms, symptoms that occur in all healthy persons. They know too that he argued that dreams, including anxiety and "punishment" dreams, are surrogates for the fulfillment of wishes. Is there an equal awareness of how comprehensible and useful Freud judged those surrogate fulfillments to be? Again, it is widely known that Freud held that all or nearly all parapraxes are symptomatic, and that he construed them as intentional and meaningful. Is it sufficiently appreciated that in taking them to be meaningful he saw them as clues to needs that their perpetrators possessed but of which they were more or less unaware? Another example: readers of Freud are familiar with his attempt to show that even the most innocent and nontendentious jokes are instances of reverting to archaic kinds of pleasure. Do those readers have an adequate sense of Freud's understanding not only of the persistence but also of the importance of those kinds of pleasure? Another example: Freud's emphasis on the secondary or paranoiac gain of every neurotic symptom is unmistakable; although such gains cannot compensate for the losses entailed by the disabling character of the symptoms, is Freud's stress on their utility amply recognized?

I have not meant these questions merely rhetorically. Although I am confident that the answers to them are sometimes affirmative, I very much doubt that it is at all common to assemble these questions—to assemble them and related reminders—and thereby enable oneself to grasp the various ways in which Freud's vision was a vision of the normalcy and health that, however obstructed or baffled, lie behind neurosis and psychosis. I have said that on Freud's view the unconscious maddens us and keeps us mad; but he also held that if we could come to terms with it, it would prove the agent and preserver of sanity. That he did thus see it is, I believe, unquestionable. And if, as I have urged, he treated all anomalies of emotion and feeling as only ostensible, taking it as it were for granted that beneath each of those incongruities there is an unconscious but real congruity, it is the more unquestionable.[11]

[11] I am grateful for help and encouragement given me by Philippa Foot, Rogers Albritton and by my students Paul Mayfield, Katherine Menton, and Benjamin Smith.

Freud's Anatomies of the Self

IRVING THALBERG

1. *The philosophical knot.* If we study clinically the sorts of behavior Freud dealt with, we may feel justifiably tempted to say that they manifest conflict of the agent with himself. And then it would be natural to see this self-conflict as a clash between forces within the agent. Thus we might wonder, as Freud did: What items contend inside a person? What is their source of energy? What forms do their struggles take? Freud put forth quite heterogenous theories of the mind's components, and how their operations result in various kinds of normal as well as disturbed behavior. Yet I'm afraid none of his ingenious and suggestive partitioning explanations turn out to be both illuminating and coherent. I plan to illustrate why it was nevertheless reasonable of him to propose such 'dynamic' accounts of human activity and affliction. It will be instructive to see which features of behavior threw Freud into conceptual confusion. These few deep muddles are no discredit to Freud's radically innovative thinking. Our appreciation of them should advance our understanding, in philosophy of mind and action, of the person and his reflexive acts.

I realize that the doctrinal thickets I want to rummage in have been staked out by a legion of Freud experts. Most of the skeptical *cognoscenti* have not argued their case in detail. Those who have done so devote insufficient attention to Freud's, and our own, profound theoretical need to subdivide the self. Few distill conceptual vaccines from his philosophically enlightening confusions.

Freud is best remembered for his tripartite divisions of the individual into unconscious, preconscious and conscious "systems,"[1] from roughly 1900 until 1923, and id, ego and superego thereafter. But his accounts of our deeds and aberrations made use of many other items within us. Freud went along with tradition and assumed that there are "ideas" populating our minds and their compartments. By the slippery term "idea" he seemed to mean images,

---

[1] Throughout I shall reserve quotation marks for expressions used by Freud himself, as translated in the Standard Edition. I have to quote Freud at length because I want readers to be able to judge for themselves what his words could mean.

concepts, propositions and thoughts. Freud always supposed that our mental apparatus and its parts run on some kind of "energy"— which is inexplicably similar to, but not a form of, electrical current. In the guise of emotive "affect" and conative pushiness, this psychic energy adheres to some of our ideas. From the start Freud conceded that "we have no means of measuring" psychic current (1894a, III, 60). A posthumous monograph reiterates his confidence that "in mental life some kind of energy is at work"; but he confesses "nothing . . . will enable us to come nearer to a knowledge of it by analogies with other forms of energy" (1940a [1938], XXIII, 163 f.).

Freud also consistently gave top explanatory billing to our drives, impulses or "instincts" (*Triebe*), which he considered somehow derivative from psychic energy. Occasionally he writes of "energy, neutral in itself," which is "added to" an "impulse" (1923b, XIX, 44; cf. 1926f, XX, 265 f.; 1933a, XXII, 18 f.). This complicates matters. For while Freud recognizes just one kind of psychic energy, from relatively early he makes it a methodological principle that "instincts occur in pairs of opposites" (1910a, XI, 243). Only by their "concurrent or opposing action," he declares, "can the motley variety of vital phenomena be explained" (1937c, XXIII, 243). In this sense, *not* the mind-matter sense, Freud's subdividing explanations of behavior are 'dualistic.' One warring instinct he always casts as libido, which propels us toward erotic endeavors. At first its rival is the "ego instinct" of self-preservation (1910i, XI, 214). From 1920 on, the destructive instinct, directed at oneself and others, becomes the antagonist of libido.

Since I mentioned the ego instinct, I should post a warning. Freud's conception of the ego (*das Ich*) was unsettled prior to 1923. Frequently he seems to mean by "ego" the whole person (1894a, III, 54; 1920g, XVIII, 11). Other passages, occasionally in the same works, suggest that the ego is a component of one's mind, and that Freud is contrasting the ego with parts of which one is unconscious (1894a, III, 48; 1950a [1895], I, 209; 1895d, II, 122 ff.; 1920g, XVIII, 19). At times Freud makes the ego a delegate within us of morality, which censors our ideas. It keeps shameful items away from our "consciousness" (1900a, V, 526). Here Freud cannot be contrasting our ego with parts of our mind which elude our awareness. A person is no more aware that his ego is engaged in censorship than he is of what it excludes from his consciousness (see section 10). Finally, in his *Project* of 1895, Freud presents the ego as nothing but a sub-system of "neurones" whose job it is to maximize "discharge" of psychic energy from our whole homeostatic mental apparatus (1950a, I, 323–26).

2. *Physicalistic subdividing hypotheses.* While we are taking a census of the components which Freud uses to explain reflexive deeds and attitudes, we should notice that he portrays their dynamic interrelations in correspondingly varied terms. His topographical account "has reference . . . to regions in the mental apparatus, wherever they may be situated in the body" (1915e, XIV, 175). Everyone remembers his mechanistic imagery of tensions and tugs: "the repressed exercises a continuous pressure in the direction of consciousness, so that this pressure must be balanced by an unceasing counter-pressure" (1915d, XIV, 151). Equally familiar is Freud's hydraulic talk of flow and "blockages" (1923b, XIX, 45). Libidinal instincts pour through "channels" (1916–17, XVI, 345). If it is dammed up, after leaving its "reservoir," libido "may . . . move on a backward course . . . along infantile lines" (1912c, XII, 232). Freud invokes crystallography to depict the fusion of repressed hysterogenic memories around a "nucleus" (1895d, II, 123). When we dream, a childhood experience may be a "nucleus of crystallization attracting the material of the dream thoughts to itself" (1901a, V, 659). Speaking botanically, Freud compares a repressed idea, with its charge of affect, to a fungus which "proliferates in the dark" (1915d, XIV, 149). A recurring zoological simile is that libido goes out to objects and returns like an amoeba's pseudopods (1914c, XIV, 75; etc.). From pathology he draws the notion of "strangulated affects" (1895d, II, 17), along with the comparison between a repressed memory-idea and a wound that contains some irritating "foreign body" (ibid., 139, 165). Toxicology also enriches Freud's explanations. For example, libidinal currents, or "sexual substances" (1923b, XIX, 47), become poisonous if they do not escape from our mental apparatus (1894a, III, 107 ff.; see 1908d, IX, 185).

3. *Animistic stories.* It will round out our view of Freud's subdividing explanations if we recall the array of anthropomorphic models he takes from social life. When one performs an "erroneous action," Freud says that "control over the body" passes from one's ego, and its "will," to an opposing "counter-will" (1892–93b, I, 122–28). Freud regularly tells of "two thought-constructing agencies" within our minds, "of which the second enjoys the privilege of having free access to consciousness for its products" (1901a, V,

676). Other political and social conventions besides "privilege" spice the contacts between parts of the self. There are upheavals too. Freud says:

> [T]his soul . . . is a hierarchy of superordinated and subordinated agents, a labyrinth of impulses striving independently of one another towards action . . .
>
> . . . Psychoanalysis . . . can say to the ego: ". . . a part of the activity of your own mind has been withdrawn from your knowledge and from the command of your will . . . [S]exual instincts . . . have rebelled . . . to rid themselves of . . . oppression; they have extorted their rights in a manner that you cannot sanction." (1917a, XVII, 141 f.)

Neurotic symptoms, for example, an hysterical affliction, slips of the tongue, and dreams, Freud constantly explains as a political "compromise" between impulse and some moralistic component.

Freud characterizes many of his theories as "economic." Twice he deploys financial imagery, likening an instinct to a "capitalist" who loans us energy for our undertakings (1905e, VII, 87; 1916–17, XV, 226). At times he describes an individual, or his ego, as acting on "economic" grounds when they maximize pleasure (1920g, XVIII, 7; 1924c, XIX, 159). Mostly, however, Freud means by "economic" an explanation of conflict behavior by reference to the relative "strength" or "pressure" which psychic components and instincts exert upon each other (1950a [1895], I, 283; 1915e, XIV, 181; 1924b, XIX, 152).

Even erotic relationships have a place in Freud's component explanations. Narcissism occurs when the ego "offers itself . . . as a libidinal object to the id, and aims at attaching the id's libido to itself" (1923b, XIX, 56; also 30, 46). In melancholia, by contrast, "the ego . . . feels itself hated . . . by the superego, instead of loved" (1923b, XIX, 58). Finally there is the Platonic 'mastery' model. Freud considers that the ego "in its relation to the id is like a man on horseback, who has to hold in check the superior strength of the horse" (1923b, XIX, 25; cf. 1933a, XXII, 77).

4. *Is there any common structure* to Freud's anthropomorphic and mechanistic narratives? For one thing, whenever a person's act or attitude is reflexive—directed toward himself—Freud usually explains this as a transaction between different parts of the man's mind, or between the whole individual and one of his mental components. This is also Freud's approach to dreaming, which is not reflexive in

any obvious way. Curiously enough, we find that when your conduct involves a second agent, Freud reduces this straightforwardly interpersonal transaction to an encounter among your mental components and the other's. One droll example appears in a letter to Fliess. Freud writes: "Bisexuality! I am sure you are right . . . And I am accustoming myself to regarding every sexual act as an event between four individuals."[2] I hope that these "four individuals" are not themselves bisexual! However that may be, we notice the same reductive view when Freud elucidates psychotherapy: "the physician . . . works hand in hand with one part of the pathologically divided personality, against the other partner in the conflict" (1920a, XVIII, 150); it is the analyst's political goal to "give . . . back . . . command over the id" to the neurotic's ego (1926e, XX, 205).

I trust that my hurried conspectus of Freud's partitioning schemes for explaining conflict behavior has exhibited their diversity, sophistication and attractiveness. Before I start evaluating them, I must anticipate a complaint. The grumble would be that these are just metaphors, not meant to have any literal application, and hence not liable to philosophical prosecution. Freud himself cautions: "What is psychical is something so unique . . . that no one comparison can reflect its nature" (1919a, XVII, 161). But far from being a prohibition, this is an encouragement to consider seriously as many images as possible. For Freud continues: "The [therapeutic] work of psychoanalysis suggests analogies with chemical analysis, but just as much with the incursions of a surgeon or the manipulations of an orthopedist or the influence of an educator." Regarding one of his favorite topographical and social models, Freud says:

> These crude hypotheses, the two chambers, the doorkeeper on the threshold between them, and consciousness as a spectator at the end of the second room, must indicate an extensive approximation to the actual reality. (1916–17, XVI, 296)

In any case, if a metaphor is to be at all enlightening, must there not be some points of contact between one's model and what it explains?

With this stage setting and rationale behind us, we can turn to the first aspect of our puzzle about Freud's subdivisions of the mind.

5. *Why partition the self?* As an observer in psychiatric hospitals, and as a practitioner, Freud said he was not "pledged to any

[2] Letter 113 (1899), in Ernst Kris et al., eds., *The Origins of Psychoanalysis* (Imàgo, London, 1954).

particular psychological system"; he "proceeded to adjust [his] views until they seemed adapted for giving an account of . . . the facts which had been observed" (1905e, VII, 112 f.). Did he encounter any behavior which especially demanded partitioning explanations? An early paper gives us his theoretical response to hysteria patients undergoing an attack:

> [I]f I find someone in a state which bears all the signs of a painful affect—weeping, screaming and raging—the conclusion seems probable that a mental process is going on in him of which those physical phenomena are the appropriate expression . . . The problem would at once arise of how it is that a hysterical patient is overcome by an affect about whose cause he asserts that he knows nothing . . . He is behaving as though he *does* know about it. (1893f, III, 19)

At the time Freud believed that hysterical afflictions, including "absences," result mainly from a "summation of traumas"—as a rule, sexual experiences. At the beginning of treatment, Freud's patients seemed to have forgotten these traumas. But when they were led to recall them, their hysterical disorders vanished. Freud is driven toward a partition theory:

> [E]verything points to one solution: the patient is in a special state of mind in which all his impressions or his recollections . . . are no longer held together by an associative chain . . . in which it is possible for a recollection to express its affect by means of somatic phenomena without the group of the other mental process, the ego, knowing about it or being able to intervene to prevent it. (1893f, III, 20)

Another rationale for subdividing, Freud takes from well-established experiments with hysterically blind patients:

> Excitations of the blind eye may . . . produce affects . . . though they do not become conscious. Thus hysterically blind people are only blind as far as consciousness is concerned; in their unconscious they see. . . . [O]bservations such as this compel us to distinguish between conscious and unconscious mental processes. (1910i, XI, 212)

Freud says in the same essay that hypnotic experiments also prove that other sorts of mental activity take place within us than those which we monitor. Elsewhere he maintains that a posthypnotic suggestion must be "present in the mind," since a subject will obey it while candidly disclaiming knowledge of its origin (1912g, XII, 261; cf. 1916–17, XVI, 277; 1926e, XX, 197; 1940b, XXIII, 285). I return to this notion of 'presence' in sections 11 and 12.

Dreaming particularly seemed to call for a 'divided soul' hypotheses. Freud insists: "There must be a force here which is seeking to express something and another which is striving to prevent the expression" (1933a, XXII, 14). Another late discussion turns upon the memory we show in dreams of incidents we cannot recall when awake (1940a, XXIII, 160 f.). Isn't this proof that such recollections must have been "present" all along, but inaccessible?

One typical phase of analytic treatment impressed Freud as needing an 'inner conflict' explanation. Sincere patients who are progressing steadily come all at once to a halt. Abruptly they find themselves unable to bring forth dreams and associations. Or they become too obliging, and produce whatever material their analyst seems to expect. Freud thought such "resistance" behavior demonstrated that some internal agency is holding back. He remarks:

> The existence of this force could be assumed with certainty, since one became aware of an effort corresponding to it if, in opposition to it, one tried to introduce the unconscious memories into the patient's consciousness. (1910a, XI, 23; see 1933a, XXII, 13 f.)

Later Freud amplifies:

> There can be no question but that . . . resistance emanates from the ego. (1923b, XIX, 17; see 49)

> No stronger impression arises from the resistances during the work of analysis than of there being a force which is defending itself by every possible means against recovery and which is absolutely resolved to hold onto illness and suffering. (1937c, XXIII, 242 f.)

A final source of divided soul theories we might call 'respect for the ordinary language of psychotics.' Freud considers paranoid, individuals who are afflicted by delusions that they are being observed and criticized, who constantly 'hear' unfavorable comments upon their acts and attitudes. He asks:

> How would it be if these insane people were right, if in each of us there is present an agency [viz., the superego] which observes and threatens to punish . . . [and which they have] mistakenly displaced into external reality? (1933a, XXII, 59; cf. 1914c, XIV, 95; 1940d [1892], I, 208 f.)

In his last systematic work Freud derives theoretical justification from the fact that victims of hallucinatory confusion, following recovery, often say that throughout their most disturbed periods, "in some corner of their mind . . . there was a normal person hidden, who . . . watched the hubbub of illness go past him" (1940a [1938], XXIII, 201 f.).

Two recent commentators on Freud argue along similar lines from the ordinary self-representational thinking of less deranged people. Jerome Bruner says that the id-ego-superego theory exemplifies 'the dramatic technique of decomposition, the play whose actors are parts of a single life'; its 'imagery . . . has an immediate resonance with the dialectic of experience.'[3] Richard Wollheim is more explicit. He declares that Freud's tripartite theory

> not only provides a model of the mind and its working, but also coincides with, or reproduces, the kind of picture or representation that we consciously or unconsciously make to ourselves of our mental processes.[4]

Although Freud's partition plans are thus rooted in clinical and everyday experience, I am afraid they do not work. His consistently non-anthropomorphic explanations make sense, but fail to elucidate those aspects of reflexive and other behavior which most baffle us. I won't take up the much belabored question whether Freud's physicalistic theories of mind qualify as 'scientific.' With regard to Freud's animistic accounts, I would concur with Bruner and Wollheim that these provide us illumination—no doubt because we have a practical and theoretical grasp of social life, from which Freud draws his animistic models. But careful assessment will show these explanations to be instructively incoherent. The question whether they are unscientific does not come up. I start with an early physicalistic theory which ranges over considerably more than the conflict behavior which mainly interests me.

6. *A mental apparatus and its component "neurones."* Freud's homeostatic theory, as we would call it nowadays, seems to me a paradigm of relative cogency together with explanatory emptiness. This doctrine seems to be taking shape in his earliest metapsychological works. He elaborates it with a treasury of details in his *Proj-*

[3] Jerome Bruner, "The Freudian Conception of Man and the Continuity of Nature," in M. Brodbeck, ed., *Readings in the Philosophy of the Social Sciences* (Macmillan, New York, 1968), p. 710.

[4] Richard Wollheim, *Sigmund Freud* (Viking, New York, 1971), p. 234.

ect of 1895 (1950a, I, 295–387), and its silhouette hovers behind many of his subsequent writings. In outline, we have a "mental apparatus" composed of three kinds of "neurones," classed according to how "permeable" they are to currents of psychic energy. Freud's *Project* gives the latter the title "Quantity," or "Q." The system of least permeable neurones Freud labels "the ego." As I noted above, this "ego" system operates to maximize "discharge" of Q from the whole apparatus—hence the comparison with present-day homeostatic devices. But more philosophically intriguing is Freud's dubbing of the most permeable system, which receives "stimuli" from the "external" environment, as "consciousness."

Presumably when this system is affected by the flow of Q through other neurone systems composing our mental apparatus, and when it passes on "stimuli," we are conscious. The hypothesis is meaningful enough. My reservation, however, is that it furnishes us no clues regarding features of our consciousness, and its theoretical partner, our unconscious mental activity, which are most puzzling to curious laymen and to practising therapists. When our super-permeable neurone system is activated, Freud cannot say that *it* is conscious—aware of stimuli or flowing Q. Nor would it be meaningful to attribute consciousness at such moments to the "ego" neurone group. Epistemic notions like 'awareness' or 'being unaware of something' seem out of place amid reports of neurones and their quasi-electrical activity. And the latter just tell us what goes on inside a vital mechanism when we achieve or fall short of various kinds of awareness.

I have similar reservations about another chapter in Freud's story of our mental apparatus. He gives a rather inflated description of its homeostatic tendencies. He says it is governed by "the principle of constancy or stability." For this term of Fechner's (see 1920g, XVIII, 8 f.), Freud eventually substituted his own: "the pleasure principle." But what does it mean to say that a mechanism follows a principle? Just as neurones cannot be said to be conscious or unconscious, an apparatus cannot be said to adopt and follow principles —or to be unprincipled either. Freud must mean only that it, or a part of it, usually runs in a way which maximizes discharge of Q. On his view, our overt activity, conscious thinking, dreaming and neurotic symptoms all release Q.

Pleasure comes into the picture because Freud attaches this label to the discharge of Q from our mental mechanism. The buildup of Q he calls "unpleasure" (*Unlust*). But as we noticed with his neurone-system explanation of consciousness, this cannot be more than an interesting speculation about what electrical happenings occur within our brains when we are distressed or pleased. It would make no sense to suppose we enjoy releasing Q from our mental apparatus, or that our "ego" neurones do. From the other side, we gain little enlightenment regarding what we dislike and relish, or how these emotions depend upon our beliefs and our social conditioning, if we study the flow of Q through neurones. I would heartily agree with Freud, and mind-brain 'identity' theorists of today, that a single event can be an instance of current—psychic or other—leaving my mental apparatus, as well as an instance of my being aware that it is cocktail time, and glad that it is. My objection is that to account for the event's electro-mechanical features is not to explain its epistemic and hedonic dimensions.

I have no transcendental proof that one cannot possibly account for consciousness, pleasure or conflict-behavior through mechanistic-sounding hypotheses like Freud's. I certainly cannot define, in general, what it is to explain an individual occurrence or a type of event. But I want to illustrate how explanations become incoherent if you try to blend into them talk of electrical mechanisms and talk of conscious agency. This will also bring us to conflict-behavior.

7. *A mixed account of hysterical symptoms.* Perhaps because he sensed that mechanistic stories left important aspects of neurosis unexplained, Freud often threw in anthropomorphic details. Thus his early theory of hysteria begins with the doctrine that a form of psychic energy, emotional "affect," clings to some of our "ideas." Freud thought that a series of "traumatic" happenings in life, usually during childhood and sexual in nature, could leave behind highly charged memory traces. But this load of affect may fail to be discharged, or "abreacted," though our overt actions, including emotional outbursts, and our conscious thinking about the traumatic incidents.

What is it for affect to build up, and what happens to it when it does? As Freud approaches this central theme of repression, and how it results in hysterical afflictions, his account begins to sound anthropomorphic. He says the traumatic memory is "objectionable." The person's "ego . . . decides on the repudiation of the incompatible idea" (1895d, II, 123). He reports that one early patient "repressed her erotic idea from consciousness and transformed the amount of its affect into physical sensations of pain" (ibid., 164).

At the same time he tries to maintain a purely electromagnetic outlook. He envisions

> Contrary thoughts . . . paired off in such a way that *the one thought is excessively intensely conscious while its counterpart is repressed and unconscious.* This . . . is an effect . . . of repression. For repression is often achieved by means of an excessive reinforcement of the thought contrary to the one which is to be repressed . . . [T]he thought which asserts itself . . . in consciousness . . . I call a *reactive thought.* The two thoughts then act towards each other much like the two needles of an astatic galvanometer. The reactive thought keeps the objectionable one under repression by means of a certain surplus of intensity; but for that reason it itself is 'damped' and proof against conscious efforts of thought. (1905e, VII, 55; cf. 1893a, II, 12; 1940d [1892], I, 153)

Obviously it is a theoretical temptation to weave notions of agency into the electronic tapestry. If you hold to the standpoint of psychical mechanics, all you have is one entity bouncing another from a part of the mental apparatus which is inexplicably labeled "consciousness." You cannot express, in the vocabulary of electromagnetics, the fact that the 'repressing' entity is the *person's* deeply held evaluative principle; that the entity it knocks away is erotic; that the two are logically or morally "incompatible"; that the resulting hysterical symptom is a "mnemic symbol" of the original erotic traumas (1895d, II, 90; see 5, etc.); and that it is less unpleasant for the hysteric to be afflicted by the symptom than to continue repressing his affect-laden idea altogether. Moreover, these non-electronic facts would probably have the greatest significance for the hysteric, his sympathizers and his analyst. The hysteric might say: 'Now I'm beginning to put things together.' But if you limit yourself to a purely electromagnetic story, are any of these participants likely to exclaim, 'At last I understand what's happening!'?

So much for our urge to introduce the person, his moral outlook, sexuality, symbolism and pleasure. Why won't these be at home in an electro-mechanical story? As we will see with further parallel cases, it makes no sense to suppose that a person—or a mini-person—enters his mental apparatus, struggles electronically with ideas he finds there, and turns excess current into muscle cramps, hoarseness or abasia. On this last point, Freud admits:

> I cannot . . . give any hint of how a conversion [of affect into symptom] . . . is brought about. It is obviously not carried out in

the same way as an intentional and voluntary action. It is a process
which occurs under the pressure of the motive of defense in someone whose organization . . . has a proclivity in that direction.
(1895d, II, 166; cp. 1905e, VII, 54)

Now we should consider undiluted anthropomorphic explanations
of conflict behavior like hysteria, and see if they fare better than
mixed accounts. I think Freud's theory of dreaming, along with its
magnificent insights and suggestions, really hides many intriguing
forms of incoherence. I shall start from it, and explore concepts in
it which seem muddled. A question will focus some of my puzzlement:

8. *Is our ego awake or asleep when we dream?*   This is a dilemma for every Freudian account of dreaming, whether one means
by "ego" the whole person who dreams, or a part. I cannot see any
way around it, as long as we explain what it is for an individual to
dream by specifying what agencies within him do, or what he does to
items within his mind. A casual reader of Freud's pellucid prose
might not be jolted by his inconsistencies and other lapses of cogency
on this score. So here are samples, numbered to facilitate discussion:

(i)   [T]he wish to sleep (which the conscious ego is concentrated
upon, and which . . . is part of the conscious ego's share in dreaming) must . . . be . . . one of the motives for the formation of
dreams . . . (1900a, IV, 234)

(ii)   [D]reams are given their shape by the operation of two psychical forces . . . one of these forces constructs the wish which is
expressed by the dream, while the other exercises a censorship upon
this dream-wish and . . . brings about a distortion of the expression of the wish. (Ibid., 144)

(iii)   [C]riticism . . . involved . . . exclusion from consciousness.
The critical agency [has] . . . a closer relation to consciousness
than the agency criticized . . . [T]he critical agency . . . directs
our waking life and determines our voluntary, conscious actions.
(1900a, V, 540)

(iv)   [T]he ego . . . goes to sleep at night, even though then it
exercises the censorship on dreams. (1923b, XIX, 17)

(v)   The critically disapproving agency does not entirely cease to
function during sleep. (1923a, XVIII, 268)

(vi)   A dream may be described as . . . fantasy working on behalf
of the maintenance of sleep . . . It is . . . a matter of indifference

to the sleeping ego what may be dreamt . . . so long as the dream performs its task. (1925i, XIX, 126)

(vii) [B]etween the two agencies . . . a censorship . . . only allows what is agreeable to it to pass through to consciousness . . . [T]he repressed material must submit to certain alterations which mitigate its offensive features . . .
. . . [T]he formation of obscure dreams occurs *as though* one person who was dependent upon a second person had to make a remark which was bound to be disagreeable in the [latter's] ears . . . and it is on the basis of this simile that we have arrived at the concepts of dream distortion and censorship. (1901a, V, 676; see 1900a, V, 526)

(viii) Now while this second agency, in which we recognize our normal ego, is concentrated on the wish to sleep, it appears to be compelled by the psycho-physiological conditions of sleep to relax the energy with which . . . [it holds] down the repressed material during the day . . . The danger of sleep being disturbed by [the repressed material] . . . must . . . be guarded against by the ego . . . [E]ven during deep sleep a certain amount of free attention is on duty to guard against sensory stimuli, and . . . this guard may sometimes consider waking more advisable than a continuation of sleep. (1901a, V, 679; see 1933a, XXII, 16)

(ix) [O]ur ego . . . gives credence to the dream images, as though what it wanted to say was: "Yes, yes! You're quite right, but let me go on sleeping!" The low estimate which we form of dreams when we are awake . . . is probably . . . the judgment passed by our sleeping ego . . .
. . . [A]nxiety dreams . . . can no longer [prevent] . . . an interruption of sleep but . . . [bring] sleep to an end. In doing so it [*sic*] is merely behaving like a conscientious night watchman . . . suppressing disturbances so that the townsmen may not be waked up . . . [He] awakens them, if the causes seem to him serious and of a kind that he cannot cope with alone. (1901a, V, 680; see 1933a, XXII, 17; 1940a, XXIII, 171)

I shall devote the next three sections of this paper to 'Who?' questions about characters in this story, and to enigmas about "consciousness" which pervade it. I shall not even worry that at some junctures Freud's narrative implies a vicious regress. In (ix), for example, it sounds very much as if the ego were not only sleeping, but dreaming too! This section will be concerned only with the ego's sleeping or waking.

Freud's account of dreaming meshes with his theory of psychic energy because he assumes that instincts, loaded with counter-cathexis, make up the "repressed material" (vii). When we are awake, our alert ego prevents repressed instincts from gaining discharge through our actions (iii). That is why they seek to escape through our "consciousness" while we sleep (ii, iii). Like an hysterical symptom, a dream is a "compromise" (1933a, XXII, 15). Partly disguised instincts escape through our groggy consciousness, usually without interrupting our repose (vi, vii, viii, ix). Hence Freud's motto that dreams are "guardians of sleep" (1900a, IV, 233, 238; 1901a, V, 678; 1915c, XIV, 129). But the main point is that in Freud's theory of dreaming, instincts are not mere electrified ideas; they are quasi-persons, striving for personal freedom.

This brings us to our opening question whether our ego is awake or asleep when we dream. Obviously our repressed instincts are on the *qui vive,* waiting to break out. It sounds much odder to say our ego is in the same alert condition. That is because we tend to think of our ego as the real us, or at least the kernel of what we are. When we dream, we sleep; shouldn't our ego slumber too? Freud says so (iv, vi, ix). On the other hand, it is almost a 'dramatic' necessity of Freud's anthropomorphic theories that each character in them should 'do' something. If you are going to explain a psychological occurrence, such as dreaming, as a transaction between parts of our mind, these parts ought to be on the move. Freud could say that our instincts assume complete control when we dream. But then there would be insufficient dramatic tension, as required by his dualistic methodology (section 1).

If this reconstruction is near the mark, then we can see why Freud inconsistently portrays our ego as sleeping but actively censoring, and why he sometimes tries to avoid this dilemma with a drowsy ego (v, vii, viii). But this is still a form of wakefulness.

It is at worst self-contradictory for Freud to assert that our ego censors while snoozing. The riddles about identity and consciousness which I deal with next arouse our suspicion that other statements by Freud are meaningless.

9. *'Who?' questions.* I shall branch out now from the numbered sample statements about dreaming. If we try to gain any understanding of theories which endow parts of our mind with personal characteristics, we are bound to ask: Who are these mini-individuals? Do they care about us? Will their fate affect us? Take a

repressed instinct. To say that an erotic urge is active in my mind is to say that I 'want,' in some as yet unexplained sense, to engage in sexual activity. Whatever the status of this desire, it is a desire that I, a flesh and blood human being, should act. But now consider my newly personified instinct. Does it want *me* to participate in sexual undertakings? Why should it be concerned with me? Yet what could Freud mean if he said that instincts desire to engage in sexual activity themselves?

If we turn to the gratification of our instincts, which Freud equates with our pleasure, we confront the same enigmas. Freud's account of all instincts—repressed or not—is that "these processes strive toward gaining pleasure; psychical activity draws back from any event which might arouse unpleasure" (1911b, XII, 219). But whose pleasure do they "strive" for? It would go against Freud's general outlook if we suppose these mini-people work for the satisfaction of another, namely myself. Yet it would be unintelligible to say that they themselves enjoy escaping from my mental apparatus, and that this pleasure is what they seek. Would you give a homeostatic account of the pleasure felt by instincts whose escape constitutes my delight? Then each impulse would have to possess its own mental apparatus, with its own instincts pressing for freedom, and so on *ad infinitum!* What is left for Freud to mean when he compares our instincts to tiny people? Most things we can assert or deny with regard to people are inadmissible here.

Since we tend to think of our ego as representing ourselves, we ought to have less trouble when we personify our ego. Unfortunately for Freud's subdividing theory, we run into similar bogs. Consider my ego's "wish to sleep" (i, viii). For *whose* sleep does it yearn? Mine? Just its own? In this case there are additional sources of bafflement. Who is the owner of the "free attention" which is "on duty" (viii)? Whose "waking" may the attentive "guard" consider "more advisable than a continuation of sleep" (viii)? His own? Mine? When we hear of the sleeping "townsmen" (ix), we should raise further questions. On his overall view of human motivation, can Freud suppose that any "watchman" is "conscientious" enough to care about his fellow townsmen? Does he call them from sleep just to help him put down rowdy instincts? What harm can the most licentious instincts do him? If Freud were talking about ordinary sentinels and sleeping townsmen, we would be able to answer. So we must wonder what Freud's analogy comes to here.

Our bewilderment should become more general when we remember Freud's functional characterization of the ego. To the ego he always assigns "the task of self-preservation," which it carries out "by learning to bring about changes in the external world to its own advantage (through activity)" (1940a [1938], XXIII, 145–46). Again we ought to ask: Which "self" does my ego have the "task" of preserving? Why should my ego seek *my* "advantage"? But what would it mean if we said that it presses for its *own* advantage? Freud's notion of the ego now seems very hard to understand.

It is not the only denizen of our minds in this situation. Let us put Freud's theory of dreaming aside for a moment. We recall the "ego ideal," which Freud says it is the superego's job to "impose" upon the ego (1923b, XIX, 34–39, 48–57; cf. 1914e, XIV, 93 f.). Generally, our superego has the "functions of self-observation, of conscience and of maintaining the ideal" (1933a, XXII, 66). But if this characterization is going to help us, we should have some notion of the goals an "ego ideal" can specify for a mini-person. Furthermore, we ought to ask: Whom does my superego watch when it engages in "self-observation"? How can it watch my ego? Why does it care about *my* ideals, or my ego's falling short of them?

As we move further away from dreaming, we notice the same puzzles. Discussing anxiety and inhibitions, Freud asserts that "the ego is the actual seat of anxiety" (1923b, XIX, 57; see 1926d, XX, 93, 109). Is Freud offering the partition theory that when a person is overcome by dread, so is his ego? That reading gains support when Freud declares that an inhibition is "a restriction which [the] ego had imposed on itself so as not to arouse the anxiety symptom" (1926d, XX, 101). Here we should ask: Whose anxiety does my ego want to avoid? Even if it were meaningful to speak of my ego placing a "restriction . . . on itself," why should it do so to prevent *my* anxiety? Yet it would be no easy task to explain what it might be like if my ego itself were overwhelmed by dread.

Freud's notion of responsibility has only a small niche in his metapsychology, but what he says about it shows us how to elude such embarrassing 'Who?' questions. His remarks also guide us back to dreams, because Freud concentrated on our accountability for what we dream. His view is sufficiently general, however, to fit any situation where our repressed instincts bring about some untoward result. Freud's problem is whom to blame for the result. His solution is

marvelously cogent, and incidentally quite at variance with the outlook of 'hard determinist' philosophers who invoke his name. Freud
reasons:

> Obviously one must hold oneself responsible for the evil impulses
> of one's dreams . . . [T]he content of the dream . . . is a part of
> my own being . . .
>   . . . [I]n the metapsychological sense this bad repressed content
> does not belong to my "ego" . . . but to an "id" on which my ego is
> seated. But this ego developed out of the id, it forms with it a single
> biological unit . . . it . . . obeys . . . the id.
>   . . . [I]f for purposes of moral valuation I . . . do not make
> my ego responsible for it, what use would that be to me? . . . I
> . . . do take that responsibility . . . Psychoanalysis has made us
> familiar with . . . obsessional neurosis, in which the poor ego feels
> itself responsible for . . . evil impulses . . . which it is unable to
> acknowledge. Something of this is present in every normal per-
> son . . .
>   The physician will leave it to the jurist to construct a respon-
> sibility that is artificially limited to the metapsychological ego.
> (1925i, XIX, 133 f.)

I would generalize Freud's conclusion: Just as we cannot mean-
ingfully say who, among the denizens of our mind, is a responsible
agent, we cannot make any of the other personal attributions which
Freud himself made. The best way to forestall 'Who?' questions is
to avoid personifying whatever the components are which operate
within us.

Now we turn to some overlapping difficulties about consciousness.
Again we branch out from Freud's remarks about dreaming, which
I numbered. Eventually we shall zero in on the question:

10. *Can there be multiple centers of consciousness within the
dreamer?* We have stored up riddles about consciousness throughout this investigation. In section 6, we noticed that Freud called a
system of "permeable" neurones "consciousness," and we found this
honorific title inappropriate. We discovered in section 7 that Freud's
theoretical *mélange* of electronics and anthropomorphism did not
make sense of hysteria—particularly of Freud's suggestion that the
hysteric has a memory-idea of a traumatic event, but because of its
"charged" sexual content, the idea is pushed from his "consciousness." When we examined Freud's thoroughly anthropomorphic
model for dreaming, in section 8, we immediately noticed that he

had to say whether or not our ego is endowed with waking consciousness when we dream. If he says either, or compromises on drowsy
wakefulness, Freud's theory begins to sound unintelligible.

Now we also notice that Freud's animistic stories of dreaming, as
well as hysteria, tacitly separate our "consciousness" from the alert
or drowsy consciousness of our ego. For doesn't our ego consciously
"censor" and "repress" ideas? Doesn't it have to be conscious enough
to spot those which are dangerously erotic? As our ego does these
things, during the buildup of hysterogenic tension within us, or when
we dream, we remain in ignorance. We are not aware of the banished
ideas, or of our ego's conscious behavior toward them. Furthermore,
our repressed but freedom-seeking ideas act like conscious goal-
directed agencies themselves. Even if our watchful ego is aware of
their endeavors, we are not. Thus Freud's account of dreaming and
hysteria implies that there are at least two other centers of consciousness within us besides our own.

I do not think it is unintelligible or self-contradictory if we merely
envisage many independent loci of awareness in each person. Nonsense begins, as we saw in section 9, when we attempt to characterize
the tiny bearers of consciousness. Freud briefly took over a 'multiple
centers' view from Charcot, and during the 1890's wrote of an hysteric's "second consciousness" (1940d [1892], I, 153; 1893a, II, 15;
1893h, III, 39). Afterwards he developed strong methodological objections to such views. He vigorously denies that

> instead of subscribing to the hypothesis of unconscious ideas of
> which we know nothing, we had better assume that consciousness
> can be split up, so that certain ideas or other psychical acts may
> constitute a consciousness apart . . .

Freud considers this proposal

> a gratuitous assumption, based on abuse of the word "conscious".
> We have no right to extend the meaning of this word . . . to . . .
> include a consciousness of which its owner himself is not aware.
> If philosophers find difficulty in accepting . . . unconscious ideas
> . . . an unconscious consciousness seems to me even more objec-
> tionable. The cases described as splitting of consciousness . . .
> might better be denoted as shifting of consciousness between two
> different psychical complexes which become conscious and uncon-
> scious in alternation. (1912g, XII, 263; see 1915e, XIV, 170; 1925d,
> XX, 3)

If we glance back at Freud's statements about dreaming, however, we see that (i), (ii), (iii), (iv), (v), (vii), (viii) and (ix) all record activities which require a conscious mini-agent, of whose capers the dreamer himself is unaware. I doubt that any other anthropomorphic model would enable Freud to withhold independent consciousness from the citizens of our mind. This is due, *inter alia,* to Freud's novel and pervasive notion of repression. As I have emphasized, if you want to say that one part of the mind keeps another part away from the *owner's* consciousness, then *he* cannot be conscious of the repressed item. Now you have a choice about how to characterize the part which represses. If you depict it as some inanimate force, then you fail to explain why it picked on, say, an erotic idea. But if you introduce a repressing agency—a censoring ego—then you have to assume that it is conscious of what it represses. Otherwise it is no better, explanatorily speaking, than an insentient force. Yet since the repressed idea does not, by definition, reach the consciousness of the person in whom all this goes on, the repressing ego's consciousness of the idea is separate from the person's consciousness. Thus it is inevitable that Freud should ascribe independent cognitive capers to our ego.

I shall not uncritically adopt Freud's objection to multiple centers of consciousness, merely because it undermines his own anthropomorphic theories. Are there good reasons not to proliferate? Freud remarks that "the assumption of consciousness" in our fellow men "rests upon an inference and cannot share the direct certainty we have of our own consciousness" (1915e, XIV, 169). Suppose we accept this inferential account of our knowledge of other minds. Then would other centers of consciousness within us be any more dubious? My non-Freudian reply would be that crucial disparities remain. We can perceptually discriminate the body of another person. We can watch his facial expressions and the motion of his limbs. He sometimes displays—or betrays—his moods and emotions. Above all, he can tell us—candidly, or perhaps exaggerating, understating or distorting—whatever he believes, feels and wants. We have all these grounds for attributing conscious actions and mental states to other people. Even if the attribution were somehow inferential, it is rooted in our epistemic language games of observing and conversing. By contrast, the putative independent centers of consciousness within us cannot participate in any of these language games. They have no bodies for us to observe. They do not talk. When my analyst learns about the agencies he thinks I shelter, he must listen to *me* report my dreams and free associate.

I suppose this is a kind of 'unverifiability' charge against the 'multiple consciousness' implication of Freud's anthropomorphic theories. It is not as decisive a proof that Freud's animistic theories are unintelligible as the arguments in sections 7, 8 and 9; but it strengthens the case against Freud's subdividing method.

11. *Is Freud clear about our consciousness?*   Before we leave this topic, we should ask what Freud means generally when he says an idea, with its load of "affect" and "instinct," is present to our consciousness. This may help us evaluate, in the concluding section, Freud's assumption that some ideas are "present" in our minds, but not to our consciousness. I discern three Freudian accounts of consciousness.

Freud's simplest theory follows tradition. He proposes to "compare the perception of" our ideas "by consciousness with the perception of the outside world through the sense organs" (1915e, XIV, 171). What could he mean? There may be some parallel between our awareness of what goes on inside our bodies—digestion or indigestion, for example—and our tactile, auditory and other perception of extra-somatic items. At least there is the possibility of non-awareness and error in both cases. We might altogether fail to notice some occurrence within our bodies, and we could misdiagnose it—just as we sometimes overlook and misperceive extra-cutaneous happenings. But what would it be like for an idea to be in the line of our consciousness, in contact with it, or within its range, yet go unnoticed? What analogues are there to tricks of lighting, perspective, refraction and Doppler effects, which might cause us to be misconscious of an idea we have spotted? As long as these points remain unclarified, Freud's comparison between our awareness of our own ideas and sensory perception has little meaning.

His second account of consciousness might be called 'the attention theory.' He suggests:

> . . . Becoming conscious is connected with the application of . . . attention . . . which, as it seems, is only available in a specific quantity, and this may have been diverted from the train of thought in question on to some other purpose . . . If . . . we come upon an idea which will not bear criticism, we break off: We drop the cathexis of attention . . . [But] the train of thought . . . can continue to spin itself out without attention being turned to it again,

unless . . . it reaches a specially high degree of intensity which forces attention to it. (1900a, V, 593–94; see 1915e, XIV, 192)

This attention theory is vulnerable to 'Who?' questions and charges of 'multiplying.' Do we direct our own attention to the ideas running through our minds, or does a mini-agency have this job? Is this aiming done consciously? Unwittingly? Does the attention-directing agency know beforehand what our attention will strike? Who continues thinking our unattended train of thought? Is it perhaps not entertained by any agency when our attention moves from it? Can it become "intense" while there is no one attending to it whom it bothers intensely? Moreover, isn't this account patently circular? Attending to X is one specific way of being conscious of X. So even if Freud's attention theory were intelligible, it would be useless as an explanation of consciousness.

A third and last doctrine about consciousness we can derive from Freud's attempt to mark off "preconscious" ideas. These are ideas which, in some sense, we can bring before our consciousness at will. By contrast, we are unable to be conscious of our repressed "unconscious" ideas. The peculiarity of preconscious ideas, according to Freud, is that they are

> . . . brought into connection with word presentations . . .
> These word presentations are residues of memories; they were at one time perceptions . . . [O]nly something which has been a *Cs.* [conscious] perception can become conscious, and . . . anything arising from within (apart from feelings) that seeks to become conscious must try to transform itself into external perceptions: this becomes possible by means of memory traces. . . .
> The part played by word presentations now becomes perfectly clear. By their interposition internal thought-processes are made into perceptions . . . When a hyper-cathexis of the process of thinking takes place, thoughts are *actually* perceived—as if they came from without—and are consequently held to be true. (1923b, XIX, 20–23; see 1915e, XIV, 201)

As we illustrated above, it makes no sense to say our ideas are "perceived." Furthermore it is empirically doubtful that all the thoughts of which we are conscious "are . . . held to be true." Sometimes we hold an opinion tentatively, allowing that it may well be erroneous. The rest of Freud's story is infected with the kind of anthropomorphic nonsense that we diagnosed in sections 7 through 10.

For these reasons, we should not casually accept Freud's bifurcation of ideas which are "present in the mind": those which are, and those which are not, before our consciousness. We must be wary of agreeing that the latter are 'before' or "in" our unconscious. I think one source of Freud's partitioning theories, both mechanistic and animistic, is his assumption that our minds contain "unconscious" as well as "conscious" ideas—and by extension, instincts and whatever mechanisms or agencies work upon our ideas and instincts. Since we are unaware of the majority of these *dramatis personae,* and their interactions, Freud's scenarios have to list them as "unconscious," or more tendentiously, "in the unconscious." Having noticed how obscure Freud's notion of consciousness is, we ought to scrutinize what he says about its opposite.

12. *Inferring unconscious ideas and their receptacle.* Freud mostly rebuts objections against the unconscious. He never spells out what it means to say there are ideas and other things in our mind of which we are not conscious. The closest he comes to furnishing a positive argument for his assumption is when he discusses one of Bernheim's experiments with hypnosis. Freud reports that the hypnotized subject

> was ordered to execute a certain action at a certain fixed moment after his awakening . . . He awakes . . . he has no recollection of his hypnotic state, and yet at the pre-arranged moment there rushes into his mind the impulse to do such and such a thing, and he does it consciously, though not knowing why. It seems impossible to give any other description of the phenomenon than to say that the order had been present in the mind of the person in a condition of latency, or had been present unconsciously, until the given moment came . . . (1912g, XII, 261)

Freud then proposes a more "dynamic view of the phenomenon":

> this idea became *active* . . . The real stimulus to the action being the order of the physician, it is hard not to concede that the idea of the physician's order became active too. Yet this idea did not reveal itself to consciousness . . . it remained unconscious, and so it was *active and unconscious* at the same time. (Ibid.; see 1940b [1938], XXIII, 285)

Perhaps we will understand Freud's general notion of "unconscious ideas" if we ask what his "description of the phenomenon," and especially his "dynamic view," amounts to in this case. Does

Freud mean that the *subject* of this experiment was thinking about Bernheim's order in between times? No, because Freud says the man was unaware that he had received the order until its 'content' rushed into his consciousness. Does Freud mean that part of the subject's mind—for instance, the receptacle of such hidden ideas—was pondering Bernheim's order? Then Freud would have to face embarrassing 'Who?' questions, and recognize another center of consciousness within the subject besides his own. We noticed this difficulty in section 11, when we came across Freud's statement, "the train of thought . . . can continue to spin itself out without attention being turned to it again . . ." I cannot guess what happens to an idea which has nobody—not even an id, an "unconscious" or an ego—to think about it. Surely it does not contemplate itself!

A defender of Freud might reply that neither the subject, nor a part of him dwells upon the hypnotically injected idea: it is simply laid up within his mind, outside the range of his consciousness, "until the given moment." I have two grumbles against this 'warehouse' interpretation of Freud's "description of the phenomenon":

(i) As we showed in section 11, it is already unclear enough what goes on, according to Freud, when an idea parades before a person's consciousness. We fall into perfect obscurity when we try to specify what happens with a stored idea. To say that one thinks of his idea when it is before his consciousness, but does not think of it when it is stored, may be truistic. However, our question merely shifts. Now we should ask: what transpires with a stored idea when we do not think about it—when it is "not apprehended by the conscious mind"? (1915e, XIV, 161). In what sense does the hypnotist's order "continue to spin itself out"? To assert there is a "permanent trace" of it in our unconscious (1925a, XIX, 230), is not to elucidate the key notion of this spinning out.

(ii) Whatever happens in storage, a warehoused idea does not seem to be "present" in a sufficiently "active" manner to vindicate Freud's "dynamic view" of this hypnotic experiment by Bernheim.

I am equally unimpressed by Freud's appeal to our capacity for calling up ideas which we have not been conscious of for a while—ideas he calls "preconscious." Freud bluntly asserts: "When all our latent memories are taken into consideration, it becomes totally incomprehensible how the existence of the unconscious can be denied" (1915e, XIV, 167). No doubt human powers of recollection are mystifying, and we need some explanation of them. But we shall only compound our bafflement if we explain these powers by offering either an unintelligible "active" theory, or a vague 'storage' doctrine.

Freudians may protest at this: 'How else can we account for these occurrences, as well as dreams, associations, parapraxes and neurotic symptoms, unless we assume the presence of preconscious and unconscious ideas?' This 'How else?' begs the very 'presence' question at issue. Besides, nonsense explains nothing.

My investigation of what Freud might mean when he classifies the ideas in our mind as being either "conscious" or "unconscious" fits neatly with my attack upon his subdividing theories. Both his mechanistic and his anthropomorphic 'component' stories require that there should be things within us of which we are not conscious: streams of energy, high voltage ideas, pressing instincts, struggling agencies. If Freud is going to explain people's conflict behavior as a clash of inanimate forces, or of contentious actors within the mental arena, he must provide for the existence of more than what we are aware of. There must be parties to the conflict which are not registered by our consciousness. So this cluster of notions gives indispensable support to Freud's partitioning plans. However, if these notions are obscure or confused in Freud's theorizing, then he should not even begin to tell us about things within our mind of which we are unconscious. I am not objecting that our ideas and so on are never unconscious. I haven't enough understanding of what Freud means by saying a man is conscious of an idea. Therefore I do not know what to make of his implied contrast with ideas having some other status. Since all Freud's partition schemes take this contrast for granted, they would be unjustifiably premature even if they were both relevant and coherent.

My goal has been to explore some curious implications of the mechanistic and anthropomorphic models used by Freud to elucidate conflict behavior. I remain convinced that his imagery of the mind, its components, and their interplay, is original as well as suggestive. But I think we should spell out exactly what his models suggest. Along with all the fruitful perspectives they encourage us to take toward disturbed and 'normal' conduct, we should be on the lookout for unilluminating and unintelligible implications they carry. His detailed accounts of our mental apparatus, hysterical symptoms, dreaming, consciousness, the unconscious and so on, have the merit of bringing these difficulties out into the open. None of the deep conceptual snags I have assessed here are due to shortcomings on Freud's part. Whatever anatomy of the self you propose, I believe you will be saddled with doctrines which are either not germane to the psychological phenomena, or else not cogent. Those in search of edification might conclude that we seem to have no alternative but to assume the unity of the self.[5]

[5] I read a version of this paper at a Michigan State University Philosophy Colloquium, November 28, 1972, and I am grateful to many listeners for constructive criticisms. I thank Richard Wollheim for perceptive editorial comments on my penultimate draft.

Identification and Imagination: the Inner Structure of a Psychic Mechanism

RICHARD WOLLHEIM

1. Freud in a number of passages, all to be found in his mature work,[1] describes and contrasts two ways in which the infant—and subsequently the adult as formed by his infantile experiences—may establish a libidinal tie or attachment. One of these ways is object-choice proper, the other is identification. Identification is the more primitive of the two: hence from the adult's point of view it invariably represents a regression. For Freud it is in origin a continuation, a kind of lateral continuation, of primary narcissism. It is a sideways move out of loving oneself into loving another: in that the infant who until then had been exclusively attached to himself now puts the other in the place of his own self or ego. It was out of consideration for the origins, as well as more obviously for the aims, of identification that Freud felt himself able on more than one occasion to distinguish between the two modes of attachment thus: When the infant chooses another (say, his mother) as his first love-object, he wishes to *have* her; but when, more archaically, he identifies himself with another (say, his father), he wishes to *be* him.[2] To have versus to be: in this distinction rightly understood we have, according to Freud, a clue to the difference between object-choice and identification, and so promise of entry into the understanding of each.

Now, identification, like comparable notions such as projection and regression, undergoes a systematic extension in Freud's thinking, which is of the utmost significance. Identification makes its first appearance as a mechanism of defence: as a means by which the ego deals with objectionable, or (an expression with changing meaning) "incompatible," wishes or desires. Soon, however, identification assumes a further role. For it becomes a method by means of which a trait or feature of the personality is fixed. Nor are these two functions unrelated: on the contrary, the most intimate connection between the two may be observed. For a defence which is constantly iterated conditions or constitutes the character.

---

[1] 1905d, VII, 222 n. (added 1915); 1910c, XI, ii–100; 1917e, XIV, 248–50; 1921c, XVIII, 105–8.
[2] E.g., 1921c, XVIII, 106; 1933a, XXII, 63.

This extension of function on the part of identification is elaborately illustrated in "From the History of an Infantile Neurosis," written in 1914 and published in a slightly expanded form in 1918: the so-called Wolf-Man case.[3] However, the shift is already in evidence in what is in effect Freud's first sustained application of the notion: that is to say, in his appeal to identification in order to provide an explanation of Leonardo da Vinci's homosexuality[4]—an explanation which when generalized eventually became one part of a disjunctive explanation that Freud produced for the incidence of homosexuality.[5] In the case of Leonardo the explanation goes something like this: Up to his fifth year or so Leonardo, the love-child of the notary Ser Piero da Vinci and the servant-girl Caterina, had lived alone with his mother and thus enjoyed her undivided love. Then he was required to leave his mother's house and move to the more elevated household maintained by his father: for Ser Piero's marriage to a certain Donna Albiera had proved childless, and it therefore seemed now appropriate for him to bring his illegitimate son under his roof. To Leonardo the move was a clear threat to the love in which he had enjoyed such intense bliss. To defend himself against the threatened loss of love—as well as, it turns out, against an excess of love on his part, the latter doubtless augmenting the former—Leonardo identified himself with his mother. He put himself in her place. And, having done so, he then took on, or found himself taking on, a number of her roles, including those of a libidinal character. More specifically, he found it natural to love boys just as she had loved him; and to love them in just the way in which she had loved him—that is, in an idealized or "pure" fashion. In his effort to conserve his love for his mother, and his mother's love for him, Leonardo became a homosexual.

The most general structure of the case is that one libidinal attachment, undertaken defensively, leads on to further libidinal attachments, which are constitutive of the character. By a special and powerful coincidence the secondary attachments into which Leonardo is drawn exhibit a property that is also exhibited by, indeed is intrinsic to, the primary attachment: narcissism. It is in consequence

---

[3] For this case now see also *The Wolf-Man and Sigmund Freud*, ed. Muriel Gardiner (Basic Bks., New York, 1971; Hogarth, London, 1972).
[4] 1910c, XI, 98–101.
[5] 1922b, XVIII, 230–32; 1923b, XIX, 37, 43.

of this that Leonardo loves boys; or that his history, as we have it so far, is a history of *homosexuality*. But, of course—though in the Leonardo essay Freud is perhaps not so clear on this point as one might have wished—the coincidence need not have held. It came about because it was with his *mother* that Leonardo identified himself. And we can see this more clearly when we consider other cases of identification to which a different outcome is assigned: where the secondary attachments do not share in the narcissism predicated of the primary attachment. For instance, in the early history of the Wolf-Man, identification with the *father* is an important theme. Now, so long as the Wolf-Man maintained himself in his active attitude, and did not lapse into masochism, the identification led on to heterosexual attachments: most notably, the heavily sadistic longing for the servant-girl Grusha, glimpsed in a moment not to be forgotten, bending over a pail of water, a broom of twigs by her side. But the identification itself is a narcissistic or homosexual attachment.[6] And, more generally, in his revised account of feminine sexuality,[7] Freud accorded the girl's identification with her mother a vital role in the development of her heterosexuality. Through a relation which is intrinsically narcissistic she transcends narcissism.

However, if the original identification and the subsequent libidinal attachments that it generates can differ in the kind of sexual object that they take, they are intimately linked in that they are in effect merely different phases of the same continuing process. And this linkage we can observe whichever way round we look at the process: forwards or backwards in time. Forwards: in that, if identification is to be operative, then it must transform the sexual life of the individual who employs it. Identification, Freud says in *Group Psychology and the Analysis of the Ego,* "remoulds the ego . . . in its sexual character."[8] Backwards: for every time the individual involves himself in a libidinal attachment, we can see at work the same redirection of desire and impulse that occurred around the original identification. The sexual transformation that the individual imposes on himself has never been so complete that that part of the process does not have to be constantly re-enacted. So, for instance, Freud speculated that, in each case of homosexual attraction, what happens is that the

[6] 1918b, XVII, 27, 63, 90–97, 107–8.
[7] E.g., 1933a, XXII, 117–35; 1940a [1938], XXIII, 193.
[8] 1921c, XVIII, 108.

homosexual has first experienced the charms of a woman and then, to preserve his loving relations with his mother, he transfers the excitation on to a man. "In this manner" Freud writes, "he repeats over and over again the mechanism by which he acquired his homosexuality."[9]

It is considerations such as these that make what I have called the extension of function assigned to identification comprehensible and natural.

2. The phenomenon of identification, both in its initial or defensive function and in its extended or constitutive function, is certainly very complex, and no analysis of the corresponding concept will be adequate unless it reproduces this complexity. However, in both its functions it seems reasonable to associate identification with imagination. The association has an intuitive appeal, but reflection supports the soundness of this intuition.

In the first place, identification must be regarded as containing essentially an internal component. It cannot, in other words, be elucidated in exclusively behavioural terms: no matter how generous a view we take of the notion of behaviour itself. One reason why this is so is that otherwise we would not be able to distinguish between identification and imitation. And this we need to do. For even when imitation and identification go together, the two are not identical in that identification provides the explanation of imitation. And there are other cases where imitation occurs without identification and it finds its explanation in, e.g., conditioning, intimacy or aggression. Now, if I am right and we are required to find an internal component for identification, imagination is the most likely candidate.

Secondly, identification is closely connected in Freud's thinking with phantasy, and phantasy, once again, plausibly associates itself with imagination. Phantasy, it should be pointed out, is connected with identification twice over. For, on the one hand, it occurs as a concomitant—though, I have suggested, an essential concomitant—of identification. (It is in this connection that this essay will be concerned with the relations between identification and imagination.) And, on the other hand, phantasy occurs as, or as part of, the initiating event in identification. From the beginning Freud seems to have been inclined to associate identification with the oral phase of libidi-

---

[9] 1910c, XI, 100. The same expression occurs, almost verbatim, in a footnote added at this time to the *Three Essays on the Theory of Sexuality*, 1905d, VII, 145 n. (added 1910).

nal development[10]—an association in which he was encouraged by the thinking of Karl Abraham. However, it was a step towards greater specificity—though not one which it is easy to date—when Freud located the origin of identification in a phantasy of oral incorporation or a piece of psychic cannibalism. The son, say, phantasises the taking in of the father through the mouth when he identifies himself with him. "Introjection" is used in this sense in *Group Psychology and the Analysis of the Ego,* and from then onwards Freud brought introjection and identification into a conceptual linkage in much the same way as years earlier, at the very beginning of psychoanalysis, he had linked repression and resistance. I shall have nothing further to say about this second connection, and I mention it here only to show how identification depends upon phantasy for its genesis as well as for its ongoing nature. And this I do only, in turn, to stress the case for the association between identification and imagination, which is my theme.

In developing the theme I shall follow a lengthy detour. For I want first to set out an account or analysis of imagination which I shall then apply to the more abstruse problem of identification. My account will fall into two parts: one dealing with the content of imagination, the other dealing with its nature. What I shall say about imagination will, I believe, be found to have most bearing upon identification where the two parts meet: or—to put it another way—where the topics of content and nature intersect.

3. First, the content of imagination.

Traditionally, it has been maintained that the imagination of man knows no limits, except the limits of possibility: the limits, that is, of logical possibility. There is nothing that can be that cannot be imagined. However, even if the objects of imagination cannot be circumscribed, they can be classified. And I mean this not just in the uninteresting sense in which it follows from the fact that objects, or possible objects, in the world can be classified: but in some more constructive sense, in which the classification would be worked out by reference to the imagination itself. Or, to put it another way, the different types of object of imagination in which the classification would issue would correspond to, or could be correlated with, what independently we might think of as different types of imagining.

---

[10] 1905d, VII, 198 (added 1915); 1915c, XIV, 113–40; 1917e [1915], XIV, 249–50; 1918b, XVII, 106–7.

Let me now make a suggestion, which might also bring out more clearly what I have in mind. I suggest the following classification, which I intend to be exclusive but not exhaustive. When I engage in imagination it might be that:

I imagine doing something or other

or that

I imagine my doing something or other

or that

I imagine someone else's doing something or other. Or, to fill in the examples, it might be that

I imagine setting foot on the moon

or that

I imagine my setting foot on the moon

or that

I imagine Goethe's setting foot on the moon.

"Doing something or other," "my doing something or other," "someone else's doing something or other" would, on the view that I am suggesting, instantiate different types of object imagined, and these different types of object would in turn be objects of three different types of imagining.

In this essay I shall not be concerned again with the first type of imagining. I shall be concerned only with the second and third types of imagining.

4. My suggested classification might be clarified by considering an objection that could be raised against it, or that, more specifically, could be raised against the way in which it distinguishes between the second and third types of imagining. There is no real difference, the objection would run, between my imagining my doing something or other and my imagining someone else's doing something or other, in that these cannot reasonably be conceived of as different types of imagining. There may be some kind of difference, but there is not the difference in principle that my classification supposes. For consider cases which might ordinarily be thought of as cases of my imagining myself doing something or other. Now, when I imagine myself doing something or other, is there not often someone else around whom I also imagine doing something or other? Or, when I imagine someone else's doing something or other, am I not often also in the act and imagined to be doing something or other? And, in such cases, are not the two pieces of imagining often integrally linked so that I

may be said to imagine one in imagining the other? For instance, I imagine myself hurling insults at an enemy, and I *therein* imagine the enemy's writhing under my insults. Or I imagine a foreign agent's slipping me some money, and I *therein* imagine myself pocketing the money. And if this is so, whether I describe what I imagine by saying that I imagine *myself* doing something or other (to someone else) or by saying that I imagine *someone else's* doing something or other (to me) seems a matter of indifference. For all that is at stake is the point of view from which I choose to describe my imaginings, and this (the objection will continue) cannot give rise to a real difference in the type of imagining involved. Whatever difference there is cannot coincide with a difference in principle. In other cases, it is true, there will not be this choice of description open to me. It will not be open: either because I do not imagine both myself and someone else at the same time, or I do imagine both myself and someone else but not engaged in any interlocking activity. I imagine myself, like the poet in German *Lieder,* wandering alone by the brook in springtime; or I imagine myself and another seated in front of a fire, each deep in silent study. But between these cases and the cases we were considering a few moments back—myself and the enemy, the secret agent and me—there seems (again) no difference in principle. So, if the cases where there is a choice of description do not generate different types of imagining, neither do the cases where there isn't such a choice. So my classification is in doubt.

But there is something most important that this objection overlooks; and the objection is worth considering if only because consideration of it is likely to bring out this factor. The objection is quite right to link the difference between my imagining myself doing something or other and my imagining someone else's doing something or other with a difference in the point of view from which I describe what I imagine. But it is wrong to express this by talking of the point of view from which I *choose* to describe what I imagine. For often —not always, but often—I imagine what I do from a certain point of view. And in such cases a description of what I imagine must, if it is to do justice to this feature of my imagining, be from that same point of view. If it isn't, then there is some part of my imaginative experience that it will omit. When I imagine something from a certain point of view, I cannot *choose* the point of view from which I describe what I imagine: I cannot, that is, if my description is to be faithful.

In supposing just now how I might imagine myself hurling insults at an enemy, or a foreign agent's slipping me some money, I had suggested, though I had not asserted—I had not asserted because I was not yet in a position to do so—that in each case my imagining involved a point of view. The scene of foolhardiness at the front, the backstreet incident of petty corruption, were imagined, the first from my point of view, the second from the secret agent's. If this is now made explicit, then we can see that in each case there is a valid reason why the point of view from which I describe what I imagine is not optional. "My hurling insults at the enemy," "the agent's slipping me the money" now emerge as the canonical descriptions of what on these two occasions I imagine.

To register this last point, I shall introduce a new distinction. The distinction is between "centrally imagining someone's doing something or other" and "peripherally imagining someone's doing something or other"—where "someone" now ranges over both me and someone else. When I imagine someone's doing something or other and I imagine this from his point of view, I centrally imagine his doing something or other; and it is often the case that when I centrally imagine someone's doing something or other, there will be another or others whom I peripherally imagine doing something or other. (There will be cases, which involve interesting complexities, which I shall not pursue, where the person whom I centrally imagine shifts in the course of my imagining whatever it is. And there will be other cases, at the opposite end of the spectrum, involving a simplification, which I shall also not pursue, where there is no one whom I centrally imagine, and *a fortiori* no one whom I peripherally imagine. These latter cases have, I suspect, a considerable affinity with the first type of imagining, which I introduced only to put to one side.)

Now, when I offered a classification of imagination into different types of imagining by reference to whom I imagine, what I had in mind was a classification by reference to the person whom I centrally imagine. My second and third types of imagining must be understood as, respectively,

I centrally imagine myself doing something or other

and

I centrally imagine someone else's doing something or other. And neither the fact that, when I centrally imagine myself doing something or other, there may well be someone else whom I peripherally imagine doing something or other, nor the fact that, when I centrally imagine someone else's doing something or other, I may well peripherally imagine myself doing something or other—neither of these two facts does anything to dispute my classification. Yet it should now be clear that it is on just these facts that the objection to my classification that I have been considering in this section rests its case.

5.   However, it is one thing to introduce the notion of centrally imagining someone doing something or other—e.g., setting foot on the moon, provoking an enemy, handing over a bribe—and another thing to say what it consists in.

I want to indicate two marks by which the phenomenon can be identified. One I shall suggest now while I am talking about the content of imagination. The other will have to wait a little until I have said something, as I intend to next, about the nature of imagination.

The first mark is this: That when I centrally imagine someone doing something or other I liberally and systematically intersperse imagining his *doing* certain things with imagining his *feeling and thinking* certain things. I say "liberally and systematically," and both words need to be taken seriously. By "liberally" I mean "quite a lot." By "systematically" I mean something like "as and when they occur"— that is, as and when the feelings and thoughts occur. For when I centrally imagine myself doing something or other, I am quite likely to imagine another thinking or feeling something—but only in response or in reaction to what I imagine myself thinking or feeling. For instance, I imagine—centrally imagine—myself hurling insults at the enemy; in the course of doing so I shall most likely imagine the enemy's writhing under my insults: but this is so only because, in imagining myself hurling insults at the enemy, I shall most likely imagine myself wondering over or rejoicing at what the enemy feels. I don't imagine what the enemy feels as and when he does, but only as and when I wonder what he does. In such a case imagining what someone else feels is not incompatible with, indeed it is corroboratory of, the fact that it is myself whom I centrally imagine.

So this first mark of centrally imagining someone is that in imagining his doing certain things I *liberally* and *systematically* imagine his feeling and thinking certain things. For the second mark we must wait a little. We must wait until we have considered somewhat the *nature* of imagination.

6.   Secondly, then, the nature of imagination.

I should like to start by taking seriously a suggestion made by Wittgenstein in various places.[11] The suggestion is to the effect that, if we want to understand the nature of an inner phenomenon, we do well to consider an external counterpart of that phenomenon: a phenomenon, that is, that is external and seems somehow to match or correspond to it. I shall adopt the suggestion by assuming that a counterpart to imagination is to be found in acting. Where, we might think, could we find a better match in the outside world to the internal phenomenon of imagining than in the discharge of the actor's role?[12]

However, if this seems initially the right way to apply Wittgenstein's suggestion, we are soon brought up against certain limitations to it. For all its intrinsic plausibility, the match between acting and imagination soon runs out, for there seem to be too many aspects of the internal phenomena that go unrepresented in the external phenomenon. For instance, the actor must follow the lines and actions laid down by another whereas we, we feel, are free in ourselves to imagine what we want.

There are, as I say, a number of respects in which acting falls short of imagination, but all these respects can, I think, be gathered together and accounted for in a unitary way. Acting—real-life acting, that is—is a dependent acting. The role of the actor is intelligible only in the context of two other roles which flank it: the role of the dramatist and the role of the audience. By contrast, imagination is, comparatively speaking, an independent activity. Accordingly, if we want to find an external counterpart to imagination, we might well start with acting but we shall soon need to supplement it by bringing in the two other roles on which it, acting, is dependent. Indeed, I think that it is only when we use this broader model that the initial plausibility that it had is sustained and justified. It is only because we naturally think of acting in this more extended framework that we ever thought of acting as the counterpart of imagination.

7.   Wittgenstein's suggestion, I have said, is that we should try to understand the nature of the internal phenomenon by considering the nature of an external phenomenon. We have not, however, fully complied with Wittgenstein's suggestion when, in our efforts to grasp

[11] E.g., Ludwig Wittgenstein, *Blue and Brown Books* (Blackwell, Oxford, 1958), p. 4.
[12] Cf. Gilbert Ryle, *The Concept of Mind* (Hutchinson, London, 1949).

a certain mental state or condition, we identify its external counterpart. For, however good an understanding we may have, or we may reach, of the external phenomenon, there is always a residual difficulty in working out the implications of this for the internal phenomenon. We can always go wrong in what we think the internal version would be of the phenomenon that we have taken as providing the external counterpart.

And whatever weight we may attach to this as a general difficulty in the way of applying Wittgenstein's suggestion, I am certain that the specific difficulties involved in the case of imagination are considerable. The correlation of imagination with acting doesn't complete our task: even when we have sufficiently broadened our conception of acting. For the very real difficulty remains of what we are to make of this correlation when we turn back to imagination. For what are we to take as the internal version of this external phenomenon? It is to this question that I shall now address myself. I shall try to say something briefly about what is implied—and, more significantly, what is not implied—in thinking that imagination contains an internal version of the dramatist and an internal version of the audience: that these are both truths about its nature. I shall say something about each of the roles in turn, stressing where the pitfalls lie.

8.   To begin with, the role of the dramatist.

To say that imagination contains an internal version of the dramatist is a way of doing justice to a fact already observed: the fact that we initiate what we imagine, or that we initiate what we imagine in a sense in which the actor does not initiate what he acts. (Of course, the actor who improvises does; but then the improvisatory actor fills more roles than that of actor.)

But it is important to see what does not follow from, or what is not implied in, thinking that imagination contains an internal version of the dramatist. What is not implied is that I am quite untrammelled in my imaginings. If, for instance, I imagine some friends of mine arriving together in a foreign city, a city unknown to them but known to me, I am not at liberty in the sequence of what I imagine. I experience certain constraints, which might in the present case be subsumed under two general headings. I am constrained by *whom* it is whom I imagine, and I am constrained by *what* it is that I imagine their doing: that it is John and Jane whom I imagine, and that it is Cairo where I imagine them arriving, and I imagine them arriving by train.

The point might be put by saying that in imagination I draw upon a repertoire, where the repertoire consists in knowledge of or beliefs about what or whom I imagine. It is, indeed, for this reason—because, that is, of the connection between imagination and a repertoire—that imagination is such a potent source of new information: a source so often overlooked by philosophers. For in imagining people in unfamiliar or unexperienced circumstances my awareness of them expands.

However, when one thinks it over, it is not really so surprising that to postulate an internal version of the dramatist in imagination does not imply that we are quite untrammelled in our imaginings. For we could have arrived at this same conclusion by reflecting more closely on the position of the real-life dramatist. For when a dramatist—a real-life dramatist, as I call him—has invented a certain character and placed him in a certain setting, he is not untrammelled in the words or actions that he can attribute to his character. He, too, is constrained, he too has a repertoire from which he must draw, and the fact that the repertoire is substantially one of his own invention does not affect the principle at issue.

And the introduction of the real-life dramatist at this point has another possible advantage for the development of my argument. For it may make us think again about the question which we are even now perhaps eager to raise. In talking of the constraints which we are under in our imaginings, am I talking of merely psychological or of logical constraints? Well, of what nature are the dramatist's constraints? Is it in the psychological or in the logical sense of "couldn't" that Shakespeare couldn't have let Lear give way to Kent's remonstrations, or that Ibsen couldn't have made Rebecca West go straight ahead and marry Rosmer? The question about the nature of the constraints upon our imaginings still remains, but perhaps the simple dichotomy of answer does not.

9.   Now, let me turn to the role of the audience.

What is the implication of saying that imagination contains an internal version of the audience? The question is hard: harder, I think, than the corresponding question about the dramatist. And once again let me concentrate on something that isn't implied, or that doesn't follow.

To say that there is in imagination an internal version of the audience is intended to do justice to the fact that, when we imagine someone doing something or other, there is a state or condition which we are in at the end of imagining this and which we are in as the result of what we have imagined. This is the force of talking about the internal version of an audience. But this point needs to be distinguished from another, quite different point; and that is that, after imagining someone doing something or other, we may find ourselves in a certain state and be in it as the result of having observed or reflected upon what we have imagined.

An example may bring out the distinction I have in mind. Let us take a familiar use of imagination: in erotic phantasy. Let us suppose that I imagine myself engaging in some specific piece of sexual activity, something really quite ingeniously elaborated. Now, a likely outcome of this is a condition on my part of sexual arousal: at the end of imagining whatever it is, and as a result of imagining this, excitement supervenes. However, when the excitement has died down, or perhaps while it still continues, I might step back from my imaginings and survey them. "So I've been imagining myself doing *that*"—I might think. And then, if the sexual content is something to which I am not reconciled, I might feel disgusted or appalled. Another possible reaction would be to feel admiration for my powers of invention or my lack of inhibition. My hope is that these two kinds of case allow us to see clearly the difference between a condition that is where my imagination leaves me and another that is subsequent upon, or a consequence of, my imagination. My erotic phantasy leaves me aroused, and a consequence for me of having indulged in it is that I am shocked, alternatively a hero to myself. With this distinction clear we may then observe the following: that of these two conditions it is only the first that supports the claim that imagination contains an internal version of the audience, and it requires no mediating event between what I have just imagined and the state I am in. By contrast, the second of these two conditions does involve such a mediating event and just for that reason it is a consequence, rather than a part, of my imagining.

The distinction has, interestingly, a rather wide application. For there would seem to be a number of mental phenomena which characteristically bring in train, as part of themselves, some terminal condition. As a result of the mental phenomenon, or of the activity or activities that comprise it, I am in a specific state, and my being in that state belongs to the phenomenon. But as an alternative, I can detach myself from whatever mental phenomenon it may be, observe or reflect upon it, and then find myself in a certain state, where my being in this state lies in consequence outside the mental phenomenon. In both cases, the later condition results from the preceding mental phenonenon. But, in the one case, it is integral to the mental phenomenon, and therefore it is unmediated by any event. In the other case, it is mediated by a piece of observation, and therefore is a consequence of the mental phenomenon. (Of course, that there is such a mediating event is a sufficient, but not a necessary, condition of the later state being a consequence of the mental phenomenon: mental phenomena have many consequences that do not arise through reflection upon them.)

As examples of the first kind of case, consider the following: Having composed a piece of prose which I intend to use later—say, in a political address—I then say it over to myself, and suddenly I don't like the sound of it at all. Or, having forgotten a line from a favourite poem, I start reciting the poem to myself until I come to the words

Aux yeux de souvenir que le monde est petit!

and then I have recalled what up till then I could not remember. In such cases it is neither necessary nor plausible to interpose as a mediating event my listening to what I say to myself where this is distinct from my saying whatever it is to myself. Rather, I take against my carefully turned phrase, I remember the line of Baudelaire, *in* saying it to myself.

As to the second kind of case, the delusions of observation, of being observed, which provided the material for Freud's earliest speculations about the superego,[13] provide extreme examples. For, though phenomenologically, these are experiences of being watched by another, the other who watches me is also part of myself. But equally good and less controversial examples are provided by the phenomena of shame or guilt: shame or guilt, that is, at or over a thought or feeling that I have entertained. And in all such cases the reflexive mental phenomenon is no part of the mental phenomenon upon which it subsequently reflects. Shame and guilt are consequences of shameful or guilty thoughts or feelings.

The point that I want to make about what isn't implied by saying that imagination contains an internal version of the audience might be put by emphasising that what imagination contains is an internal

[13] 1914c, XIV, 94–96.

version of *an audience,* not an internal version of a *spectator* or an *observer.* If we do observe what we imagine, that is no part of the imagination.

10.   There is, however, more to be said about the internal version of the audience in imagination. But to do so I need a further distinction: a distinction which applies in the first instance to the real-life audience but can be usefully extended to the audience-constituent of imagination. The distinction I have in mind I shall express by means of the contrast "empathic"/"sympathetic"; though I must point out that I shall not be using these terms exactly as they are used in dramatic theory—if, that is, they have an exact use. How I shall use them, my examples should make clear.

The audience is concentrated upon a character who, momentarily at any rate, dominates the action. Now, if the audience is empathic, then its reactions can be characterized thus: If the hero (let's call him that) feels terror, then his audience, if it feels anything, will feel terror. If the hero feels courage, then the audience, if it feels anything, will feel courage. The reactions of the empathic audience will match the feelings of the hero. If, however, the audience is sympathetic, then what its reactions will be will in part depend on a prior estimate it makes of, or attitude it adopts towards, the hero. If the attitude is favourable, the characterization of the reactions will go thus: If the hero feels terror, then the audience, if it feels anything, will feel pity. If the hero feels courage, then the audience, if it feels anything, will feel admiration. If, however, the attitude to the hero is unfavourable, the reactions of the sympathetic audience will be characterized thus: If the hero (let us still call him that) feels terror, it, if it feels anything, will feel delight. If the hero feels courage, it, if it feels anything, will feel terror. The reactions of the sympathetic audience will be, I shall say, appropriate to the feelings of the hero. Thus—if we assume feeling throughout—the empathic audience will feel terror when Gloucester is blinded and excitement when Iago poisons Othello's mind. By contrast, the sympathetic audience will (given normal attitudes) feel pity when Gloucester is blinded, and terror when Iago appears to be succeeding in his malevolent designs.

Let us now transport this distinction between the empathic and the sympathetic audience from the domain of the real-life audience to that of the internal audience, or the audience-constituent in imagination. For there surely is a distinction to be observed between the cases where I empathise, and those where I sympathise, with the person whom I imagine: where my imaginings leave me feeling (if I feel anything at all) just as I imagine him feeling, and where they leave me feeling in a way that responds to what I imagine him feeling. If this is conceded, then I am now in a position to indicate the second mark of centrally imagining someone. It is that, when we centrally imagine someone feeling something or other—and that we do so, liberally and systematically, is, you will recall, the first mark of centrally imagining someone—then the internal version of the audience in imagination will be of the empathic type. If it were not, if it were of the sympathetic type, then the tendency to feel in a way that is appropriate to, rather than identical with, the way the person imagined feels would, of course, destroy the centrality of that person in our imaginings. He would be, as it were, momentarily displaced. (It is, of course, quite compatible with this that, after centrally imagining someone doing something, I should feel about it, or about him, in a way that runs quite counter to what he would feel. But this would be a consequence, and no part, of what I imagine. A considerable imaginative effort often provokes such a reaction.)

If we put the two marks together, we might say that they add up to this: that the person centrally imagined—if there is such a person—is imagined *from the inside*. And if you now ask why I didn't say this in the first place, my response would be that I could not trust that phrase, so abused in philosophy, if I had not gone through this lengthy argument which establishes its meaning in the context of my argument.

11.   And now at last we are in a position to return to the phenomenon of identification, and to pursue the connection between identification and imagination. It is my hope that the points that I have been making about imagination will have clarified the connection. For, if there is, as I suggested, a *prima facie* plausibility in associating identification with imagination, this plausibility is surely only enhanced when we think of imagination in terms of centrally imagining. A piece of centrally imagining—a sustained or dispositional piece, of course—seems to slip into place so smoothly at the heart of identification. To return to our original example: When Leonardo identified himself with his mother, and what followed followed, is it not natural to suppose that the core of this identification was provided by his centrally imagining himself behaving and feeling in certain ways: that is, lovingly and tenderly towards young men?

But if this seems a natural supposition, care is required in its application. We must take note of certain significant differences that exist between centrally imagining as I have so far characterized it, in what might be called its normal form, and centrally imagining as it occurs within, or as a constituent of, identification. Indeed, in the example above, in which I tried to apply the supposition to the Leonardo case, the first of these differences manifests itself. One important feature of centrally imagining undergoes transposition. For I have maintained that if, outside identification, I imagine someone's doing something or other, I am bound in my imaginings; and if this is true when I imagine someone's doing something or other, it is *a fortiori* true when I centrally imagine someone's doing something or other. I have expressed this necessary fact about imagination by saying that my imaginings come out of a repertoire, where the repertoire is constituted by what I know, or (more generally) what I believe, about the person whom I imagine. Now, when Leonardo in identifying himself with his mother centrally imagines himself doing various things, he too is bound in what he imagines, in that his imaginings also come out of a repertoire. But the case exhibits this difference: that the repertoire upon which he draws in centrally imagining himself is not, as the normal form would lead us to expect, his, but another's. The constraints upon what Leonardo may imagine himself doing are provided by what he knows of, or believes about, his mother, not himself. It is himself whom he centrally imagines but she who provides the material.

And this, I want to maintain, goes for all cases of identification. In all such cases there is this transposition within the imaginative project. The person who identifies himself with another may invariably be held to imagine himself doing and thinking and feeling things that he has reason to suppose that the other would do or think or feel. That is essential to identification.

(At this point I may expose myself to a charge of inconsistency. For, a while back, I suggested that the question whether the connection between the identity of the person imagined and the repertoire employed in imagination was contingent or necessary did not admit of a straightforward answer. But what I have just said about the transposition of repertoire within identification might seem to call this in doubt. It might seem to imply that there is a straightforward answer, and that is, Contingent. However, I don't think that this is right, and a little later I shall very briefly say why. But what the transposition of repertoire within identification does show is that at no time does the repertoire employed in imagination determine the identity of the person imagined: even if it is (or is sometimes) determined by it. My own somewhat cryptic answer to the question what determines the identity of the person imagined would be "The person who imagines him.")

And now we need to add to this first difference between centrally imagining as it occurs outside, and centrally imagining as it occurs inside, identification a second difference. In both cases, as we have seen, a repertoire obtains. A repertoire is (roughly) a stock of beliefs, and, if the first difference between the two cases of centrally imagining concerns who the beliefs are about, the second difference concerns the status or stability of these beliefs. For in the ordinary case the repertoire is tantamount to the beliefs that the person in general or in an overall way holds about whomever it is he imagines: the repertoire is the stock of persisting or long-term beliefs. But in cases of identification this need not be so. For the person who identifies with another may draw on beliefs about the other which he holds only for the period of the identification; the repertoire may, in other words, be a temporarily adjusted stock of beliefs. And this is so because it is likely that identification will follow directly upon some other psychic mechanism, such as projection or idealization; and idealization and projection have, characteristically, the effect of adjusting beliefs about the person who has been idealized or projected upon—at least for the period during which they are effective.[14]

The classic use that Freud makes of identification occurring in the context of adjusted belief is the account, first given in *Civilization and Its Discontents,* of the genesis of the super-ego. Accepting the observations of Melanie Klein and "other English writers" that the severity of the child's super-ego might be quite incommensurate with the actual behaviour of the parents, Freud explained the deviation by supposing that the child first projects on to the parent the aggression that it would have liked to express against it, and then introjects, or identifies itself with, the parents so modified in thought.[15] I shall, however, not pursue this phenomenon. I shall not do so for the reason that the identification involved in the formation of the super-ego is somewhat special, in that the super-ego once introjected remains peculiarly distinct from the ego—as Freud puts it, "It confronts

[14] I am grateful for this observation to Mr. Keith Campbell.
[15] 1930a, XXI, 129–30.

the other contents of the ego"[16]—whereas ordinarily in identification the introject becomes very much part of the ego. (It is in this way that the ego is, in another well-known phrase of Freud's, "a precipitate of abandoned object-cathexes.")[17] Accordingly, to illustrate the way in which identification may draw upon an adjusted repertoire, I shall consider another phenomenon that Freud connects with identification: that is (male) epilepsy and the epileptic attack, and I shall base myself on Freud's discussion of these in the essay "Dostoievsky and Parricide."

The significance of the epileptic attack lies, Freud suggests, in the epileptic's identification with his father. The identification occurs against the background of a wish—a wish originally entertained in infancy but constantly revived in memory. The wish is a wish about the father, and we may assume the function of the identification to be, in the first instance, that of a defence against this wish. Now, from our point of view, the crucial feature about this wish is that like all infantile wishes—or, perhaps more accurately, like all wishes as opposed to the desires of later life—it was in the omnipotent mode, and consequently it gave rise to a belief: the belief that the wished-for outcome was so. It is this belief that constitutes the adjustment in the repertoire on which the epileptic draws when he comes to identify himself with his father. More specifically: the epileptic had wished that his father should die; in wishing this, he believed that his father had died; and so in identifying himself with his father, he centrally imagines himself dead.

Thus far the explanatory value of combining identification with an adjusted repertoire should be obvious. That in identifying himself with his father the epileptic draws on an adjusted repertoire accounts for the content or nature that the epileptic attack happens to have. It accounts for the fact that the attack is like an artificial or induced death. But this does not exhaust the use to which Freud puts the idea. That identification can occur on the basis of an adjusted repertoire is also used by Freud to account for a secondary function that the epileptic's identification with his father fulfils: that is, that it serves as a form of self-punishment. In identifying himself with a father wished dead the epileptic not only defends himself against this wish, he also punishes himself for it. And this further function could not be discharged without the adjusted repertoire. It is not simply that wish

[16] 1923b, XIX, 34; cf. 1928b, XXI, 184–85.
[17] 1923b, XIX, 29.

generates belief, what is vital is that belief colours identification: for the specific colour that the belief gives to the identification is what allows it to expiate the wish that generated the belief. It is thus that, as Freud puts it, "One has wished another dead, and now one *is* this other person and is dead oneself."[18]

However, the Freudian account of epilepsy also brings out very clearly a third, and surely the most significant, difference between centrally imagining as it occurs outside, and centrally imagining as it occurs inside, identification. And that is that in the latter case it has an efficacy for which nothing about the former case prepares us. When Leonardo, identifying himself with his mother, centrally imagines himself feeling tenderly and lovingly towards young men, he becomes a homosexual; when Dostoievsky, identifying himself with his father, centrally imagines himself dead, he has an epileptic attack. Homosexuality and epilepsy are phenomena that far transcend the world of the imagination. How can this be? How can imagination have such long-range effects?

Initially we might observe—though this observation gives us only the beginning of an answer to our question—how well adapted centrally imagining as it occurs inside the context of identification is to the task of self-modification. With the transposed, or with the adjusted and transposed, repertoire on which to draw it has precisely the right complex structure for bringing about the changes in character that are typical of identification—at any rate of identification in its extended or constitutive function. To see this consider, first, the chain that standardly runs from the internal version of the dramatist through the internal version of the actor to the internal version of the audience; and then add the fact that in this case the dramatist in devising what shall pass along this chain has a special licence to depart from verisimilitude. In effect what we do when we identify with another is that we write a part for ourselves, based upon that other, in the hope that, when we act it to ourselves, we shall be carried away by the performance.

But all this does is to explain how such performances could be successful, it doesn't explain why they are generally successful; it doesn't explain—to put it another way—why the internal audience is not only responsive to what is enacted for its benefit, but is singularly so. The degree to which identification is efficacious remains a mys-

[18] 1928b, XXI, 183.

tery. However, in referring a moment back to the hope in which we enter into the imaginative experience when we resort to identification, I may, I think, have dropped a clue as to the lines along which such an explanation is to be found. And more than that: for along these same lines we may arrive at a more precise or more detailed understanding of how centrally imagining fits into the overall structure of identification.

12.   For it cannot be that centrally imagining taken by itself—even with all the special features that we now know to hold of it as it occurs within identification: that is, that one type of imagining is combined with a repertoire appropriate to another, and that this repertoire may be adjusted from the norm, and that the imaginings have a special potency—just *is* identification. There is more to identification than that.

I now want to suggest that we need to add to what we have already, another element: an element which, though of some importance in all mental phenomena, gains in importance as we approach or move towards the pathological end of the spectrum. The new element I shall call the Master Thought.[19] What I have in mind by this phrase is (very roughly) the way in which we conceive or in which we represent to ourselves our mental processes, or the conception under which a mental process occurs. In the identification of himself with his mother, the imaginings in which Leonardo engages and which, as has been seen, are modelled not upon *his* but upon *her* thoughts and feelings, are conceived of in a certain way; more specifically, they are conceived of as a means by which, having once taken her into himself, he can retain her and lovingly merge with her. And by saying that this is how the imaginings are conceived of, I mean not just that this is why Leonardo imagines whatever he does, but, more directly, that this is what he imagines he is doing when he imagines whatever he does. An account of Leonardo's imaginative experiences that made no reference to the Master Thought would be to that degree incomplete—although, of course, the only account that Leonardo himself would have been able to give—if, that is, he would have been able to give one at all—would be one that omitted it. It would omit it because Leonardo, whether conscious or not of the imaginative experiences themselves, would not have been conscious of the Master

[19] Cf. Richard Wollheim, "The Mind and the Mind's Image of Itself," *International Journal of Psycho-Analysis* 50 (1969), pp. 209–20, reprinted in my *On Art and the Mind* (Allen Lane, London, 1973).

Thought under which they occurred. More generally, there is reason to think that the Master Thought and the thoughts it subsumes will not arise on the same level of consciousness.

The notion of the Master Thought—as well as, most likely, the Master Thought itself—is complex, and I shall simply take up one aspect of the Master Thought as far as its role in identification is concerned. (But before I do even this, a brief observation, which will honour a promise. Some while back I said that the fact that imagination could base itself on a transposed repertoire didn't—contrary to what one might initially suppose—settle the question whether in centrally imagining someone one necessarily or only contingently drew upon his repertoire. It didn't follow from the fact that a transposed repertoire might be invoked that the connection was merely contingent. What I had in mind was this: that it might be that the connection between the imaginative project and the repertoire should be seen as mediated by the Master Thought. And this I now want to suggest is the case. In other words, in determining what repertoire is employed, we have to appeal not only to what is imagined but to the Master Thought under which the imaginings in which he figures are entertained. And once the Master Thought is introduced, the question once more remains open whether the relevant repertoire is not fully determined; for it remains possible that the repertoire to be employed is fully determined by these two factors in conjunction.)

I said that there is only one aspect of the role played by the Master Thought in identification that I intend to take up; and that is that the Master Thought can be invoked to explain the peculiar efficacy of the imaginings that occur within identification or the fact that I expressed by saying that in identification the internalized audience is so singularly responsive to the internalized actor. For that fact can, I think, be connected with the way in which the internalized acting has itself been conceived. It is no serious distortion of the situation to say that the fact that the internalized acting has been conceived of as a way of modifying or transforming oneself can be used to account for, or to provide a partial explanation of, the fact that it does so.

Initially this might seem a most unsatisfactory form of explanation. How, we might ask, can the success of an action of ours be explained by the fact that we think of it as achieving a certain end? Now this question would be pertinent if it were a matter of an external action or of our efforts to secure something in the outer world. But internally the situation may well be different. And to see this I suggest that we consider mental phenomena that include a Master Thought but that lie at the opposite end of the spectrum from the pathological. In this connection I can appeal to two phenomena already considered. For the fact that I do indeed come to criticise certain phrases of mine, or the fact that I do indeed come to remember a line of Baudelaire, seem to be clearly connected with the respective ways in which I conceive of the internal recitations: that is, as a trial run in the one case, or as a mnemic device in the other. It is because I conceive of them in this way that they have the efficacy they have.

But we have only to put together the two kinds of case, pathological and normal, for immediately a further, and a major, difference between them to emerge. For if in both kinds of case a Master Thought is involved, and if in both the Master Thought is invoked to explain the efficacy of the mental phenomenon, the efficacy itself is very different in the two kinds of case. In both something (it is true) is achieved. But whereas in the case of the internal recitations what is achieved is identical with what is attempted, in the Leonardo case it isn't. Leonardo certainly modifies or transforms himself, but the transformation or modification is not that which Leonardo wishes for. Setting out to merge with his mother, Leonardo becomes not a woman but a homosexual: he remains a man and the closest he gets to being a woman is that he becomes and remains a lover of men. Now, the obvious explanation why he doesn't achieve what he intends is that he couldn't: he sets out to achieve the impossible. But if this explanation is right, it also needs examination. It isn't simply that what Leonardo intends has the facts of anatomy against it; though that does come into it. What is really significant is that the method he selects, the mechanism to which he resorts, is essentially inadequate to the end he desires. For the most general way of describing what Leonardo sets out to do is to change the real world through the resources of the psychic world. Whether Leonardo could or could not become a woman, whether he could or could not merge with his mother, whether he could or could not preserve the love in which he had known such intense happiness, the transformation could not be effected in the internal theatre of the mind: by a piece of impersonation designed for his own admiring gaze.

However, it must in conclusion be pointed out that it is no part of Freud's account of the matter to suggest that the lack of measure between what Leonardo intends and how he sets out to achieve it is a mere coincidence. On the contrary, it would seem that Leonardo resorts to psychic mechanisms to attain his intention precisely because he misconceives their efficacy. And the most evident way to account for this is to assume that the gross over-estimation that he places upon them is already implicit in the way in which he represents them to himself. He represents them to himself as ways of realizing external aims. And this assumption will not merely account for the fact that Leonardo systematically selects inappropriate means to ends, it will also explain why he is debarred from recognising their inappropriateness.

In other words, we may assume that the unsuitability of Leonardo's imaginings to Leonardo's intentions is already grounded in the Master Thought under which these imaginings occur. The Master Thought—and we might generalize this to cover all pathological phenomena—is formulated within what is for Freud the typically infantile —and so from the adult's point of view the typically regressive—theory of the mind: the theory, that is, in which the "omnipotence of thoughts" is a central tenet.[20] Within this theory a thought, in any of its various modes, is represented as adequate for bringing about that which it is of.

If I am right in my reconstruction of Freud's thinking on this last point, it would be a significant, though also a neglected, discovery of his that mental disorder is not only disorder in, it is also disorder about, the mind.

[20] E.g., 1909d, X, 233–34; 1911b, XII, 218–26; 1912–13, XIII, 78–90. It is a further link in the overall account of identification that Freud expressly connected the infantile theory of the mind, or the over-valuation of psychical acts (as he also referred to it), with primary narcissism, out of which identification originated. Cf. 1912–13, XIII, 89; 1914c, XIV, 75, 100.

Norms and the Normal

RONALD DE SOUSA

A System must have its utopia. For psychoanalysis, the utopia is "genitality."

E. ERIKSON

Freud denied that psychoanalysis has "moral" implications beyond those of the scientific attitude in general (1933a, XXII, 158 ff.). Yet any comprehensive vision of human nature such as he provides must have implications for the nature of happiness, and for the relation of man's natural capacities to his normal or ideal state. Classical theories of man might be forced into a dichotomy between what we might tag the "biological" and the "theological." The former derive normative conclusions from the innate and specific endowments of man, the latter start from an ideal model somehow revealed. (In this sense Aristotle's vision is biological, Plato's theological.) Freud's view contrasts with both: the normal man in maturity is not "natural," he is the outcome of a complex development the course of which is not determined by innate capacities alone. Yet no source exists, outside that development itself, for an ideal of maturity. This third way blurs the venerable distinction between Fact and Value: in the developmental vision of the normal human, we should find both a source of therapeutic values—whether or not these coincide with conventional morals—and a relative measure of the worth, in relation to happiness, of different levels of experience and activity. My central object in these pages is to give a qualified defense of this approach, and to show how Freud's version of it fares in the face of criticism. A particular charge I shall consider is that of "reductionism," often levelled against psychoanalysis: that the effect of Freud's theory is to degrade the higher manifestations of human life by reducing them to lower ones.[1]

---

[1] This view finds both support and disavowal in Freud's own writings: "Man's judgments of value . . . are an attempt to support his illusions with arguments." (1930a, XXI, 145); but " 'to blacken the radiant and drag the sublime into the dust' is no part of [the] purpose" of psychoanalysis (1910c, XI, 63).

I THE PLEASURE PRINCIPLE, WANTS, AND HAPPINESS

In the opening sentence of *Civilization and Its Discontents,* Freud remarks: "It is impossible to escape the impression that people commonly use false standards of measurement . . . and that they underestimate what is of true value in life" (1930a, XXI, 64). How is the implied distinction to be made? "The idea of life having a purpose stands and falls with the religious system" (ibid., 76): if value is determined by life's "purpose," the idea of "true value" must then fall. Instead of questions about transcendent purpose or value, Freud asks "what men themselves show by their behaviour to be the purpose and intention of their lives" (ibid.). His conception of value is a naturalistic one, grounded in experienced wants. But if people's actual wants are the measures of value, what criteria can be used to show that they are using "false standards of measurement"?

We might interpret Freud's view thus: wants are conceived as a mode of perception having as its proper object pleasure-at-a-future-time (or rather: on-a-possible-occasion) (cf. 1900a, V, 565–66); then wanting is *veridical* if the experience it envisages is, when it occurs, actually pleasurable, otherwise *mistaken.* But could one not be mistaken about the value of *occurrent* pleasure? The present assumptions leave room for a mis-estimation of this only where there is a mistake in the perception of the pleasure itself; and perhaps such a mistake could not occur unless pleasure were somehow experienced without adequate awareness. And Freud does not seem to allow for such a possibility. For pleasure is an affect, and "strictly speaking," he says (though in a somewhat different context), "there are no unconscious affects" (1915e, XIV, 178). So far then, this essentially utilitarian account of value seems to work. Still, there are fatal difficulties for the view that what is of value for man is determined by what his choices and behaviour *show* him to want. Both his choices and behaviour may belie his *real* wants. First, because a man may be mistaken at the moment of choice about the pleasurable qualities of the object chosen: wants are sometimes not "veridical." Second, in so far as the reality principle takes the place of the pleasure principle in determining rational choice (1933a, XXII, 76), we cannot infer from any given choice that its object is of "genuine value" (or genuinely wanted): it might be chosen as a compromise or for the sake of something else.

These difficulties appear to stand in the way of distinguishing, on Freud's assumptions, between real and illusory wants. Yet Freud offers a way. Through the theory of instinct and development, the variegation of human tastes becomes encompassed in a system; different balances of elements give us different normal types (1931a, XXI, 215), from which deviations are more or less pathological. This results in a subtle shift: it is not individual men who "show by their behaviour" what the purpose of their life is. A *theory,* based on facts about individuals, to be sure, but which need not reflect the subjective preferences of any particular one, determines the normal wants and pleasures of men in general. This is how the developmental perspective provides a "third way" contrasting both with the "biological" and with the "theological." The account is rooted in natural fact: Freud calls instinctual stimulus "need" (1915c, XIV, 119). But for a capital reason we cannot simply identify even instinctual wants with biological needs. Some needs are without corresponding felt wants (say, the need for vitamins), and we are interested just in those needs that have a "psychical representative" (1905d, VII, 168). For only those can ground an account of the vicissitudes of mental phenomena. Moreover it follows from the long helplessness of human infants that the development of their instincts must be shaped by social influences. Normal development, therefore, cannot be *reduced* to natural fact: "We may characterize [the development of civilization] with reference to the changes which it brings about in the familiar instinctual dispositions of human beings" (1930a, XXI, 96). And in so far as happiness "is a problem of the economics of the individual's libido" (ibid., 83), we have an answer to the question: How is *normal development* to be defined? Namely, by reference to the best economic solution both within the individual and between the claims of the individual and those of the group (ibid., 96).[2]

This line of thought ties in with the determination of value by "pleasure and unpleasure." But it suggests that the relation between

---

[2] Note that there is something misleading about this opposition between the individual and the group. Though the claims of the group impinge on the freedom of the individual, they are derivative of the claims of the group's member individuals. Only individual consciousness can experience "pleasure and unpleasure."

only in a utopia

developmental theory and human values is not a simple one. For while a moment ago developmental psychology promised to justify a distinction between real and illusory wants, we are now led to the curious conception of a psychology itself partly grounded in a Utilitarian theory of value. Yet, as we shall see, the psychological theory obscures rather than clarifies the basic notion on which Utilitarianism must rest: that of pleasure or satisfaction. To see why this is, let us turn first to a cursory sketch of instinct theory.

II THE THEORY OF INSTINCT

Instinct, Freud repeatedly emphasized, is "the most important and the most obscure element of psychological research" (1920g, XVIII, 34. Cf. 1915c, XIV, 118; 1930a, XXI, 117). The most basic part of psychological theory must exhibit the relation between our mental life and its roots in our organic constitution. More particularly it should relate the physiological mechanisms operative in our bodies to the intentionality of mental life and behaviour. This is the fundamental task of instinct theory: "although instincts are wholly determined by their origin in a somatic source, in mental life we know them only by their aims" (1915c, XIV, 123). It is "a concept on the frontier between the mental and the somatic" (ibid., 122; cf. 1905d, VII, 168).[3]

This frontier role of instinct may help us to understand the point of asserting that "the course of mental events is automatically regulated by the pleasure principle" (1920g, XVIII, 7). The pleasure principle is often attacked as either false or vacuous. As a psychological principle perhaps it is indefensible. Yet Freud is only one of many thinkers who have felt its attraction. Its true role may be not its ostensible one of explanation, but rather to remind us that in explaining behaviour we need to use mentalistic terms even where our explanation refers to natural needs or chemical facts. Freud postulates that the task of the nervous system is to reduce stimuli

3 Actually Freud's terminology is not consistent: he says elsewhere that "an instinct can never become an object of consciousness—only the idea that represents the instinct can" (1915e, XIV, 177). In those terms what interests us is the representative idea. What he there calls an instinct is what he usually terms its (somatic) *source* (see below, p. 201), an exact knowledge of which is "not invariably necessary for psychological investigation" (1915c, XIV, 123). This matter is discussed by Strachey in his Note to 1915c.

(1915c, XIV, 120) and adds: "We can hardly reject the further hypothesis that [feelings belonging to the pleasure-unpleasure series] reflect the manner in which the process of mastering stimuli takes place." The regions amenable to explanation in terms of instinct are those in which this parallelism may be expected to hold: the area of what we do, as opposed to what our organism achieves in response to needs that lack a "psychical representative" (e.g., digestion). (One may well feel, however, that in so far as the theory of instincts aims to *explain* this passage from the organic to the mental as well as draw attention to it, the task it sets itself is an impossible one. This point will be pursued below, pp. 211 ff.).

Outside psychoanalysis, "instinct" usually means something like "fixed and innate determinant of behaviour," where what is innate is what is not changed by learning.[4] Freud, on the contrary, is interested in the transformation of instinct into modes of experience and behaviour that are not innate. He defines instinct as a stimulus that differs from others in being *internal* and *continuous*. This carries the idea of innateness, since if the stimulus is strictly continuous it does not have an onset, and if it is internal its source must be genetic. But the emphasis is first on function not on origin, though, of course, from a developmental and evolutionary point of view the two converge.

For his definition Freud claims two benefits: explanations, first, of the distinction between "outside" and "inside," and, second, of the complicated development of higher animals. Both rest on the "necessary" (ibid., 124) postulate cited above (p. 199) about the biological role of instinct in controlling stimuli. Outside stimuli are picked out as those that can be controlled by mere locomotion. (It might be more prudent, to avoid a Kantian objection, to speak of how objects of experience are classed as inner or outer, rather than of the origin of the distinction itself.) The second point is meant to be a corollary: the satisfaction of hunger or sex requires more complex manipulation of the outside world than the mere avoidance of its impingement (ibid., 120).

The postulate that the aim of instinct is to master stimuli applies to all instincts. They differ, however, from each other in their *force,* "the measure of the demand for work which [they] represent" (ibid., 122). They differ also in their intermediate *aims,* which are means

[4] N. Tinbergen, *The Study of Instinct* (Oxford. London, 1951), p. 2.

to the general aim of satisfaction, and are in turn determined by their organic *source*. (This simply means that, while both hunger and sex demand to be satisfied, we don't generally go about it in the same way.) However, this distinction between instincts is blurred by the fact that these intermediate aims "are combined or interchanged with one another" (ibid.). This will prove to have important consequences.

The aim of instinct is different from its *object*, defined as "the thing in regard to which or through which the instinct is able to achieve its aim." The object is not intrinsically attached to an instinct, but "becomes assigned to it in consequence of being peculiarly fitted to make satisfaction possible" (ibid.). The intermediate aims of instinct (the manner in which the object is used to provide satisfaction) are more narrowly limited by genetic disposition, but still admit of a wide range of conditioned variation. On this point note the contrast with the ethologist's conception, which posits specific aims ("responses") and predetermined objects (or "innate releasing mechanisms"). To be sure, these are hardly real objects: the animals concerned are easily fooled by dummies. But their responses are highly specific and tied to innately determined sign stimuli.[5] For Freud, on the other hand, the factors determining the connection of instinct with its aims and objects are complex. Maturation, environmental repression, and "organic" repression (1905d, VII, 177–78) all play a part, as does an associationist mechanism that would not disgrace Hume or Russell: you learn what you like by induction from experiences of satisfaction (1900a, V, 565–66). The question of the relative importance of these various factors receives no settled answer (cf. pp. 204–5 below). What is clear is that no set of innate predispositions wholly determines a "natural" relation between instincts and their aims and objects. Nevertheless, the character of that relation is crucial to the psychoanalytic conception of "normal" development.

Within the development of the sexual instinct, different choices of object and aim are regarded in very different lights. An adult

[5] See ibid., pp. 37 ff. After prolonged absence of stimuli the threshold at which they become effective may become lowered so far as to reach zero. This results in what are sometimes called "vacuum activities" (K. Lorenz, *On Aggression* [New York, 1967], p. 49). It has led Lorenz and Tinbergen to a view that on this point is rather close to Freud's: that "automatic centres . . . send out a continuous flow of impulses to central nervous mechanisms" (Tinbergen, op. cit., p. 75).

choice that reproduces too closely and exclusively the choice of an earlier stage of development is a "fixation" (1905d, VII, 155 ff.). But the convergence of the sexual "component instincts" on a single heterosexual object choice and their subordination to the genital aim is True Love and the "utopia" of genitality (1915c, XIV, 138). Thus the theory of development imposes criteria of normality on those choices, though they are not determined by the nature of the instincts. Freud says this clearly, in a long footnote about bisexuality:

> . . . psychoanalysis considers that . . . freedom to range equally over male and female objects . . . is the original basis from which, as a result of restriction in one direction or the other, both the normal and the inverted types develop. Thus from the point of view of psychoanalysis the exclusive sexual interest felt by men for women is also a problem that needs elucidating and is not a self-evident fact based upon an attraction that is ultimately of a chemical nature. (1905d, VII, 145–46)

This illustrates the theme sketched in the last section: the developmental story gives rise to judgments of value, but does not do so simply by laying down what is "natural": for that is insufficiently determinate. How then is the range of the "natural" narrowed down to yield the "normal"?

A clue to the answer may be obtained if we consider the notion of *regression.* Freud distinguishes three sorts of regression: a) *topographical,* in terms of the model of the mind in which the systems *Pcpt* (Perception), *Mnem* (Memory), *Ucs* (Unconscious), *Pcs* (Preconscious), and *M* (Motor) are arranged in sequential order; b) *temporal:* "harking back to older psychical structures," both in terms of the individual and in terms of the race; c) *formal:* "where primitive methods of expression and representation take the place of the usual ones." "All these three kinds of regression," Freud observes, "are one at bottom and occur together as a rule;[6] for what is older in time is more primitive in form and in psychical topography lies nearer to the perceptual end" (1900a, V, 548). Here the language carries an almost inevitable evaluative force: the view that associates "primitive" with earlier and primary processes seems naturally to go with a comparative judgment which exalts what is later in de-

---

[6] Though—according to a later paper—"not necessarily always" (1917d, XIV, 227). This is a general statement which applies to the aims and objects of instinct, and also to the aspects of the ego that are not directly manifestations of instinct (1917d, XIV, 222).

velopment, more complex, and closer to conscious thought than to perception.

In their context, which concerns dreams, the observations just quoted imply the superiority of waking life to dreaming. But what does this consist in? Clearly, in the capacity to *act rationally* in the *real world*. This suggests a rationale for the additional determinants of normality: behind the value judgments implied in the developmental view are the ideals of *objectivity* and *rationality*. Yet it is quite unclear how this rationale applies to judgments of normality relating to genitality and the component sexual instincts. This is a central theme to which I shall return below (sections V and VI).

III PERVERSION

I now turn to the concept that provides the most obvious foil for normality: the concept of perversion. It will throw light on Freud's approach to see how his treatment of perversion, in contrast to some others, carries legitimate implications of value.

Broadly speaking there are five possible approaches to perversion: 1) Denial: the notion is purely theological and once God is removed there is no more to be said. This view seems to me intellectually fainthearted: I ignore it. 2) The moral view: judgments of perversion are neither more nor less than moral judgments. 3) The biological (or Roman) view: anything is a perversion which interferes with the ascertainable biological ends of some act or process. 4) The phenomenological view: once the phenomenological essence of an experience is discovered by careful disciplined attention, anything is a perversion which leads away from that essential experience.[7] 5) The developmental view: perversions are "seen to be on the one hand inhibitions, and on the other hand dissociations, of normal development" (1905d, VII, 231).

The second view must be wrong, as Thomas Nagel has pointed out, since it is assuredly not a sufficient condition of being a perversion that an act be morally wrong. Nagel also argues that the third view is wrong, because it omits the essential element of mentality: otherwise the accidental death of a pregnant mother would be a perversion. Once more: we are on the frontier between the

---

[7] This is the view defended by Thomas Nagel in "Sexual Perversion," *Journal of Philosophy* 66 (1969), pp. 5–17.

mental and the physical. However, this element could easily enough be built into the Roman view, and then—apart from the silly choice of reproduction as the end of sex—the Roman view comes rather close to Freud's. But there remains a crucial difference, as we shall see. As for the phenomenological view, it suffers from the fault for which Freud repeatedly criticized Jung (perhaps wrongly): it "loosens the connection of the phenomena with instinctual life" (1914d, XIV, 60), and so hangs in an explanatory void. Moreover, it harbors its own refutation. For, if consciousness is the only guide to the essence of sex, one cannot exclude the possibility that some will experience sex in terms, for example, of the intention to procreate. Or simply that they will not recognize the characterization of that essence which Nagel discovers when he practices sex with *epoche*. To show that such people are missing something, we require the sort of shift from individual experience to human nature in general which we saw to be characteristic of the developmental view (cf. p. 198 above). But this mere phenomenology cannot provide.

I am less concerned, however, with the relative merits of these approaches than with a contrast that can be drawn between the developmental view on one side and the two extreme views—the biological and phenomenological—on the other. The Freudian view, in spite of its scientific stance, implies moral judgments: the extreme views do not. I take "moral" here in the broad sense of "evaluative in relation to the happiness of men as such"; and I shall argue that taken in this sense the approach involving moral judgment is the right one.

It may sound surprising to hear that the Roman view is morally neutral. For it generally comes firmly backed by a doctrine of Natural Law from which it follows that what is against nature is immoral. Even if that doctrine were coherent, however, the identification of perversion by the biological criterion could be independent of its moral evaluation. It is not hard to think of examples in Roman doctrine of matters where "conforming to biological nature" and "morally good" are not equivalent. The point applies even more obviously to the phenomenological view. Determining the essence of sex may ground a scale on which to measure how good something is *as sex*. But this bears no special relation to moral questions until it is determined what role is played by sex in the happiness of men.[8] By contrast, Freudian theory does attempt to determine that role. It

8 Cf. ibid., p. 16.

turns out to be so central that we are justified in inferring that, *if* there is a sexual norm, a deviation from it will have moral import. The condition is secured by the developmental theory of the sexual instinct.

(This argument exhibits the shift of which I spoke, from the individual consciousness to the race or culture, in the determination of standards of happiness. If the developmental theory is correct, this shift involves no fallacy. It implies that, even if the individual experiences no awareness of frustration, he would experience more satisfaction if his desires were different in specifiable ways. This move, however, transfers the burden of defining normality to the notion of satisfaction. And as we shall see, the theory is not clear enough on this point to yield practical precepts of any great precision. [Cf. section IV below.])

If the argument just given for the moral significance of sexuality sounds too short and deductive, there are further considerations that are suitably complicating. The developmental history in terms of which normality is contrasted with perversion is not, as I have already pointed out, merely a process of maturation.[9] It is highly dependent on social interaction, and it involves the sacrifice of instinctual gratification of the purest sort. So even though the control of instinct allows some satisfactions, they are not comparable to those afforded by "the wild instinctual impulse untamed by the ego. . . . The irresistibility of perverse instincts . . . finds an economic explanation here." (1930a, XXI, 79). In this context, "perverse" means "natural": such is the distance that separates the natural from the normal:

A disposition to perversion is an original and universal disposition of the human sexual instinct and . . . normal sexual behaviour is developed out of it as a result of organic changes and psychical inhibitions occurring in the course of maturation . . . [including] the structures of morality and authority erected by society. (1905d, VII, 231)

Alteration or removal of these structures cannot eliminate anxiety.[10]

[9] Like locomotion in birds, for example, which seems to have nothing to do with learning or imitation. Cf. Tinbergen, op. cit., pp. 128 ff.
[10] Freud himself seems to have become less optimistic on this point in later years. In 1907c and 1908d, he seems to imply that the removal of repression would also do away with neurotic anxiety. But in 1926d this view is retracted and anxiety, traced primarily to the demands of the libido, is itself what "sets

206 RONALD DE SOUSA

Nevertheless, we are led to expect that character traits predominant in a given culture, and institutions—such as property—have been fostered by particular infant-rearing techniques. And it appears that cross-cultural studies confirm this.[11]

Although socialization takes different forms in different cultural contexts, the bare fact of socialization is necessarily a part of human "nature." There is no reason to suppose that babies can survive its absence any better than monkeys,[12] and what may be their most important innate skill can only mature in a social environment. I mean language. To learn to speak requires a passage from the primary processes to the secondary ones. This passage, according to Freudian theory, involves limitations on the pleasure principle and transformations of instinct (1911b, XII, esp. 221–22). The way seems open to make a distinction between the amount of repression (or suppression) necessary to perpetuate *some* sort of social organization and civilization, and the "surplus repression" which serves only to maintain the dominance of a particular segment of society.[13] Occasionally Freud is inclined to take such a view: "neurosis could be avoided if . . . the child's sexual life were allowed free play" (1940a [1938], XXIII, 200; cf. 1912d, XI, 187; and 1908d). But mostly he adopts a standoffish attitude:

---

the repression going" (1926d, XX, 109). More recent writers agree. Cf. Anna Freud, *Normality and Pathology in Childhood* (Hogarth, London, 1969), p. 8; D. W. Winnicott, *The Child, the Family, and the Outside World* (Penguin, London, 1964), chap. 15.

[11] Cf. E. Erikson, *Childhood and Society* (Norton, New York, 1950, 1963). Erikson is careful not to attribute simple causation to such factors:

We are not saying . . . that their treatment in babyhood *causes* a group of adults to have certain traits—as if you turned a few knobs in your child-rearing system and you fabricated this or that kind of tribal or national character. . . . We are speaking of goals and values and of the energy put at their disposal by child training systems. Such values persist because the cultural ethos continues to consider them "natural" . . . (pp. 137–38).

Doubtless what raises the problem of normality so acutely for us is that we have no "culture" in the relevant sense. Insofar as our psychological make-up is conditioned by the ethics of the containing culture, we are therefore without guidance as to *who* we are. Conversely, of course, one's identity conditions one's values: so we are uncertain about those. Hence the familiar talk of an Age of Anxiety, of Alienation, and so forth. The problem is real, for there is no philosophical mistake in the underlying tendency for ethics and psychology to pass the buck back and forth. Such is the burden of much of this paper.

[12] See H. H. Harlow and M. K. Harlow, "Social Deprivation in Monkeys," *Scientific American* 207 (1955), pp. 136–46.

[13] Cf. H. Marcuse, *Eros and Civilization, a Philosophical Inquiry into Freud* (Beacon Press, New York, 1955), esp. p. 40.

Psychoanalysis has no aim but that of disclosing connections. It can but be satisfied if what it has brought to light is of use in effecting reforms. . . . It cannot, however, predict whether other, perhaps even greater sacrifices may not result from other institutions. (1912d, XI, 187)

And again: "For a wide variety of reasons, it is very far from my intention to express an opinion upon the value of human civilization" (1930a, XXI, 144). This attitude is in part grounded on the conviction that interpersonal comparisons cannot rationally be made. For in attempting to compare ourselves with people in alien situations,

It is . . . impossible . . . to divine the changes which original obtuseness of mind, a gradual stupefying process, the cessation of expectations . . . have produced upon their receptivity to sensations of pleasure and unpleasure. (1930a, XXI, 89)

Yet isn't psychoanalytic theory precisely designed to provide rational grounds for such "divination"? Inferences of this sort would not seem impossible if we had a complete account of instincts, their modes of satisfaction, and the transformations to which their objects and aims are susceptible. So I now return to the theory of instincts, and its bearing on the normative implications of developmental theory. The transformations of instinct raise the following issue: Does Freud propose a reduction of man's higher activities to his "lower" instincts, in such a way as to impugn the difference of value between the two?

IV   REDUCTIONISM AND THE AIMS OF INSTINCT

On the exact nature and number of instincts that should be postulated Freud is not firm; but in the strict sense "only primal instincts—those which cannot be further dissected—can lay claim to importance" (1915c, XIV, 124). His conception of these primal instincts evolved over time. He first distinguished a self-preservative instinct, or group of instincts, from a sexual one. This distinction was supposedly grounded in biology, with the observation that "all our provisional ideas in psychology will presumably some day be based on an organic substructure" (1914c, XIV, 78). But Freud admits that we have no access at present to the underlying biochemical facts. We can only speculate. The speculation is that the two groups of instincts are chemically different by reason of their different evolutionary function (ibid.). But this has little plausibility. For the fact that individual and phyletic survival are different ends does not show that the two must be secured by different means. An additional minimal criterion of distinction seems implied, namely, that two instincts are different if they can conflict. We shall shortly see how much weight can be placed on this test.

Later the concept of narcissism threatened the dualism of ego and sexual instincts. But the dualism survived, and in 1920 a new theoretical postulate led to its reformulation in terms of Eros or Libido and Thanatos or the Death Instinct. Here again there were (somewhat abstruse) biological considerations (1920g, XVIII, 45 ff.), and the more straightforward arguments appealed to the "ubiquity of non-erotic aggressivity" (1930a, XXI, 120). This fact might simply have suggested an instinct of aggression, but for rather abstract theoretical reasons Freud chose to interpret it differently.

This is not the place for a critique of the death instinct; nor is one necessary. But it will serve as a particularly good illustration for some points of more general relevance.

In its absurdity the death instinct once more shows Freud to be negligent about the bearing of evolution. If there had been organisms endowed with the capacity for self-destruction, their ability to propagate this trait would, by necessity of evolutionary mechanisms, have been inversely proportional to its efficiency. Thus if any trace of such an instinct by chance survived it would be guaranteed to be quite ineffectual. No wonder it "was not easy . . . to demonstrate the activities of this supposed death instinct" (1930a, XXI, 119).

Still, it might be retorted that the aim of this instinct has undergone transformations, so that it is mostly manifest in aggressiveness. This brings me to the central point. Freud's characterization of the aims of *all* instincts—including the libidinal—is unacceptably vague. He is not unaware of this: we have seen that he frequently laments that instinct theory is insufficiently developed, and in 1933a he says: "Instincts are mythical entities, magnificent in their indefiniteness" (1933a, XXII, 95). But this indefiniteness has more important consequences than he allows.

It is generally assumed to be the chief strength of Freud's theory of sexuality that it displays the sexual instincts in their bewildering variety of forms. The explanatory power of psychoanalysis owes much to their interchangeability and the pervasiveness of their influence on our mental life.[14] Yet this strength is, as many critics have pointed out, too great for the theory's own good. There are no criteria for distinguishing one instinct from another. Conflict does not provide a sufficient criterion of difference, for two component instincts of the libidinal group can have opposite effects. This is particularly obvious once the libido comes to include both of the originally contrasting groups, the sexual and the ego instincts (1923a, XVIII, 257). Nor does Freud himself invariably assume that conflict proves distinctness. For though he seems to have assumed that the conflict leading to the transference neuroses "compelled" him to posit two independent groups (1914c, XIV, 77), he was also willing to consider, at about the same time, the possibility that in repression "it is precisely the cathexis which is withdrawn from the idea that is used for anticathexis" (1915e, XIV, 181). In other words, the force repressed and the repressing force might have the very same source.

It might be suggested here that only a certain kind of conflict is strong enough to provide the needed criterion of distinctness: essential conflict, conflict between the pure or primal forms of instinct. But this would be a mistake. For, strictly speaking, instincts cannot conflict at all as mental entities in their primal forms. For they belong to the *Ucs* (later, the id), which is indifferent to contradiction (ibid., 187). Therefore the only conflicts to which instincts are subject are practical conflicts, conflicts of effects.

If Freud gives us no adequate criterion of distinctness for his two main groups of instincts, we may still hope for a criterion of identity (or kinship) between instincts of the *same* group. We might then get a criterion of difference as a corollary. Let us see what links the "components" of the sexual instinct to each other.

Each component instinct is tied to an erotogenic zone, and none, even that connected with the genital zone, is intrinsically related to reproduction. All acquire this link as a result of a development which brings them under the dominance of the genital zone, and of its mature aim and object (1905d, VII, 197). In these respects they are comparable to the "tool activities" which, according to Lorenz, serve the "big drives."[15] Tool activities are decomposable into a

[14] Cf. Richard Wollheim, *Freud*, (Collins, London, 1971), chap. 4, esp. p. 118.
[15] See Lorenz, op. cit., p. 85, and cf. Tinbergen, op. cit., pp. 102 ff. Tinbergen gives a more refined account of the hierarchical organization of the mechanisms that contribute to biological functions.

number of specific mechanisms which develop and can operate independently of each other. They have evolved into hierarchical systems serving some biological purpose. All of this is indeed reminiscent of the role of the component instincts: but the differences are crucial.

First, Freud's component instincts are not innate mechanisms of specific response, but only internal stimuli. The responses provoked by these stimuli (the aim and object of the instinct) are determined at least in part by association. Apart from the location of the zone with which their intermediate aims are associated, there is therefore nothing to differentiate one component instinct from another:

> In itself an instinct is without quality. . . . What distinguishes the instincts from one another and endows them with specific qualities is their relation to their somatic source and to their aims. (1905d, VII, 168)

The second difference is this. We can presume that "tool activities" became organized under a "big drive" by the same process of selection and mutation that ensures the complex organization of an organ. The appearance of teleology is reducible to the mechanism of evolution. But Freud's instincts become parts of a hierarchy which is not only a biological one, and which is organized partly as a result of social conditioning. The teleology involved here is, therefore, of the very different sort, which must be traced to intentions, conscious purposes—in short, the mental rather than the organic life (cf. 1913j, XIII, 188). The unity of aim achieved in the genital organization can therefore not be viewed, as can the role of "tool activities," as a simple functional convergence of biological traits. Both Freud and the ethologists are interested in explaining complex behaviour in terms of hierarchies of simpler elements. Freud's task, however, is more ambitious in that his explicanda are essentially mental (cf. p. 198 above). He must therefore meet two more stringent adequacy conditions. First, the nature and scope of the elementary instinct—including its mental aspect—must be made precise. Second, it must be clear just how the instinct *explains* manifestations that go beyond its organic base: in sublimated forms of instinct, do we simply have another *effect* of the *same* instinct, or is there something more abstract which all forms have in common but which is not identical with any one form?

Unfortunately Freud's theory does not satisfy either requirement. The first is most obviously violated by the death instinct, which lacks a somatic source and has an excessively abstract aim. But, as we have seen, it is true also of the libido that the identity of its parts is assured only by the fact that they are all involved in a process which, under certain conditions, leads to their subordination to the monogamic reproductive aim. Given the vaunted versatility of the libido, it is also unclear what exactly happens in the case of sublimation. This is defined as a "diversion of sexual instinctual forces from sexual aims and their direction to new ones" (1905d, VII, 178). If the second adequacy condition is to be met, we must know the nature of the "forces" involved precisely enough to recognize them in a different guise. In fact, all we are told is that there is a source of "neutral energy" which is "desexualized Eros" (1923b, XIX, 44), but we are not told what marks it still as *Eros* when desexualized. It is clearly not enough to observe causal-like ("economic") correlations between forms of the libido: for the existence of causal relations argues no underlying substantial identity of "energy."

This presents us with a dilemma: if we are reasonably precise about the nature of this energy, and so satisfy the first of the two requirements just mentioned, then we are all the less likely to satisfy the second. On the other hand, if we manage a sufficiently abstract characterization of the instinct to cover all its forms ("uniting and binding"), for example (ibid., 45), then we fail of the first adequacy condition. Actually we fail in the second too: for such vague characterization cannot be said to *explain* the relation between direct and sublimated expressions of instinct. The attempt to explain too much results in a blurring of the concept of instinct which finally explains nothing at all. Much would be gained by narrowing the concept of instinct in such a way as to bring the psychoanalytic theory close to that of the ethologists. If we tie instinct firmly to somatic sources, there can be no death instinct, and we place limits on the plasticity of sublimation. We would then be free to contrast instincts with other innate characteristics, such as, for example, the disposition to play.[16]

Perhaps the second of our adequacy conditions cannot be met by any theory. We have seen that the sort of explanation we require

---

[16] See D. W. Winnicott, *Playing and Reality* (Tavistock, London, 1971), esp. chap. 3. For Winnicott, the urge to play is innate, but not instinctual. Instinct and play compete for a child's attention and are thus far incompatible (p. 39). But play is not a transform or sublimation of instinct; nor is the former essentially linked to the repression of the latter.

is a psychological one: yet instinct is "determined by its somatic source" (cf. p. 199 above). The hardest problem is therefore prior to any questions about sublimation. It concerns the relation between the somatic source and its "representative idea" even in its simplest form. A striking and notorious example of this is provided by Freud's treatment of femininity. He assumes, plausibly, that there are "psychical consequences of the anatomical distinction between the sexes" (1925j), but there is no satisfactory account of the relation between anatomy and its consequences. I am not asking here for a justification of the claim that a girl's penis envy has "permanent effects on the development of her character" (1940a, XXIII, 155), but for an explanation of the claim that the lack of a penis must lead to penis envy in the first place. There is no *a priori* reason for the penis to be judged more enviable than the compact smoothness of a girl's external genitals. (There is no *a priori* reason for white to be more beautiful than black.) Of course, it may be replied that Freud does not know the subjective meaning of this lack *a priori*, but by analytic experience. But this misses the point, which is that the existence of penis envy is not explained simply by the lack of a penis. It may be— implausibly—that there is an innate expectation in every male and female to find a penis appended to every human being: so everyone is *naturally* disappointed. The mental factor for which we are looking would then be innately determined as is its source, but could not strictly be claimed to be determined *by* its source: for the organic fact *might* have had a different *sense*. On the other hand, it is more likely that the sense of the anatomical difference is given to the child by his environment. In that case, once again, it is not true that the lack of a penis determined penis envy. Still less does the sublimation of penis envy explain "a capacity, for instance, to carry on an intellectual profession" (1933a, XXII, 125). On the contrary, the penis may act merely as a symbol of male freedom, and something else would have taken its place if anatomy had been different.

All this has important consequences for the issue of "reduction." "Reduction" sometimes means simply "explanation" ("Is chemistry reducible to physics?"): reduction in this sense establishes a causal dependence. But in a stronger sense reduction can establish an ontological dependence ("Are physical objects reducible to—nothing but—constructions out of sense data?"). It is safe to say that the Freudian account of mental life in general aims at reduction in the first sense. Even such weak reduction can, in practice, affect our attitude; but it is probably only in the strong sense that a reduction can legitimately show up a mistake in our conception of the nature and value of the reduced phenomenon. To sustain a charge of strong reductionism against psychoanalysis, one would have to show not merely that the "higher" mental functions are explicable in terms of their origin in "lower" instincts, but that the former are "nothing more" than inhibited avatars of the latter.

We have seen that it is not clear enough what THE (natural) aim of an instinct is for this charge to be clearly assessed. And the considerations of the last page suggest that even the weaker form of reduction has not been shown to be involved. For it is not clear whether organic factors actually cause psychological ones; the possibility remains open that the role of the mental is to give a sense to the relevant organic facts without being caused by them.[17] Moreover, the process of sublimation, whether it leads to real transformations of instinct or merely to novel manifestations of the same instincts, may entail a modification of the value of satisfaction. We need a criterion of assessment over and above the determination of instinctual origins for human experience and activity.

In pursuit of such criteria, let us look at some Freudian explanations of particular states which are explicitly and pejoratively reductive. We shall see that they impugn the value of the states concerned not merely by tracing their origin in instinct, but for more specific reasons. By this route we shall be led to a partial answer to our earlier question about the character of Freud's "normal" or ideal man.

V THE EPISTEMIC CRITERION

In Freud's view religious belief, "so patently infantile, so foreign to reality" (1930a, XXI, 74), is thoroughly discredited by his explanation of it in terms of wish. Art is not, though it too is an indulgence in illusion: "the mild narcosis induced in us by art can do no more than bring about a transient withdrawal from the pressure of vital needs" (ibid., 81). The crucial difference is that the illusions of art

17 This would not, of course, contradict the hypothesis of some sort of general psycho-physical parallelism. It would only cast doubt on the causal primacy of organic features (such as the presence, etc., of a penis) which affect the mental through one's *perception* of them.

are recognized as such (ibid., 80; cf. 1908e, IX, 144), whereas religion is a mass delusion: "No one, needless to say, who shares a delusion ever recognizes it as such" (1930a, XXI, 81).

The rationale is clear: wherever such a criterion can find application, the worth of a mental state is assessed in terms of *truth*, in terms of the extent of correspondence between the subjective and *reality*.[18]

One might seek to justify the value of truth itself in terms of its contribution to happiness, in so far as any enterprise will have greater chances of success if it is undertaken in the light of realistic appraisal rather than wish-fulfilling phantasy (cf. 1937c, XXIII, 237). But in that case truth will never be preferred to satisfaction in case of conflict, except by dint of the rule-utilitarian fallacy which infers a universal from a general truth. (Realism is usually advantageous, so it should be preferred even when it isn't.) In spite of what I have called Freud's Utilitarianism, however, it is clear that in his mind truth is an independent value which might even dominate the value of happiness. The fact that Freud did not assume that everyone shared this value explains in part his scorn for "the great majority of mortals [who] will never be able to rise above [the religious] view of life" (1930a, XXI, 74). Whatever its justification, this concern for truth yields a criterion of value for those states or activities that are epistemically committed—such as psychoanalysis itself: "psychoanalytic treatment is founded on truthfulness. In this fact lies a great part of its educative effect and its ethical value" (1915a, XII, 164). This epistemic criterion does not dismiss a belief merely because it is susceptible of a genetic explanation. On the contrary, the right kind of genetic explanation establishes a belief as legitimate. A belief constitutes knowledge if its coming into being can be explained in terms of the truth of its object. Its genesis can then be adduced as justification. But "we call a belief an illusion when a wish-fulfillment is a prominent factor in its motivation, and in so doing we disregard its relations to reality, just as the illusion itself sets no store by verification" (1927c, XXI, 31).

The application of this epistemic criterion is straightforward in

18 This finds an illustration in Freud's praise of work: "No other technique for the conduct of life attaches the individual so firmly to reality" (1930a, XXI, 80). The fact that realism does not always coincide with utility is attested by the fact that "as a path to happiness, work is not highly prized by men" (ibid.).

the case of epistemic states. But how does it extend beyond the realm of belief? Consider the contrast between *character* and *neurosis*. In a number of papers Freud traced the development of certain character types from the predominance of certain stages in the development of the libido—particularly anal-erotism (e.g., 1908b, 1917c). In theory every particular character is determined by some particular combination of dispositional and accidental factors. But neurotic symptoms are also explained in terms of such an interaction of factors. Whatever derogatory connotation attaches to neurosis, then, tends to spread over to character through the similarity of form in their explanations. Thus it may appear that psychoanalytic explanation *per se* is derogatory. But we have seen that this is a mistake: such evaluative implications are legitimate, if at all, only where the explanation shows a character trait, like a neurotic symptom, to be *irrational*.[19]

The epistemic criterion clarifies the difference between character and neurosis in so far as pejorative reductions are based on imputations of irrationality. Neurotic symptoms are obviously irrational, considered as actions in the light of the agent's beliefs and desires. For example, in those neuroses that are traceable to the repression of sexual impulses, the repressed impulses

> find expression in other ways, which are quite as injurious to the subject and make him quite as useless for society as satisfaction of the suppressed instincts in an unmodified form would have done. (1908d, IX, 191)

By contrast, character traits cannot be assessed so simply for rationality: they do not merely select means to independently established ends, but find their expression in the choice of ends themselves as well as styles of action. The epistemic criterion seems inadequate to assess such choices. Its applicability can therefore be taken to differentiate neurotic from character traits. Intuitively, however, character can also be evaluated in terms of rationality. It is now time to

---

[19] One reason why the explanation of character in analytic terms is felt as degrading is that the development of instinct is frequently described in terms implying identity between its primal and its "aim-inhibited" forms (cf. 1917c, XVII, esp. 128). But we have already seen that the sense of such identity is too unclear to bear much weight. Besides, the feeling that such explanations are degrading is itself subject to psychoanalytic explanation. Since the moral sentiments have their roots in the superego, it is to be expected that they should feel degraded by their origin in the Oedipal phase. For the superego itself has precisely come into being by repression of the Oedipus complex (1923b, XIX, 34).

press the search for a broader notion of rationality which will make sense of this. We shall find that psychoanalysis is in the same ambiguous dialectical position in relation to rationality as in relation to pleasure and instinctual satisfaction. That is to say, while the notion is fundamental to the theory, the theory in a sense obscures it.

VI THE RATIONAL AND THE REAL

What are the criteria that govern rationality of *emotion?* Freud speaks of the lover's "overvaluation of the sexual object" (1905d, VII, 150), and presumably an overvaluation is an irrational valuation. In Simone de Beauvoir's *Les Mandarins* there is a character who is "cured" of a life-long passion by its analytical interpretation as "transference"; and presumably transference too is irrational. But what is *adequate* valuation? And when is love not transference? On the one hand, Freud says, "it is the essential character of every state of being in love [to] . . . reproduce infantile prototypes" (1915a, XII, 168); but elsewhere, "not every good relation . . . [is] to be regarded as a transference; there [are] also friendly relations which [are] based on reality. . . ." (1937c, XXIII, 222). To be *based on reality* is at least to satisfy the epistemic criterion. In some cases, therefore, the rationality of emotion seems reducible to the rationality of the beliefs with which it is associated. Thus the lover's overvaluation consists in "credulity"; "his powers of judgment are weakened" (1905d, VII, 150). Similarly with the distinction between (normal) mourning and (pathological) melancholia: "although mourning involves grave departures from the normal attitude to life, it never occurs to us to regard it as a pathological condition" (1917e, XIV, 243). In melancholia, by contrast, the characteristic "self-reproaches are reproaches against a love object which have been shifted away from it onto the patient's own ego" (ibid., 248); this shift of object gives the attitude an automaticity and ineffectiveness which precludes the achievement of any relevant goals.

The systematic failure to secure an end is by definition irrational. Neurotic behaviour is in this sense irrational, as we saw. Nevertheless, this characterization is inadequate to define the ideal man of psychoanalysis. Under certain circumstances, frustration provides the energy for greater achievement:

What appears . . . as an untiring impulsion towards further perfection can easily be understood as a result of the instinctual repression upon which is based all that is precious in human civilization. The repressed instinct never ceases to strive for complete satisfaction, which would consist in the repetition of a primary experience of satisfaction. (1920g, XVIII, 42)

To measure the relative worth of the frustration and the resulting achievements, we need to evaluate *ends*. The "economic" point of view affords definite standards only if it is grounded on meaningful calculations of utility. But such calculations make clear sense only if the pleasure principle makes clear sense. The difference between satisfactions of different *kinds* has always caused trouble for systems akin to Utilitarianism. The usual solution offered, from Plato to Mill, is the appeal to the experienced judge: he who has experienced both can make the distinction between real and illusory wants, and higher and lower pleasures. This device has its Freudian counterpart in the *analysed man*. But the various factors I have discussed confuse the issues. One factor is Freud's tendency to treat satisfactions other than primary as mere "surrogates," from which one might infer that if any want is "unreal" it is the sublimated want, not the primal instinct from which it derives its energy. Working against this is the lack of any clear criterion of identity through change for instincts. This means that no clear "economic" relations between different modes of satisfaction can be defined. I have already mentioned the political scepticism that Freud derives from the difficulties of interpersonal comparisons. Indeed the modern practice of psychoanalysis, and Freud himself, have often been accused of taking an excessively conservative attitude to politics, morals, and society.[20] In Freud, the conservative stance stems not from approval of the social order as it is, but from scepticism about the effects of institutional reforms (see p. 207 above). Yet such scepticism is quite unexpected from someone inclined to Utilitarianism and equipped with a theory of satisfaction.

Another important factor is the difficulty attaching to the word "Reality": what the "reality principle" has to contend with is shaped

[20] See, for example, Marcuse, op. cit. It should in fairness be observed that Marcuse's charge applies chiefly to the "Neo-Freudian revisionists" (Fromm, Horney, Sullivan) rather than to Freud himself, and that apart from the orthodox Marxist line the most serious attacks of this sort have been aimed at psychiatrists outside the analytic tradition. Cf., for example, T. Szasz, *The Manufacture of Madness* (Harper & Row, New York, 1970).

by the containing society's expectations and sanctions. But these are partly determined by the characters of the society's members. The neurotic's behaviour may cause him suffering not because it is based on false beliefs about physical reality, but "by raising difficulties in his relations with his environment and the society he belongs to" (1930a, XXI, 108).[21]

All these factors limit the applicability of the reality principle. But in his late works Freud brings to it a qualification from a different perspective. The ideal of rationality is often formulated in terms of the control of the whole person by the ego: "Psychoanalysis is an instrument to enable the ego to achieve a progressive conquest of the id" (1923b, XIX, 56; cf. 1933a, XXII, 80). But the conquest can never be completed: not merely in practice, but as a matter of logic. For the ego, like the rider of a horse, "has borrowed its energies from the id" (ibid., 77). To conquer it altogether would be for the rider to kill off his horse the better to control him. Nor is the ideal type the one whose superego is dominant, the "obsessional type," "though from the social standpoint [men of this type] are the true, pre-eminently conservative vehicles of civilization" (1931a, XXI, 218). The ideal is the "erotic-obsessional-narcissistic" who balances the claims of all three agencies:

> such a type would no longer be a type at all: it would be the absolute norm, the ideal harmony. We thus realize that the phenomenon of types arises precisely from the fact that, of the three main ways of employing the libido in the economy of the mind, one or two have been favoured at the expense of the others. (Ibid., 219)

This represents an acknowledgement that the "reality" faced by the ego includes both inner and outer reality. Freud occasionally seems to imply the contrary, as when he contrasts "real" and "instinctual" danger, and correspondingly "realistic" and "neurotic" anxiety (1926d, XX, 166). But this is misleading: the true basis of the distinction turns out to be whether the danger is *known* or *unknown*, and Freud recognizes that "in so far as the instinctual demand is

---

[21] In this way, of superficially identical patterns of behaviour that admit of analogous psychological explanations, such as obsessive or religious ceremonials (1907b), the one may be normal and the other pathological. Erikson (op. cit.) differentiates neurosis from primitive mentality as follows:
Neurosis is an individual state in which irrational trends are irreconcilably split off from a relatively advanced rationality; while primitivity is a state of human organization in which pre-rational thinking is integrated with whatever rationality is made possible by the technology. [P. 184]

something real, his neurotic anxiety, too, can be admitted to have a realistic basis" (ibid., 167).[22] It is here, no doubt, that we might seek the unexplained link between rationality and the developmental view of normal mature sexuality (cf. p. 202 above). In man's total situation—faced with id, society, and external world—genitality is taken to be the most satisfactory compromise. This may or may not fit in with fact and theory; but at least it displays the unified perspective behind the "norms" based on the developmental view.

The need for the ego to deal both with inner and with outer reality brings a new complication to the problem of "real wants" or "true values" with which I began. If we attempt to apply what I have called the "epistemic criterion" of rationality to desires, we shall find the result particularly ambiguous. From the point of view of external reality, it is natural (though admittedly not necessary) to consider "realistic" desires to be those that are likely to be fulfilled. From the point of view of internal reality, on the other hand, a realistic desire is one—as I suggested above, p. 197—which strives for something that is actually satisfying: a correct perception of possible pleasure. Unfortunately the two sorts of "realism" often conflict: what is of true value may be very unlikely to be attained, whilst what is "realistically" desired in the light of external reality may bring but puny pleasure. There is no obviously acceptable principle of rationality that can reconcile these two sorts of "realism." So we have here another essential limitation on the ideal of rationality.

An adequate conception of rationality should recognize not only the multiplicity of human ends, but the existence of incomparable ends. It is on this point that there is a tension within Freudian theory. On the one hand, there is an insistence on an "economic" point of view which presupposes the comparability of all ends, and perhaps hints at a measure of desire in instinctual "force" (p. 200 above). On the other hand, Freud's account of the vicissitudes of instinct fails to provide instructions on how to apply any single measure to different sorts of satisfaction. Moreover, the separate demands of inner and outer reality cannot be brought together under a unified principle of rationality. Both these points hint at an im-

---

22 Freud speculates in two short papers (1924b, 1924e) that the difference between neurosis and psychosis lies in the fact that the former begins with a denial of the claims of the id, whereas the latter begins with a denial of (external) reality. Though he uses the word "reality" to mean external reality, it is clear that the other demands on the ego are equally real.

plicit recognition that principles of rationality may conflict in the pursuit of incomparable goals. Thus they undermine the narrowly "economic" point of view.

VII SUMMARY

I have argued that Freud's comprehensive developmental view of human nature carries legitimate implications of value, but that these are severely limited by the detail and the defects of the theory itself.

The first reason was this: The theory aims to trace our mental life to its simplest elements, where these are intimately bound up with biological functions. Broadly speaking, this programme is obviously sound, though in carrying it out Freud is rather free with his assumptions about the mechanism of evolution. But he tends to conflate the kind of teleology involved in evolutionary explanations and that are inherent in intentional explanations. Since the main point of the "frontier concept" of instinct is the explanation of intentionality in terms of its relation to biological finalities, this weakens the argument at the most crucial point. Primal instincts cannot adequately be characterized merely by reference to their somatic source. Their *psychological* nature demands to be identified in terms of *aims*. And the specifications of these aims are either too narrow to provide the far-reaching explanations demanded of them, or too vague and abstract to show their organic origins.

This may point to a limitation of principle on the whole enterprise. Perhaps some of our mental endowments are simply tied to maturational properties of our nervous and endocrine systems, without any more specific links with any particular bodily zone or independently identified biological function. The best hope for the notion of instinct may lie in not forcing it to explain too much.

The second reason was a corollary of the first. Freud's theory lacks criteria of reidentification for instinctual forces, and partly as a consequence it lacks principles for the relative evaluation of the satisfactions correlated with different forms of instinct. It cannot, therefore, fulfill its promise to extract from a developmental account of the human mind an objective distinction between basic and derived wants, nor derive from such a distinction criteria for telling real from illusory values. By drawing attention to the complexity and obscurity of the fundamental notion of *satisfaction,* the theory undermines its own implicit Utilitarianism.

Nevertheless, there is a value clearly bound up with psychoanalysis, though the attempt to deduce it strictly from a conception of satisfaction or happiness must fail. This is the value of truth and rationality. In so far as rationality in behaviour can only be defined with reference to specific ends, or to a method for selecting ends, this notion is infected with the unclarities of instinct theory. It further suffers from the relativity of the "reality" with which it is the business of the ego to contend. Finally, it is limited by the need to balance against each other the claims of the individual and of society, as well as the three agencies of the individual mind. Freud's theory provides no procedure for regulating these balances, and no hint as to how one might construct a fully unified and integrated notion of rationality.

The accusation of reductionism, however, should now be seen to be without foundation. Instinct theory is not a firm enough base for any degrading reduction, and in any case the charge is based on a confusion between eliminative (ontological) reduction and mere explanation.

On the other hand, it is also wrong to credit—or discredit—Freudian theory with a rigid model of ideal man. The normative implications of Freud's vision first present themselves as epistemological norms: they consist in the erection of standards of normality in a sense common in biology, and without which classification cannot proceed. Since what is being classified concerns the nature of man, however, these norms automatically acquire moral import, in a broad sense of the term. But it would be a misinterpretation of these norms to assume that they are bound to work in a rigid or conservative way. The complex relativities to which "reality" is subject account sufficiently for Freud's inclination—and that of many of his followers —to a conservative stance: some variables have to be fixed in practice. Yet the only true utopia of psychoanalysis is rationality; at the same time, it teaches us how difficult an ideal this is to interpret.[23]

23 I am grateful to the Canada Council, who provided a research grant in the summer of 1970, during which preliminary research for this paper was done.

I also wish to thank Richard Wollheim for many valuable criticisms of an earlier draft.

The Id and the Thinking Process

BRIAN O'SHAUGHNESSY

A. INTRODUCTION

The concept of the id was formulated by Freud in 1923, in a work entitled *The Ego and the Id,* and it marked the culmination of almost thirty years of empirical investigation and meta-psychological thought concerning the unconscious part of the mind. It is remarkably similar to concepts found in the nineteenth-century German philosophical movement, most especially to Schopenhauerian Will and the Dionysiac of the early Nietzsche; indeed, we must in some sense accept that those two great explorers of the mind had stumbled upon the truth of the id. But I think we can, in addition, discern significant likenesses between the Freudian id and concepts ranging as far afield as Lockean material substratum and the Kantian noumenon.

It is important to notice the sharp distinction which Freud drew—though not perhaps in so many words—between *a part of* and *a system within* the mind. The id, in Freudian theory, is the mental system that is the repository of the two ultimate instincts, the life and death instincts, Eros and Thanatos. Then while these instinctual contents of the id are in themselves invariably unconscious, so that an entry on their part into consciousness would be possible only in symbolic form, the Freudian concept of the unconscious is not the concept of a particular mental system like the id. Rather, greater or lesser sectors of discrete mental systems jointly constitute the unconscious part of the mind, and do so simply through being something of which people are unconscious. Thus the province of the unconscious encompasses the unconscious part of the ego, which is responsible for mentally self-protective measures like repression; the unconscious part of the super-ego, which is responsible, for example, for the unconscious sense of guilt which may drive an habitual criminal to commit the crimes that repeatedly land him in jail; and, most important of all, it includes the id in its entirety. These unconscious parts of discrete systems form, not one system that is the unconscious, not one system that is the unconscious part of the mind, but the unconscious part of the one system of systems that is—the mind.

In this essay I shall venture to take for granted two basic facts about the mind: the first is its totalised or holistic character, the second is the impossibility of what might be called "mental physics." The holism of mental phenomena implies the absence of an *absolute autonomy* on the part of mental events; for the identity of these undeniably real and unquestionably individual events stands essentially behoven to the mental setting in which they occur: that is, they would be other than themselves were the setting to depart from what it is in various specifiable ways. And by "the impossibility of 'mental physics,'" I mean no more than the inapplicability within the mind of a mental scientific explanatory system structured analogously to physics.

My intention is to examine certain phenomena in mental life that make plausible such a theory as that of the id. I shall be concerned with the various forms taken by the central phenomenal process in the mind, the thinking process, and my account will be conditioned by a double preoccupation. One of these preoccupations is *the will,* for I hope to form a clear estimate of the will-status of such thinking processes as creative thinking, the day-dream and the dream. The other is the Freudian account of *mental structure,* for I shall try to characterise these processes in terms of the mental systems, the ego and the id. Indeed, I will try to unite these enterprises, and make evident the close relation that holds between will-status and the locus of the determining centre of the mind; for these are essentially linked. Thus, all acting or willing proceeds exclusively from the ego, never from the id. Action springs from the "I" in one, never from the "It."

Now, the impossibility of "mental physics" is a direct consequence of the holistic character of the mind (though I do not propose to attempt a demonstration of this thesis here). In fact, it may seem astonishing that causal relations can hold within holistic totalities of the kind of the mind. But they can, and between individual events, despite these apparent counter indications. For mental explanations of mental phenomena, of the utmost certainty, do and must exist; and in depth too, if one thinks of the insights of a non-scientific and gifted observer like Dostoevsky. Paradoxically, however, the region of the mind that offers the greatest resistance to the explanatory enterprise, is the most developed and most characteristically mental of mental phenomena: the thinking process! But what has impressed me, is that a continuity links the *most* self-determined of these, attending, and the *least* self-determined, dreaming; and that as one moves along this spectrum, *pari passu* the will fades from the scene.

But the will is itself a form of mental cause. Therefore as we move across in the direction of the dream, one mental agency is deleted from the causal picture. Moreover, it is the causally central mental agency. Indeed, it is in man the very organ or instrument of reason, being the psychic thrust through which rational self-determination objectifies itself either in the mind or in physical nature.

What, then, is left as sleep descends and the will departs? Or are we to suppose that, with the arrival of sleep, non-mental causes are *all* that operate? But this is highly implausible, for the dream is a describable, even an intelligible, process unity; and this makes it all but impossible to suppose that the early stages of a dream could be of *no* causal relevance to the later stages. It seems that there must be non-rational non-self-determining mental causal forces at work in the generation of the dream. These must at least partially explain, in holistic rather than lawlike manner, why the dream takes the course that it does. Not lying in consciousness, they lie in unconsciousness; and being neither rational nor entirely intellectual, they require as origin something in unconsciousness at least akin to the id. This is the general line of the succeeding argument.

Like the continuity or spectrum mentioned above, this paper also travels in the direction: from self-determination (of the mind's processes) to id-determination (of its processes). The former is the concern of section B, the latter of section C. But in depicting self-determination in B, I want to lay open for inspection the role open to the id in a mind that determines its own movement. It is for this reason that I have seen fit to discuss the problem of *mental creativity,* for the mentally creative situation is *par excellence* a situation in which the id is subordinated to the ego. This is my concern in B; and in C I will consider the dream, where the situation is reversed, and *par excellence* the ego is subordinated to the id.

B. MENTAL CREATIVITY: THE INTERNALISATION BY THE EGO OF ID FORCES

The id most reveals itself when the self least determines itself

We will be concerned with those mental phenomena that, as we shall argue, most require explanation in terms of the id. I take these phenomena to be marked by the following features. They are those mental phenomena, of which we are conscious, in which ego-function is at its lowest ebb (which is certainly not to say entirely absent). The most noteworthy example is dreaming. But of course there are others. Thus, while Freud described dreams as "the royal road to the unconscious," he thought that alongside dreams one could range neurotic and psychotic symptoms, parapraxes and free-associative trains of thought, as the places where the id pre-eminently revealed its existence. Then this is to say that the course of processes like the dream or free-associative trains could be rendered intelligible only through the invocation of some occurrent mental process factor other than the processes occurring in the conscious and unconscious parts of the ego. This factor consists in the so-called primary processes, the processes native to the id. So the theory goes.

Why did Freud think that these phenomena were the sites in which the presence of the id most clearly "showed through"? If, as is my intention, we confine the question to the central thinking processes of the mind, then the answer is not hard to find. It is because in these processes the *will,* or *choice* or *say,* is least operative. For it is evident that I have less say in what happens in my dreams than in what words will appear in this paper, and there can be no doubt that this is why the dream *must be* the "royal road" to the unconscious and *probably will be* the "royal road" to the id. Now, it is true that I have no direct say in determining what will be my visual impression when a certain image impinges on my retina, and it is also true that the formation of that visual impression out of that visual data is the work of unconscious parts of the ego. Therefore an absence of self-determination, taken in the sense of choice or will, is no certain mark of the active presence of the id; and this looks to run counter to the above formula. But the difficulty is resolved if we confine ourselves to the thinking process, for there it seems certain, as a matter of empirical fact, that the less say I have over what happens the more in general the id has say. This is because reason, understanding, intellect, play a less central determining role in such cases. And so I suggest that we proceed with the following simple formula: that the id most reveals itself when self-determination of the mind's thinking processes, taken in the sense of will or say, is at its lowest ebb.

A simple physical image of this mental force situation

Let me illustrate this claim by means of a simple image. Thus it is somewhat as if we were to notice perturbations in the orbits of the more outlying members of a planetary system, and were to argue from the position and character of these deviations to the presence of a hidden disturbing magnetic source lying beyond the outer confines of that system. Thereafter as a result of this discovery we would seek to explain and compute the paths of *all* planets in that system in terms of two variables: an outwardly directed magnetic force; an inwardly directed gravitational force. And the existence, and magnetic character, of the hidden disturbing force will be more nakedly evident the farther the planet under scrutiny lies from the sun. Then in our image the sun is the Apollonian ego, and the dark magnetic source the Dionysiac id.

Thus being in the neighbourhood of that magnetic source is in many ways analogous to being relatively much determined by processes in the id. And being close to the sun resembles being relatively much determined by ego-processes: either the conscious ego-processes of self-determination or choice, or unconscious ego-processes of an intellectual character. The process of intentionally attending to an item, which I think we must rate as a completely pure example of self-determination, lies, so to say, as near to the sun as possible; an authentic free-associative flow in a psychoanalytic session is situated somewhere in the middle; and hallucinatory processes and dreams, and most especially the dreams of young children and perhaps of great artists, lie as near to that magnetic source as is consistent with remaining within the sway of the sun. We might as well labour the image a little and make this latter requirement, of continuing to describe computable orbits around the sun, stand for the inevitable "secondary elaboration" that the existence of consciousness strictly demands. (It might even be conjectured, falsely, as I would suppose, that the extremest possible katatonia is the analogue of collapsing into that source!)

Certainly this planetary image is seriously misleading. Yet it helps us appreciate that the id "shows through" in just those places where the ego is least efficacious. Indeed, adapting one romantic usage, we might say that id most shows through where will is most asleep; for the will, in the romantic sense of *mental force,* is *the* manifestation of an ego that is both large *and* strong; for such an ego is an instrument that is essentially gifted in the sustained art of applying mental force. Then as that magnetic source will be most studied through observation of the paths of outer planets, so it is that from the dream especially we argue both to *the existence* and *the characteristic ways of working* of the primary process. Thus it was from interpreting dreams, as well as symptoms, that Freud was able to say that the primary process was above all noteworthy for two properties that bespeak a tendency towards Dionysian undifferentiation: condensation and displacement.

Mental creativity: the shadow of Dionysus

A process like attending to a sensation, however deep its origins, must if intentional be a pure self-determining. For here a process occurs in my mind simply because I choose that it shall, and the line of its development is determined by nothing but will. Thus far we are concerned entirely with ego-processes. But we take a first step in the direction of the id, and therefore towards a form of *psychic dualism,* when we approach the problem of *mental creativity.*

At once we encounter facts which point towards the presence of more than one ruling deity in the mind. For a deep problem is posed by the fact that much mental activity, and certainly always the most creative, harbours within itself an element that departs from the above simple model of self-determination. I refer to the fact that creative mental activities involve the occurrence of phenomena for which one is responsible *only via the mediation of the activity itself.* I have in mind: those mental events that constitute the advance of the creative activity; for these occur only because that activity brings them into being. For example, thoughts in the course of thinking. In consequence, it may truly be said of the thinking process that it interposes itself between the thinker and his thoughts. Indeed, in general the creative activity must incorporate as an element of itself that which stands at just such a remove of one from the self-determiner creator. The very concept of inspiration demands this. Thus the perpetuation of the creative process depends on the creator's granting a controlled measure of freedom to mental processes upon which he depends. And it involves the un-chosen occurrence of ideas which occur only through the mediation of the activity—which is by contrast most assuredly chosen. In the light of this, such a self-determining may be said to gather up into itself the unself-determined. That is, it integrates it into itself.

The power to create exists only because a requisite liberty reigns in part of a mind that is *strong enough* to retain its purposes in the face of such liberty. Indeed, the more exploratory the process, and thus the more of value, the more it occurs only because of this accommodated liberty. But, it might be objected, does not one simply switch on these subordinate mental processes at will? Certainly one does, for it is an activity. Then is it not absolutely analogous to switching on the requisite muscle processes in one's body when one chooses to raise an arm? The answer to this important objection has already been given above. Namely, these two situations differ in the crucial respect that, while one intends the perpetuation of the mental process, one does not intend the mental events its progress involves; and there is simply no analogue of this in the physical situation. Expressing the matter in vague-ish but still revealing language, we might say that this means that those subordinate mental processes have *a life of their own,* and while they move only because we set them in motion they are not the mere instruments of our purposes. They do *our* bidding, but go *their own* way; and this living relationship involves an harmonious division of labour within the psyche. A properly human form of authority is established in such a mind. But so also is duality.

Even the purest ratiocination, if creative, leaves room for the id

We have drawn attention to a quasi-antinomy in the concept of mentally creative self-determination. This led to the realisation that some self-determination integrates into itself the unself-determined. But what has that to do with the id? Supposing this true of an exemplary example of ratiocination, do we not explain each thought in that process when we exhaustively delineate the rational links that tie it to the problem itself, and to the preceding phase of the ratiocinative process? But the truth is, that while we thereby explain *the thought* that we thought, we give thereby no more than a partial explanation of our *thinking that thought.* For having explained a thought by relating it to a problem, we have yet to answer these questions. Why not another thought of equal relevance? Why not nothing of any relevance at all?

It is precisely because the process is creative, as opposed to being something like a mere listing of names, in which case the succeeding phases of the activity would be preordained, that these questions remain unanswered long after we have explained the thought. Of course we can attempt to answer them, invoking relevant factors like the intelligence and talent, the era and training of the thinker. Inevitably, much remains unexplained.

But to this it might be protested: must not these imponderables be intellectual processes, if the thought advances a ratiocinative process? And must they not therefore be unconscious ego-processes, and therefore not id-processes? Now, there can be no doubt that no unconscious intellectual processes are id-processes. But why cannot non-intellectual factors play a causal role in exemplary examples of ratiocination? For example, mental energy. And why should not mental energy be evoked by non-rational forces? Think of the type of mental soil out of which grew certain Newtonian ideas or some of the poems of Yeats. And concerning philosophy, as Nietzsche observed: "anyone who hears only a 'will to truth' in the background surely does not enjoy the keenest hearing."[1] Then could not non-rational causal factors determine which of a number of equally fruitful lines of inquiry is followed? I conclude that the quasi-antinomy in ratiocination at least allows a gap within which the id might conceivably play a determining role.

While what we have asserted concerning creative activities, holds equally of intellectual and artistic creation; and while in all creative activities the ego is the ringmaster in a psyche wherein unconscious mental processes play a determining role; it would be a mistake to suppose that intellectual and artistic creations emerge out of the same kind of mental processes. I know too little about the mental-structural differences between scientist, philosopher and artist, to be able to speak definitively here, but significant differences in the nature of their creative processes seem more or less to be guaranteed. Thus it seems certain that the id is a more powerful determining force in art than in either philosophy or science. This should hardly surprise us if we bear in mind the kinship between artistic creation and dreaming. It is supported by the fact that, just as the emotions are never rational, (which is not to suggest that they are irrational), so it is in the case of the ideas which occur in the creation of a work of art. After all, predominant purposes in art are the *moving* and even the *entertaining* of the spectator. Thus pre-eminently in the case of art we find that the near antinomy in all mental creative processes owes its existence at least in part to the working of the id. Whereas all that we know in the case of intellectual processes is that it is due

[1] Friedrich Nietzsche, *Beyond Good and Evil*, par. 10, trans. Marianne Cowan, (Henry Ragnery Company, Chicago, 1965).

to the necessary presence of unconscious phenomena. But, as already suggested, no contradiction results from supposing these also to be id-processes.

The parts of the self, bound by Eros, form diverse structures in mental creativity and dream

Our interest in creative mental processes derives primarily from the fact that here, as opposed to pure self-determinings like attendings, there exists a strange explanatory gap, an *hiatus,* within which the id might perhaps function. But what is most interesting is the way it vividly displays the element of *structural hierarchy* in the mind. Thus, while the id doubtless plays a role in creative activity, that role is always enacted *under the auspices of the ego,* which is the focal point of the self that actively creates; for this is a necessary condition of free activity. By contrast, while the ego plays a determining role in dreaming, that role is always enacted *under the auspices of the id,* which is the focal point of the self when consciousness of the world is in abeyance; and this ensures that the dream is not free activity. And so we see the focal point of the self shifting as the state of consciousness alters. I would now like to make a little clearer these twin notions: focal point of the self; structural hierarchy in the mind.

We suppose that id-processes partially determine the course both of the dream and the creative psychical process. Yet a highly significant mental structural alteration occurs as we switch from dream to creative activity. I shall endeavour to shed light on this structural situation by comparing it to an *inter-personal relation;* and, because Freud believed that Eros held the parts of the self together, which may therefore be thought of in personalised terms, I will make that personal relation one of love. Thus it is somewhat as if a lover were selflessly to declaim to his beloved the altruistic message that "your purposes are mine," only to receive the similarly selfless declamation that "it is not *mine* that are yours, it is rather that yours are mine." This possibly archaic situation is to be likened to be above structural switch; and, trite as the comparison may seem, we shall see that it has much to recommend it.

The value of this comparison resides in its capacity to illustrate for us an important property of love. Namely, the capacity of love to create unities in which *the kind of the love* and *the kind of the*

linked lovers mutually condition one another, leading to mutual freedom and a predestined division of labour. And so it is in the mind,
where Eros holds together parts of the self which perform predestined
tasks. We shall find that this holds of creativity and dreaming, but
in fact it holds throughout any mind not totally wrecked by illness.
Thus the free ego, working harmoniously with a super-ego from
which it is barely distinct, is free only because the latter is benign or
loving; while by contrast the ego of the melancholic labours, as Freud
remarked in *The Ego and the Id,* under a super-ego that has become
"a pure culture of the death instinct."[2] Similarly, the communication
between ego and id that Freud talked of in "The Unconscious" as a
prerequisite of mental health,[3] is possible only where the id is not
overloaded with the forces of evil and death. Thus, according to
Freudian structural theory, the healthy mind harbours within itself
various channels of communication, together with divisions of labour
that are thereby made possible. And, ultimately, both are made possible only through the synthesising influence of the benign forces of
love or life, the instinct Eros, originating in the id.

The id as the psychic matter or psychic fuel of mental creation

Let us return to the structural hierarchical differences between
dream and creative mental process. We compared the unified parts
of the mind to united lovers, the divergent character of those parts
of the self corresponding to the diverse natures of the lovers. This
is because we supposed there to be two possible mental focal points.
These will now be displayed in structural accounts of free creative
action, and dreaming, taken in that order.

(1)   Concerning free creative action we might say this: "The
creative processes in the mind have their own purposes, and these
are those of the *self*." And what we mean is that the mind of the
creator spontaneously travels along the inspired paths it follows, only
because that creative person has chosen to engage in the creative
enterprise. Whereas (2) concerning the dream, the following rather
seems apposite: "While the self that dreams has goals that are its
own, these are those of the *dream*." And we mean that the self that
is sleeping has the goals that it has only because the dream determines that it shall. That is, it merely dreams them.

[2] 1923b, XIX, 53.
[3] 1915e, XVI, 194.

This switch corresponds to a significant structural difference. In the former case, (1), the id is subordinated to the ego, which exploits the id's creative forces in the generation of the active creative process; so that while the ego goes where it wishes, it depends upon the id that it uses. In the latter case, (2), it is the ego that is subordinated to the id, which makes use of the ego's powers of secondary elaboration, and thereby ensures for itself a place in the consciousness of the sleeper and thus an avenue to expression; so that while the id goes where it wishes, it depends for its expression upon the ego that it uses. In those two great phases of the life of the mind, wakefulness and sleep, a different structural relation and division of labour is in each case established, and ego and id perform divergent tasks. More, in either case the focal point or pre-eminent determining centre in the mind correspondingly shifts its locus. For the wakeful it lies in the ego, for the sleeping it is centred in the id.

We assume the id plays a determining role, not merely in the least rational mental processes, such as dreams and hallucinatory psychoses, but in the deepest and most creative human occupations. Then because this generic source of creative impulse finds its naturally appointed (or healthy) role in consciousness in being organised by the active ego, its place in conscious mental life may be likened to that of the raw material or material stuff in the construction of the artefact. For while the id is not entirely without structure, there is much about it that would recommend this construing of it, or else of the life instinct it harbours, as the sheer formless matter or fuel of the mind.

I think we may justly suppose, following our characterisation of creative and therefore relatively integrated activity, that a rich id is ideally subordinated to an ego that possesses the strength, and in consequence the required communicative links with the id, to marshall and put to its uses the untapped riches resident in these mental resources. Rather like a nineteenth-century industrialist harnessing the forces of nature, or like a rider on a horse (as Freud observed),[4] the power of a powerful ego consists in its capacity to summon up at will, and simultaneously to control and structure, powerful sources lying deep in the id; and in this sense to internalise these psychic forces, thereby assimilating them into the self. For it is in many respects a nineteenth-century image, and I am reminded most vividly of

4 1923b, XIX, 25.

Ibsen's tragic character John Gabriel Borkman, towards the end of the play of that name, addressing by night the minerals buried deep in the nearby mountains: "I can see the veins of metal stretch out their winding, branching, luring arms to me . . . You begged to be liberated and I tried to free you. But my strength failed me, and the treasure sank back into the deep again. (With outstretched hands.) But I will whisper it to you here in the stillness of the night: I love you, as you lie there spellbound in the deeps and the darkness! I love you, unborn treasures, yearning for the light! I love you with all your shining train of power and glory."[5] The loss of those now quite inaccessible yet still loved materials, a loss that is explicitly interpreted as symbolic of Borkman's mental tragedy, is the "objective correlative" of the failure of his ego to establish constructive communicative links with his id, which is in effect that in which his mental tragedy consisted. Those minerals are his own unrealised-forever mental deeps or resources. Indeed, the situation could even be said to represent an ego addressing with love an id which it has proved too weak to harness to its purposes. As Freud observed, in speaking of mental development: "Where id was, there ego shall be";[6] and what he was referring to was the internalising, as it were, the mapping and harnessing and civilising, of the natural and primaeval regions in the psyche.

C. Dreaming: The Subordination of Ego to Id

We shall now pass on from the consideration of controlled pure self-determinings like attending, or controlled impure self-determinings like the creative mental processes of pure thought or art. Instead, we shall turn our attention onto those central thinking processes which are marked by an increasing absence of self-control. That is, day-dream, deep pre-sleep phantasy and dream. Here, as we have already remarked, the id is increasingly visible to eyes that can see. It becomes the focal or determining point in the structural hierarchy in the mind.

We shall, however, begin by examining one important element of the dream. Namely, the unconscious shaping by the ego, the Apol-

[5] Henrik Ibsen, *John Gabriel Borkman*, trans. William Archer (Heinemann, London, 1910), act 4.
[6] 1933a, XXII, 80.

Ionian dream-work,[7] as a result of which the deep instinctual phenomena buried in the id enter in symbolic form into the consciousness of the sleeper. This is none other than the famous "secondary elaboration" of Freudian theory.

"Secondary elaboration": like a bridge between the atomic and the visible realm

We have spoken of the theory of the "secondary elaboration" of the primary process. While to many this may seem a somewhat creaking piece of theoretical machinery, conjuring up the image of a perpetually active stage manager scurrying around in the psychic wings, Freud's acceptance of the principle that all thinking processes require perspicuous mental explanation more or less forced him to postulate this theory. I say so for two reasons. First, because the above principle compelled him to postulate id-processes in order to explain the dream (etc.); and secondly, as we shall soon see, because once one accepts the existence of id-processes one cannot but endorse the theory of secondary elaboration.

There is a close analogue between the explanatory role of the id, and that of fundamental particles in present-day physical theory. These last make possible a deep complete explanation of the properties of material stuffs only through contriving to inhabit a categorical limbo lying between matter and energy, for the electron is at once the quantum of negative electricity *and* endowed with mass. Because the most minute speck of sulphur (say), visible only under a microscope as a yellow dot, possesses all the chemical properties of a chunk of sulphur, of sulphur in short, we are compelled to hypothesise explanatory factors lying beyond the visible, which are themselves inevitably lacking in the properties of the sulphur to be explained. The realm of the electron cannot be a duplication *in minutiae* of the macroscopic or microscopic realm it explains, if it is to function as a totally comprehensive explanation.

[7] Compare: Nietzsche, still under the influence of Schopenhauer but already wonderfully original, speaking of the lyric poet: "As Dionysian artist he is in the first place become altogether one with the Primordial Unity, its pain and contradiction, and he produces the copy of this Primordial Unity as music, granting that music has been correctly termed a repetition and a recast of the world; but now, under the Apollonian dream-inspiration, this music again becomes visible to him as in a *symbolic dream picture*" (Friedrich Nietzsche, *The Birth of Tragedy* [Foulis, London, 1910], p. 45).

So, I suggest, it is, in the case of the primary processes in the id. If these were a sort of subterranean second conscious mind, wherein reason, self-determination and values held sway, they would fail to perform the deep explanatory task assigned them by Freud. *A priori*, from the very structure of these two theories, it is no more possible to introspect or recall id-processes than it is to see the electron or the sulphur atom. As one must lie outside the range of the perceptible, so the other must forever defy the powers of introspectible consciousness. The invisibility of the atom may be likened to the inaccessibility of the id. Both doctrines run counter to common sense, and they are at one in rejecting a philosophy of nature that would be content to regard established surface regularities as final explanatory ultimates. They look for the source of those regularities in something whose ontological status is novel, and whose instances lie outside experience. They continue the pursuit of ultimate truth, knowing they will never arrive at their goal but opting regardless for the search.

Processes in the id could never conceivably fill consciousness

Let me now say why *a priori* id-processes must defy the powers of introspectible or recollective consciousness. Because the consciousness of rational creatures constitutively requires the existence of at least some measure of rational sensitivity to the world,[8] whereas the id is assigned the task of explaining those mental phenomena for which neither intellect nor self-determining choice can be held responsible, it follows that if a mind could be filled with nothing but the primary process, then not even a psychotic consciousness could inhabit the mind at the time. Now, to this it might be objected that people who are completely unconscious sometimes experience dreams, and from this it could be argued that a mind filled with primary process might conceivably be dreaming.

To see why this is impossible, is to see why the secondary elaboration of id-processes is a necessity in the generation of any conscious process that is partly id-determined; and if the dream matches this specification, this must hold of the dream as well. The point turns on the crucially important distinction between consciousness-of-an-item and consciousness-of-the-world, the latter being the condition

[8] See Brian O'Shaughnessy, "Mental Structure and Self-Consciousness," *Inquiry* 15 (1972), p. 43.

of wakefulness.[9] Thus a man who dreams is at once unconscious of the world, and conscious of the contents of his dream, even though he is doubtless unaware that those dream contents *are* dream contents. More, because the dream contents are objects of consciousness, there must exist the possibility of recollecting that dream, which is to say, of recollecting a process that he must be capable of describing in intelligible narrative. Then that narrative narrates what seemed at the time to him to be true, and this means that in rational creatures the dream takes place under the heading, the true. The conjunction of these two features of human, but not animal, conscious life, is no accident: namely, occurring under the aspect of the true, occurring under the concepts made available to him by the language that he knows. But this is already to locate those dream experiences within the orbit of the ego. It follows that no dream can *consist in* id-processes.

Thus it must be true of any id-determined process of which we are aware, whether contemporaneously or retrospectively, whether when conscious or in a state of unconsciousness, that it owes its place in awareness entirely to the labours of the unconscious portion of the ego. And this is to say that processes of secondary elaboration have occurred. However close certain processes may seem to the id itself, phenomena like hallucinatory episodes or peculiarly raw dreams, it would be impossible for us *ever* to become aware of them unless *at the time* of their occurrence their id-content had already undergone processes of secondary elaboration. Clearly this holds of present phenomena; and it must hold of the past, since it is through memory that those past phenomena enter awareness, and what we now remember must at the time have been an object of our consciousness.

Therefore, were it the case that the mind of the extremest possible katatonic was filled with pure destructive id-processes—which is, I daresay, far from true—it would be logically impossible that he should ever be aware of them. Actually, I suspect that there exist decisive theoretical considerations, most readily expressible in the powerful conceptual framework constructed by Melanie Klein, why this must be a false account of the extremes of schizophrenia. For one thing, it seems to be a case of mental death, for if the forces of death entirely possess something, then that something is dead. But the schizo-

9 Ibid., p. 41–42.

phrenic can part with his schizophrenia only through cure of it. Nevertheless, it would be a mistake to conclude from this that the id lies outside time (like its grandfather concept, Schopenhauerian Will). The id must be temporally diverse, for it must at least in part have its origin in the impact of somatic phenomena on the brain, and it makes its presence felt in the temporally ordered phenomena of consciousness. Thus Freud speaks of primary *processes*, as he was compelled to do, and while id-processes lack the rational structure of ego-processes, in being processes they must be temporally diverse. Therefore, however close it may get to it, the concept of the id is not the concept of a kind of *psychic matter*. It is, as it were, the mere filling of a psychic form that is entirely the work of the ego. It, too, has structure.

Dreaming is thinking when consciousness is unaware of the world

We pass from a consideration of the unconscious ego-processes, the Apollonian dream-work of "secondary elaboration," as a result of which id-processes in symbolic form enter the consciousness of the sleeper who dreams. And we shall now attempt to characterise, first, the dream, then the day-dream, finally, the deep pre-sleep phantasy. In particular, we shall be concerned to assess *the will-status* of these three phenomena.

The dream is the form that thinking cannot but take, always supposing it continues, as one's state of consciousness switches from wakefulness to sleep. For the dream is a natural continuation of the thinking processes occurring just prior to the onset of sleep. I say so in part because of resemblance between these processes, in part because in either case the state of consciousness is consistent with no other form of thinking. Thus it is surely no contingency, as we reach that rapt state in which we are already well embarked on the road downwards into sleep, that the thinking processes which were unfolding as we first closed our eyes should by then have acquired that peculiar amalgam of drift, intensity and symbolism, all in the absence of words, that marks the transition to sleep and dream. That our thought processes should be of this kind, and the state of consciousness wherein they occur should be as it is, are not distinct states of affairs, since neither could occur without the other. Now, the situation is both similar and strikingly different with the dream: for we can dream when stunned, and fail to dream when asleep; and this shows that dreaming and sleeping must be distinct processes with distinct causes. This is a significant difference between dream and pre-sleep phantasy. Where they are alike is in the fact that sleep is consistent with no other thinking process than dreaming, for one whose thinking processes are as one who is awake must himself be awake! (*Let us not forget that the criteria of consciousness must be internal.*) Therefore I feel entitled to say that dreaming is the form that thinking cannot but take, always supposing it continues, as one's state of consciousness switches from wakefulness to sleep.

So long as we are awake, the onward rush of thought cannot conceivably stop, and therefore *a fortiori* cannot be stopped at will. That is, one awake has no choice but to be thinking (taking "think" in a sufficiently wide sense). More, if we are awake, then necessarily we have *the power,* call it *P,* actively to govern the direction of flow of the inevitable stream of ideas. Yet phenomena like day-dreaming suggest that it may be possible to *decline* to put *P* to use. Even if this is so, there is something else, namely responsibility for our mental processes, which we cannot evade. Thus, because of the special setting in which power *P* occurs, for it is a power of which we cannot be unaware, it follows that if we are awake then necessarily we must be exercising what might be described as our *say,* call it *S,* over what thinking processes shall occupy our mind. I use this watered-down term, "say," to indicate our continuing responsibility for our mind's processes, for it seems to me that because of the self-conscious power *P* we must *either* choose *or* permit the mind's processes to be what they are. Thus, at the very least, we exercise this say *S* through *knowingly declining* to put the power *P* to use, which means through permitting a process to occur; while we standardly exercise *S* through *using P* in choosing which processes shall occur.

Therefore the state of wakefulness, over which we have no immediate control, is essentially conjoined with our being not-free not to exercise say over what thinking processes shall occur in our mind. Indeed, the only respect in which we are free in this domain is in our continuing possession of power *P:* namely, the power actively to govern the direction of flow of the inevitable stream of ideas. This power we always have, and are condemned to have, so long as we are awake; and there is no third alternative to either using it or declining to use it. For the state of wakefulness, over which we have no immediate say, is a state marked by the self-conscious possession of that power. In sum: when awake we can choose neither to stop thinking, nor to cease arbiting or exercising responsible say over the processes in the mind. We can merely choose that one or another mental process shall occur.

The day-dream passively and permissively self-determines the day-dream

I introduce the concept of "say," S, the concept of immediate responsibility, as a supplement to that of power to choose, P, in order to do justice to the day-dream. For it seems to me that the day-dream is the limiting, and perhaps even the degenerative, case of the self-determination of the thinking process. Now, it is not clear to me whether the day-dreamer exercises his power P to determine by choice the thinking process; and this I must emphasise. But what is certain is that the day-dreamer is responsible for the contents of his day-dream, and thus that he is exercising his say S over the thinking process in day-dreaming. For if a religious edict were to say, "One must not permit one's thoughts to stray onto sacred topic T," would not one who day-dreams about T have disobeyed? Further, in failing to believe in the contents of his day-dream images, the day-dreamer reveals thereby that he knows he is day-dreaming; and this is confirmed by the fact that one who is roused from a day-dream does not at that moment *discover* that he has just been day-dreaming. Now, if we conjoin with this the fact of the continuing presence of the self-conscious power P to determine what mental processes shall obtain at any moment, then I think it becomes evident that, in a quite strict sense, the day-dreamer has responsibility for the contents of his day-dream.

At this point I shall hazard a brief, tentative and highly fallible account of the nature of day-dreaming. It seems to me that the day-dreamer, moved by familiarity (association) and agreeableness (inclination), passively self-determines the day-dream in the mode of permissiveness. That is, the day-dreamer self-consciously permits his thoughts to stray the way that familiarity and agreeableness take them. It is an active consenting to what is at once agreeable, familiar, unchosen; and the best comparison I can offer is that of feminine sexual consent. Its course is desired and permitted, and while it is not initiated it would not have eventuated were it not for that free consent. The conscious day-dreaming self passively conspires with its own easy inclinations. This is the nearest one can get to opting out of the necessity, imposed by sheer wakeful consciousness, of exercising say over the course of one's thinking processes. Indeed, it may even be that the self is active in day-dreaming, but if it is it may be active only in that reduced sense in which the free passive recipient accomplice in an activity engages in that activity.

By contrast, the pre-sleep phantasy pursues its course in a mind not in a self-conscious state. The person on the verge of sleep has not the responsibility or say encountered in the day-dreamer, and this is because he does not know he is merely phantasising. The proof of this lies in the fact that when one suddenly starts out of such a state, "coming awake again," one *does* then make the discovery that one was merely phantasising and, indeed, almost asleep. Therefore in not knowing as he phantasises that it is mere phantasy, he fails to be in possession of an item of knowledge, "this process is one that I could control"; and so, peculiarly, it fails to be that which he could control, which is to say that he lacks the power P. Like the dream, it genuinely assumes *the mantle of reality;* whereas the day-dream is seen as *an immediate representation,* now of the past and actual, now of the past and might-have-been, now of the impossible and future, etc. It follows that the pre-sleeper, who is by his state of consciousness compulsorily reduced to the modalities of the here and now and actual, like the dreamer, has not given his consent to what happens in this seeming reality that is a product of his mind. *Mental freedom, and modal sophistication or modal self-consciousness, go together.* For without this, there would be nothing in the mind, as there must be, that relates to the actual processes as does the architect's blueprint to the realised edifice. Therefore the pre-sleeper's conscious values play no overt or chosen role in the genesis of the phantasy. In thus phantasising, he can be said neither to have abided by, nor to have flouted, his conscious values.

A summary of the issues arising from this discussion

At the beginning of section B, we stated that we would be concerned with those mental phenomena most requiring explanation in terms of the id. We took these to be those thinking processes in which ego-function or self-determining will was at its lowest ebb. We saw that in the purest examples of self-determination, such as listening, we were in possession of a total mental explanation of a simple mental state of affairs. For example, it is because I chose to listen to the sound that my attention and the sound are in conjunction. Therefore while my choice may be determined by id-phenomena, it is choice and not id that immediately and completely determines that sound and attention shall conjoin. Therefore the explanation of this conjunction lies entirely in the will of the listener, even if the explanation both of the choice and of the capacity to listen is obscure. Thus the explanatory gap is entirely closed in the case of listening. In consequence, there is little reason to mention the id. And while the id is, in mental creation, a significant factor, the ego and its will determine as organising forces the terms of reference under which those id-phenomena take place.

How different it is with dreams! Nothing there is predetermined in advance by the choice of the subject. And so the normal causal explanatory factor, present to a greater or lesser degree in our daily waking mental life, is in the dream largely and probably completely absent. I mean: that mental cause—the will of the subject. We suggested that it was this absence that, to Freud, constituted powerful evidence that pre-eminently in the dream the primary processes in the id "showed through." Because the normal causal explanation of the course of self-composed thinking processes in waking life is unavailable in the case of the dream, Freud felt that if the dream was to be mentally explained he had to turn to an entirely different processive explanation, one in terms of the primary process. Something whose existence did not depend on that mental cause: the will. Theoretically, it would be open to him to see the dream as nothing but the product of unconscious processes in the ego. But the openly instinctual character of many dreams, in fact of much in human and animal life in general, the close kinship between the work of art and the dream, the similarity of dream contents to neurotic symptoms, jointly constitute a powerful argument for supposing that the missing determining process must be of a different order altogether from the reasoning and organisational phenomena present in the ego.

Freudian Mechanisms of Defence:
A Programming Perspective

MARGARET A. BODEN

Psychoanalysis is not a specialized branch of medicine. I cannot see how it is possible to dispute this. Psychoanalysis is a part of psychology; not of medical psychology in the old sense, not of the psychology of morbid processes, but simply of psychology.

Postscript to *The Question of Lay Analysis* (1926e).

I INTRODUCTION

The relevance of programs to paranoia is not immediately apparent. It is not evident that the mechanism of computers could incorporate the mechanisms of defence. Indeed, it is commonly believed that computer research is radically antithetical to and necessarily destructive of an adequate image of man, and that computer models therefore can have no real significance for the understanding of the human mind.

I hope to show the falsity of this opinion by reference to current programs concerned with the sorts of repressive processes which Freud considered to be "the corner-stone on which the whole structure of psychoanalysis rests" (1914d, XIV, 16). These specific examples should illustrate two general points: that appeal to cybernetic analogies in scientific and philosophical discussions of man need not have dehumanizing consequences, and that computer science can provide powerful and structurally complex models of the mental processes underlying observable and introspectible psychological phenomena.[1]

The absolute clarity required for writing computer programs forces to the surface questions which remain latent in the natural language formulations and intuitive applications of the "equivalent" psychological theories. For this type of theoretical illumination the computer itself is in principle unnecessary, although the best way of detecting

[1] For a fuller discussion of these two points see M. A. Boden, *Purposive Explanation in Psychology.* (Harvard Univ. Press, Cambridge, Mass., 1972).

hidden ambiguities and hiatuses in a program is to run it on a computer and then to test the debugged version in a similar fashion. But the computational power of a functioning computer is invaluable in demonstrating the detailed implications of a given program (or theory), since the programmer (or psychologist) himself is unable to continue the theoretical analysis to the same degree of complexity. (It is in this sense that something new and surprising can result from running a program, even though every instruction in it was provided by the programmer.)[2] A corollary of this point is that a highly complex set of initial conditions can be input to the programmed computer, which will then infer the specific theoretical conclusions appropriate to this particular set. For instance, the beliefs or delusions of an individual person, originally expressed in a long series of psychoanalytic sessions, can be fed into a program which represents neurosis in general. Thus the uniqueness of human minds can now be approached in ways as rigorous as the strictest methodologist could require. Clinical psychologists, who rightly decry the trivial generalizations that result from statistical descriptions culled from large samples of individuals, need have no fear that the individuality of their patients must be similarly ignored by a cybernetic approach.[3]

Triviality, of course, there may still be. The programs I shall discuss are no match for the human clinician. To say they are *no* match is strictly untrue, for we shall see that professional psychiatrists are unable to distinguish the initial diagnostic interviews of paranoid patients from psychiatric interviews of a "paranoid" program. Nevertheless, current programs have many limitations as compared to the equivalent theories utilized by human psychologists. In some cases this rests on technological limitations such as availability of data-storage space, or on "extraneous" factors which can be taken for granted where human theoreticians are concerned. For example, it would hardly occur to anyone to remark that Freud's

[2] One of the earliest attempts at programming "machine intelligence" succeeded in proving geometric theorems in ways which were not specifically foreseen by the programmers: H. L. Gelernter, J. R. Hansen, and D. W. Loveland, "Empirical Exploration of the Geometry Theorem Machine," *Proc. Western Joint Computer Conference* (1960), 143–47.

[3] For the individually and the statistically orientated approaches to clinical psychology, see P. E. Meehl, *Clinical Versus Statistical Prediction: A Theoretical Analysis and a Review of the Evidence* (Univ. of Minn. Press, Minneapolis, 1954).

theoretical insights were crucially dependent on his background understanding of natural language; but computer programs employing oversimple models of language-use sometimes make "absurd" errors in psychological interpretation which are directly attributable to this linguistic crudity. In other cases, however, the triviality of a programming parallel rests rather on a lack of clarity in the original theory concerned. Human clinicians do not make comparable mistakes because their implicit assumptions and intuitive applications of psychological theory are a good deal more subtle, and more sensible, than their explicit theoretical statements. If a "trivial" program acts as a spur to making human psychological intuition more explicit, and to clarifying the insights of a Freud for the benefit of lesser mortals, it is not to be dismissed as wholly irrelevant to psychological understanding.

From the defence of computers, let us now turn to "defence" in computers: I shall first give an outline sketch of the Freudian concept of defensive mechanisms, and shall then discuss some relevant programs.

II   Defence Mechanisms in Freudian Theory

That the defence mechanisms play a crucial role in Freud's theory of mental function may be stated without qualification. But it is impossible to make a similarly straightforward statement of their nature, normality, or number. This difficulty arises partly from the shifts and alternations in Freud's usage of his theoretical vocabulary: the vicissitudes of Freud's terminology are almost as complex as the postulated vicissitudes of the instincts.[4] Moreover, his examples of

[4] For instance, the closely related concepts of "repression" and "defence" were introduced into Freud's writings very early, in 1893 and 1894 respectively; by 1895 they were being used as synonyms; after a few years, "defence" virtually disappeared—only to be reintroduced in 1926 as a psychological phenomenon of which "repression" was then said to be a special case. See Joseph Breuer and Sigmund Freud, "On the Psychical Mechanism of Hysterical Phenomena: Preliminary Communication" (1893a, II, 10). Also Freud, "The Neuro-Psychoses of Defence" (1894a, I, 59–75); Joseph Breuer and Sigmund Freud, Studies on Hysteria (1895d, II, xxix); Freud, Inhibitions, Symptoms and Anxiety (1926d, XX, 163–64).

However, the effective equivalence or non-equivalence for Freud of these two concepts at various stages in his work is itself a controversial matter. See Peter Madison, Freud's Concept of Repression and Defence, Its Theoretical and Observational Language. (Univ. of Minn. Press, Minneapolis, 1961), esp. pp. 3–30.

specific defensive mechanisms are scattered throughout his work, there being no definitive listing of them; lists drawn up by his exegetists vary. Further confusion arises because independent theorists within the Freudian tradition, including the neo-Freudians and ego-psychologists, differ among themselves not only about what should ideally be said about psychological defence, but also about what Freud himself actually said on the topic. For the purposes of this essay, such exegetical and theoretical niceties will be ignored. It will suffice to sketch a general account of defence mechanisms, on the assumption that readers are already reasonably familiar with the concept from everyday or more specialized contexts.

The nature of defence mechanisms can be briefly expressed by recalling Freud's definition of *defence* as "a general designation for all the techniques which the ego makes use of in conflicts which may lead to a neurosis," and his observation that the purpose of defensive processes is "the protection of the ego against instinctual demands" (1926d, XX, 163–64). The ego is "protected" in the sense that it is prevented from consciously recognizing and acknowledging the existence of the forbidden and anxiety-ridden instinctual impulses. It follows that the activation and operation of mechanisms of defence must typically occur unconsciously; even though defensive techniques are attributed to the *ego,* they involve unconscious transformations within its deep structure rather than introspectively accessible processes that can be consciously monitored and reported.

These hidden transformations may or may not lead to psychological "end-points" in consciousness. If they do so, the conscious representations that result are somehow distorted with respect to those which would have occurred in the absence of defensive function, so that the anxiety or conflict which would otherwise be experienced is reduced. Sometimes the anxiety associated with a particular topic is so great that it is totally repressed, so that there is no conscious representation expressing it even in a disguised fashion. This state of affairs is unstable in the sense that the repressed impulse persists and continually instigates conscious expression of the forbidden topic, at least in some distorted form; but since *ex hypothesi* the level of anxiety is intolerable even after considerable distortion, a further cycle of repression supervenes to remove the conflict-ridden derivative from consciousness.

Ideally, the reduction of anxiety is great enough to hold experienced conflict down to a minimal level. But in practice many different degrees of anxiety attend conscious beliefs and ideas that have been defensively disguised. Unless a belief is in a phase of total repression, it is attended by anxiety of a "psychologically tolerable" level. But if it is close to the threshold of tolerance it is likely to undergo further defensive transformations, including repression as a last resort. Accordingly, a slight rise in anxiety level caused by a remark in a conversation (or an analytic session) can have very different effects on the activation of defence mechanisms at different times or for different individuals.

Although the defence mechanisms are often thought of as characteristically neurotic, it follows from Freud's definition previously cited that mechanisms of defence are employed by "normal" as well as "neurotic" personalities, the former being the more successful in controlling conflict by means of them. Indeed, Freud himself postulated similar symbolic transformations underlying dreams, jokes, and slips of the tongue; and the ego-psychologists stress the generally adaptive role of thought-patterns and behaviours which were clearly defensive in origin.[5] Successful defences allow the instinctual impulses to be expressed in a form that is psychologically acceptable to the person concerned. Particular individuals differ not only in their degree of defensive success, but also in their customary reliance on one defensive technique (or set of techniques) rather than another. One might expect, for example, that a student or professional academic would have ready access to defensive *intellectualization* regarding unpleasant facts, whereas a non-intellectually inclined person might defend himself against anxiety by the use rather of *denial*. (This hypothesis has been ingeniously confirmed in one of the more elegant experimental investigations of psychological defence.)[6] Even certain forms of psychosis were characterized by

[5] See Heinz Hartmann, *Ego Psychology and the Problem of Adaptation.* (Int. Univ. Press, New York, 1958).

[6] Speisman took two groups of subjects: students with outside interests of a markedly intellectual nature, and businessmen with non-intellectual hobbies. He measured their GSR (an electrophysiological indicator of anxiety) while they were watching a film of a rather nasty tribal circumcision-initiation rite. There were three experimental situations: film alone, no commentary; film with added sound-track providing an *intellectualizing* but non-denying commentary ("the rite is a fascinating example of this, that, and the other anthropological concept, even though it does hurt the boys"); and film with added *denying* commentary ("it doesn't really hurt, and anyway the boys are looking forward to joining the adult community"). The GSR of all subjects was reduced by each added sound-track; but the intellectualizing commentary worked better with the

Freud with reference to particular mechanisms of defence; thus he interpreted the delusional beliefs typical of paranoia as resulting from the combination of *denial, projection,* and *reversal* (1911c, XII, 9–82). Insofar as defence mechanisms are employed by normal, neurotic, and psychotic personalities, they may be regarded as universal features of the human mind.

Precise enumeration of Freudian defensive techniques is difficult for textual reasons that have already been mentioned. They certainly include repression, regression, reaction-formation, isolation, undoing, projection, introjection, turning against the self, reversal, and sublimation; and they are often held to include also denial, displacement, splitting, fixation, condemnation, neutralization, intellectualization, and rationalization.[7] Specific examples cannot be detailed here, but many of these concepts have entered into common parlance and a number of instances should spring readily to mind; some illustrative examples will be given later, in the discussion of programs intended as representations of belief-systems employing psychological defences.

The operation of defence mechanisms, then, was described by Freud in terms pertaining to cognitive psychology or epistemological structures—in terms, that is, of distortive transformations of beliefs and concepts. And the aim, activation, and success of defences were characterized by him in affective psychological terms, by ref-

---

student group and the denying commentary with the businessmen (indeed, the effect of denial on the students was hardly noticeable). See J. C. Speisman, "Autonomic Monitoring of Ego Defense Process," in N. S. Greenfield and W. C. Lewis, eds., *Psychoanalysis and Current Biological Thought.* (Univ. of Wis. Press, Madison, 1965), pp. 227–44.

[7] The first ten are listed (with clear examples) by Anna Freud, who regards the first nine as characteristic of neurosis, while sublimation "pertains rather to the study of the normal." Her list keeps closely to her father's writings, but her interpretation of introjection as "identification with the aggressor" constitutes theoretical development rather than faithful exegesis; she apparently uses "denial" interchangeably with "reversal"; and sublimation is equated with "displacement of instinctual aims"—but the defensive displacement involved in kicking the cat just after a quarrel with another person would hardly be called "sublimation." See Anna Freud, *The Ego and the Mechanisms of Defence.* (Hogarth, London, 1937), esp. chap. 4.

The last eight are not specifically listed by Anna Freud, but each is sometimes cited as a Freudian defence mechanism. See, e.g., Charles Rycroft, *A Critical Dictionary of Psychoanalysis.* (Nelson, London, 1968).

Largely because of the terminological shifts described in note 4 above, "repression" is sometimes used to cover the operation of *any* mechanism of defence.

erence to the level of anxiety associated with particular ideas within those structures. But Freud also described the functioning of these mechanisms in *meta*-psychological terms, and it is important to realize the potential theoretical independence of his psychology from his meta-psychology if the one is not to be rejected because of inadequacies in the other. Many of Freud's meta-psychological claims would be questioned by psychologists of a broadly "Freudian" cast of mind, and still more would be criticized by psychologists basically suspicious of the Freudian paradigm. The interpretations of "cathexis" and "countercathexis," for instance, as involving actual psychic energy flowing within a self-equilibrating system comprising a fixed quantity of *libido,* may be rejected both on psychological and on physiological grounds: drive-reduction or purely homeostatic theories of motivation are clearly inadequate to the psychophysiological reality.[8] This has been agreed by a number of psychologists of markedly Freudian sympathies, who have also rejected the concept of *psychic energy* in its orthodox Freudian interpretation, preferring a structural theory of psychological phenomena to Freud's dynamic and economic formulations.[9] And Freud's tendency to hypostatize the *ego* has been similarly faulted by some psychotherapists within the Freudian tradition, for introducing an unanalyzed anthro-

[8] For relevant psychological evidence see H. F. Harlow, "Mice, Monkeys, Men, and Motives," *Psychol. Rev.* 60 (1953), pp. 25–32; D. E. Berlyne, *Conflict, Arousal, and Curiosity.* (McGraw, New York, 1960); R. W. White, "Motivation Reconsidered: The Concept of Competence," *Psychol. Rev.* 66 (1959), pp. 297–333; D. O. Hebb, "Drives and the CNS (Conceptual Nervous System)," *Psychol. Rev.* 62 (1955), pp. 243–54. For physiological evidence see: James Olds and Peter Milner, "Positive Reinforcement Produced by Electrical Stimulation of Septal Area and Other Regions of Rat Brain," *J. Comp. Physiol. Psychol.* 47 (1954), pp. 419–27; M. P. Bishop, S. T. Elder, and R. G. Heath, "Intracranial Self-Stimulation in Man," *Science* 140 (1963), pp. 394–96; C. T. Morgan, "Physiological Theory of Drive," in I, Sensory, Perceptual, and Physiological Formulations, *Psychology: A Study of a Science,* ed. Sigmund Koch, (McGraw, New York, 1959), pp. 644–72.

[9] For critiques of psychic energy from a broadly Freudian point of view, with the suggestion that a *structural* theory of motivation be preferred, see K. M. Colby, *Energy and Structure in Psychoanalysis* (Ronald, New York, 1955); M. M. Gill, "The Present State of Psychoanalytic Theory," *J. Abn. Soc. Psychol.* 58 (1959), pp. 1–8; R. R. Holt, "A Review of Some of Freud's Biological Assumptions and Their Influence on His Theories," in *Psychoanalysis and Current Biological Thought,* eds. N. S. Greenfield and W. C. Lewis, (Univ. of Wis. Press, Madison, 1965), pp. 93–124; Louis Breger, "Dream Function: An Information Processing Model," in Louis Breger, ed., *Clinical-Cognitive Psychology.* (Prentice-Hall, Englewood-Cliffs, N.J., 1969), pp. 182–227.

pomorphic—and so hardly explanatory—homunculus into human psychology.[10]

Given that the power-engineering theories appropriate to cybernetic machines likewise exclude explanatory reference to computer libido, cybernetic energy, or machine egos, it remains to ask whether the relevant information-engineering (information processing) theories can illuminate Freud's theory of repression in any way. The question is not merely whether general concepts drawn from information theory, or systems theory, can be useful in describing the overall nature of the human mind. The question, rather, is whether there can be specific programmed parallels to the detailed cognitive and affective aspects of defensive thought which have been outlined in this section, and whether such cybernetic parallels would be wholly trivial or potentially fruitful from the psychologist's point of view.[11]

III COMPUTER SIMULATIONS OF DEFENCE MECHANISMS

There are a number of groups, attached to artificial intelligence laboratories around the world, who are working towards the computer simulation of different aspects of normal and psychopathological thinking. I shall try to indicate the general nature of some of their programs, but my discussion can only be sketchy in the extreme, and the original papers should be consulted for further details. This is especially important if the reader is disturbed by the apparent anthropomorphisms in my account. For the sake of convenience I shall speak of programmed computers as demonstrating, believing, defending themselves against anxiety, and the like. If the reader's philosophical sensibilities dictate the notional addition of heavy scare-quotes in every such case, my argument will be in no way affected. My claim is not that computers, or programs, *really* believe, *really* defend themselves, and so on, but that

[10] See Emanuel Peterfreund, *Information, Systems, and Psychoanalysis: An Evolutionary Biological Approach to Psychoanalytic Theory,* Psychological Issues, *7,* Monograph 25/26 (Int. Univ. Press, New York, 1971), esp. pp. 66–74.

[11] Freud's account of the motivational aetiology of defensive thought-systems was an important part of his theory; but it is irrelevant here, where the concern is with the current defensive functioning of an established structure of beliefs rather than its psychodynamic origins. This is because the relevant programs simulate adult thought-structures rather than their childhood development. It is of course possible that future programs might attempt representation of these features also.

there are significant analogies between the information processing within certain symbol-manipulating machines and the psychological processes of human thought. Reference to actual programs should help to clarify the nature and extent of the analogies and the sense in which anthropomorphic terminology is used and justified in a cybernetic context. In every case, the *precise* meaning of the convenient anthropomorphic abbreviation can be given in terms of the functional details of the program concerned.

Attempts to model defence mechanisms include some that are based on conventional mathematical techniques[12] and others which rely rather on manipulating semantic symbols and relations approximating those of natural language. The most developed computer representation of Freudian defences to date is that of K. M. Colby, whose "Simulation of a Neurotic Process" is described in a series of papers from 1962 on.[13] Later versions of Colby's neurotic program have incorporated some of the ideas of R. P. Abelson, whose simulation of affectively influenced everyday cognition derives from the "cognitive balance" theorists such as Fritz Heider rather than

[12] E.g., Moser et al. use variable density-functions as mathematical representations of psychoanalytic concepts such as: oral, anal, phallic, and genital pleasure gain; the primacy of genitality (the fusion of the four previous component drives); anxiety; repression and its derivatives, functioning as countercathexis mechanisms; emergency defence mechanisms; and specific forms of neurosis. See Ulrich Moser, Werner Schneider, and Ilka von Zeppelin, "Computer Simulation of a Model of Neurotic Defence Mechanism. (Clinical Paper and Technical Paper.)," *Bull. Psychol. Inst. Univ. Zurich* 2 (1968), pp. 1–77; Ulrich Moser, Ilka von Zeppelin, and Werner Schneider, "Computer Simulation of a Model of Neurotic Defence Processes," *Int. J. Psycho-Anal.* 50 (1969), pp. 53–64; Ulrich Moser, "Discussion of 'Computer Simulation of a Model of Neurotic Defence Processes,'" *Int. J. Psycho-Anal.* 51 (1970), pp. 167–73; Ulrich Moser, Ilka von Zeppelin, and Werner Schneider, "Computer Simulation of a Model of Neurotic Defense Processes," *Behavioral Science* 15 (1970), pp. 194–202; W. R. Blackmore, "Some Comments on 'Computer Simulation of a Model of Neurotic Processes,'" *Behavioral Science* 17 (1972), pp. 229–32; Ulrich Moser, Ilka von Zeppelin, and Werner Schneider, "Reply to W. R. Blackmore," *Behavioral Science* 17 (1972), pp. 232–34.

[13] K. M. Colby, "Computer Simulation of a Neurotic Process," in S. S. Tomkins and Samuel Messick, eds., *Computer Simulation of Personality: Frontier of Psychological Theory* (Wiley, New York, 1963), pp. 165–80; K. M. Colby and J. P. Gilbert, "Programming a Computer Model of Neurosis," *J. Math. Psychol.* 1 (1964), pp. 405–17; K. M. Colby, "Experimental Treatment of Neurotic Computer Programs," *Arch. Gen. Psychiatry* 10 (1964), pp. 220–27; K. M. Colby, "Computer Simulation of Neurotic Processes," in *Computers in Biomedical Research*, Vol. 1, ed. R. W. Stacy and B. D. Waxman, (Academic Press, New York, 1965), pp. 491–503; K. M. Colby, "Computer Simulation of Change in Personal Belief Systems," *Behavorial Science* 12 (1967), pp. 248–53.

Freud, but whose program involves a type of rationalization which is commonly dubbed "Freudian" or "neurotic," particularly when it occurs unconsciously.[14]

This theoretical similarity and interchange should come as no surprise to those who take seriously Freud's remark cited as the motto of this paper. As Gertrude Stein might have said, but doubtless didn't, a belief-system is a belief-system, is a belief-system. Processes of cognitive organization and transformation are unlikely to be totally different in cases of psychopathology and of normal psychology, and a number of interesting questions arise if one asks how the same general principles of thought (the same basic program) should be differentially "set" or adjusted so as to result in normal, neurotic, or psychotic phenomena.

Colby himself was for many years a practising psychoanalyst, and the original impetus of his program was his desire to produce a clear theoretical model of the process of free association in psychotherapy. The earliest ("output") version of the program simulates the patient's spontaneous free association or introspection; later ("input-output") versions simulate also the patient's response to the conversational and interpretative remarks of the analyst. Colby hopes that future developments may be of use in studying the (currently obscure) ways in which belief-systems and defensive habits of thought can be modified by particular conceptual inputs—in other words, how a neurosis can be ameliorated or cured by some of the analyst's interventions and left unaffected or aggravated by others. Simulation of an individual person undergoing analysis, by feeding in his idiosyncratic thematic beliefs as expressed over hundreds of hours of therapy, might allow for preliminary "testing" of therapeutic strategies: if a certain input precipitates a crisis in the simulation, this may provide a warning practically appropriate to the specific person-to-person context. Colby also suggests that the program might eventually be used for initial training purposes: getting a neophyte analyst to try out his word-magic on a computer would have some distinct advantages over current practice. Above all, Colby believes that his programming efforts—whether or not they ever achieve the sorts of therapeutic usefulness just listed—can

---

[14] For the original formulation of cognitive balance theory, see Fritz Heider, *The Psychology of Interpersonal Relations* (Wiley, New York, 1958). For a clear discussion of this and related theories of attitude change, see Roger Brown, *Social Psychology* (Free Press, New York, 1965), chap. 11.

clarify considerably the implicit assumptions and explicit theories which analysts and other psychologists bring to bear on the intrapersonal and interpersonal phenomena concerned.

Very briefly, and very drily, Colby's simulation consists of a system of propositions, each associated with a varying numerical index or "charge"; a set of symbol-manipulating routines which can effect changes of different types in these propositions or their interrelations; and five numerical monitors which vary continuously in quantity with operation of the aforesaid routines, and which serve to guide the direction of the information processing in the system.

In more readily intelligible, and more obviously Freudian, terms: the simulation represents a system of beliefs, each emotionally cathected to varying degrees; a set of defence mechanisms which can distort beliefs by effecting cognitive transformations on them; and various affects or anxiety-measures indicating danger, excitation, self-esteem, pleasure, and well-being, which influence the fate of individual beliefs (expression, distortion, or repression) and which determine the selective activation of the defences. Operation of a defence mechanism produces a distorted belief whose emotional charge is a percentage of the charge on the original belief—but the degree of countercathexis involved varies according to the mechanism concerned. Expression of a belief (whether distorted or not) reduces its charge to zero; but if it is a distorted belief which is expressed, the original (repressed) belief remains in the system with some residual emotional charge. The beliefs provided by Colby to the program represent those of one of his patients in long-term analysis; examples include *I am defective, Father abandoned me, I descend from royalty,* and *Mother is helpless.*

The program attempts to express its beliefs in the form of a printout. Its first step is to choose a belief of high emotional charge for consideration (the "regnant" belief). Next, a complex, or pool, of relevant (topic-related) beliefs is drawn from the background belief-system, and processing now continues with respect to this pool alone. The program initiates a random search of the pool for a belief conflicting with the current regnant; for instance, *I hate father* conflicts with *I must love father,* according to the dictionary definitions provided of *love* and *hate.* If no conflicting belief is found, the original belief is expressed as output. If one is found—and particularly if this belief itself is of high affective charge (as "super-ego" beliefs involving *must* all are)—a defensive routine is chosen from the set available to effect a distortion of the regnant.

The defensive techniques available to Colby's early program include eight "transform" routines which change the symbolic content of an old belief in forming a new derivative, and routines of isolation, denial, and rationalization which operate on interrelations between beliefs rather than beliefs taken singly. Colby's list of transforms is as follows:

(1)   Deflection: Shift Object (Not Self)

(2)   Substitution: Cascade Verb

(3)   Displacement: Combine (1) and (2)

(4)   Neutralization: Neutralize Verb

(5)   Reversal: Reverse Verb

(6)   Negation: Insert *Not* Before Verb and Do (5)

(7)   Reflexion: Shift Object to Self

(8)   Projection: Switch Subject (Self) and Object (Not Self)[15]

Let us suppose that the original belief selected as a candidate for expression is *I hate father.* Transform (1) would change this to *I hate the boss,* or *I hate Mrs. Smith.* Transform (2) relies on a dictionary of weak to strong "synonyms" of verbs, and in this case might give *I see faults in father.* Transform (3) could give *I see faults in Mrs. Smith* as the final distorted version of the regnant. Both (1) and (3) would qualify as "displacement" in the Freudian sense. Transform (4) may give *I couldn't care less about father;* (5) gives *I love father;* and (6) gives *I do not love father.* These three transforms are analogous to what Freud called "reaction formation" of varying strengths. The use of (7) gives *I hate self,* and echoes introjection, or turning against the self. Finally, (8) gives *Father hates me,* a classic case of simple projection.

These being the alternative distorting transforms available to the program (ignoring, for the moment, rationalization, isolation, and denial), how does it decide which transformation to express? Indeed, how does it decide to express any derivative at all, rather than entirely repressing the matter? And in the case of those transforms whose operation allows some latitude of choice—namely, the first

[15] Colby, "Computer Simulation of a Neurotic Process," p. 172. The list of transforms is slightly different in Colby and Gilbert, "Programming a Computer Model of Neurosis," p. 412.

four—how does the program select one application of the transform rather than another?

A trivial way of answering these questions would be to program a random operator (like that which selects beliefs from pools for comparison with the regnant belief) to activate and operate defence mechanisms. However, this would have little psychological interest or plausibility. For it is at least possible, perhaps even probable, that different techniques achieve defensive purposes to different degrees in the same or different situations. Crucial questions necessarily arise, then, as to the relative power of the various mechanisms in reducing anxiety and in effecting discharge of the underlying impulse.

Consider the first transform, which Colby terms "deflection." The syntactical (and psychological) object of the belief-sentence is to be altered. The new object must be chosen from a list of objects represented in the dictionary provided to the program. In Colby's simulation, only objects classed as persons by the dictionary are allowed as object-substitutes in operating the transforms, persons being the most commonly occurring objects of neurotic beliefs encountered in analysis. Let us suppose that there are only five persons listed in the dictionary: *father, mother, self, boss, Mrs. Smith.* The new object cannot be *self,* since there is a universal constraint attached to transform (1) forbidding this; shifting to the self would in fact be a case of transform (7), reflexion. Shifting to *mother* would conflict with the highly charged *I must love mother,* and would improve the situation not at all. Shifting to *boss* or to *Mrs. Smith* are both prima facie admissible.

If one considers a human being who unconsciously hates his father, it seems theoretically and phenomenologically plausible that greater satisfaction of the underlying impulse would be achieved by his consciously hating a male, dictatorial, high-status authority-figure than by his hating a gentle and obscure female. But the high anxiety level of boss-hate (based in these very attributes of the boss) may be too close for comfort to the even higher anxiety level of father-hate, so that the inoffensive Mrs. Smith may be hated instead. In programming terms, if one wishes to avoid a random search through the list of persons, necessitating continual "affective experimentation" of ensuing anxiety levels, then specific constraints must be built into the program. One might decide, for instance, to limit the search for a substitute to those persons having attributes (such as gender, age, status, personal habits) in common with the original object of the belief, with the caveat that not more than four common attributes are allowed. Colby's program (or, rather, Colby himself) solves this problem by use of a routine called *Findanalog*.[16] This procedure computes the number of properties two nouns have in common by referring to the dictionary. The dictionary is an information-matrix which codes (among other things) superordinate and subordinate categories for nouns; it provides the information, for example, that *man* and *woman* are each instances of the class *person,* and that *Joe* is an instance of *man*. The strength of analogy required between the original and the substitute object is represented by a numerical index which varies according to the specific psychological nature of the conflict-situation. Thus *Findanalog2* might be content with deflection to *Mrs. Smith* in the previous example, whereas *Findanalog5* would not. If no appropriate object can be found, the program then turns to consider a different transform entirely. But which one should it pick?

The nature of the transform selected depends on the degree of danger signalled by the *Danger* monitor at the time, and also on whether or not self-esteem is involved (the *self-esteem* monitor is adjusted whenever expression of the regnant would violate an *ought* or *must* sentence in the pool). A procedure called *Pick-transform* takes these monitors into account in deciding which transform to activate. Successful operation of a given transform results in a greater probability of its being used on future occasions. Thus a preferred style of defence develops over a series of runs, depending on the idiosyncratic nature and processing history of the belief-system currently being simulated. The example of hating the boss *or* hating Mrs. Smith shows that a defensive operation which is efficient in reducing anxiety may be less satisfactory in discharging the original impulse. Colby commits himself to the theoretical position that this is generally true, for he describes the eightfold list of defensive transforms as rank ordered from low to high according to their effectiveness in reducing anxiety, and from high to low in respect of their effectiveness in providing discharge of the charge on each belief. Projection, for example, involves such gross distortion that it is highly efficient in reducing anxiety levels, but poor in reducing charges. In general, he says, "the need for discharge

[16] This procedure is described on pp. 412–13 of the most detailed published account of the program: Colby and Gilbert, "Programming a Computer Model of Neurosis."

through expression drives the program down the list of transforms, while the need to reduce anxiety drives the program up. The sequence of derivatives created as output will represent a compromise formation between these processes."[17]

Distorted versions of beliefs always carry a lower charge than their original, so that expression of them may be possible. The more distorted the derivative, the lower its percentage of the original charge. Degree of distortion depends on which transform was responsible for producing the delusional derivative, deflection being the least and projection the most distortive. If the maximal distortion available fails to lower the charge below the anxiety threshold—something which can happen only when the charge on the regnant is exceptionally high—no output whatever is produced, and the program changes the subject by (randomly) choosing a fresh regnant for processing. In the latter case, the original belief, having been totally repressed, remains latent in the pool with a continuing high charge which results in its being chosen again and again for processing—a cybernetic version of the neurotic's "repetition without remembering."

Colby summarizes the neurotic character of his early "output" program in this way:

> The essentials of this neurotic process are conflict, producing a danger signal which in turn produces a transformation of belief until the danger is eliminated. The safety-first postulate of avoiding danger takes precedence over the discharge through expression postulate. The transforms are adjustive mechanisms, but they are maladaptive since they result in loss of information, misrepresentations of beliefs, and insufficient discharge leading to increasing repetitive preoccupation with conflictual areas. If the program attempts to interrogate itself about its own information, it cannot express directly some of its most highly charged beliefs and it receives as answers distorted derivatives of those beliefs.[18]

Later versions of the simulation incorporate a number of further subtleties, such as the admissibility of compound beliefs whose subject or object is itself a belief (for example, *Mother says father abandoned us*); representations of the credibility and degree of subjective certainty of beliefs; and "self-corrective" ways of *con*tending (rather than *de*fending) by facing conflicts and working on them

[17] Colby, "Computer Simulation of a Neurotic Process," pp. 172–73.
[18] Ibid., p. 173.

in various ways. For instance, a troublesome belief can be deliberately weakened in influence by finding reasons (and reasons for reasons) for disbelieving it: even though the belief is retained, it is simultaneously "denied" to such an extent that it may cause little psychological disturbance. This complex type of denial is more flexible, and potentially more stable, than those which rely on simple negation or on total repression of anxiety-ridden beliefs.

An additional development of the program is that the later versions are able not only to produce output but to respond to input, thus giving a closer analogy to the actual therapeutic situation. The sentence functioning as input is not added as such to the belief-system. Rather, the system is searched for a topic-relevant belief, which is examined for agreement or disagreement with the input sentence and is also used as the core of a pool of beliefs (as described above). Consequently, the effect of the input sentence is selectively to activate specific belief-structures already present in the model, even though it is not itself accepted into the system of beliefs. Similarly, a remark about policemen's pay, or the duty owed to one's parents, will have very different effects on the inner thoughts of a "neutral" listener and one with a neurotic preoccupation with authority-figures, whether the said remark is overheard in the café or endured in the consulting room. Meanwhile, the program replies to the input with *Yes, No,* or *Maybe*—but as the flow diagram in Figure 2 clearly shows, a *No* should not always be taken at its face value.[19] Analogously, a patient's rejection of his analyst's suggested interpretation may or may not derive from defensive resistance, may or may not be reliable. Those who complain that psychoanalytic interpretations are scientifically empty because they are "verified" if the patient accepts them but are not necessarily falsified if he rejects them, should ponder the flow diagram carefully. The highly structured program which it summarizes may be a false picture of the human psychological reality, but is certainly not "empty."

An early computer simulation of the process of rationalization was related not to Freudian theory in particular, but to the psychology of attitude-change in general. Abelson's simulation of "hot,"

[19] The two flow diagrams are taken from Colby, "Experimental Treatment of Neurotic Computer Programs." What Colby had earlier called a "pool," he now calls a "complex" of beliefs. Note that the diagram of Figure 2 flows directly into the diagram of Figure 1 by way of the box "Process Complex." Note also the *alternative* ways of arriving at a box for "Reply 'no'" provided for in Figure 2.

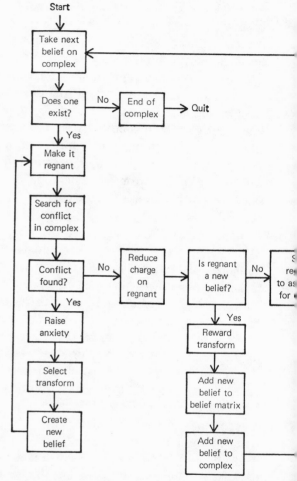

Flow diagram for processing a complex of belief

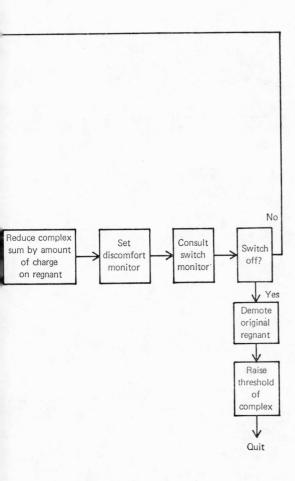

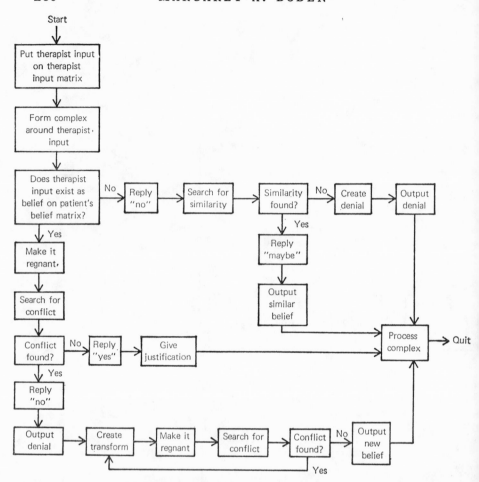

Flow diagram for response to therapist input.

or affect-laden, cognition modelled the theory of cognitive balance deriving from Heider and later elaborated by Abelson himself.[20] This program also has developed over the years, but the basic form of the rationalization subroutines is relevant to the present discussion. Abelson's program, even in its early form, is designed to deal with the

[20] See R. P. Abelson, "Computer Simulation of 'Hot' Cognition" in Tomkins and Messick, eds., *Computer Simulation of Personality*, pp. 277–98; R. P. Abelson and J. D. Carroll, "Computer Simulation of Individual Belief Systems," *Amer. Behav. Scientist* 8 (1965), pp. 24–30. Abelson's program is described in more detail, and is compared with that of Colby, in J. C. Loehlin, *Computer Models of Personality*. (Random House, New York, 1968), esp. chaps. 5–8.

input of beliefs into a pre-existing system. A new belief is assessed first for its prima facie credibility, and then for its evaluative balance with respect to the values coded in the belief-system. Certain types of imbalance initiate the defensive process of rationalization, which has three subvarieties: *reinterpret final goal, accidental by-product,* and *find the prime mover.*

Abelson gives the example of the cognitively imbalanced input sentence, *My simulation produced silly results.* My simulation, being mine, is positively valued—but silly results are negatively valued, so the sentence as it stands is imbalanced. The subroutine called "reinterpret final goal" searches for a positively valued implication of the concept *silly results.* The first implication generated by the program may be *non-publishable;* if the belief-system represented is one of those which abhors non-publishability even more than silliness, then *My simulation is unpublishable* will be rejected as unsuitable for purposes of rationalization. The next implication of *silly results* may be *enrichment of understanding;* since *My simulation enriched my understanding* is cognitively balanced, it is accepted. Analogously, the subroutine "accidental by-product" searches for a factor which explains the silly results by attributing them to a negatively valued source accidentally interposed between subject and object: thus *My simulation had program bugs* is an acceptable rationalization. Finally, "find the prime mover" replaces the subject by a disvalued substitute, as in *That crazy programmer produced the silly results.* The routines are much more subtle than this brief description suggests, but it should be clear that complex cognitive transformations are represented by this program, and that they serve a psychologically defensive function. In real life such rationalization may be largely conscious: if one considers the belief *Einstein produced silly results,* one may well mutter "Impossible! There must be some other explanation," and then quite deliberately think one up. "Neurotic" rationalization is probably basically similar to the conscious variety, but as well as being hidden to introspection, it is maladaptive, in that it accepts relatively unrealistic alternatives to the unacceptable belief.

The relatively unrealistic nature of the neurotic's defensive beliefs is one of the psychological characteristics distinguishing him from a "normal" person, but he still has a considerable grip on what his society accepts as reality. In this he differs from the psychotic, whose view of the world (or some pervasive aspect of it) differs markedly from that of most members of his community. The paranoid person, for instance, has a delusive belief-system about being persecuted and is unusually suspicious of other people accordingly. These delusions and mistrust influence his conversation in telltale ways, and the clinical diagnosis of paranoia rests largely on the paranoid's suspicious and hostile responses to perfectly innocent remarks. As an aid to understanding this psychological syndrome, Colby has recently programmed a case of "Artificial Paranoia."[21] This program responds to input sentences with both "inner thought" and "outward expression" and, as in the case of artificial neurosis previously described, the latter does not always faithfully reflect the former.

The paranoid program scans input sentences for explicit or implicit harms and threats of various kinds. This scanning constitutes a very severe scrutiny—indeed, an oversevere scrutiny—for it often involves the transformation of the input sentence into a distorted form which results in an interpretation of malevolence where none was intended. The inner transformations are not random, but are in many cases so far-fetched by normal standards that a nonparanoid person would be tempted to dismiss them as wholly irrational. One of the strategies employed by the program is to scrutinize the conversation for "flare" topics, which tend to activate the delusional complex concerned. These sensitive concepts are represented within the program in the form of a directed graph, one flare leading eventually to all the others according to their semantic interrelations. The graph functions as a cognitive core providing detailed tactics for leading the conversation around to the paranoid preoccupation, by way of appropriate prompts and hints output to the interlocutor. Analogously, one can expect trouble and misunderstanding if, while talking to a person paranoically convinced that he is being hunted by the Mafia, one mentions crime, police, Italians, or even spaghetti. Moreover, one does not have to mention any of these things: the chance remark that one enjoys Chinese food may enable the deluded person to lead up to his persecution complex

[21] For a description of the program, with some sample dialogues, see K. M. Colby, Sylvia Weber, and F. D. Hilf, "Artificial Paranoia," *Artificial Intelligence* 2 (1971), pp. 1–25. For an account of directed graphs like those used by the paranoid program, see Lawrence Tesler, Horace Enea, and K. M. Colby, "A Directed Graph Representation for Computer Simulation of Belief Systems," *Mathematical Biosciences* 2 (1968), 19–40.

by way of an apparently disinterested critique of the town's restaurants.

As in the programmed model of defence mechanisms, Colby's paranoid program incorporates quantitative parameters representing affect-states (fear, anger, and mistrust) which monitor and direct the details of the information processing going on. For a given input sentence, the transformation (if any) effected on it and the output in response to it are dependent on the values of these parameters, which themselves depend on the semantic content of the preceding dialogue. The program has two modes of function, which are differentiated primarily by the "setting" of the level and rate of change of the three affective monitors. The weakly paranoid mode involves general suspiciousness regarding certain topics, but no actual delusions. The strongly paranoid mode represents intense suspicion and hostility, backed up by an integrated delusional system of *idées fixes*. The dialogue produced by these two versions of the program is subtly different in either case, and in both cases differs from the dialogue of normal persons.

One might suspect at this point that the paranoid program (in either mode) produces dialogue which differs from the conversation of *all* persons, that it is "abnormal" in a sense quite other than the sense in which the human paranoiac's speech is "abnormal." If this were so, it would cast doubt on the relevance of the program to the study of actual paranoia, if not on its intrinsic fascination as an intellectual pastime. These questions have been raised by Colby himself, who has carried out a series of "Turing tests" of his artificial paranoiac.[22] The first step was to have a group of psychiatrists interview mental patients by teletype so as to arrive at a psychiatric diagnosis. From their point of view, the rationale for using a teletype had to do with efficient use of doctors' time: they did not know of the existence of the simulation. In some cases, of course, they were not communicating with mental patients at all, but with the

[22] For Turing's original concept, see A. M. Turing, "Computing Machinery and Intelligence," *Mind* 59 (1950), pp. 439–42. For Colby's applications, see K. M. Colby, F. D. Hilf, Sylvia Weber, and H. C. Kraemer, "Turing-Like Indistinguishability Tests for the Validation of a Computer Simulation of Paranoid Processes," *Artificial Intelligence* 3 (1972), pp. 199–221; K. M. Colby and F. D. Hilf, "Can Expert Judges, Using Transcripts of Teletyped Psychiatric Interviews, Distinguish Human Paranoid Patients from a Computer Simulation of Paranoid Processes?", *Stanford Artificial Intelligence Project, Memo AIM-182*, December 1972.

program. As the second step, another group of psychiatrists (similarly ignorant of the project) were asked to rate the transcripts of the interviews for presence (and degree) or absence of paranoia. Lastly, a third group (picked randomly from the professional psychiatric register) were sent the transcripts, were told that some were interviews of patients while others were interviews of a program, and were asked to decide which was which.

The results were striking. No interviewer realized that he was diagnosing a computer. Interviews with the "weak" mode of the program were reliably judged to be less paranoid than interviews with the "strong" mode. This remained true in the second phase, when transcripts were sent to uninvolved psychiatrists for rating. (It is worth pointing out that the interjudge reliability of the concept of paranoia is unusually high—nearly 90 per cent—relative to other psychiatric categories.) Finally, the guesses of the psychiatrists in the third phase were successful at no better than a chance level. In other words, on the basis of these diagnostic interviews they could not distinguish the delusive defences of a "paranoid" program from those of a paranoid patient.

Strictly, this was not a Turing test in the accepted sense, since the psychiatrists doing the interviewing were not asked to judge which teletypes were attached to men and which to machines. They were not even informed that an "imitation game" was going on. Colby justifies this by pointing out that if the interviewer is informed at the start that a computer may be involved he tends to change his normal interviewing strategy; that is, he asks questions designed to test which respondent is a program, rather than asking questions specifically relevant to the diagnostic dimension (paranoia) being studied. Colby also points out that, even in such a case, the program does not necessarily fail the Turing test: "We have found in informal experiments that if a human-respondent does not follow standards of the interviewer's expectations [does not answer honestly and candidly], jokes around, or plays other games, ordinary judges cannot distinguish him from a computer program with limited natural language understanding."[23] It has already been remarked that the conversation of paranoid psychotics typically does seem "irrational" when judged by everyday standards.

Talk of "Turing tests" inevitably raises the question of how suc-

23 Colby, "Turing-Like Indistinguishability Tests," p. 203.

cessful current simulations actually are in modelling the human mind. In this section I have tried to present the strengths of the defensive programs I have described. In the next, something must be said about their weaknesses.

IV LIMITATIONS OF CURRENT PROGRAMS

With respect to the weaknesses of computer models of psychological phenomena I am tempted to quote Colby's words without further elaboration:

> The criticisms of the approach should be familiar to you since they are the criticisms which are applied to all approaches to problems. One could assert that the hypotheses are questionable, the postulates are naive, the boundary conditions are too narrow (or too wide), there is too much (or too little) structural detail in the model, there are better ways of solving the empirical problem, and the data are unreliable.[24]

If elaboration there must be, it should be confined to a critique of limitations that are directly attributable to the cybernetic context of theorizing, rather than to the psychological theories themselves.

The subtlety of the cybernetic models of neurosis and paranoia clearly depends heavily on the quantity and quality of data supplied to the program. The relevant data include beliefs, each with its specific charge; relations (such as *reason for*) between beliefs; dictionary entries such as verbs, nouns, and their respective modifiers; "cascading" relations between verbs coding relative strength; lists of instances, synonyms, and antonyms of verbs; and subordinate and superordinate relations between nouns.

The quantity of data is in principle limited only by the storage capacity of the machine being used to run the program, and so far this has not proved a problem. The quantity is in practice restricted, however, by the enormous effort required to write a datum —especially a belief—into the program. To believe that p is not merely to assent to p considered as an isolated proposition, and the systematic nature of belief must be somehow paralleled in the simulation. The coding and cross-referencing problems involved are immense, and the early neurotic program had only twenty beliefs

[24] Colby, "Experimental Treatment of Neurotic Computer Programs," p. 226.

to worry about. Later versions have over one hundred beliefs, and nearly three hundred dictionary entries. Satisfactory representation of human idiosyncracy would presumably require more data than this, even though many of a person's beliefs are irrelevant to his neurosis.

The quality of the dictionary data depends on the programmer's sensitivity to ordinary (rarely to technical) language. Decisions have to be made about how to program the semantic relations between words and how to represent the function of individual words. For instance, one has to settle for a particular cascade of verbs, such as *abhor, detest, hate, dislike, disapprove, reject* (should *see faults in* be included in this list, or should it not?). And one has to face the problem of how to write a program which could reply to a phrase like "a *good* knife," or "a *good* husband," with a statement containing an appropriate inference.[25] Philosophical analyses of the terms involved may sometimes be helpful, but the necessity of making unambiguous decisions will usually result in less subtle usage of the term concerned than is found in everyday discourse. For theoretical purposes, of course, many such subtleties are luxuries, not necessities. The real problem is how to avoid those semantic crudities which can lead to important psychological misunderstandings.

The quality of the data in the *belief* and *reason* matrices depends on the clinical ability of the person supplying these data to the programmer. In Colby's case, clinician and programmer are one and the same. The significance of a given model considered as a hypothetical case reflects his clinical insight in general, while its significance as a representation of a particular patient in analysis rests on his success in perceiving and summarizing the idiosyncratic neurotic themes concerned. Colby has considered the time-saving (and, he claims, perhaps even psychotherapeutic) possibility of using computers to interview individuals and to effect an initial listing of their neurotic concerns. To this end he has written an interviewing program, basically similar to Joseph Weizenbaum's ELIZA, which simulates the therapist in non-directive Rogerian therapy.[26] Some-

25 K. M. Colby and Horace Enea, "Machine Utilization of the Natural Language Word 'Good,'" *Mathematical Biosciences* 2 (1968), pp. 159–63.

26 K. M. Colby, J. B. Watt, and J. P. Gilbert, "A Computer Method of Psychotherapy: Preliminary Communication," *J. Nerv. Mental Disease* 142 (1966), pp. 148–52; K. M. Colby and Horace Enea, "Heuristic Methods for Computer

times Colby's program successfully elicits from its interlocutor a sustained expression of psychologically significant feelings and beliefs; sometimes, however, the "conversation" is ludicrous in the extreme. Consequently, the program in its early stage is of no practical use. Moreover, one may doubt whether the psychological *ambience* of dropping one's defences in communicating with a computer could ever be sufficiently similar to that of the analytic situation to make future versions of the program useful as a psychotherapeutic tool.

The basic reason for the absurdities that sometimes occur in dialogues with the interview program is its failure to understand natural language. It responds to language, rather than understanding it. That is, like the paranoid program and the "input" version of artificial neurosis, its general linguistic strategy is to react in fairly inflexible ways to certain "key" words or phrases. Common examples include *father, mother, I should, I feel, I seem, worried,* and the like; idiosyncratic additions such as *Joey, Mafia,* and *spaghetti* are also allowed for. These key words selectively trigger certain types of information processing in the program, whether in the form of "inner thoughts" or "outward expression." This does not matter too much in the "input" neurotic program, since ongoing conversation is not attempted and the input sentence is not even accepted into the belief-system. Even the paranoid program, which does engage in dialogue, is not too badly flawed by its reliance on this "mechanical" model of language-use, since it is precisely characteristic of a paranoid person that he will respond "irrationally" to flare concepts, irrespective of the conversational context (although the program was occasionally diagnosed by the interviewing psychiatrist as *brain-damaged*—literally—because of its linguistic incompetence). However, this crude model of language constitutes a grave drawback to the interview program. And if the paranoid program were to be given more than an *initial* diagnostic interview, it could not rely so heavily on its expectations of particular questions like *What sort of work do you do?* and *Why are you in the hospital?*

Colby has suggested that an essential step in overcoming the cru-

Understanding of Natural Language in Context-Restricted On-Line Dialogues," *Mathematical Biosciences* 1 (1967), pp. 1–25. See also Joseph Weizenbaum, "ELIZA—A Computer Program for the Study of Natural Language Communication Between Man and Machine," *Commun. Assoc. Computing Machinery* 9 (1966), pp. 36–45.

dity of the current man-machine dialogues is for the machine to be provided with—or, still better, to build up for itself—a detailed cognitive model of the person with whom it is communicating.[27] In order to build up such a model through interchanges with the person, the program must initially have an extensive built-in model (or theory) of human psychology in general. Since he made this suggestion, a great advance has occurred in the programming of language-use: Terry Winograd's "Program for Understanding Natural Language."[28] It is impossible even to indicate the nature of this program here; suffice it to say that it is greatly superior to its predecessors, which rely on key words, semantic networks, and the like. And, what is of particular relevance, it "understands" natural language largely by exploiting its reasoning abilities within a cognitive model of its world of action. Since its world of action is restricted to cubes, blocks, and pyramids of various colours, which can be moved and stacked on a table or placed in a box nearby, there is no question of directly "plugging-in" Winograd's program to Colby's program. The point, rather, is that Winograd's program provides some promising insights into precisely how a simulation can use theoretical (and factual) knowledge about a universe of discourse in interpreting natural language statements about that universe. The possibility arises, then, of building Colby's psychological theory of defence mechanisms into a program based on Winograd's model. The result would be a computer simulation of neurosis considerably more powerful than any now in existence.

V CONCLUSION

Some personality theorists believe that "attempts to study personality by observing the behavior of computers programmed by humans to simulate other humans is the crudest form of projection— a most primitive and maladaptive method of defense."[29] If the study of computer models were regarded as a *substitute* for the anxiety-

[27] Colby and Enea, "Heuristic Methods for Computer Understanding of Natural Language," p. 22.

[28] Terry Winograd, *Understanding Natural Language* (Edinburgh Univ. Press, Edinburgh, 1972).

[29] G. S. Blum, "Programming People to Simulate Machines," in Tomkins and Messick, eds., *Computer Simulation of Personality*, pp. 127–57. Quote from p. 127.

ridden personal investigation of other people which until now has provided the prime data-base for theoretical psychology, this response would be perfectly in order. But no such suggestion is involved in the claim that computer simulation can be a useful complement to the psychologist's intuitive theorizing.

Expressing one's theory in the form of a computer program sharpens and clarifies questions even though it does not in itself provide answers to them. For example, Colby was forced to make theoretical decisions as to the relative power of the various defence mechanisms in reducing anxiety and effecting motivational discharge. In principle, of course, these questions could have been as clearly raised by "armchair" theorizing: Freud himself made a number of remarks pertaining to these very issues. But clarity is unavoidable in a programming context, and questions must be given answers.

Theoretical decisions such as these can then be taken as hypotheses about actual psychological functioning, and can be investigated with or without the mediation of a programmed model of the processes concerned. In this sense the program aids in the development of what Imre Lakatos has called a "scientific research programme."[30] Experimental investigations of a broadly "positivist" type have provided some general validation of the Freudian concept of defence mechanisms, but they have not fully justified detailed individual applications of it and nor is it easy to see how they ever could do so.[31] The enormous complexity and perverse idiosyncracy of human personal belief-systems prevent operationalization of "defensive" concepts except at a relatively coarse or trivial level. The structure and complexity of computer programs, by contrast, are well suited to representation both of the general phenomena of defence and of their specific instantiations in particular cases. There is reason to hope that extended clinical studies of (for example) free association, or responses to the therapist's interventions in analysis, can be increasingly fruitful if guided and monitored by reference to the precise theoretical models made available by computer science. Since similar research possibilities in principle exist for theories

[30] Imre Lakatos, "Falsification and the Methodology of Scientific Research Programmes," in Imre Lakatos and Alan Musgrave, eds., *Criticism and the Growth of Knowledge* (Cambridge Univ. Press, Cambridge, 1970), pp. 91–196.

[31] For a recent survey of experimental work relevant to Freud's theory of defence, see Paul Kline, *Fact and Fantasy in Freudian Theory* (Methuen, London, 1972), chap. 8.

concerning any psychological phenomenon, computer simulations have a considerable potential for deepening our understanding of the human mind.

Above all, one must insist on the total irrelevance of objections to the effect that computers cannot *really* defend themselves against anxiety, cannot *really* believe and infer or feel suspicious and afraid. Parameters in computer programs are used to represent theoretical concepts such as "belief" and "anger," which themselves represent the actual phenomena of belief and anger in human minds. More-over, "mistrust," "fear," and "anxiety"—as employed, for instance, in Colby's programmed models of neurosis and paranoia—are not mere labels, but are functional aspects of the program. The theoret-ical interest is not in questions about the felt nature of fear as such, but rather in what difference fear makes to the information process-ing going on—for example, to the paranoiac's interpretation of and reaction to specific remarks from his interlocutor. This functional view of affect is not a monstrous brain-child of overambitious pro-grammers, but an established part of "respectable" psychology. Freud himself was interested not so much in the subjective experience of anxiety as in the cognitive structures and affective monitoring proc-esses contributing to the complex phenomena of defence.

Computer simulations, then, attempt theoretical modelling of psychological function and structure rather than ontological mimicry of mental reality, and it is in these terms alone that they should be assessed. In these terms, programs may be more like paranoia than ravens are like writing-desks. And the question why a program is like paranoia—unlike the Mad Hatter's unanswerable riddle—allows of a precise and definite reply.

Psychoanalytic Theory and Evidence*

WESLEY C. SALMON

The distinction between considerations which are in a broad sense logical and those which are empirical is a fundamental one for the philosophy of science; indeed, this distinction constitutes the basis for differentiating philosophy from the empirical sciences. It is the business of the philosopher of science to investigate and explicate the logical criteria a scientific theory must satisfy and, in cooperation with the empirical scientist, to determine whether a particular theory does satisfy them. Failure to meet these logical criteria would be an insuperable objection against any scientific theory. If it satisfies the logical criteria it must still pass the test of empirical confirmation. The logical criteria are within the domain of philosophy, but the actual empirical confirmation is not. The collection, evaluation, and interpretation of the evidence is strictly the business of the empirical scientist.

It is not the aim of the present essay to formulate and discuss the general philosophical principles which are applicable to all of the empirical sciences. Rather, the attempt will be made to apply some of the more familiar and relatively noncontroversial principles specifically to parts of psychoanalytic theory.[1] The general area of investigation will be the logical relations between observational evidence and hypothesis or theory. No attempt will be made to deal

* This paper originally appeared in *Psychoanalysis, Scientific Method and Philosophy*, ed. Sidney Hook (N. Y. Univ. Press, New York, 1959). Reprinted by kind permission of the author and publisher.

[1] Terminological note: In this essay the term "psychoanalytic theory" will be used to denote the empirical theory in a general way and to distinguish it from psychoanalysis as a therapeutic technique. I make no attempt to state precisely what I take to be the content of psychoanalytic theory—that in itself would be a colossal task. I appeal only to those parts of the theory which are accepted by analytic theorists of a relatively orthodox Freudian kind. "Hypothesis" is used to refer to statements about individual cases; presumably such statements result from the application of the theory to these cases. Hypotheses are not directly verifiable by observation; they are indirectly confirmable on the basis of observational evidence. "Theory" is reserved for the generalizations which are supposed to hold for all cases and which constitute the substance of the scientific discipline. "Logical" is used in a broad enough sense to comprehend both inductive and deductive considerations as well as semantic ones.

comprehensively with the nature of the evidence which supports psychoanalytic theory as a whole. The discussion will take up some restricted but important issues concerning the confirmability of psychoanalytic theories and hypotheses.

I

Freud and his followers have repeatedly emphasized the fundamental role of a principle of determinism in psychoanalytic theory.[2] Since the concept of determinism has had a long and varied philosophical history, it may be useful to distinguish several of the more important philosophical doctrines of determinism, indicate the roles these doctrines have been intended to fulfill, and show how the psychoanalytic principle differs from them in content and function.[3] I hope to show that the philosophical interpretations of determinism are inappropriate to psychoanalytic theory, and I hope to present a formulation which will be appropriate. In reformulating the psychoanalytic principle I am not attempting to state what Freud or any other psychoanalytic theorist had in mind when he referred to a principle of determinism.[4] I shall be attempting to state with reasonable precision a principle which will have the theoretical import required by psychoanalytic theory. This formulation bears directly upon the problem of evidence, the subject of this essay as a whole.

(1)   Philosophers have often taken determinism as an a priori principle. Some of these philosophers have used the principle to circumvent the Humean problem of the justification of induction. To avoid the circularity of using inductive reasoning to establish a principle which would serve to justify induction, the principle of determinism has been regarded as a priori. In psychoanalytic theory there is no problem of the justification of induction; like any other empirical science, it makes use of inductive methods without involve-

[2] Statements to this effect abound. For example, see 1916–17, XV, 28, 49, 106; 1901b, VI, *passim;* and Charles Brenner, *An Elementary Textbook of Psychoanalysis* (Doubleday, New York, 1957), chap. 1.

[3] Two of the most famous classical statements are those of Kant and Laplace: *Immanuel Kant's Critique of Pure Reason,* ed. Norman Kemp Smith (Macmillan, London, 1933), p. 218; P. S. Laplace, *A Philosophical Essay on Probabilities* (Dover, New York, 1949), pp. 3–5.

[4] Quite possibly Freud associated the psychoanalytic principle of determinism with a philosophical doctrine; indeed, he seems to regard determinism as a presupposition of empirical science. See 1916–17, XV, 28, 106–9.

ment in the problem of their justification. The problem of induction is a problem in the philosophy of science, and one that should in my opinion be taken seriously, but it is not a problem in any one of the empirical sciences. Hence, no empirical science need include a special a priori principle to secure for itself a justification of the inductive method.

If the principle of determinism were a priori, either it would be a synthetic a priori metaphysical presupposition of science[5] or it would be an analytic a priori truth of logic. It has been argued effectively by many authors that neither science in general nor any particular science has need of metaphysical presuppositions.[6] On the other hand, if the principle of determinism were a truth of logic it would be tautological and therefore empirically empty. In neither case would it be required as a basic principle within the empirical discipline of psychoanalytic theory; it could be deleted from the theory without affecting the empirical content of the theory in any way.

In psychoanalytic theory the principle of determinism is a posteriori. In Freud's work it is supported by a large body of empirical evidence taken, for example, from the investigation of slips of the tongue or pen, dreams, and neurotic symptoms. Whether or not this evidence can be regarded as conclusive, it is the kind of evidence upon which the principle rests.

(2)   The philosophical doctrine of determinism has often been stated in a very general way which may be rendered somewhat inaccurately as "Every event has a cause." Apart from the fact that determinism in the inanimate world is irrelevant to psychoanalytic theory, there are two important reasons why this sort of formulation misses the psychoanalytic principle. First, it need not be taken as a basic postulate of an empirical science that every event in the range of the subject matter of that science be subject to causal determination and explanation. Even if we adopt the dubious assumption that it is the business of science to discover causal relations, we do not need to postulate beforehand that such relations exist. The most we need is a regulative principle that the discovery of such relations is important to the scientific discipline in question—that it is worth

---

[5] Kant is probably the most important historical representative of this point of view.

[6] Herbert Feigl, "Scientific Method without Metaphysical Presuppositions," *Philosophical Studies* 5, no. 2 (February 1954); Arthur Pap, *Elements of Analytic Philosophy* (Macmillan, New York, 1949), chap. 16.

while hunting for such relations. A regulative principle would be a directive for the conduct of science, not part of the content of a particular science. Whether such relations exist need not be decided beforehand; it may be left to the investigators to see whether they can be found. There is nothing logically peculiar in looking for something even though we cannot be given iron-bound assurance that it exists. We merely need to know that it would be worth finding if it did exist. Of course, we would not undertake the search if we knew ahead of time that the object did not exist. But we are certainly justified in the search if we simply do not know whether it exists or not. Furthermore, even if it were not true that every event is subject to complete causal determination, it might still be true that some very interesting causal relations exist. The investigation of these relations would unquestionably form an appropriate part of a scientific discipline.

Second, psychoanalytic theory is not content merely with the statement that certain events, such as slips of the tongue, have some cause or other. For psychoanalysis it is important that these causes be psychic causes. If such events were completely determined by physiological causes, this would not be sufficient for psychoanalytic theory. Psychoanalytic theory holds that such events as slips, dreams, and neurotic symptoms have as their causes such occurrences as conscious or unconscious impulses, wishes, desires, etc.[7] This point will be discussed more thoroughly below; here it is sufficient to point out that the psychoanalytic principle specifies the *kinds* of causes involved whereas a philosophical principle would not.

(3) The philosophical doctrine of determinism has often been related to ethical issues, and often in conflicting ways. It has sometimes been argued that determinism excludes freedom and moral responsibility; at other times it has been held that determinism is a necessary condition of freedom and moral responsibility. Philosophical disputes of this sort are perennial; there is no need to enter upon them here.[8] We need only remark that such ethical issues are irrelevant to the methodology and empirical content of psychoanalytic theory. We cannot countenance the acceptance or rejection of a fun-

---

[7] Antony Flew, "Motives and the Unconscious" in *Minnesota Studies in the Philosophy of Science*, Vol. I, ed. Herbert Feigl and Michael Scriven (Univ. of Minn. Press, Minneapolis, 1956).

[8] For discussions of this topic see *Determinism and Freedom in the Age of Modern Science*, ed. Sidney Hook (N.Y. Univ. Press, New York, 1958).

damental principle of an empirical theory on grounds of alleged desirable or undesirable ethical consequences.

(4) In philosophy of science the controversy over determinism has often been a controversy over the kinds of laws that are fundamental in science. Those who reject determinism hold that statistical laws are fundamental and that events are determined probabilistically. At least, the opponent of determinism holds we have no good ground for asserting that deterministic laws must be fundamental and that all probabilistic relations must be explainable in terms of deterministic ones. The determinist, on the other hand, maintains that all events are governed by unexceptionable and non-statistical laws. We may use statistical laws because it would be impractical to trace out all the causal determinants of some events or because of our ignorance of some of the causal laws, but the determinist maintains that complete causal determination obtains in the real world nevertheless.

The issue of determinism is widely discussed in the philosophy of quantum mechanics, but it is doubtful that psychoanalytic theory needs to make a commitment on this sort of issue. It is one thing to deny that certain events are completely haphazard and unrelated to previous events. It is quite another to claim that events of a certain kind are related to their predecessors by deterministic laws. It is a distinct possibility that there are stable probability relations between events and their predecessors in which the degree of probability is sometimes high. There would hardly be grounds for complaint if psychoanalytic theories could be shown to be well-confirmed statements of probabilistic relations which would enable us to explain any event as following from certain predecessors with a high degree of probability. In such a case we would have every right to deny that events such as slips, dreams, and neurotic symptoms are haphazard and meaningless, and this is what the psychoanalytic principle of determinism is concerned to deny.

The foregoing discussion has not been intended as an exhaustive survey of philosophical principles, doctrines, or controversies; it has been intended to show that these are quite irrelevant to the psychoanalytic principle of determinism. We might characterize the psychoanalytic principle provisionally in the following way: it is an empirical postulate subject to confirmation or disconfirmation by empirical evidence; it asserts the existence of definite relations among events; but the relation may be either deterministic or probabilistic; and it specifies that the "causes" involved are of a rather specific sort. Perhaps it is misleading even to call a principle that fits this description a "principle of determinism"; however, the usage is so well established it would be futile to recommend a change at this point. It is better to emphasize the difference between philosophical determinism and psychoanalytic determinism and hope that confusion will be minimized. It is probably advisable always to speak of psychic determinism when the latter principle is involved.

There is a good deal to be done before we can state the principle of psychic determinism in a satisfactory form. It is not sufficient to say that all psychic events have psychic causes, even if we understand the statement probabilistically. In many cases, at least, when we apply the principle of psychic determinism, only the determinants are psychic while the event which is probabilistically determined is an event of behavior—a movement of the body, for example. On the other hand, we do not wish to say that every event of human behavior has psychic determinants; blushing has, but flushing often has not. Nor will it do to say merely that voluntary behavior has psychic determinants. In the ordinary sense of "voluntary," such behavior as a nervous tic is not considered voluntary, yet we would hold that it has psychic determinants. Rather, what we want to say is that the organism's responses to stimuli fall into two classes; first, responses which are mediated only by constitutional mechanisms, i.e., mechanisms which cannot be modified by stimuli (except perhaps of a physically traumatic sort), and second, responses which are not thus mediated by constitutional mechanisms. Psychoanalytic theory says that there are psychic mechanisms in such cases, whether or not there are neurophysiological mechanisms. Roughly, if there are neurophysiological mechanisms, they can be modified by experience.

Stimuli and responses are publicly observable phenomena.[9] In addition, there may be certain privately observable psychic phenomena such as conscious wishes, feelings, and emotions; this is a matter of controversy with which we need not become involved here. However, on any theory whatsoever, unconscious psychic phenomena

[9] This seems to be the point of departure adopted by Ellis, who, incidentally, emphasized the probabilistic character of his reformulations. Albert Ellis, "An Operational Reformulation of some of the Basic Principles of Psychoanalysis" in Feigl and Scriven, eds., op. cit.

are not directly observable by anyone, subject or other observer. They are inferred entities or events.

If we begin by thinking of the organism as a container whose surface and environment we can observe but whose interior cannot be directly observed, then our problem can be regarded as that of understanding the output of the organism.[10] It becomes obvious that the output is conditioned by the input; there is a relationship between stimulus and response. In some cases the relationship is constant— a certain type of stimulus is followed by a certain type of response with a high degree of probability, unless a definite physical pathology can be discovered. In such cases we have simple reflexes and the like—stimulus and response are mediated by a constitutional mechanism. Perhaps it is possible to give a completely physiological explanation of this mechanism; whether it is or not is beside the point here. In other cases a psychic mechanism can readily be found; at least, the organism can report the existence of such a mechanism which he claims is an object of his immediate awareness. "He called me a fool, and this made me angry so I left the room." Conscious anger is the mechanism according to this report. It may be desirable to investigate this mechanism further, since being called a fool does not always lead to conscious anger, and conscious anger under these circumstances does not always lead to leaving the room, but at least we have a good start toward an understanding of the behavior when we realize that conscious anger occurred. When behavior occurs which is not the result of a stimulus setting off a constitutional mechanism and which cannot be explained in terms of a psychic mechanism which the subject can report, then, according to the principle of psychic determinism, there is an unconscious psychic mechanism which causes the behavior in question. The existence of this unconscious psychic mechanism cannot be established by direct observation (including introspection); it can only be inferred on the basis of indirect evidence. In order for the principle of psychic determinism to be empirically meaningful, then, it is necessary that there be independent evidence for the existence of this psychic mechanism, apart from the specific item of behavior it is supposed to explain. If no such independent evidence were possible, then the

[10] For a discussion of such models see Egon Brunswik, *The Conceptual Framework of Psychology, International Encyclopedia of Unified Science* (Univ. of Chicago Press, Chicago, 1955), Vol. I, no. 10, pt. IV. See also Otto Fenichel, *The Psychoanalytic Theory of Neurosis* (Norton, New York, 1945), pt. I-A.

assertion of the existence of the mechanism would add nothing to the statement of the behavior to be explained. Other parts of psychoanalytic theory indicate what the independent evidence is. The theory gives a limited list of inferred entities such as unconscious feelings, desires, impulses, conflicts, and defense mechanisms. In some cases, at least, the theory states that such entities are created (with a high degree of probability) under certain specifiable conditions. The occurrence of such conditions constitutes independent inductive evidence for the existence of the entity. Furthermore, according to the theory, if one of these unconscious psychic entities exists, it is possible under specifiable conditions to elicit a certain kind of conscious entity (which may go under the same name without the qualification "unconscious"). Free association, hypnosis, and narco-synthesis are ways of eliciting the conscious entity. It is not that the subject becomes aware of an unconscious entity—there is a sense in which this is impossible by definition. Rather, according to the theory, the occurrence of the conscious entity (or the report of it if one insists upon excluding introspective evidence) under the specified conditions constitutes inductive evidence for the existence of the inferred entity at an earlier time. Other items of behavior such as slips, dreams, and neurotic symptoms constitute further inductive evidence for the existence of the inferred entity. It may be, and often is, the case that none of these items of evidence is by itself very conclusive, but we must keep in mind that inductive inferences often involve a concatenation of evidence each item of which is quite inconclusive. Nevertheless, the whole body of such evidence may well be conclusive.

In view of the preceding discussion, then, we may attempt a formulation of the principle of psychic determinism. It will be quite different from any formulation of a philosophical doctrine of determinism.

Every item of human behavior constitutes indirect inductive evidence concerning the inferred mechanisms by which the organism mediates between stimulus and response. Particularly, behavior which cannot be explained on the basis of constitutional mechanisms alone constitutes indirect inductive evidence for the existence of conscious or unconscious psychic mechanisms for which other indirect inductive evidence is also theoretically available. In short, no item of behavior is inductively irrelevant as evidence concerning the mecha-

nisms by which the organism mediates between stimulus and re-sponse.

I offer the foregoing formulation, tentatively, as an adequate statement of the principle of psychic determinism. Whether this is what psychoanalytic theorists have always meant is beside the point. It is offered as an empirically verifiable statement which will fulfill the required function in psychoanalytic theory. It is empirically verifiable in the sense that it asserts the existence of certain objective probability relations. These relations are fundamental to psychoanalytic theory.

II

In the preceding section I have spoken of psychoanalytic theory as a theory of the mechanisms which mediate between stimulus and response. It is a theory which postulates the existence of certain unobservable events, entities, and mechanisms. In that section I spoke of indirect inductive evidence for the existence and nature of these unobservables. The charge has sometimes been made that all of this is vacuous because the relationship between observables and unobservables is stated in such a way that *any* evidence supports *any* hypothesis about the unobservables. In this section I wish to examine such criticism.

The kind of situation I shall take up is this. A subject X is observed by a psychoanalyst. On the basis of his observation of X and on the basis of psychoanalytic theory the psychoanalyst hypothesizes that X has a certain unconscious feeling. For example, from his knowledge of X's childhood he may hypothesize that X has an unresolved oedipal conflict. On the basis of this hypothesis he may derive the conclusion that X has unconscious hostility toward his father. This latter statement is another hypothesis, for unconscious hostility cannot be observed directly. When it comes to confirming this hypothesis, trouble may arise. Suppose X is observed to treat his father with a great deal of affection and solicitude. Rather than withdrawing the hypothesis that X has unconscious hostility toward his father, the psychoanalyst may say that X also has unconscious fear of hostility and exhibits behavior of the opposite extreme in defense against his own feelings of hostility. At this point the critic will very likely rise in objection and say that the psychoanalyst is making his hypothesis about unobservables immune to any negative observational evidence; hence the hypothesis is empty. If affectionate behavior is not evidence against hostility, the critic might say, then nothing could be.

If it were true that the hypothesis is compatible with any conceivable evidence, then it would be empirically empty and thus useless from the point of view of empirical science. In order to be nontautological a hypothesis must be falsifiable in principle. If it is impossible consistently to describe observable conditions which would, if they occurred, falsify or render improbable a psychoanalytic hypothesis, then the hypothesis could not be considered an empirical one.

There are at least two ways to answer the objection in the specific instance cited above. First, we might point out that overt hostility and extreme affection and solicitude do not exhaust the possible modes of behavior of X toward his father. The modes of response cover a continuum ranging from the one extreme to the other and including more moderate forms of behavior such as appropriate filial affection, indifference, and covertly hostile neglect. One way to answer the above objection is to maintain that behavior at either extreme of the continuum is evidence for the existence of hostility, while the more moderate forms would constitute evidence against the hypothesis. This answer can be made rather plausible by citing a great deal of clinical and everyday evidence for the fact that behavior at one extreme of a continuum often replaces that of the other extreme.

A second and better answer can be given. Rather than maintaining that a few restricted items of behavior can constitute conclusive evidence for or against the hypothesis, we can point out that a large range of facts is relevant to the hypothesis and the hypothesis must be judged on the weight of total evidence. Any single item of behavior or any small sample may be compatible with the hypothesis that X has unconscious hostility. We know that conscious hostility can be expressed and handled in a wide variety of ways. According to psychoanalytic theory, unconscious hostility can be dealt with in an even wider variety of ways. The unobserved mechanisms are extremely complex, and this means that the variety of modes of response is large. But it does not mean that every total behavior pattern is compatible with the hypothesis of unconscious hostility. It does mean that a good deal of evidence is required to determine whether the unconscious hostility exists, and this evidence must be taken in conjunction with a complex set of theories and hypotheses. A dialectically clever psychoanalyst might be able to argue rather convincingly that any given behavior pattern is compatible with any hypothesis concerning unconscious entities, but such forensics are no part of psychoanalytic theory and are not sanctioned by it.

What, then, is the character of the total evidence bearing upon the hypothesis that X has unconscious hostility? What counts as evidence for the hypothesis, and, more important, what would count as evidence against? It is, of course, impossible to give a complete and detailed answer to these questions, but it is not too difficult to give a fairly clear indication of what the answer must be. Here are some kinds of relevant considerations. How does X generally deal with anger and hostility? Does he express conscious anger or does he suppress it? Do situations which would arouse conscious anger in most people arouse conscious anger in X? If X generally avoids the expression of conscious anger and tends not to feel conscious anger in situations which would ordinarily arouse conscious anger, then this would tend to confirm the hypothesis that X's hostility will be unconscious if he has any. On the other hand, if X does not show tendencies to suppress and repress anger, that would tend to count against the hypothesis. Does X have dreams in which violence occurs, and in which the object of the violence is associated by X with his father? Does X make slips of the tongue which are associated with anger toward or abuse of his father? Does X "unwittingly" hurt his father's feelings? Does X "accidentally" break things belonging to his father? In the process of psychoanalysis does X develop conscious hostility toward his father? If the answers to all the foregoing sorts of questions are negative, then the hypothesis of unconscious hostility toward his father is disconfirmed; if there are a fairly large number of affirmative answers, then the hypothesis tends to be highly confirmed.

If criteria like those roughly indicated above are applied to a large number of subjects and it is found that with a high degree of probability a subject with a certain type of background turns out to have unconscious hostility toward his father, this tends to confirm the larger theory which would yield the prediction of hostility in such cases. When the larger theory has been confirmed, then the very fact that the subject X has a certain background lends weight to the hypothesis of his unconscious hostility. Indeed, if the larger theory is well enough confirmed, this may be the greatest evidence there is for the hypothesis of unconscious hostility. Then, the fact that a subject Y whose background is similar to that of X developed conscious hostility toward his father in the course of psychoanalytic treatment will lend weight to the hypothesis that X has unconscious hostility.

The ideal that the theory attempts to approach is, of course, to be able to predict with a high degree of reliability which individuals will have unconscious hostility toward their fathers and which will not, and then to predict, with respect to those who do have such hostility, the exact mode in which they will deal with it. Some progress has been made in this direction, but a good deal is left to be done.

The whole point of this section of this essay is well illustrated by an example taken from Freud's work. In Chapter IV of *The Interpretation of Dreams* Freud attempts to defend his thesis that all dreams are wish fulfillments. He explains how many dreams which appear not to be wish fulfillments can be shown to be wish fulfillments upon analysis. But there is one type of dream that he calls "counterwish dreams." These can be explained as wish fulfillments only by interpreting them as fulfilling the wish to produce a dream which does not fulfill any wish, that is, as fulfilling the wish to refute the theory that all dreams are wish fulfillments. The critic of psychoanalytic theory may look upon this as almost a paradigm of the interpretation of any evidence, however adverse, as compatible with or even supportive to psychoanalytic theory. Surely, the critic might say, the hypothesis that every dream is a wish fulfillment is a tautology if we are allowed to count as wish fulfillment dreams any dream which cannot be the fulfillment of any other wish than the wish to have a dream which is not a wish fulfillment. Any possible evidence contrary to the theory is thus automatically made compatible; negative instances are automatically transformed into positive instances.

Such a criticism would be superficial and unjustified. First, we must note that the wish to refute a scientific theory is a genuine wish in every sense of the word. It would be an unexplained peculiarity in the theory if it held that this particular type of wish is somehow incapable of being expressed in a dream. When we consider the emotional fervor that rose in opposition to Freud's theories during his lifetime, and when we consider, in terms of psychoanalytic theory, how important it must be to patients in psychoanalysis to deny the existence of certain wishes, such an exception would seem even stranger. The wish to deny the thesis that all dreams are wish fulfillments is no casual wish. However, this does not answer the critic's charge. In order to answer his criticism we must state what would constitute evidence against the theory: First, if one of these dreams which cannot be explained as any other kind of wish fulfillment were to occur to someone who had never heard of Freud's theory, this would be most damaging. Second, if a counterwish dream were to occur to someone who had not been negatively inclined toward Freud's theory, that would count as negative evidence. Freud points out carefully that every such counterwish dream occurred to someone who gave ample independent evidence of being negatively disposed toward the theory. In particular, these dreams were had by persons hearing Freud's lectures for the first time and reacting negatively to them, and by patients in analytic treatment who were experiencing strong resistance. Freud said he could almost predict when a patient would have such a dream. Third, if such a dream occurred to someone who was negatively disposed toward Freud's theory, but at a time when the issue was not under consideration, that also would count as negative evidence. Freud explicitly states that events of the previous day constitute the occasion for a dream. Furthermore, he points out that oftentimes the counterwish dreams occur the very night after the individual first heard Freud's theory. In other cases, perhaps, this happens when the issue has arisen during the day. But, according to the theory, these dreams can occur only to those who vehemently reject the theory and only when the day preceding the dream has occasioned resistance to the theory. Such a dream, occurring under any other circumstances, must count as negative evidence.

Psychoanalytic theory has been discussed as a theory of the unobservable mechanisms which mediate between stimulus and response in the human organism. According to the theory the mechanisms are complex, and they undergo changes which constitute a complex history. The main point of this essay has been to indicate the wide range of evidence which is relevant to the inference concerning these mechanisms, and to show that it is in principle possible to state the kind of evidence which should count as positive and that which should count as negative. In so far as this kind of case can be made for the various parts of psychoanalytic theory, to that extent the theory is shown to be empirically meaningful. Whether it is empirically *confirmed* is an entirely different question, and one which can be answered only by empirical investigation.

Freud, Kepler, and the Clinical Evidence

CLARK GLYMOUR

I

Whether or not we should think psychoanalysis a reasonable theory, or even a theory at all in the usual sense, depends on what we think to be the evidence for and against it, and that, in turn, depends on how we think theory and evidence go together generally. On one very influential view of scientific testing what is required in order to obtain evidence for or against psychoanalysis, as with any other theory, is that we deduce from it some claim regarding the correlation of two or more properties—which are of a kind that can be identified without using any psychoanalytic hypotheses—and then subject this claim to the rigors of statistical hypothesis testing. This strategy has been used to test psychoanalysis with very mixed and unpromising results.[1] For several reasons, analysts tend to oppose evaluating their theory solely on the basis of such evidence. In the first place, they claim that the experimentalists' bias for easily manipulated and easily controlled factors results in an undue emphasis on testing psychoanalytic hypotheses that are peripheral to the main tenets of the theory; even worse, the hypotheses tested by experimentalists are often no more than surrogates for the genuine article, and inferences from the falsity of such ersatz hypotheses to the falsity of psychoanalysis are not legitimate.[2] Further, the procedures of experimental psychologists are largely framed within a hypothetico-deductive view of theory testing which, when experiment and theory conflict, does not inform us whether the fault is with some readily abandoned thesis or with the most central tenets of the theory. But the most frequent and most controversial complaint is that evaluations of psychoanalysis which consider only experimental results ignore the evidence available from clinical observations. Analysts contend that the observation of neurotics receiving therapy, of children,

[1] See R. Sears, *A Survey of Objective Studies of Psychoanalysis* (Social Science Research Council, New York, 1943).

[2] These problems and others are discussed in, for example, D. Mackinnon and Wm. Dukes, "Repression" in L. Postman, ed., *Psychology in the Making* (Knopf, New York, 1962).

and particularly the contents of psychoanalytic case studies, provide the principal sources of evidence for psychoanalysis. Their view was put very bluntly by Freud himself. In the early thirties an American psychologist, S. Rosenzweig, carried out a series of experiments which he thought provided experimental support for psychoanalytic claims about repression. Rosenzweig sent a report of his results to Freud, who replied as follows:

> My dear Sir
>
> I have examined your experimental studies for the verification of the psychoanalytic assertions with interest. I cannot put much value on these confirmations because the wealth of reliable observations on which these assertions rest make them independent of experimental verification. Still, it can do no harm.
>
> Sincerely yours
>
> Freud[3]

By contrast, I think the majority of experimental psychologists who have an opinion regard psychoanalysis as nearly bereft of evidence, and that is because they think clinical evidence worthless. That opinion is evidenced by the title of Sears's survey, a book which does not discuss a single psychoanalytic case study. H. J. Eysenck's statement is unusually vivid but not atypical in its conclusions:

> What then is the evidence on which psychoanalysis is based? Essentially it is clinical rather than experimental . . . Suffice it to remember that clinical work is often very productive of theories and hypotheses, but weak on proof and verification; that in fact the clinical method by itself cannot produce such proof because investigations are carried out for the avowed purpose of aiding the patient, not of putting searching questions to nature. Even when a special experiment is carefully planned to test the adequacy of a given hypothesis there often arise almost insuperable difficulties in ruling out irrelevant factors and in isolating the desired effect; in clinical work such isolation is all but impossible. The often-heard claim that 'psychoanalytic hypotheses are tested on the couch' (i.e., the couch on which the patient lies during the analytic session) shows a clear misunderstanding of what is meant in science by 'testing' hypotheses. We can no more test Freudian hypotheses 'on

[3] Quoted from D. Shakow and D. Rapaport, *The Influence of Freud on American Psychology* (World Pub., Cleveland, 1968), p. 129.

the couch' than we can adjudicate between the rival hypotheses of Newton and Einstein by going to sleep under an apple tree.[4]

This is not much of an argument, but it is a common enough view. It stems in part, I think, from what are genuine drawbacks to clinical testing; for example, the problem of ensuring that a patient's responses are not *simply* the result of suggestion, or the feeling, not without foundation, that the "basic data" obtained from clinical sessions—the patient's introspective reports of his own feelings, reports of dreams, memories of childhood and adolescence—are less reliable than we should like. But neither of these considerations seems sufficient to reject the clinical method generally, although they may of course be sufficient to warrant us in rejecting particular clinical results. Clinicians can hopefully be trained so as not to elicit by suggestion the expected responses from their patients; patients' reports can sometimes be checked independently, as in the case of memories, and even when they cannot be so checked there is no good reason to distrust them generally. But I think condemnations like Eysenck's derive from a belief about clinical testing which goes considerably beyond either of these points: the belief that clinical sessions, even cleansed of suggestibility and of doubts about the reliability of patients' reports, can involve no rational strategy for testing theories. The reasons for such an opinion are not difficult to surmise. Most theories, and psychoanalysis is no exception, deal with putative entities and processes which cannot be identified readily, which are not "observable." It may well be thought that the view that psychoanalytic hypotheses are tested on the couch involves the claim that such theoretical entities and processes suddenly and mysteriously become discernible within the analytic hour. Further, although Freud wrote a good deal about method, there is still no treatment of clinical testing which compares in clarity, let alone detail, with standard accounts of statistical hypothesis testing and experimental design. Without such a treatment, clinical testing is bound to seem mysterious and arbitrary to those nurtured on statistical methods.

I think that Eysenck's claim is wrong. I think there is a rational strategy for testing important parts of psychoanalysis, a strategy that relies almost exclusively on clinical evidence; moreover, I think this strategy is immanent in at least one of Freud's case studies, that

[4] H. J. Eysenck, *The Uses and Abuses of Psychology* (Penguin, London, 1959), p. 228–29.

of the Rat Man. Indeed, I want to make a much bolder claim. The strategy involved in the Rat Man case is essentially the same as a strategy very frequently used in testing physical theories. Further, this strategy, while simple enough, is more powerful than the hypothetico-deductive-falsification strategy described for us by so many philosophers of science.

Before trying to make my case, I would enter two cautions. I am not proposing a theory of the confirmation of theories, only of their testing. I do not know how one puts tests together to establish any degree of confirmation, or if one does at all. Further, I am certainly not claiming that there is good clinical evidence for Freud's theory; I am claiming that if one wants to test psychoanalysis, there is a reasonable strategy for doing so which can be, and to some degree has been, effected through clinical sessions.

II

When considering the objection that psychoanalytic procedures do not provide experimental evidence, Freud sometimes compared psychoanalysis with astronomy: there, too, we must rely on observation since we cannot manipulate and control the heavens. Very well, how do astronomers test their theories? Let us consider the theory comprised of Kepler's laws and their consequences. The laws are these:

1. Each planet and comet moves in a fixed plane in which the centre of the sun is situated; the orbit of such a body is a conic section.
2. For any such body, the ratio of the space described about the sun in an interval of time (i.e., the area of the conic section swept out by the position vector with the sun as origin) to that interval of time is a constant particular to the body.
3. For any two such bodies, moving in closed orbits, the ratio of the squares or their orbital periods is equal to the ratio of the cubes of their average distances from the sun.

Certainly it is very implausible to say, as some philosophers seem recently to have said, that astronomers can look through their telescopes and just *see* the orbits of planets, or their periods or their distances from the sun. And even if we are willing to say such a thing, that is not how astronomers report their observations. What astronomers have claimed to observe, at least in contexts where we and they would agree that Kepler's laws might be tested, are right ascensions and declinations—that is, the locations of a planet on the celestial sphere—at various times, as well as the locations of other bodies (such as the sun) at the same or related times. How are these observations to be used to compare the actual orbits and periods with those required by Kepler's laws? On the deductive account of theory testing they are not to be so used at all. Instead, one deduces from Kepler's laws (together with Euclidean geometry, etc.) some "purely observational" statement; in this case perhaps some statement roughly of the form "If the planet is located at x,y (on the celestial sphere) at t, then it is located at $f(x,y, t', t)$ at t'," where 'f' is some explicit function. This "observational consequence" is then compared with observations in order to test the theory. The disadvantages of such a strategy are well known. Chief among them is the fact that it does not enable us to say anything about which of Kepler's laws are tested by a set of observations. For example, observations of the positions of Mars at various times clearly should not of themselves count as a test of Kepler's third law, but on the deductive account there seems no way to make this exclusion. It is of no avail to claim that the third law is not needed for the deduction of the "observation statement" since we can trivially reformulate the theory so that none of Kepler's laws are required for the deduction.

If we look at the astronomical writings concerned to show how to compare Kepler's theory with astronomical observations we find a rather different strategy employed.[5] From Kepler's laws there are deduced a vast body of relations among geometrical quantities associated with an orbit. It is shown that given the values of six quantities, called the elements of the orbit, by using various of these relations one can compute the complete orbit of a body in three-dimensional space and also its location in the orbit at any time. Further, again by using these derived relations, which we must think of as forming an integral part of Kepler's theory, we can from as few as three suitably chosen observations of a body compute the elements of its orbit. The strategy for testing Kepler's laws which emerges from these considerations is then roughly as follows: There

[5] My remarks here and subsequently on this topic are based on Karl F. Gauss's *Theory of the Motion of Heavenly Bodies Moving About the Sun in Conic Sections* (Dover, New York, 1963), and on modern treatments of the orbit problem. I have not read Kepler.

is a set of quantities, in this case the locations of planets on the celestial sphere, which can normally be determined to good approximation without using (or without assuming the truth of) any of the hypotheses which form Kepler's theory.[6] From a set of values of these *non-theoretical* quantities we can by using certain of the relations occurring in Kepler's theory compute values for other, *theoretical,* quantities such as the orbital elements, period, and so on. Of course it will not necessarily be the case that every set of observations permits the calculation of every theoretical quantity. From values of these theoretical quantities we can, again by using the relations of the theory, compute the values required of other observations. Actually it is important to look at this last step in reverse. From one set of observations we can compute the values of various theoretical quantities by using some of the laws of the theory; we can do the same for another, different, set of observations. If the theory is correct, then the results must be the same in both cases. We can think of the strategy of testing as a kind of logical pincer movement: for various of the laws asserting the equality of two quantities, observed values of non-theoretical quantities enable us to use some of the laws of the theory to compute values for the two quantities independently. Our results must then either instantiate the law in question or contradict it; in either case the law has been tested. The crucial point is that *which* laws we can perform this pincer movement on is determined by (a) the other laws in the theory and (b) the particular set of observed quantities. For example, if we have, say, half a dozen complete, suitably chosen observations of the position of Mars on the celestial sphere we can use these data to test many of the relations of Kepler's theory via a logical pincer: we use one triple of observations to calculate a quantity on one side of an equality and another triple of observations to calculate a quantity on the other side of the equality. But we cannot so test Kepler's third law using only these observations. Using either of the triples we can calculate Mars's period and average distance from the sun,

[6] I have discussed this distinction in "On Some Patterns of Reduction" *Philosophy of Science* 37 (September 1970) pp. 340–53. I there refer to it as a distinction between "primary" and "secondary" quantities, a terminology which seems to me now to be cumbersome and unrevealing. I think very nearly the same distinction is introduced by J. Sneed in his recent book, *The Logical Structure of Physical Theories,* (Reidel, Dordrecht, Netherlands, 1971), as a distinction between "theoretical" and "non-theoretical" quantities. Both his terminology and his discussion of the distinction seem to be superior to mine.

but we cannot calculate the ratio of Mars's period to that of any other planet.

I do not suppose that all of this is intelligible; perhaps more of it will be if we consider a simple, entirely contrived example. Suppose that *a, b,* and *e* are three quantities which we know how to determine without using the theory below

1) $c = R(a)$
2) $d = S(b)$
3) $e = T(f)$
4) $f = U(c)$
5) $d = V(c)$

where *c, d,* and *f* are *theoretical* quantities and *R, S, T, U, V* are explicit functions and, for simplicity, we will assume all of them to have inverses. Suppose now that by performing some physical operations we obtain values *A* and *B* for quantities *a* and *b* respectively. Which of the hypotheses are tested by this pair of measurements? It is easy to see that 1, 2, and 5 are tested but hypotheses 3 and 4 are not. From *A* and *B* using hypothesis 1 we obtain

$$C = R(A)$$

and using 2 we obtain

$$D = S(B).$$

The derived pair of values *C, D,* is either in accord with or else contradicts hypothesis 5, accordingly as $D = V(C)$ or not, and therefore provides a test of that hypothesis. In a similar way, from these same data, we can test hypotheses 1 and 2. By using only measured values of quantities *a* and *b* and whatever hypotheses we please we cannot test hypotheses 3 and 4. For given only values of *a* and *b* there is only *one* way to compute a value of *f*, and that is by using hypothesis 4; similarly, there is only *one* way to compute a value of *e*, and that is by using 3.

If we had measured and obtained values *A* and *E* for quantities *a* and *e* respectively, then our measurements would provide a test of hypotheses 1, 3, and 4 but not of 2 and 5. Again, if we have *B* and *E* as values of *b* and *e,* respectively, then we can test every hypothesis except hypothesis 1.

A satisfactory account of this testing strategy must do a number of things. It must provide a general and precise account of when an arbitrary hypothesis within an arbitrary theory is tested by an arbitrary set of data; it must determine whether, and under what conditions, we can regard those hypotheses used in testing a hypothesis as themselves tested indirectly; it must combine with a theory of error to inform us as to what imprecision is introduced into the computed values of theoretical quantities by imprecision in the values of non-theoretical quantities or by the use of approximation procedures in computing the values of theoretical quantities. I cannot yet give such an account but I am convinced that one can be given. For the present I wish merely to point out that there is here a discernible strategy instances of which we should be able to recognize when we come across them, and that the strategy is apparently superior to the deductivist one for several reasons. It is superior because it permits us to test particular laws, or at least particular subsets of the laws, of a theory, and because it sometimes permits us, when theory and experiment conflict, to identify the faulty hypotheses simply by the use of Mill's methods.[7] Even more, the strategy reveals an apparently unnoticed reason for demanding that our theories be tested on a variety of different kinds of instances, and it provides a framework for understanding the role of approximations in testing theories.

I do not think that the use of this strategy is confined to Kepler's laws, or to astronomy, or even to observational sciences. I think it is frequently a central part of the over-all argument for or against a theory, even in the experimental sciences. Its use is particularly apparent whenever an experimenter attempts to test a theory containing quantities which the experimenter does not know how to determine save by measuring other quantities and computing using some of the very hypotheses to be tested. More pertinent to our topic, which in case it be forgotten is Freud, I see no reason why essentially the same strategy cannot be carried out in testing theories the hypotheses of which are not quantitative. In such cases the theory will not relate quantities but, let us say, states of affairs.

By a state of affairs I intend at least such states of persons as those of consciously feeling guilt, having a cough, feeling compelled to

---

[7] To see how one might use Mill's methods suppose that in the above example we do three sets of measurements: I) of a and b; II) of a and e; III) of b and e. Suppose further that I and II conflict with the theory, but III does not. I tests hypotheses 1, 2, and 5; II tests hypotheses 1, 3, and 4. Agreement says 1 is at fault. III tests 2, 3, 4, and 5 and agrees with them, so Difference says 1 at fault.

utter certain ritual phrases, having a repressed wish, having had a sexual conflict with one's father, and so on. The distinction between theoretical and non-theoretical states of affairs seems to me as intelligible, if not perhaps as precise, as the distinction between theoretical and non-theoretical quantities. Some of the states of persons which Freud describes are of a kind that we might reasonably expect to be able to discriminate without making use of any psychoanalytic hypotheses; other states Freud discriminates only through the use of psychoanalytic theory applied to discernible states of the first kind. All unconscious states are of the second kind, that is, theoretical, and most conscious states and overt actions can reasonably be regarded as non-theoretical for psychoanalysis.

A Freudian application of the testing strategy I have described would, then, go roughly as follows: From non-theoretical states of a patient observed in a clinical setting, other states—whether themselves theoretical or non-theoretical—are inferred by using psychoanalytic hypotheses. Hypotheses which claim that these inferred states obtain only if other states obtain are then tested directly by independently determining, either by theoretical or by non-theoretical means, whether the other states do in fact obtain. The hypotheses used in the theoretical determinations involved in such a test are themselves tested indirectly. The hypotheses of psychoanalytic theory will permit us to infer some states of affairs from others, and we can, just as in the quantitative case, effect a pincer strategy to attempt to determine independently whether the states of affairs related by a conditional or biconditional sentence obtain.

However vague this may be, it is not impossibly so. I think the strategy is clear enough so that we know what it would be like to have a precise philosophical explication of it, even if we have in fact none to give. And that clarity is sufficient, I hope, to enable us to recognize the strategy when it appears in Freud's case studies, and to recognize its similarity with quantitative cases. It is true that Freud nowhere explicitly described such a strategy, although in at least one place he did come close,[8] but this is no objection to the thesis that

---

[8] In "Psychoanalysis and the Establishment of the Facts in Legal Proceedings": "And now, Gentlemen, let us return to the association experiment. In the kind of experiment we have referred to so far, it was the person under examination who explained to us the origin of his reactions, and the experiments, if they are subject to this condition, will be of no interest from the point of view of judicial procedure. But how would it be if we were to make a change in our planning of the experiment? Might we not proceed as one does in solving

the strategy is implicit in his case studies. Physicists are notoriously bad at describing their methodology and the epistemic features of their theories; there is no reason to expect a greater accuracy from psychologists. It is not even necessary that Freud used this strategy intentionally, either in the case as it actually developed or in his written account. The essential point is that in the published case study—which closely follows the clinical notes—data sufficient to test certain analytic hypotheses are presented, and the inferential steps necessary to test these hypotheses are exactly the steps Freud traces out in his discussion.

III

I think that something like the strategy I have tried to describe can be teased out of Freud's Rat Man case. More than with other case studies, perhaps, the central interpretations which Freud offers in this case are law-governed. That is, they are backed by appeal to generalizations regarding the states of affairs concerned. The generalizations are typically not the more esoteric claims of Freud's metapsychology, but instead are relatively less exciting "clinical hypotheses", e.g., that obsessive-compulsives are invariably sexually precocious. It is chiefly these clinical hypotheses which I think are tested, by the strategy I have proposed, in Freud's case study. Of course, even here it is not always entirely clear when Freud's inferences from a non-theoretical state of affairs to a theoretical one are warranted by some general lawlike claim in contrast to those cases in which the inference is only warranted by the fact that it makes a plausible story.

---

an equation which involves several quantities, where one can take any one of them as the starting point—by making *either* the *a or* the *b* into the *x* we are looking for. Up to now in our experiments it has been the *complex* that has been unknown to us. We have used stimulus-words selected at random, and the subject under examination has revealed to us the complex brought to expression by those stimulus-words. But let us now set about it differently. Let us take a complex that is *known* to us and ourselves react to it with stimulus-words deliberately chosen; and let us then transfer the *x* to the person who is reacting. Will it then be possible to decide, from the way in which he reacts, whether the complex we have chosen is also present in him? You can see that this way of planning the experiment corresponds exactly to the method adopted by an examining magistrate who is trying to find out whether something of which he is aware is also known to the accused as an agent" (1906c, IX, 105–6).

The Rat Man, Paul Lorenz, was in his late twenties when he began his treatment with Freud. He was afflicted with superstitions, feelings of guilt, compulsions, and obsessive fears. He was especially obsessed with the thought that a torture he had learned of during military service would be applied to his father, who was dead at the time the treatment began, and to a young woman with whom the patient had long been infatuated. The torture required that a person be sat upon a cage filled with starving rats, the top of the cage then slid away, and the victim devoured from the bottom up. Lorenz suffered from fears that unless he did or did not do certain things the rat torture and other unpleasant events would befall the young woman in this world and his father in the next. He developed intricate and compulsive rituals in the belief that they would protect the young woman, his father, and others from such harms.

The history Lorenz recounted began with his sixth year. Before that age he had only very fragmentary memories, but from six years on his memory was complete. As a child of six or seven he had indulged in sexual play with his nurses and had particularly strong desires to see women naked. The occurrences of these wishes were on some occasions accompanied by a fear of his father's death and by the impression that his parents could read his thoughts. Lorenz did not recall masturbating as a child, and did so only for a very brief period as an adolescent, but he did begin the practice after the death of his father. Despite his deep affection for his father, on several occasions associated with sexual desire, Lorenz nonetheless had thoughts of his father's death, always accompanied by a feeling of dread at such an event. For example, at the age of twelve the thought occurred to him that a younger girl, of whom he was fond, would show him affection if something unfortunate were to befall him, in particular if his father should die. Lorenz was able to recall only one instance of severe and overt conflict, reaching to rage, between himself and his father. At about the age of three or four he was beaten by his father—apparently for biting a nurse—and flew into a rage, calling his father, for want of a more elaborate vocabulary, "You plate, you towel, you lamp . . ." His mother, who was alive at the time of the analysis, confirmed the details of the incident and its singularity. Lorenz felt a great deal of guilt over his father's death; the reason he offered was merely that he had not been present at the moment of demise but instead had fallen into an exhausted sleep in an adjoining room.

The central features of the explanation which Freud offered for his patient's behavior are that his guilt, obsessions, and compulsions were the result of the conflict between his conscious love and unconscious hatred for his father. The unconscious hatred in turn was the consequence of an acute conflict between Lorenz and his father when the former was a small child; specifically, the hatred was first formed when the father punished young Lorenz for masturbation. Lorenz's obsessions were in fact the result of the re-emergence of repressed wishes formed in his early childhood, but permitted into consciousness only in altered, symbolic form. Of course, there is much more intriguing detail in this case study, but rather than develop it I want to examine in detail how Freud warranted the central features of his account of the case. For the most part, Freud was remarkably explicit, and his use of the testing strategy described earlier is almost obvious.

The first three sections of the case study—which correspond to the first few sessions of the analysis—are devoted to the patient's account of his sexual behavior in childhood and of a particularly exaggerated piece of adult obsessive behavior. Very little is done by way of interpreting either, save that characteristically Freud insisted that the cause of the adult behavior lies in the infantile sexual practices. Freud put his view in perfectly general terms:

> (1) Such cases [obsessional neuroses], unlike those of hysteria, invariably possess the characteristic of premature sexual activity. Obsessional neuroses make it much more obvious than hysterias that the factors which go to form a psychoneurosis are to be found in the patient's *infantile* sexual life and not in his present one.[9]

In the fourth section of the case study, Lorenz recounted the "criminal guilt" he felt at his father's death, and Freud used a psychoanalytic generalization to infer an unconscious state:

> (2) Hearing this, I took the opportunity of giving him a first glance at the underlying principles of psycho-analytic therapy. When there is a mésalliance, I began, between an affect and its ideational content (in this instance, between the intensity of the self reproach and the occasion for it) . . . the analytic physician says 'No. The affect is justified. The sense of guilt is not in itself open to further

[9] 1909d, X, 165.

criticism. But it belongs to some other content, which is unknown (unconscious), and which requires to be looked for . . .'[10]

The generalization Freud used in this instance had been stated as early as 1894.[11] In the present case, the use is quite clearly to infer the existence of an unconscious thought for which a feeling of guilt would in fact be appropriate. The generalization in question would, on the account proposed earlier, be tested positively if a state of affairs could be found which, together perhaps with other psychoanalytic hypotheses, entailed the existence of an unconscious thought for which guilt would ordinarily be appropriate. In the very next analytic session, Freud proceeded to establish just such a state of affairs; Lorenz recounted his occasional but recurrent fears and Freud interpreted.

(3) These thoughts [of benefits to Lorenz from his father's death] surprised him very much, for he was quite certain that his father's death could never have been an object of his desire but only of his fear . . . According to psycho-analytic theory, I told him, every fear corresponded to a former wish which was now repressed; we were therefore obliged to believe the exact contrary of what he had asserted. This would also fit in with another theoretical requirement, namely that the unconscious must be the precise contrary of the conscious.[12]

A desire for the death of one's father is evidently something which would warrant feelings of guilt. Thus Freud has already given us a small example of a qualitative application of the testing strategy described earlier. Freud proceeded to apply his theory to infer the cause of the patient's unconscious hatred for his father. At this point Freud's discussion loses something of the terse, straightforward character of the previous steps and becomes slightly rambling. Nonetheless it is clear that Freud was making an inference under the compulsion of his theoretical principles:

(4) The unconscious, I explained, *was* the infantile; it was that part of the self which had become separated off from it in infancy, which had not shared the later stages of its development, and which had in consequence become *repressed*. It was the derivatives of this

---

[10] Ibid., 174–75.
[11] In "The Neuro-Psychoses of Defence," 1894a, III, 45–61.
[12] 1909d, X, 179–80.

repressed unconscious that were responsible for the involuntary thoughts which constituted his illness.[13]

This generalization, together with the hypothesis contained in the first quotation, requires the conclusion that Lorenz's unconscious hatred for his father resulted from the repression of a conscious hatred for his father during infancy or early childhood, and moreover a hatred which in turn resulted from the young Lorenz's sexual behavior. The only possibility allowed by Freudian theory is that Lorenz came to hate his father because the latter had interfered with his sexual activities. That is exactly what Freud concluded:

(5) The source from which his hostility to his father derived its indestructibility was evidently something in the nature of *sensual desires,* and in that connection he must have felt his father as in some way or other an *interference.* A conflict of this kind, I added, between sensuality and childish love was entirely typical.[14]

Moreover, using the non-theoretical fact that Lorenz's infantile amnesia ended with his sixth year, and using as well the psychoanalytic characterization of the unconscious given in the fourth quotation, Freud was able to locate the time of the original conflict.

(6) This wish (to get rid of his father as being an interference) must have originated at a time when circumstances had been very different . . . It must have been in his very early childhood, therefore, before he had reached the age of six, and before the date at which his memory became continuous.[15]

At this point in the case study, Freud used the information he had obtained about Lorenz to provide explanations of the significance of the patient's various symptoms. He proceeded to conjecture as to the nature of the "precipitating cause" which triggered the illness in adulthood. These discussions involve few general lawlike claims, and they appear to be irrelevant to the testing strategy we are considering. In section g the main lines were taken up again. Freud noted several features of his patient's masturbatory behavior, in particular the fact that as an adult he resumed masturbation after his father's death. Freud put his conclusions as follows:

[13] Ibid., 177–78.
[14] Ibid., 182.
[15] Ibid., 183.

(7)   Starting from these indications and from other data of a similar kind, I ventured to put forward a construction to the effect that when he was a child of under six he had been guilty of some sexual misdemeanor connected with masturbation and had been soundly castigated for it by his father. The punishment, according to my hypothesis, had, it was true, put an end to his masturbating, but on the other hand it had left behind it an ineradicable grudge against his father and had established him for all time in his role of an interferer with the patient's sexual enjoyment.[16]

Freud makes it sound as though this construction was but a conjecture peculiar to this case, and not required by psychoanalytic theory. But that is not correct. For by 1905, two years before the treatment of Lorenz was begun and four years before the case study was published, Freud was already committed to the primacy of masturbation as a form of sexual gratification in infancy and early childhood and as an aetiological factor in neurosis.[17] Indeed, he repeats this commitment in the very same section of the case study from which the previous quotation is taken:

(8)   Infantile masturbation reaches a kind of climax, as a rule, between the ages of three and four or five; and it is the clearest expression of a child's sexual constitution, in which the aetiology of subsequent neuroses must be sought.[18]

Let us review what has happened. Starting with the patient's reports Freud used various psychoanalytic hypotheses to determine, first, certain unconscious thoughts and the character of at least one event in the patient's early childhood. The first inference, to the existence of an unconscious thought which would warrant guilt, was tested indirectly and so too was the hypothesis used to make that inference. The states of affairs subsequently inferred are, however, unchecked and their laws thus far untested. Freud had nonetheless arrived at an inferred non-theoretical state of affairs, namely the patient's having been punished by his father for masturbation. Checking independently for the presence or absence of this state of affairs would provide a test of the laws used in making the inference:

[16] Ibid., 205.
[17] See the concluding summary in *Three Essays on the Theory of Sexuality,* (1905d, VII, 234).
[18] 1909d, X, 202.

positive if such an event could be located, negative if it could not be after some reasonable effort. For clarity we can put these several inferences into a kind of diagram:

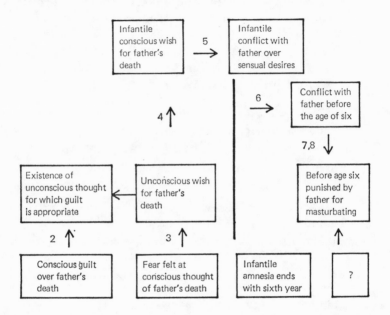

The lower boxes indicate non-theoretical states of affairs which are determined in the case study without the use of psychoanalytic hypotheses; the numbers associated with the arrows are to indicate which quoted passage warrants the inference. The crucial question is whether or not Lorenz was in fact punished by his father for masturbation. Freud reported that immediately after he told Lorenz of his conjecture, the patient recalled the "You plate, you towel . . ." incident and reported it. Could this be the very event required? Unfortunately, the patient's only memory of the incident was through his mother, who had repeatedly told him of it. But when she was consulted as to the reason for the punishment "there was no suggestion of his misdeed having been of a sexual character."[19] Moreover, this was apparently the *only* time the father beat the child.

The chief conclusion I should like to draw from this discussion is that the Rat Man case did provide a test of certain psychoanalytic hypotheses, and in fact a positive test of some hypotheses and a

[19] Ibid., 206.

negative test of others. That the inferred castigation for sexual misbehavior was not revealed by the most reliable available means—the
memory of an adult observer—is presumptive evidence that something was wrong with Freud's account of the role of psychosexual
development in the aetiology of psychoneurosis. The memories of
adults are not, of course, infallible; it could have been, as Freud
suggested in a footnote, that Lorenz's mother suppressed the sexual
character of the incident for which the young Lorenz was punished,
but some special evidence would be required to make this suggestion
as credible as the alternative, and none was forthcoming.

Whether the clinical evidence of the Rat Man case tested views
Freud actually held is bound to be of more interest than whether the
clinical evidence tested views Freud could have held. The strategy
of testing I have described is so elementary that it is difficult to believe that Freud could have failed to see that the Rat Man case
had implications for his views of psychosexual development, if the
views I have ascribed to him were his in fact. Nor is it likely that
Freud would simply have ignored such implications, for throughout
his career Freud remained critical of his own views and seems always to have tried to judge them by the clinical evidence. We
should, then, expect some significant shift in Freud's account of psychosexual development, and a shift of a kind that would be compatible
with the Rat Man case.

Exactly at the point in the case study that Lorenz's mother's memory of the scene between Lorenz and his father is reported, Freud
included a long footnote, running to three pages in the Standard
Edition. He there made several points, including the following:
The punishment Lorenz in fact received *could have* been either for
a sexual misdeed or for some non-sexual misbehavior; interpretation
of one of Lorenz's dreams indicated that, unconsciously, he regarded
his father as a sexual antagonist; in constructing phantasies about
childhood, one sexualizes his memories, "that is, he brings commonplace experiences into relation with his sexual activity and extends
his sexual interest to them—though in doing this he is *probably*
following upon the traces of a really existing connection";[20] and
finally, Freud writes that "It is entirely characteristic of the nuclear
complex of infancy that the child's father should be assigned the part
of a sexual opponent and of an interferer with auto-erotic sexual

[20] Ibid., 207 (italics mine).

activities; and real events are *usually* to a large extent responsible for bringing this about."[21]

The qualifiers "probably" and "usually" block any requirement of a *real* conflict between Lorenz and his father, and suggest that, at this period, Freud thought that either real sexual experiences in childhood, or phantasies of them, could serve as aetiological factors in neurosis. If so, then the Rat Man case would not provide a negative test of Freud's hypotheses regarding psychosexual development, but only a negative test of some ersatz theory. I think rather the opposite is the case; I think the qualifications cited above are rather novel in Freud's writings, and are best understood as the very change Freud thought his theory required in view of the negative evidence of the Rat Man case. I shall argue that prior to the Rat Man case, phantasies of childhood sexual experiences were regarded as, at best, screens for memories of real sexual experiences of a different kind. Increasingly after 1909, Freud thought phantasies themselves, even when derived from no real sexual experience, could serve as aetiological factors.

The theory of the psychoneuroses that Freud published in 1896 took the specific cause of hysteria and of obsessional neuroses to be seduction in childhood.[22] In 1897, in a letter to his friend Wilhelm Fliess, Freud renounced the seduction theory, and concluded that many of the seductions reported by his patients were phantasies.[23] But he did not give up the view that the cause specific to psychoneurosis is some kind of sexual experience in childhood. In his first properly psychoanalytic case study, an account published in 1905 of a case undertaken five years before, Freud referred to his view as a "trauma theory"[24] and took the specific cause of hysteria to be precocious and excessive masturbation subjected to severe repression:

> Hysterical symptoms hardly ever appear so long as children are masturbating, but only after a period of abstinence has set in; they form a substitute for masturbatory satisfaction, the desire for which continues to persist in the unconscious until another and more normal kind of satisfaction appears—where that is still possible. For upon

[21] Ibid., 208 (italics mine).
[22] 1896b, III, 162–85.
[23] M. Bonaparte, A. Freud, E. Kris, *The Origins of Psychoanalysis* (Doubleday, New York, 1957), p. 218 f.
[24] 1905e, VII, 27.

whether it is still attainable or not depends the possibility of hysteria being cured by marriage and sexual intercourse. But if the satisfaction afforded in marriage is again removed—as it may be owing to *coitus interruptus,* psychological estrangement, or other causes—then the libido flows back again into its old channel and manifests itself once more in hysterical symptoms.[25]

In the first edition of *Three Essays on Sexuality,* Freud proposed, citing Binet on fetishism, that in both neurosis and perversion the libido is fixated by some precocious sexual experience or other, the outcome being determined by the subjects' constitutionally determined psychological reaction to those experiences.[26] In an essay published a year later, in fact the very essay in which Freud first publicly renounced the seduction hypothesis, Freud claimed that seduction phantasies generally serve as screen memories for real infantile auto-erotic activity,[27] and he reiterated the view that it is a constitutionally determined psychological reaction (excessive repression) to infantile sexual experience which brings about a disposition to neurosis in adulthood.[28]

After the turn of the century and before 1909, Freud's views on the aetiology of neurosis placed decreased emphasis on *traumatic* sexual encounters in childhood, strong emphasis on childhood sexuality, especially masturbation, and regarded the psychological reaction to such experiences as the determining factor in the generation of a neurotic disposition. In this period, and before, there is no statement of the view that sexual phantasies formed in childhood or subsequently, having no real basis in fact, may themselves serve *in place of* sexual experiences as aetiological factors. Then, in 1909 there appeared the footnote discussed above, even while the text of the Rat Man case contains no hint that the events in question may have been phantasized rather than real. Yet after the Rat Man case the view that either infantile sexual experiences *or* phantasies of them may equally serve as aetiological factors became a standard part of Freud's theory. In *Totem and Taboo,* four years after the Rat Man case appeared, Freud emphasized that the guilt that obsessional neurotics feel is guilt over a happening that is psychically real

[25] Ibid., 79. Two pages later, however, Freud indicates uncertainty as to the universality of masturbation as a cause of hysteria.
[26] 1905d, VII, 154, 190, and 242.
[27] 1906a, VII, 274.
[28] Ibid., 276–77.

but need not actually have occurred.[29] By 1917 Freud not only listed phantasies themselves as aetiological factors alternative to real childhood sexual experiences, but omitted even the claim that the former are usually or probably based on the latter.[30] Whatever the merits of Freud's revised theory, I think it reasonable to conclude that, to his credit, Freud learned from the experience of the Rat Man case.

The kind of testing a theory admits depends largely on the strength of that theory itself. Weak theories which embody no putative laws, which concern only causal factors or correlations, may perhaps have to be tested with great regard for statistical methods and experimental controls. But the theory Johannes Kepler proposed long ago was strong enough to be tested in the observatory, and the theory Sigmund Freud developed at the turn of this century was strong enough to be tested on the couch.

[29] 1912–13, XIII.
[30] 1916–17, XVI, 370.

Rational Behaviour and Psychoanalytic Explanation*

PETER ALEXANDER

I

It is often said that psychoanalysis has drawn our attention to the irrational springs of human behaviour. Recently, however, I have heard it said[1] that, on the contrary, psychoanalysis has revealed that our behaviour is more rational than we usually suppose it to be. The neurotic, according to this view, is radically misinformed but on the information he has he behaves rationally and if he discovers, or is supplied with, information he lacks he does the rational thing and alters his behaviour accordingly. This is a tempting and persuasive view but, it seems to me, a misleading one which calls for a detailed examination. I shall first show why the view appears to have some force, then discuss the notion of rational behaviour and finally raise some objections to the view.

In *The Psychopathology of Everyday Life*, and many other places, Freud argued that many pieces of apparently accidental, haphazard or purposeless behaviour could be explained in terms of unconscious wishes or purposes. I give three of his examples which will be convenient for testing the view in question.

(1) A woman patient always read "storks" instead of "stocks" and did not know why she did so. Freud explained this by discovering that she had no children but badly wanted them.[2]

(2) Freud found that on a sheet of notes about his daily engagements he had himself written the correct date, September 20th, and, under it in brackets, October 20th. He could not remember doing this and was, at first, completely mystified by it. He finally explained it in terms of an unconscious wish. He had just returned from a holiday, feeling fit and ready for work, but he had very few patients. He had, however, a letter from a patient saying that she

---

* Reprinted from *Mind* 71, no. 283 (July 1962), pp. 326–41, by kind permission of the editor.

[1] By Mr. J. W. N. Watkins and others, in discussion and conversation.

[2] This example comes from A. A. Brill's translation of *The Psychopathology of Everyday Life* and is not to be found in Freud's text. Ed.

would come to see him on October 20th. He concluded that his mistake sprang from a wish that the intervening month had passed. He accounts for his easy discovery of the explanation by the fact that the "disturbing thought" was not unpleasant (1901b, VI, 116–17).

(3) A young woman with a jealous husband danced a can-can at a party. Everyone was full of praise except the husband who accused her of behaving like a harlot ("once again"). The next day she went driving in a carriage, jumped from the carriage because, she said, she was afraid that the horses were going to bolt, and broke her leg. Her unconscious purpose, Freud says, was to punish herself for her forwardness and make it impossible for her to dance the can-can in the immediate future. (There is a good deal more supporting evidence for Freud's explanation [1901b, VI, 179–80].)

The idea that apparently purposeless and innocent slips of tongue and pen can be explained in terms of unconscious wishes and purposes is connected with the Freudian theory of the generation and cure of neuroses. Even the simple examples I have quoted involve minor neurotic symptoms but in the fully blown neuroses greater stress is laid on the unconsciousness of the purposes and wishes and the difficulty of discovering them. The general theory is, briefly, that a person who has desires of which he is ashamed or frightened protects himself from them by "pushing them into the unconscious," forgetting them beyond all normal power of recall, and substituting for the behaviour which would satisfy them some more innocent behaviour which, however, is mysterious both to himself and to the ordinary observer. Such behaviour is often referred to as a "symbolic" satisfying of the forbidden desire and is also regarded as inflicting a punishment for the repressed wish. It is mysterious because it does not appear to serve any purpose and no adequate reasons for it are obvious.

The view I am considering stresses the central assertion of the Freudian theory that it is possible to explain much of our behaviour in terms of unconscious wishes, purposes, and so on. The behaviour which we usually call "irrational" can be shown to be based on reasons which can be unearthed by psychoanalysis. The examples I have given show typical, though elementary, explanations of this sort. At first sight it seems plausible to say that since reasons can be given for pieces of behaviour we usually call "irrational," even this behaviour is, after all, rational, but at the unconscious level. It is a short step to the conclusion that Freud has shown irrational behaviour to be "really" rational and that we are, therefore, more rational than we usually suppose. I am inclined to think that the step, though short, is in the wrong direction.

The view is connected with a general account of human behaviour according to which the only way to explain an *action*, as distinct from a mere physical movement, is by showing that it was the rational thing to do. Attempts to explain actions in terms of physical causes are, at best, no more than explanations of physical movements: attempts to explain them in terms of forgetfulness or clumsiness, or some other such factor, amount to admissions that the actions cannot be explained or to assertions that they were not actions at all. I do not intend to discuss, here, this general view but only its application to psychoanalytic explanation.

It is important, here, to mention the distinction, to which I shall return, between rational *beliefs* and rational *behaviour*. It may be rational or irrational to hold a given belief but given that I hold it, I may act rationally or irrationally on its basis. If I firmly believe, falsely and on insufficient evidence, that my neighbour is planning to poison me, that is irrational. But it is rational, *given* my firm belief, to avoid drinking tea in his house and to instruct my wife not to leave him alone in our kitchen.

The view in question is that the neurotic behaves rationally in this sense. He unconsciously holds a number of irrational beliefs but, given these beliefs, he behaves rationally. Psychoanalytic explanation, it is argued, involves discovering these beliefs. The theory of cure is that if the neurotic discovers, or is provided with, the information he lacks he will abandon these beliefs because he will see that they are irrational. He will, in consequence, stop behaving in a neurotic way. It is sometimes even argued that to dispel these beliefs, and to bring about a cure, it is *sufficient* to bring them to light, when their absurdity will be evident to the patient.

I am concerned chiefly with the alleged rationality of the behaviour rather than the unquestioned irrationality of the beliefs, and with psychoanalytic explanation rather than cure. It is necessary for my purpose to examine the distinction between rational and irrational behaviour and to say something about explaining behaviour. These topics are the subjects of my next two sections.

II RATIONAL AND IRRATIONAL

It may well be that there are various senses in which the word "rational" is used in connection with behaviour. I shall discuss here what appears to me to be a central and important sense in which it is commonly so used and try to show that, at least in this sense, the view I am considering is mistaken or misleading.

There is a difference between saying that a given piece of behaviour would be rational in a given situation and saying that A's behaviour in that situation was rational. What makes a given piece of behaviour rational in a given situation is that there are good reasons for behaving thus; what makes A's behaviour rational is that he behaved in the way he did *for* those good reasons. The good reasons were *his* reasons. He *had* those reasons for behaving thus. I shall mainly be working towards a closer analysis of what it is for a given person's behaviour to be rational. I shall not, I am afraid, arrive at a complete analysis of rational behaviour in this sense; but it will be sufficient for my purpose if I can correctly establish certain of its characteristics.

As a first approximation I might suggest that A behaved rationally if he behaved thus for a reason. But this clearly will not do because we should not say this if A's reason was a bad one. I may do something for a reason without its being the reasonable thing to do or, *a fortiori*, rational. This is implicit in the fact that I can correctly say that y was *my* reason for doing x while admitting that y is not *a* reason or *a good* reason for doing x. I may, for instance, have done x because I thought it would achieve y but now I see that it could not possibly have done so.

Thus we must add to the first suggestion that the reason was a *good* reason. But this is still inadequate since any reason *for* doing x cannot be a very bad reason and a reason for doing x may be good without being sufficient. One good reason for doing x may be outweighed by several good reasons against doing x or it may not *by itself* (i.e., without other good reasons) constitute a sufficient reason for doing x. In order for x to be rational I must have sufficient reason for doing x, that is a reason or collection of reasons which is strong enough to stand even after weighing the important reasons for and against doing x. There may be a reason, a good reason or good reasons for doing *x* without there being sufficient reason. So we have at least one further necessary modification of the original suggestion. Let me say that *a piece of behaviour was rational if it was done for reasons which constitute a sufficient reason.*

I must now consider what it is for something to be a reason and to be a sufficient reason for certain behaviour. If I say that *y* is a reason for doing *x* I imply that *x* will achieve, or help to achieve, *y*, that the behaviour is somehow appropriate to what it is intended to achieve; if I say that *y* is not a reason, or is a bad reason, I imply that *x* will not achieve or help to achieve, *y, or* that it is unlikely to do so *or* that it will not do so as economically as some other behaviour would *or* that it will also produce other undesired consequences. If *x* is very unlikely to achieve *y* or could not possibly do so we could not correctly say, "*y* is a reason for doing *x*," although *I* could still say, "My reason for doing *x* was *y*." If I say that *y* (which now may be complex) is sufficient reason for doing *x* I mean that *x* is likely to achieve *y* and that *y* is valued above all other things which may be brought about by doing *x* but which I do not want to bring about or which I want *not* to bring about.

There are some difficult cases which do not at first sight seem to fit into this account of reasons. It might be said, for example, that when I thank someone for a present I do not aim to achieve anything and even that it is not correct to say that I had any reason. I think that there are perhaps cases in which thanking someone for a gift is just a spontaneous gesture which would appear to be too calculated if we said it was done for a reason.[3] I doubt if this behaviour would be said to be either rational or irrational, but I am very unsure about this. Of other cases it might be said that the fact that someone gave me a present was a reason, and perhaps sufficient reason for thanking him, and that no mention need be made of my wishing to achieve anything. But in such a case I think we can always say that a reason for thanking him was that I wanted to show him that I was pleased, or grateful (or that I wanted to conform to convention or . . .). The question "Why did you thank him?" can be answered by "Because he gave me a present," but it can then be asked again in expectation of some such answer as "because I wanted to show my gratitude." I am inclined to think that whenever it is appropriate to ask for a reason for a piece of behaviour, it is possible to give

[3] My thanks are due to Paul Ziff for convincing me of this.

a reason in terms of someone's wanting or intending to achieve something, even if in certain cases what it is intended to achieve is consistency or appropriateness or a state of mind in someone else.

I can now expand my account of rational behaviour. A piece of behaviour was rational if it was done for reasons which constitute a sufficient reason, that is, if it was likely to achieve what was intended and unlikely to lead to other consequences whose undesirability outweighs the desirability of what it was intended to achieve. It was irrational if it was not done for reasons which constitute a sufficient reason, that is, if it was unlikely to achieve what was intended, or less likely to achieve it than some other piece of behaviour, or was likely to lead to other consequences whose undesirability outweighs the desirability of what it was intended to achieve.

There is, of course, a scale of rationality between the most rational and the most irrational. Clearly it is irrational to do something which cannot possibly achieve what is intended and clearly it is rational to do something which is very likely to achieve it without any unwanted side-effects. In between we often have to contrast alternative ways of behaving between which it is not easy to decide. In a given situation, other things being equal, it is rational to behave in a way which is more likely to achieve what is intended, less rational or irrational to behave in a way which is less likely or unlikely to achieve it.

There may *be* a sufficient reason for behaving in a certain way in a given situation but if this is not my reason for behaving in that way then I cannot be said to have behaved rationally, by reference to *that* reason. It is therefore necessary to be clear about what it means to act *for* a reason or with a reason in mind, to *have* a reason or to say that a given reason was *my* reason. An inarticulate person may sometimes be said to behave in a certain way for a reason, and even for a good or sufficient reason even though he is unable to say what this reason was. Habitual actions and those performed during the exercise of a craft may be done for good reasons and constitute rational behaviour although the agent was not conscious of the reasons before, during or after the actions. I may have a reason in mind without attending to it. However, I think that it is a necessary condition of my acting for a reason that I should be able to become aware of my reason if I think about my behaviour, although I need not be able to state it. To say that a given reason was *my* reason is to imply that, if I think of that reason or someone suggests it to me I can recognize it *as my* reason, or one of my reasons, for that behaviour (or as having influenced my behaviour). I doubt if it is correct to say, "I acted for a reason," and at the same time to confess that, however hard I think about it, I cannot discover the reason and that, however many possible reasons are put to me, I cannot recognize any of them as *my* reason. If this is true of having a reason it is true of having a good or a sufficient reason. Having a reason, at least in this sense, is a necessary condition of behaving rationally.

It would be as well to mention here a consideration which will become important later. There is a perfectly ordinary, everyday sense of "unconscious" in which while I am not thinking of something I may be said to be unconscious of it. I am at the moment unconscious of what I had for breakfast this morning because I am not thinking of it or trying to recall it, but if I did try I could probably recall it. Similarly I may have a reason for behaving in a certain way and yet be unconscious of my reason at any given time. This is to be distinguished from the technical sense in which "unconscious" is used in psychoanalysis, according to which what is unconscious is beyond all our normal powers of recall.

If what I have said so far is correct, both rational behaviour and irrational behaviour are such that they could have been consciously planned even if they were not. My account allows, as I think we normally would allow, that some habits and learned skills may be said to be rational. Irrational behaviour resembles rational behaviour in the sense that it is the sort of behaviour which it is possible to give reasons for and against.

I have used the words "intention" and "intend" because I wish to exclude from both categories such things as reflexes and sheer accidents. For these, if we are to call them "behaviour," we need a third category which may be called "non-rational" and includes any behaviour of which it does not make sense to say either that it was or was not done for a reason. Non-rational behaviour could not be intended; for example, fainting or jumping when startled (*real* fainting and *real* jumping), or sheer accidents involving unforeseeable events, like unavoidably running over someone who runs out in front of a car. I cannot intend to faint or run a person over unavoidably.

It might be thought to be an objection that doubt can be cast upon the rationality of behaviour which tends to achieve what is desired, by questioning the rationality of seeking to achieve the particular thing desired. Behaviour which, in a narrow context, looks rational may be regarded as irrational in a wider context. Given that I wish to commit suicide it is rational to choose the gas oven rather than the electric oven but there may be more rational ways out of my difficulties than self-destruction. This is not, however, an objection to my view since suicide would be judged to be rational or irrational in the light of yet other things desired and the criteria I have outlined would simply be applied in the wider context.

Similarly, it may be rational to behave in a particular way given the beliefs I have about certain matters of fact but these beliefs may be irrational because they conflict with the evidence I have or evidence I could easily get or are based on careless or mistaken reasoning. But if I believe that w is the case and that, in consequence, I ought to aim to produce y, then behaviour that tends to produce y may be rational, within the narrower context, no matter how wrong is my belief about w. The rationality of behaviour is relative to context.

This bears obliquely on my reason for *not* saying that behaviour which is rational must achieve what is intended *in the way the agent thinks it does*. Suppose that we have discovered empirically that railway lines buckle in hot weather when gaps are not left between them, although we know nothing about the relation between heat and expansion. Then it is rational to leave gaps between them so that they do not buckle, even if we think we do this in order to appeal to the aesthetic senses of the gods so that they will refrain from bending the rails and even if, when we have learnt about heat and expansion, we no longer think it is rational to leave gaps *because* the gods prefer it.

III   EXPLAINING BEHAVIOUR AND JUSTIFYING BEHAVIOUR

It is easy to mistake a justification for a piece of behaviour for an explanation of it and I suspect that such a mistake is involved in the view I am considering. The mistake may arise in this way. A person behaves in an unusual way and, without consulting him, we ask ourselves why he behaved as he did. That is, we look for reasons for his behaviour. If we are able to find a sufficient reason we may think we have explained his behaviour, but the most we can be sure we have done is to justify behaviour of this sort in this kind of situation. We have not explained *his* behaviour until we have discovered what *his* reasons were. We have discovered something that would explain it but not necessarily what does explain it. We may justify such behaviour by showing that it achieved something of which *we* approve but we can explain it only by showing what *he* intended to achieve.

Suppose, for example, that for a month our friend eats and drinks nothing but milk. We cast about for explanations and decide, since he has shown some interest in nutritional problems, that he wished to show that milk is a complete food for an adult. (There are, of course, several other reasonable conclusions we might reach.) This would be a good reason for his behaviour and sufficient, we think, to justify it. But if we are ignorant of our friend's reasons we cannot say that this was his reason and although we have justified such behaviour to ourselves we have not explained it. We have shown how behaviour of this sort might be shown to be rational but we have not shown that he behaved rationally. The most we can say is that if this *was* his reason it would both explain and justify his behaviour.

He may now deny that we have found his reason. There are two possibilities. First, he might give another good or sufficient reason, which would both explain and justify his behaviour. Second, he might give another reason which was a bad one. This would explain his behaviour but not justify it or show it to be rational, just because it was a bad reason. Thus to explain a piece of behaviour is not just to show that it was a rational thing to do and to show that it was a rational thing to do is not necessarily to explain it. To explain a piece of behaviour we have to show what reasons the agent had: to show that he behaved rationally we have also to show that these reasons were sufficient. We may therefore justify such behaviour as *A*'s without either explaining it or showing that he behaved rationally and we may explain his behaviour without showing that he behaved rationally.

There is an ambiguity about the word "reason" which I should perhaps get out of the way. I refer to the fact that we occasionally use "reason" in the sense of "cause." There is sometimes a difference between saying, "My reason for doing *x* was *y*," and, "The reason why I did *x* was *y*." The second form may be used to indicate causes as well as reasons in the strict sense I have been using. I can correctly say, "The reason why I fainted was that insufficient blood was getting to my brain." Thus a statement of the form "The reason why I did *x* was *y*" may be used either to reinforce the assertion that my behaviour was rational or for the different purpose of giving a causal account of what I did. It would be odd to say, "My reason *for* fainting was that insufficient blood was getting to my brain," because it suggests that on discovering the physiological fact I realized that the appropriate thing to do, finding no reasons against, was to faint, so I fainted. I can, however, say either, "The reason why I bought a thermometer was that I *wanted* to measure my temperature," or, "My reason for buying a thermometer was that I wanted to measure my temperature." The need to include the word "wanted," or some such word, in the description of the reason, in the strict sense, is important.

IV   CRITICISMS

When we are considering behaviour in the ordinary way, and not theorizing about it in the manner of psychoanalysis, we find two sorts of behaviour which are conveniently labelled "rational" and "irrational." It is helpful, or sometimes essential, to contrast these with one another and with the sort of behaviour which can be called "non-rational." But psychoanalytic theory implies that all the behaviour which we call "irrational" can, at least in principle, be explained in terms of unconscious purposes, and so on. If we go on to say that this shows such behaviour to be rational we blur these distinctions. There would be nothing wrong with this if it were accompanied by arguments showing these distinctions to be inaccurate or unnecessary, but such arguments do not seem to be forthcoming. As we shall see, nothing of this sort follows from psychoanalytic theory, so it is difficult to see how such arguments could be upheld.

Here it is sufficient to note that if we say that our irrational behaviour has been shown to be "really" rational we allow "rational" to be used only in contrast to "non-rational." It is not very instructive merely to distinguish our faintings and unavoidable accidents from all the rest of our behaviour, and to make no further distinctions. In making moral judgments, ascribing responsibility, assessing intelligence, cleverness, reliability and a host of other activities it is essential to make finer distinctions. Moreover, the problems in which psychoanalysis originated depend upon this distinction. The meaning of "rational" in such contexts involves the contrast with both "irrational" and "non-rational." If this is so, to assert that our irrational behaviour has been shown to be rational is to use "rational" in a new sense while pretending to use it in the familiar sense, for it leaves us no behaviour which can be said to be, either consciously or unconsciously, irrational.

This frustrates any attempt to make the view more acceptable by saying, "Freud has shown us that behaviour which is consciously irrational is unconsciously rational." This is not to say that he has shown us that we behave more rationally than we usually suppose, for it is not to say anything about the rationality about which we usually suppose. We usually, I claim, suppose people to be rational to the extent to which their behaviour fits the criterion I have outlined, or something like it: we do not, without benefit of Freud, entertain ideas about unconscious rationality. This formulation does, indeed, leave the distinction between consciously rational and consciously irrational behaviour but it weakens it by suggesting that unconscious rationality differs from conscious rationality only in being unconscious. This is misleading because Freud has not left us any behaviour which is unconsciously irrational with which to contrast that which is unconsciously rational. "Rational," I suggest, is being used in such different senses at the conscious and unconscious levels that we must be very careful how we draw an analogy between them.

We might, in an attempt to save the view, retreat still further and claim that Freud has shown our irrational behaviour to be *more like* our rational behaviour than we supposed, since whereas we formerly thought that we could not give good reasons for it we now find that we can. This is to draw an analogy between psychoanalytic explanations and certain ordinary explanations of behaviour in terms of reasons for it. The value of this analogy depends on the extent to which the good reasons for "irrational" behaviour are like the good reasons for rational behaviour. A more detailed examination will show that the reasons adduced in psychoanalytic explanations are very unlike what we would normally regard as good reasons and consequently that the behaviour in question is shown to be rational only in a new and unfamiliar sense.

I shall come to this more detailed examination by recapitulating three points I made earlier and applying them to psychoanalytic explanations. In ordinary circumstances (1) we may explain a piece of behaviour by showing that it was done for a reason or with a reason in mind and showing what that reason was; (2) to explain a piece of behaviour is not necessarily to show that it was rational; (3) to show that somebody's behaviour was rational it is necessary to show (*a*) that the agent had reasons and (*b*) that the reasons were sufficient reasons.

Thus the fact that a psychoanalytic explanation can be given for a piece of otherwise unexplained behaviour does not show that behaviour to be rational unless (*a*) the reasons given were the reasons for which the agent behaved as he did and (*b*) they were sufficient reasons. It seems to me that there is some doubt about the possibility of satisfying the first condition and that the very nature of the typical psychoanalytic explanation makes impossible the satisfying of the second. This is not to claim that psychoanalytic explanations are not explanations or are useless but only that they are of a very different kind from everyday explanations of rational behaviour. I shall discuss these two conditions separately.

(*a*)   I have argued that when we say that I did something for a reason or with a reason in mind we imply that I must be able to discover that reason or recognize it when it is suggested to me as having influenced my behaviour. It must, at least in this sense, be *my* reason. I may recognize a suggested reason as a 'good' reason without recognizing it as *my* reason and I may have to admit, if I am being honest, that *my* reason is not to be found among the good reasons.

The sense in which we normally allow that a person may be unconscious of his reasons for acting demands that he should be able to discover them by everyday methods of self-questioning or at least to recognize his reasons when they are suggested by others using similar everyday methods. But the special sense in which "unconscious" is used in psychoanalysis may make all the difference, since a person's unconscious reason, in this sense, is *ex hypothesi* beyond his power to discover without the assistance of special techniques and, usually, another person trained in these special techniques, working on the basis of a special theory. Neurotic behaviour is mystifying to both the neurotic and the ordinary observer. The discussions and other transactions necessary to dissolve the mystery are very unlike the discussions we normally go through in finding explanations for normal behaviour.

The nature of the techniques employed is very important in the present context. Are they such that the patient can be said, when he has accepted the explanation, to have *recognized the reasons* as those which in fact influenced his behaviour? This I doubt. Case histories show, again and again, that the patient meets the suggested reason as a stranger, failing to recognize it or resisting it violently, until a good deal of preparatory work, including the expounding of bits of theory, has been done by the psychoanalyst. Is this preparatory work correctly described as showing the patient that these were in fact his reasons rather than showing him that, given the theory, these reasons are "good," i.e, fit the theory? Is his acceptance more correctly described as seeing what his reasons were or as seeing what his reasons *must have been?* ("must" not, of course, implying *logical* necessity). Of course, his resistance to the reasons is explained by the theory. We are all familiar with our own inner struggles not to admit a disreputable reason for which we have acted but we are also familiar with our own reluctance to admit a disreputable reason which we are sure did not influence our action. Moreover, the importance of the transference situation suggests, very strongly, I think, that the processes involved are not just those associated with intellectual conviction.[4]

When the patient accepts or "discovers" unconscious reasons he may be saying, "Now I see what my reasons must have been, though I did not suspect it," or he may be saying, "Now I see what my reasons were but I had forgotten them." It is easy to suppose that the alleged reasons were not in fact effective reasons, did not in fact influence the behaviour, but rather that the behaviour can be interpreted *as if* they were and, moreover, that the cure can be achieved if this interpretation is accepted, whether or not it is correct. I am suggesting that the *process* may be more like the normal justifying of an action than the normal explaining of an action even though what issues from it is not very like a justification for the action. There is, of course, the connected problem of how it is possible to discover that we are remembering reasons we had forgotten, especially when the forgetting is of the Freudian type.

(*b*) Compared with the ordinary acceptance of reasons for behaviour, the acceptance of the psychoanalytic kind of reason for behaviour which before looked irrational is odd in another way, because we can never have been conscious of having *such* reasons

---

[4] Patrick Mullahy, in *Oedipus, Myth and Complex* (New York, 1935) p. 30: "Nor does enlightenment *per se* concerning the causative relation of [such] experiences to his illness effect cure."

for *such* behaviour. The theory holds that unconscious reasons are effective only because they are repressed and so unconscious in the technical sense. In the ordinary way, before we say that a piece of behaviour was rational we demand that a sufficient reason be given for it. A sufficient reason is such that we can see that it could have been a reason for this particular behaviour and, I think, that we can conceive of ourselves as behaving thus with this reason in mind. We demand appropriateness.

I doubt if the typical Freudian reason can satisfy this condition. Such a reason is a reason for this behaviour only because it was unconscious. We can never know what it would be like to act thus with this reason in mind since it does not make sense to talk of acting with unconscious (in the technical sense) reasons in mind. The typical unconscious reasons are not the sorts of reasons which would lead to that sort of behaviour if we were conscious of them. The shocked reaction "Good gracious, is that why I did it? I should never have done it if I had known" is typical and says more than the speaker, and perhaps Freud, usually realizes. The whole point of the theory is that neurotics behave as they do because they fool themselves completely about certain things; but we cannot fool ourselves completely and be aware that we are fooling ourselves. Unconscious reasons are not just possible conscious reasons for the behaviour in question: they would not be regarded as reasons for it if they were conscious.

This does not mean simply that the patient would see the reasons as disreputable if they were conscious but that he would see them as inadequate. For example, suppose that my lunging at lamp-posts with my umbrella is explained by referring to my Oedipus Complex. My alleged reasons for behaving as I do are:

(i)   I feel that my father hates me because we are rivals for my mother's love and I therefore wish to kill my father so that I do not have to share her love;

(ii)   I am ashamed of and feel guilty about this wish so I conceal it from myself;

(iii)   it is still effective so I "satisfy" it without realizing that this is what I am doing by some substitute activity such as lunging at lamp-posts;

(iv)   I want to punish myself for having this wish.

Now if my wish to kill my father were conscious it would be obvious to me that it was not adequately satisfied by my lunging at lamp-posts. If my wish to protect myself from my own guilt were conscious it would be obvious that such behaviour would not help. That is, these "reasons" can be reasons for this behaviour only if they are unconscious for they would not look like reasons if they were conscious. The fourth reason looks, at first sight, more convincing. By behaving in an odd way I upset my relations with society by leading people to treat me as odd and so punish myself for my guilty wishes. However, this is not a very effective way of punishing myself as I would no doubt see if I were conscious of my guilty wishes and my desire to punish myself for them. The reasons would not appear to be appropriate to the form of my behaviour and we might further question the belief that the mere having of certain wishes merits punishment. It is not satisfactory, moreover, to regard all these factors taken together as constituting good reasons in the ordinary sense; even if they were all conscious the behaviour would not appear to be appropriate.

It is true that if my father hates me this may be a sufficient reason for protecting myself against him, but is it a sufficient reason for the neurotic behaviour in which I indulge? Only, I suggest, in conjunction with the theory. The relation between the reasons and the behaviour is not such that we would normally say that this was a sufficient reason for this behaviour. The relation needs explaining in terms of more theory. These considerations suggest that "reason," "good reason" and "sufficient reason" are used in this context in senses very different from their usual ones. In their ordinary senses, something which would not look like a sufficient reason for doing x, if we were conscious of it, is not a sufficient reason for doing x.

I can now return to the examples I quoted from Freud. In each of these, the behaviour does not seem to be related to the alleged reason in the way in which ordinary behaviour is related to ordinary good reasons for it. The woman who read "storks" for "stocks" does not appear, by so doing, to have furthered either the end of obtaining children or of concealing from herself her own unhappiness and it is doubtful if she or others could have seen the behaviour as achieving anything except with the help of the Freudian theory.

Freud's own mistake about the date did not make the wished-for day come more quickly, nor bring him more patients, nor conceal from himself that he was short of patients. If he had been convinced that it was the correct date it might have done the last, but he was not. His behaviour would have been perfectly rational if he had meant merely to remind himself that he had no important engagements until October 20th, but he neglects entirely this possibility. If he had not been so interested in explanations which fitted his theory might he not have thought that this was his reason? Moreover, it is easy to suppose that he did not recognize the reason he gives as his reason but inferred that it was his reason because it was the kind of reason he was looking for—and, indeed, he introduces the reason by saying, "It was not difficult to explain . . ." (i.e., in terms of the theory).

The woman who jumped from the carriage could hardly have regarded her desire not to dance the can-can again or her desire to regain her husband's respect as good reasons for breaking her leg if she had been aware of them. She did, of course, punish herself for dancing the can-can and losing her husband's respect but I doubt if she would have found it the appropriate kind of punishment if she had been conscious of all this. It is true that the punishment does, in a sense, fit the crime but I doubt if many of us would regard our having danced the can-can as constituting sufficient reason for, and as being suitably punished by, the wilful breaking of our legs. Moreover, the husband's loss of respect here was due, Freud darkly hints, to more serious offences for which this is not a punishment with even this macabre kind of appropriateness.

In general, similar things can usually be said about Freud's explanations of neurotic symptoms. If I am said to do x for unconscious reason y, it is nearly always the case that y is not the sort of thing which we would normally consider a good reason for x. The theory is, of course, that y leads to x because it is repressed. The repression of the guilty thoughts is prior to the behaviour so that the behaviour cannot be thought of as fulfilling a wish to deceive oneself but only as fulfilling the repressed wish in spite of its being repressed or as punishing oneself for having the wish at all. The punishment itself seems always to be too severe, or not severe enough, or inappropriate in some other way.

It might be said that the reason given for the behaviour is the whole complex repressed-guilty-desires, that is, that the fact of repression is part of the reason. But the same arguments apply since if the neurotic could be conscious of having repressed his guilty desire this would still not look like a good reason for this behaviour. Moreover, this begins to look like an account in terms of causes rather than reasons, similar to "The reason why we hear scufflings is that there are mice in the cellarage." It seems more accurate to say, "The reason why he did this was that he had repressed certain desires of which he felt guilty," than to say, "His reason for doing this was that he *wanted* . . ." I cannot discuss this here but wish merely to point out that there is a danger of confusing these two senses of reason in this situation. I have argued elsewhere[5] in favour of a causal interpretation of psychoanalytic explanations and cure but this would clearly be incompatible with the view I have been examining.

It seems to me that we can say that Freud has shown that it is possible to construct a theory on the basis of which irrational behaviour can be interpreted *as if* it were the outcome of given unconscious reasons. There is an apparent analogy between psychoanalytic explanations of irrational behaviour and ordinary explanations of rational behaviour. But the analogy can be pushed so little that it seems more of a hindrance than a help to use "explanation" and "reason" as if these words were used in the same senses in the two contexts. I have tried to show that unconscious reasons are very unlike conscious reasons and especially unlike what we normally call "good reasons" or "sufficient reasons" for behaviour. If we do call them "good reasons" it is clear that we use these words in an unusual sense and are therefore not entitled to go on to say that such explanations show our irrational behaviour to be really rational. This would be warranted if we added that "rational" was being used in a new sense but then the original statement would lose its point. I have no objection whatever to the use of words in new or unusual senses as long as it is clear that this is what we are doing and that it is in some way helpful or illuminating.

[5] See Peter Alexander, "Cause and Cure in Psychotherapy," *Proc. Arist. Soc. Supp.*, 29 (1955), pp. 25–42.

Concerning Rational Behaviour and Psychoanalytic Explanation*

THEODORE MISCHEL

In a recent paper Mr. Alexander attacks the analogy between psycho-analytic explanations and ordinary explanations in terms of reasons.[1] His argument rests on two points concerning what is ordinarily meant by "rational behaviour": (*a*) "A piece of behaviour was rational if it was done for reasons which constitute a sufficient reason, that is, if it was likely to achieve what was intended" (p. 310); and (*b*) "What makes *A*'s behaviour rational is that . . . the good reasons were *his* reasons. He *had* those reasons for behaving thus" (p. 308; his italics). Alexander takes this to imply that *A* should be able to "recall" what his reasons were (p. 311), he should be in a position "to have *recognized the reasons* as those which in fact influenced his behaviour" (p. 317; his italics). Alexander then tries to show that neither (*a*) nor (*b*) is true when we explain in terms of Freudian "reasons" and concludes that these are nothing like ordinary reasons for action so that (1) we are not entitled "to say that such explanations show our irrational behaviour to be really rational" (p. 321); and (2) the analogy between psychoanalytic and ordinary explanations is "more of a hindrance than a help" (p. 321) because psychoanalytic explanations "are of a very different kind from everyday explanations of rational behaviour" (p. 316). Though I agree with (1), I will argue that (2) is independent of it and false; this will involve showing that (*a*) and (*b*) are inadequate criteria of rational conduct.

Alexander's examples come from the *Psychopathology of Everyday Life*. Freud there rejects the notion that certain errors, accidental injuries, etc., are "unexplainable through purposive ideas" (1901b, VI, 240); he tries to show instead that "there is a sense and purpose behind the slight functional disturbances of the daily life of healthy

* Reprinted from *Mind* 74, no. 293 (January 1965) pp. 71–78, by kind permission of the editor.

[1] Peter Alexander, "Rational Behaviour and Psychoanalytic Explanation," *Mind* 71, no. 283 (July 1962), pp. 326–41, reprinted in this volume, pp. 305–21. All bare page references are to this volume. The quotations remain in Brill's translation, though the references are to the Standard Edition.

people" (ibid., 162). In this context Freud cites an illustration: "A woman who is very anxious to have children always reads 'storks' instead of 'stocks.'" Alexander claims that this is not at all like an ordinary explanation because "the woman who read 'storks' for 'stocks' does not appear, by so doing, to have furthered either the end of obtaining children or of concealing from herself her own unhappiness" (p. 319). Since her behaviour was not "likely to achieve what was intended" it is not rational; the Freudian reason is not what we would ordinarily regard as a good, or sufficient, reason for such behaviour.

But *what* is this woman doing? She no more imagines that in reading "storks" for "stocks" she will produce children, than Freud imagines that in reading "'antiquities' on every shop sign that shows the slightest resemblance to the word" (1901b, VI, 110), he will turn a shop that does not sell antiquities into one that does. What the woman does, unaware that *that* is what she is doing, is to find in "stocks" an opportunity for mentioning "storks." Why does she do that? Because she wants to.

Alexander may object that this does not explain her behaviour. According to Freud, she makes the mistake because she wants children. And since her misreading is not likely to satisfy that desire, she does not have a good reason for her conduct. But this will not do. Though thinking is not likely to produce children, it would be silly to say that a woman who wants children has no more reason for thinking about them than one who has no interest in children. What is added to the explanation when we say that the woman mentions the stork because she wants children? Is wanting children some inner happening that causes her to say, "stork"? How would we explain what "wanting children" means? We could not do it without some reference to infants, storks, toys, nurseries, etc.—thinking of these, dreaming of them, finding opportunities to talk about them, etc. This is what a woman who wants children does. And that she does this is not a contingent fact which we learn by discovering an empirical correlation between an inner happening and overt behaviour; it is something we learn when we learn what it means to "want children." To explain that a woman mentions the stork because she wants children is not to cite the internal cause of an external effect; it is to re-describe what she is doing in such a way as to make it clearer to someone who has not yet understood *what* she is doing in seizing opportunities to talk about the stork. Perhaps he thinks it is because she has a special interest in birds. Of course, a woman might want children and yet not talk or think about the stork, etc. For she might have a reason for not doing so—e.g., to bring up the stork may also be to remind herself of her unhappiness at having no children. In that case she both does, and does not, want to mention the stork; and then she may mistake "stocks" for "storks."

Is it "rational" to keep bringing up the stork because one wants children? Consider a woman who keeps mentioning Jim, her husband, because she misses him. Though her talking might be intended to achieve something, e.g., impressing others with her devotion, suppose that it is not—she just talks about him because she misses him. Would we say that she is behaving "irrationally"?[2] We might say, e.g., "Granted that she wants to talk about Jim because she misses him, that is no reason for boring others all evening long." But in that case, talking about her husband is also boring her host. As long as talking about Jim is not also doing something else which there is reason not to do, we would not consider it irrational of her to talk of him because she misses him. Alexander's demand for the "appropriateness" of reasons—"in the ordinary way . . . a sufficient reason is such that we can see that it could have been a reason for this particular behaviour. . . . We demand appropriateness" (p. 318)—is satisfied here. It is also satisfied in the case of a woman who mentions the stork because she wants children. But neither case is covered by Alexander's account of "rational behaviour." Nor can his analysis accommodate "I play chess because I enjoy it," or "I took a walk because I felt like it." Here I am explicitly denying that what I do is means to any end; I do not intend to achieve anything—not even "consistency, or appropriateness or a state of mind in someone else" (p. 310)—by doing these things. But given an appropriate context, i.e., there is no pressing business on hand, etc., it would clearly be wrong to say that I do not behave rationally if I do such things because I enjoy them, or feel like doing them.

A woman who talks about her husband because she misses him is acting rationally even if her talk is not intended to achieve anything—at least, as long as in doing so she is not also doing something else which there is reason not to do. If she knows that talking about Jim will bore her host and does not want to do that, then she may

---

[2] It would not do to suggest that her behaviour is "non-rational." For it is not, like fainting, "behaviour of which it does not make sense to say that it was or was not done for a reason" (p. 311).

sit there missing him, wanting to talk about him, but never mentioning him. Or she might ask for another Jim when she wants another gin.

The analogy between the two cases should now be clear: Talking about the stork is not a symptom caused by wanting children, as talking about Jim is not a symptom caused by missing him. In an appropriate context, talking about the stork is wanting children, as talking about Jim is missing him. To explain that she wants to talk about Jim because she misses him is to make her conduct intelligible by making clearer *what* she is doing—her talking is that of a wife who misses her husband, not, e.g., that of a gossip; similarly, we understand why a woman wants to bring up the stork when we understand her interests and concerns—she is not an ornithologist, she is a woman who wants children. And one can see the point of mentioning "by mistake" what one both does, and does not, want to mention.

Since the other mistake cited by Alexander raises no new issues,[3] we can turn to Freud's interpretation of the accident in which a woman broke her leg after dancing the can-can. This differs from the preceding cases in that the woman is neurotic and her behaviour is an (unconscious) attempt at self-punishment. Alexander argues that this woman

> could hardly have regarded her desire not to dance the can-can again or her desire to regain her husband's respect as good reasons for breaking her leg . . . She did, of course, punish herself for dancing the can-can . . . but I doubt if many of us would regard our having danced the can-can as constituting sufficient reason for, and as being suitably punished by, the wilful breaking of our legs. [p. 320]

The first thing to note is that the relevant question is not whether *we* would regard this as suitable (sufficient reason), but whether *she* would. For even in cases where ordinary, rational conduct can be properly described as doing what "was likely to achieve what was intended," this must mean that the agent himself had good reason to

---

[3] Freud did not write "October" instead of "September" as means to an end (i.e., to "make the wished for day come . . ."). In writing it he was expressing the wish that September were over. *All* he does to support his explanation is show that he really did want this. (1901b, VI, 116–17; cf. Alexander, pp. 319–20). That someone who wants something should express a wish for it requires no theoretical explanation.

think it likely—not that it was in fact likely to do it, or that others had reason to think it would. For I acted rationally if I used the telephone in order to call someone in another city even if, without my being in any position to know it, the lines were cut so that what I did was not likely to achieve what I intended. I, who know something of vegetative processes, did not act rationally if I performed a ritualistic dance in order to make my vegetables grow—even if, without my knowing it, my eccentric neighbour was watching and sneaked in with fertilizer after the dance, so that what I did was in fact likely to achieve what I intended. (Cf. Alexander, p. 312.) If "likely to achieve" must be taken to mean "the agent had good reason to think it likely to achieve," then the rationality of a man's conduct cannot be independent of the rationality of his beliefs; the difference between "he acted rationally" and "he acted rationally *given* his beliefs" must not be slurred—a point that will be important later.

The next thing to note is that Freud presents this as one of a large number of cases where accidental injuries can be interpreted as (unconscious) attempts at self-punishment. Freud's main concern here is to adduce evidence such that "after the disclosure of these details we can hardly doubt that this accident was really contrived" (1901b, VI, 180). That is, he is interested in showing that the accident was not something that just happened to her, but something she *did*. Though Freud says that what she was doing was (unconsciously) punishing herself, this is not a complete explanation of her behaviour. Whether she had "sufficient reason" for what she did depends on *what* she was punishing herself for—what given her beliefs, concerns and situation, she did *in* dancing the can-can. Though it is not to Freud's purpose here to give a fuller explanation of her conduct, he does say that her husband's words, "Again you have behaved like a whore," "took effect" and that the accident "ushered in a long and serious neurotic illness" (1901b, VI, 179)—enough to make clear that for her this was not just a social dance. To represent Freud—or someone who interprets such Freudian explanations on an analogy with ordinary explanations—as saying that in dancing the can-can she had "sufficient reason" for breaking her leg, is to misrepresent what is being said.

This leaves us with Alexander's "self-analysis." He argues that there is no parallel between the psychoanalytic explanation of his lunging at lamp-posts with an umbrella in terms of an Oedipus Complex and an ordinary explanation, because "if my wish to kill my father were conscious it would be obvious to me that it was not adequately satisfied by my lunging at lamp-posts. . . . That is, these 'reasons' can be reasons for this behaviour only if they are unconscious for they would not look like reasons if they were conscious" (pp. 318–19). Again everything depends on *what* the "behaviour" in question is. If someone were to say that *his* reason for lunging at lamp-posts with an umbrella is that he hates his father and wants to kill him, this would not be a *bad* reason—it would, at least before Freud, be utterly unintelligible. (Cf. Alexander, pp. 310–14.) We could not understand someone whose "reason" for lunging at lamp-posts is that he wants to kill his father—unless, of course, we think of what he does in lunging as "symbolically" killing him. Hating one's father cannot be a reason for lunging at lamp-posts, but it can be a reason for killing him—and this is what the neurotic takes himself to be doing *in* lunging at lamp-posts. What Freud does—or tries to do—is to fill in enough detail of circumstances and character so as to enable us to see that the neurotic does (unconsciously) hate his father and has (unconsciously) "identified" lunging at lamp-posts with killing him. If we see what he is doing in this way, then we can see the point of his irrational behaviour, the reason in his unreason.

To be sure, if the neurotic were conscious of that of which he is unconscious, then his reasons would no longer look like reasons; for then *what* he is doing would no longer look like "killing father," but would look instead like "lunging at lamp-posts with an umbrella." Alexander's central contention that "in their ordinary senses, something which would not look like a sufficient reason for doing *x,* if we were conscious of it, is not a sufficient reason for doing *x*" (p. 319) is vitiated by his failure to recognize that in "doing *x*" someone may also be doing various other things. Is there only *one* correct description of what a man is doing when he goes downstairs, because he wants to get his gun, because he thinks he heard a burglar? Ordinarily, to understand *what* a man is doing in going through certain motions we must, to some extent, understand *him,* i.e., his purposes, beliefs, etc. But while the purposes and beliefs which normally help make clear what a man is doing are conscious, psychoanalysts contend that if we are to understand what the neurotic is doing then we must attribute to him (irrational) purposes and beliefs of which he is not conscious.[4] Given the psychoanalyst's description of what the neurotic is (unconsciously) doing in lunging at lamp-posts, it is not true that "the reasons would not appear to be appropriate to the form of my behaviour" (p. 319) if I were conscious of them. If I (unconsciously) want to kill my father and (unconsciously) identify lunging at lamp-posts with killing him, then, given this given irrational starting point, I do have good reason for lunging at lamp-posts. If I were conscious of a desire to kill my father, I would, of course, have no reason to think that it is likely to be satisfied by my lunging at lamp-posts. Nor would I be neurotic.

I have argued that Alexander fails to establish a disanalogy between psychoanalytic and ordinary explanations with respect to his point (a); it is false to say that in psychoanalytic explanations "the relation between the reasons and the behaviour is not such that we would normally say that this was a sufficient reason for this behaviour" (p. 319). I now turn to (b). Alexander's argument is that when someone accepts a psychoanalytic explanation for his behaviour he is saying, "Now I see what my reasons must have been though I did not suspect it," rather than, "Now I see what my reasons were but I had forgotten them"; the patient does not "recall" having had these reasons; he cannot be said "to have *recognized the reasons* as those which in fact influenced his behaviour" (p. 317; his italics). Alexander takes this to show that they were not really *his* reasons for acting.

I think that what Alexander says here is true, but fails to show what he thinks it shows. What is involved in "recognizing the reasons" for my action? Alexander talks as if this were a matter of trying earnestly to recall what "I had in mind" in order to see whether the alleged reasons were really mine (pp. 310, 316). But what would I be looking for? Clearly, not anything that passed through my mind when I acted. Indeed, as Alexander at one point admits (p. 310), my reason may not even be something "I had in mind" in the sense that I was conscious of it when I acted. What then must I recall in order to say that this reason was mine, I did in fact have it? Could I describe *what* I had—the mental content I am

---

[4] Since the "forgetting" of these purposes, etc., is not ordinary forgetting but "repression," what the psychoanalyst is saying involves an extension of the ordinary (pre-Freudian) use of "purpose," etc. I am not arguing that there is *no* difference between psychoanalytic and ordinary explanations, but that there is a significant analogy between them; and analogy involves difference as well as similarity.

looking for—without in some way characterizing it as "the reason why I did it"? How? If not, how could I ever find it or "recognize it when it is suggested to me" (p. 316)? If someone tells me that the reason I did this was not this but that, is he telling me that I made a mistake about what went on in my mind? How could he do that? Surely these questions suggest that discovering the reason for my action cannot be identified with recovering something I once "had in mind."

Consider a case in which doubt about the reason for my action arises. I think that I invited X because I enjoy his company. Someone else claims I invited X because he is a publisher whom I might find useful. How can I find out what my reason really was? Even if I clearly recall thinking of nothing but his charm and sincerely protest that his possible usefulness is not what "I had in mind" when I invited him, I may be mistaken. To avoid possible self-deception I must, if there is doubt about the reason for my action, fill in more and more detail—the circumstances under which I invited him, whom else I invited and for what reasons, how I acted towards him on other occasions, etc.—until I "recognize" a purposive pattern in my doings which either does, or does not, agree with my professed reason. Failure of such agreement may lead to further self-questioning which may convince me that the reason for my action is not what I thought it was.[5] And in that case I may well say, "Now I see that this is what my reason must have been, though I did not suspect it." The point is that *what* I am doing depends on the complex of circumstances in which I am acting. To know what I am doing I must attend to this complex, not just to what "I have in mind." The reason for my action is not a privileged mental content which was conjoined with my action. It is something "I had in mind" if I acted in awareness of what I was doing. But if I lack awareness of myself and my situation then I may act without being aware of *what* I am really doing and why I do *that*. I think I am issuing a friendly invitation because I am a good fellow, when I am really "cultivating" a publisher because I am ambitious. That is why someone else may be able to tell me that I am mistaken about my reason for acting. That

[5] I am not suggesting that there are no important differences between ordinary self-questioning and the self-questioning gone through in psychoanalysis. My point is that there is no failure of analogy between the two cases with respect to my discovering that the reason for my action is one I did not "suspect" before.

is also why "discovering" my reason may be seeing a pattern in my doings which I did not suspect, rather than "recognizing" or "recalling" something I once had in mind but have forgotten. To be mine, my reason does not need to be an item I can locate among my private possessions; it is mine in the sense that ultimately I must be the one to avow it. And this condition is satisfied by psychoanalytic explanations since it is expected that, if the interpretation of the patient's behaviour is correct, he will—at least ideally—come to agree with it in the long run.[6]

I have defended the analogy between psychoanalytic and ordinary explanations, but am far from believing that neurotic behaviour is "really" rational. Alexander says that this becomes "plausible" if we accept the analogy (p. 306). I suggest that such plausibility as it may have comes from slurring over the distinction between "he acted rationally" and "he acted rationally *given* his beliefs." When we have a clear case of rational conduct, we say the former; when we say the latter we are hedging—there is some hesitation about whether what he did was really rational. If we go on to say that, though what he believed was wrong, he had good reason to believe it, then we are affirming the rationality of what he did in spite of the fact that it was the wrong thing to do. If on the other hand, we go on to say that his beliefs were irrational, then we are denying that he really acted rationally. *Given* my belief that my neighbour wants to poison me, I have good reason for refusing to eat in his house. If, in spite of the fact that I have no reason to believe it, I refuse to eat in his house because I believe he wants to poison me, then my conduct is irrational. (Cf. Alexander, p. 307). In view of "the unquestioned irrationality of the beliefs" (p. 307) held by the neurotic, it is not plausible to say that his conduct is really rational. The analogy between psychoanalytic and ordinary explanations suggests, not that irrational behaviour is rational, but that it is not "non-rational"—it can be understood in a way similar to that in which we understand rational behaviour. The neurotic acts irrationally; but his conduct is not something "of which it does not make sense to say either that it was or was not done for a reason" (p. 311) so that it can only be understood in terms of causes.

---

[6] Why should it be necessary for the psychoanalyst to get his patient to agree that the "reasons" for his behaviour "fit the [psychoanalytic] theory" (Alexander, p. 317), when there is no need for a doctor to get his patient to agree that the causes of his illness fit the [medical] theory?

Finally, I do not wish to suggest that there are no differences of any kind between ordinary explanations and psychoanalytic explanations of the sort here under consideration.[7] Analogy is not identity; the psychoanalysts' use of "purpose," "reason," "belief," etc., does, I think, involve an extension of the way these terms are ordinarily used. What I have argued is that, Alexander to the contrary, there is no lack of analogy between psychoanalytic and ordinary explanations with respect to (*a*) the way conduct is explained, not in terms of causes, but in terms of considerations ("reasons") which make *what* was done intelligible, given the agent's beliefs, etc.; and (*b*) the fact that something may be *my* reason for acting even though I did not suspect it but "discover" that this is what it must have been.

[7] Alexander deals with explanations of the sort psychoanalysts often call "interpretations" of behaviour; my remarks are addressed to these and not to the sort of explanations they give when discussing symptom formation, etc.

Testing an Interpretation within a Session*

J. O. WISDOM

Psycho-analysis certainly involves huge numbers of what I may call "home-truths," the dissembling side of human nature known especially to novelists, diplomatists, business people, and in some degree to everyone who spends part of his life outside an ivory tower. Elsewhere[1] I have suggested that a considerable part of psycho-analysis consists of what I call "field-work," mapping the ground of ordinary motives, e.g., finding out that men sometimes cover up jealousy with friendliness, the workings of ulterior motives that are known more or less to anyone who has witnessed the deliberations of an important committee. Psycho-analysts have no corner in the market of home-truths, but naturally have a more extensive and more detailed knowledge of them than most students of human nature, and they have doubtless added very greatly to such knowledge. This growth has attracted no attention from critics, partly because it is not systematically set out in books, and partly because new additions are known and are added to the body of our unwritten knowledge, in the same way as men of the world find out more about the deceptions of their fellows.

TESTING UNCONSCIOUS INTERPRETATIONS

If this were all there were to psycho-analysis, there would be no controversy about it, and no differences of psychiatric opinion. Disagreement arises over explanations. In addition to home-truths that are "preconscious" or accessible to anyone, there is a whole body of similar discernments that psycho-analysts regard as unconscious, not accessible to men to discover in the daily traffic of their lives. If the mapping of home-truths is the field-work of psycho-analysis, explaining them is the problem. And psycho-analysts find the explanation in unconscious clinical hypotheses.

* This essay is based on part of a paper to the Fifth Annual Conference of Philosophy of Science, Oxford, 22 September 1961. It was originally printed in the *International Journal of Psycho-Analysis* 48 (1967), pp. 44–52. It is reprinted by permission of the author and the editor.

[1] J. O. Wisdom, "Testing a psycho-analytic interpretation," *Ratio* 8 (1966).

The most obvious example is the Oedipus complex, which, broadly speaking, is that a man is unconsciously jealous of his father, regards him as a rival, and wants to eliminate him, in order to possess his mother incestuously. How is a hypothesis like this to be tested? It goes far beyond the category I have called home-truths, but it is a hypothesis about people, their feelings, and their sentiments, i.e., it is about what actually goes on in patients' minds, and is not a remote or high-level theory. Thus it can concern clinical situations. But it would give a misleading picture of this part of psychoanalysis if certain complementary hypotheses were omitted. Thus, it is also a clinical hypothesis that a man is full of anxiety because of his parricidal wish, because of the punishment for it his father is expected to mete out. Then there is the further clinical hypothesis that, in order to escape this disaster, he adopts some defence against either his own parricidal wish, or his incestuous desire, or both; so that there will be no way of recognizing these desires in ordinary life comparable to the way home-truths can be recognized, and there is a further clinical hypothesis that certain of these defensive efforts combine to produce neurosis. These four hypotheses, perhaps with others of less importance, form one clinical theory. Nonetheless it is only the first of these, to do with parricide and incest, that constitutes the Oedipus complex. That a man may suffer because of its consequences is a further hypothesis. Clearly it is desirable to enquire into the main component hypothesis independently if possible, but the other contextual components have to be borne in mind. Can such a hypothesis be tested? This question is important in its own right, but also because on it hinges the question whether or not psycho-analysis is a science. For, whatever the status may be of the very abstract ideas to be found in it, like libido, psychical energy, or Thanatos, which perhaps constitute the core of the popular idea of the subject, the basic requirement for scientific status is that clinical hypotheses must, like those of any established science, be testable.

FAULTY METHODS

How, then, is a clinical hypothesis like the Oedipus to be tested? Two obvious methods suggest themselves: relying on intuitive insight or falling back on past experience.

It is, of course, just as important in psycho-analysis as it is in physics to have good insight. Hitting on a new clinical hypothesis is impossible without insight, just as in physics insight is essential for hitting on a new hypothesis, say to explain the magnetism of protons. But indispensable as insight is, it does not guarantee the truth of what it purports to reveal. I suppose the history of science is littered with the skeletons of insights that have turned out to be false. There are famous examples of this even in mathematics. There can be conflicting insights, as for instance over the nature of light, one being that it consists of corpuscles, the other of waves. But, even without such a conflict, an insight has, in the end, to be subjected to testing. Freud himself was most emphatic that an interpretation is always a conjecture (1937d, XXIII, 257–69).

Nor can we fall back on the great traditional misrepresentation of scientific method, that a clinical hypothesis can be derived and established from past experience. Popper[2] has made it clear that such is not the procedure of science, and his point has been interestingly elaborated in broadcasts by Medawar and Frisch.[3] But the point is strikingly plain where clinical hypotheses are concerned. There are still some logicians who hold that "All swans are white" can be derived from observations of white swans, but it is impossible to infer the Oedipus complex in this way, because instances of a combination of parricidal and incestuous wishes are not to be found reported by neurotic or normal subjects, and do not emerge however long such a person free-associates. Indeed, if discoveries of this sort, which have led people to regard Freud as a genius, were so easily made, if all one had to do was to listen to a patient free-associating until at last he produced these ideas, then it would have taken perseverance rather than genius to discover them. And it would be a relatively easy and uncontroversial matter to demonstrate them to the psychiatric world. But even psycho-analysts had difficulty at various times in accepting new clinical hypotheses made by their colleagues, even those hypotheses that later became part of the body of classical theory accepted by them all. Hence such hypotheses do not become obvious by simple observation. The view that discoveries might be obtained simply by waiting and listening would be the psycho-analytic equivalent of the traditional mis-

---

[2] K. R. Popper, *The Logic of Scientific Discovery.* (Hutchinson, London, 1959).

[3] P. B. Medawar, "Is the scientific paper a fraud?," *The Listener,* September 12, 1963; O. R. Frisch, "The magnetic proton," *The Listener,* September 26, 1963.

description of scientific method that hypotheses are established by past experience. Acquiescence in this view is virtually the only way in which analysts have departed from Freud. For, although they mostly use his method, his clinical hypotheses, and his theoretical super-structure, it has not been usual to follow his mode of scientific reflection. Freud seems to have devoted an enormous amount of thought to trying to explain the puzzling elements in what his patients told him. In other words, he did not wait for answers to be presented to him; he seems to have made endless conjectures in an attempt to find explanations, and then sought to apply these and test them. This cast of mind comes out very clearly in his early work *Studies on Hysteria,* and evidence for it is also to be found in the fact that he sought to construct episodes that must have occurred in the past life of his patients—he did not *find* these, he constructed them, and then tried to check them (e.g., from independent witnesses or diaries or subsequent evidence from his patients that confirmed them).

We can now see that it is a methodological mistake to suppose that an interpretation can be correct only if it can be derived and established from preceding associations.

THE GENERAL FRAMEWORK OF TESTING

What alternative procedure, then, might there be? Interestingly enough, the answer comes straight from analysts' own practice as found in published case-histories, and it has been mentioned by the well known American analyst Kubie, though it has almost completely escaped notice in descriptive writing about the subject: study the patient's *response* to the interpretation.[4] Freud (op. cit.) almost certainly followed this procedure. When an analyst reads a case report, it is true he looks at the associations leading up to the interpretation, for he can tell if that was the sort of interpretation he himself might have given, in the light of his experience of similar associations. But he would further look to the responses which *come after* the interpretation, and it is these that enable him to decide whether the interpretation was true or false. (The same holds good

[4] L. S. Kubie, "Problems and techniques of psychoanalytic validation and progress," in *Psychoanalysis as Science,* ed. E. Pumpian-Mindlin (Stanford Univ. Press, Stanford, 1952).

in training learners.) Now consider two possibilities. Suppose the preliminary associations make the interpretation seem very reasonable but the response is off the beam, then the interpretation will be regarded as at least partly false. Now suppose the preliminary associations do *not* make the interpretation seem reasonable to another analyst, he will nevertheless agree that the interpretation was correct if the response is definitely to the point.

Hence the practical position is that clinical interpretations are established or not by their consequences.[5] It is also a logical requirement.

To avoid misunderstanding it should be mentioned that this has nothing to do with whether the interpretation makes the patient better. A scientific test is concerned not with whether a desired change takes place, but with whether a change takes place that is to be expected or understood. So the broad principle involved is, after all, no different from what you would expect on Popper's methodology, and no different from what is involved when a member of a committee tests a conjecture about what is in a colleague's mind by making a proposal that will produce, not an admission, but a response that will disclose the truth.

The Basic Problem

This, however, is only a beginning. How does one assess whether a patient's responses confirm or refute an interpretation or clinical hypothesis? That is the basic methodological problem. Take a situation in which the patient waxes indignant about the traffic he encountered on his way to visit a married woman he had designs upon; bad as it is, he remarks, perhaps it used to be more dangerous in the days of horses because even today, he says, he saw a horse snap at a man trying to control it. The meaning that would most probably be ascribed to this little scene with the horse by analysts is that it represents hostility from the patient's father or from the analyst. Further,

---

[5] Certain psychological features of these methods are worth mentioning. The belief that intuition alone is sufficient stems from omnipotence of thought. The belief that the method of science is induction, which denies intuition any role, stems from a sense of lacking creativeness and is basically depressive. The belief that science works by means of bold ideas, i.e., intuitions, not in themselves sufficient but put to the test stems from the creativeness of fantasy constrained by reality.

the danger occurs in a context of possible adultery. So the analyst gives the Oedipus interpretation, and receives the reply from the patient that he has nothing against his father but has against his boss, who is loud and sharp tongued; still his bark is worse than his bite. This response provides a new disguised version of the interpretation: a man instead of a horse and biting replaced by barking. But emphasis has to be put on the disguise: in other words the response has itself to be interpreted before we can consider whether it confirms or refutes the interpretation being tested. And this may look like some sort of circular process, because it would hardly seem reasonable to test an interpretation by another one whose truth is just as much open to question.

The problem here is perhaps the most basic scientific or methodological problem in the entire subject. Whatever laboratory tests might be tried would establish only that people have Oedipus complexes, but a clinical test is indispensable to explain the patient's associations when they are given. So we are forced to consider the problem of testing one interpretation by another.

Let us consider the following as a possible criterion for testing: that an interpretation embodying a clinical hypothesis is corroborated if the response to it can be interpreted by means of the *same* clinical hypothesis. Thus the response about the barking boss would confirm part of the Oedipus interpretation if it in its turn could be interpreted by the Oedipus hypothesis. The broad idea is clear enough. If you were allowed (methodologically speaking) to interpret responses by means of any theory at all, then every response would confirm the one being tested. Freud by implication seems to have used the above criterion.

More specific proposals have occasionally been made, but they all seem to presuppose this more general one.[6]

The very notion of interpreting an item implies that the item is a disguise. Thus in the associations leading to the Oedipus interpretation to do with the biting horse, there is the presupposition that the

[6] Notable discussions have been given by Freud, 1937d, XXIII; S. Isaacs, "Criteria for Interpretation," *Int. J. Psycho-Anal.* 20 (1939); L. S. Kubie, op. cit.; C. Brenner, "Validation of psychoanalytic technique," *J. Amer. Psychoanal. Assoc.* 3 (1955); and H. Ezriel, "Experimentation within the psychoanalytic session," *Br. J. Phil. Sci.* VII (1956), reprinted in *Psychoanalytic Clinical Interpretation,* ed. L. Paul (Free Press, New York, 1963). Fenichel denied the possibility of unconscious interpretation: see O. Fenichel, "Problems of psychoanalytic technique, III," *Psychoanal. Q.* 8 (1939).

horse is functioning on behalf of the patient's father or is a disguised version of him. Underlying this is the hypothesis of *displacement* —the attitude towards the father is displaced on to the horse. Thus an interpretation presupposes a defence hypothesis. After all, the Oedipus hypothesis simply juxtaposes parricide and incest; it does not say that enmity towards a horse *is* parricide. The displacement hypothesis is needed for that (as a defence against the enormity of the idea). So, to turn the Oedipus hypothesis into an Oedipus interpretation, it is necessary to interpret displacements or other defences.

Likewise, when interpreting a response it is necessary to interpret a defence. There is, however, no reason why the defence in the response should be the same as the one in the prior associations.

A THEORY OF TESTING PROPOSED

Hence our criterion for testing would be, *that a response corroborates an interpretation embodying a hypothesis about clinical content provided it can be interpreted by means of the same hypothesis about clinical content even though with a different hypothesis of defence.*

This complicates our problem, for it is not a case of testing solely the Oedipus hypothesis but of testing this along with some defence hypothesis. The simplest procedure now is to seek some independent test for defences. Displacement can be very simply examined experimentally under hypnosis, but it can also be studied in free association. Very little systematic research has been attempted here, but it could be done. Still, there is a vast body of *un*systematic knowledge garnered and *un*systematically tested over many years of instances of displacement, just as people have a wide unsystematic knowledge of where it is wise to count their change and where there is no need to do so.

The position now is this. Given that displacements do take place, an Oedipus interpretation is an assertion that certain associations are, e.g., father-displacements and that there is a triangular relationship between the patient and such displacements. Can our criterion now be applied? A specific form it could assume has in fact been the subject of research by Ezriel,[7] who has systematically attempted to

[7] Clinical research on unconscious interconnexions or interpretations is a rarity. In addition to Ezriel's, there is the carefully carried out work of Malan: see D. H. Malan, *A Study of Brief Psychotherapy* (Tavistock Publications,

show that in effect the same clinical content hypothesis applies to responses with a diminution of a certain defence, illustrated by the diminution of the physical distance felt by the patient to separate the explosive factors. Methodologically (though not therapeutically) the result would be equally satisfactory if the distance increased. However, such consequences yield only a sufficient condition for confirmation of an interpretation, not a necessary one. A necessary condition, though not the only one, would seem to be the reappearance in the response of the structure of the interpretation in some guise or other.

Now this leads to the question of how we can tell that a response refutes an interpretation. The obvious answer is that a response with a structure different from that of the interpretation refutes it.

A Method of Testing

Nonetheless, if this is in order, my answer is hardly yet sufficiently elaborated. A further difficulty is that, *if an interpretation that was given had in fact been held back, the response might have been in line with the unvoiced interpretation all the same,* because continuous with the preceding associations.

To deal with this we should have to elaborate our criterion in terms of the effect of intervening. A broad answer is not too difficult: that the response should embody a predictable defence, i.e., the analyst should be able to know whether the response would express the preceding associations in a clearer form after the interpretation or whether a strong defence might be expected. He would have to be able to predict the form of defence likely to occur. But he would also have to be able to specify what defence would probably have occurred if he had made no active intervention, so as to see whether the flow of associations would be influenced by the actual giving of the interpretation. It should be possible to effect a more specific test by counting the proportion of predictions that are correct when interpretations are actually withheld and the proportion when they are given: from this one could tell the probability of influence of an interpretation.

London, 1963). John Bowlby's well-known and important research on delinquents centres on a clinical hypothesis but does not apply to clinical interpretations.

It is, of course, vital to bear in mind that the procedure put forward applies in the first place only to interpretations to do with wishes where defences are not also interpreted. It could, however, be adapted to interpretations of defence.

With these qualifications in mind, it will be seen that there is such a thing as the clinical testing of clinical hypotheses, but that it is vastly different from the testing for home-truths that goes on in day-to-day life. Moreover, on the present theory, a false interpretation is capable of being refuted. It therefore satisfies Popper's refutability criterion for science. Unfortunately the possibility of refuting a false interpretation may be undermined by one special phenomenon —suggestion. How does this come about?

THE PROBLEM OF REFUTABILITY AND SUGGESTION

Almost as old as psycho-analysis itself is the charge that it acts by suggestion. It is well known that under hypnosis suggestions are obeyed: thus if a subject in a trance is told to stand on one leg he will do so; if he is given a post-hypnotic suggestion to brush his teeth after lunch, he will do so even though he is no longer in the trance and despite the strange time of day; if told he will be able to move his (hysterically) paralyzed arm, he will be able to carry this out. Is it, then, in the same way that the psycho-analyst effects changes in patients, purely by suggestion? In other words, do the interpretations given by analysts merely implant suggestions, and is a change in a patient merely a suggestion-effect?

This is an interesting question. It has been less discussed of recent times than formerly. In the early days analysts were at considerable pains to point out that analysis is the exact opposite of suggestion. The chief ground for this was that analysis is based on insight while suggestion belies it. This answer is incomplete, however, for we should need to consider what proof there may be that an insight is true, i.e., that the sense of conviction of insight is not itself due to suggestion. Again, if an occasional patient can react as if to suggestion, how in principle can this be detected; for this is the complement of the question, how in principle can it be told that another patient is *not* reacting to suggestion? Again, if analytic therapy were suggestion, there would be no grounds for accepting the theory of psycho-analysis rather than some other. Part of the interest of the question lies in the challenge it presents to refute the suggestion view, which has never been adequately refuted; but the main point is that, unless this is done, analytic theory can have no claim to truth.

Critics down the decades have claimed that the suggestion-effect may always be present. Thus (i) it has long been argued that each type of psychotherapy leads to its own theoretical conclusions; it is implied that some of these are incompatible with each other, or at least that some are false; and the consequence reached is that the psychotherapies work by implanting suggestions. Further (ii) it is argued that each type of therapy evokes associations that fit the theories governing the type of therapy, which could only be a suggestion-effect. These criticisms amount to the same thing in the end,[8] but it may be worth discussing them separately.

(i) The variation in the conclusions reached by various schools may, however, be explained independently of suggestion. It is quite possible, indeed probable, that therapists mainly look only for *confirmations* of their interpretations, overlooking the need to seek out *refutations*. Now it is vital to distinguish between refutations that are present though not noticed and the absence of refutations. If refutation is disregarded, Popper has shown that confirmation of a hypothesis can in general be found *for any hypothesis* even though false; thus confirmation alone is valueless as support for a hypothesis. Hence different hypotheses could all be confirmed simply by seeking confirmations. Hence the phenomenon of different results could be explained by faulty methodology on the part of therapists of the various schools. *It is conceivable that no discrepant conclusions would arise if therapists sought refutations rather than confirmations.*

(ii) In the situation where the therapist gets associations that confirm his theories, it looks even more strongly as though refutations have not been sought. The associations are confirmatory but do not really strengthen his theories unless they could have been refutations.

Where the therapist does not notice refutations that are present in the material presented by a patient but marks up *confirmations,* he takes his interpretation to be confirmed even though it is in fact

---

[8] On the inductive methodology, (i) would concern conclusions arrived at inductively from a patient's associations, and (ii) would concern subsequent confirmation of conclusions; on the hypothetico-deductive methodology, however, both are tests of hypotheses.

false, i.e., he obtains confirmation for a false hypothesis.[9] And this result would flow not from suggestion but from faulty methodology.

On the other hand, where no refutations are present, this might be the result of suggestion. For, if suggestion does occur, what it must do is to abolish refutations that would otherwise be present. In such a situation confirmation would flow from a suggestion-effect.

The therapist cannot be certain that a lack of refutation is real evidence for an interpretation, unless there is some way of telling that it is free of suggestion.[10] *And the presence of confirmations might arise either through the methodology of confirmation which ignores refutation, or suggestion which sabotages refutation;* moreover no clear way of telling which is at work has yet emerged.

Before trying to go further with this, let us enquire into the psychology of the situation.

THE PSYCHOLOGY OF SUGGESTION

Suppose an interpretation works by suggestion, what is it that is happening? To answer this, let us consider certain ways in which an interpretation might have an effect upon a patient. Possible ways are in virtue (i) of the sound of the interpretation, (ii) of the meaning or content of it irrespective of its truth or falsity, or (iii) of the content because it is in fact true of the patient and felt by him to be so.

(i)   In certain states a patient may fail to attend to the meaning of what is said altogether, but may nevertheless respond to the analyst's act of speaking (when the uttering of something else would have the same effect), i.e., the patient is responding to the bare existence of a communication, in which the patient attributes to the analyst's remarks no more content than "I am here, I accept you, and I am making contact with you." This might be called "communication of presence." It might conceivably have an effect upon a patient that might be wrongly attributed to the context of the interpretation and therefore to the theory underlying it.

(ii)   If the meaning or content of an interpretation brings about

---

[9] Mr. A. S. S. el Kaffash has pointed out to me that a therapist, both when he overlooks a negative transference and when he notes it but treats it as resistance, may be overlooking the possibility of refutations of his interpretation.

[10] Contrariwise, proof that an interpretation acted as a suggestion could be obtained if it could somehow be shown to be false without being refuted by the patient.

an effect irrespective of whether it is true or false, which is solely because the analyst has asserted that content, then we have the suggestion-effect. A further feature of the suggestion-effect comes to light here. The interpretation is accepted irrespective of whether it is *recognized* by the patient to be true (or false) of himself. But it is accepted by him as true: true not on the basis of *evidence* but of *authority,* true because somebody asserts it.

(iii)   Truth of content involves recognition of evidence rather than authority, and therefore contrasts fundamentally with suggestion.

Which of these three possibilities is the mainspring of interpretations?

We may go some way towards answering this from a practical point of view by considering what sort of patient might come under the sway of the suggestion-effect. What would lead him to adopt a suggestion? He might do so, for instance, if he received a false interpretation and wanted to ingratiate himself with the therapist. Again he might do so to throw dust in the therapist's eyes, i.e., to prevent him from finding out where the real sore spots lay. Again he might accept the interpretation to avoid being terror-stricken at the idea that his therapist could possibly be wrong. In short there could be the (hysteric's) motive of control by ingratiation or the (more or less universal) motive of the safety of the false trail or the (infantile) motive of avoiding terror at helplessness—which are various facets of coping with dependence.

If these possibilities can be detected, then in their absence we should be on the road to the third one, that an important factor in the operation of an interpretation is its truth. Something can be done along these lines. The "communication of presence" may sometimes be easy to recognize intuitively, but that is not enough: how could we exclude the possibility of a more concrete meaning being communicated to the patient? To this end a test can be invented: frame an "interpretation" consisting of a meaningless string of words. (This might, of course, be therapeutically or ethically ruled out.) Then diminution of anxiety would be evidence of communication of presence alone. Again ingratiation, which may be intuitively recognized, can be tested by propounding an incompatible interpretation. The patient bent on ingratiation will swallow both, while one not so inclined will jib. The patient who is game to follow a red-herring may be intuitively recognized by his over-seriousness about it. This could be tested by going further along the false trail with an interpretation that ought to wound if the trail is genuine: if no resistance is offered, the trail is false. (Such a test could also be used for ingratiation.) Again, acceptance out of terror might be tested by making a stupid remark about the patient: he might then be expected to show mounting anxiety, yet to agree.

Supposing these possibilities of collusion are tested in a given patient and found to be absent, we have some practical grounds for being confident that the patient is not suggestible, and that the other interpretations given to him are not suggestion-implanting. Methodologically, however, this is incomplete. For there might be other ways, apart from ingratiation, false trails, and avoidance of terror, not thought of so far, by which a patient could produce a suggestion-effect. So from a methodological point of view, stronger proof is needed. Moreover, the tests indicated presuppose various psychoanalytic hypotheses which are being scrutinized for a suggestion basis.

There is another facet of a wrong interpretation. Just now we have been considering classes of patients who might acquiesce in a wrong interpretation. What about patients who might revolt against a mistake (because of fear that their troubles would not be dealt with)? Such patients might be expected to make desperate efforts to get the therapist back on the trail (their efforts might very easily look like resistance—which of course they are, though not resistance to the truth). If they can be detected, they might seem to provide definite evidence against suggestion. Alas, this conclusion founders on the possibility of such a patient's being *contra-suggestible*. That is to say, if an interpretation somehow suggests to a patient that he likes something or other, he reacts by asserting that he dislikes it.

This idea has to be considered because it might be held that, where a patient does *not* acquiesce by ingratiation or following a false trail, his reactions, so far from being true, are merely *contra-suggestion-effects*.

Such a phenomenon would spring from the opposite source to that siring suggestion, namely annihilation of authority. It could reveal an insatiable wish to annoy the therapist and reduce him to pulp. The phenomenon could also spring from an overt refusal to allow the therapist to get near to the source of the patient's troubles. And it could presuppose that to accept an interpretation as true would be the patient's doom. Here evidence can play no part; there is only a struggle between authorities: for the patient to accept an interpretation would be to lose his authority (without which he would see himself as nothing). In general, a contra-suggestion-effect might be suspected where a patient has a marked sense of omnipotence.

The first of these, the opposition-*motif*, could be tested by giving the opposite interpretation, to see whether the patient would disagree at any price, even the price of giving a response contradicting his previous one. The second, to do with avoidance of sore spots, could be tested by giving an interpretation that would touch nothing sensitive, when no opposition would normally be expected: here it would be opposed on principle. And the third, to do with loss of authority, might be tested by the therapist's saying (if it can be plausibly done) that the patient's contention was what he had really meant—to see whether the patient would then have second thoughts about his position.

But again the refutation of such contra-suggestion-effects is insufficient to establish the truth of an interpretation.

Now supposing that in a given setting there is no suggestion-effect of the kinds discussed, is the idea satisfactory of an interpretation producing an effect by reason of its being true? Psycho-analysts themselves—such authorities as Freud and Strachey[11]—have claimed that at this point suggestion plays some part. What is the meaning of such an admission, or claim, by those who also oppose the charge that psycho-analytic therapy is suggestion? Clearly "suggestion" here has an altogether different meaning, but this has never been adequately brought to light.

The occurrence of a true interpretation, which appeared by chance on a news tape in front of the patient, would not do much; it needs also to be uttered by the therapist. Thus the truth of an interpretation, while necessary, is not sufficient to produce change. Also necessary is the utterance of it by someone where there is a patient-therapist relationship. Certainly this utterance may be called a "suggestion" insofar as the authority of the therapist is invoked. But this authority is not a sufficient condition for implanting a suggestion; for the authoritative interpretation has also to be true. The whole difference between the charge of suggestion made by critics and the claim of suggestion made by psycho-analysts is that suggestion in the ordinary sense is supposed to be at work to produce ideas in the pa-

---

[11] Freud, 1925d, XX, 7–74; J. Strachey, "The nature of the therapeutic action of psycho-analysis," *Int. J. Psycho-Anal.* 15 (1934).

tient that are not already there, while suggestion in the sense used by Strachey is supposed to be at work to evoke ideas in the patient that he already has. It is likely to cause confusion, however, to speak of "suggestion" in this sense, and I shall avoid it.

ENACTIVITY AND TRUTH

Let us now look for a more decisive way of settling the matter whether or not an interpretation works by suggestion. To do this, let us revert to the general question of testing an interpretation by its effects. Earlier in this paper I have put forward the theory that an interpretation of a motive is confirmed if it fits the patient's response to it, provided that in his response the defence used to disguise the motive is different from what it would have been without the interpretation. Now Seaborn Jones discussing an earlier sketch of this view, has pointed out that, strictly speaking, this constitutes a theory not for testing the *truth* of the interpretation but for testing its power to bring about some change, i.e., it would be what Seaborn Jones called "enactive"; for the response described would confirm that the interpretation had had some effect.[12] And this could happen and yet the interpretation might actually be false. Seaborn Jones is therefore distinguishing sharply between the enactivity and the truth of an interpretation. It is a vital distinction.

The significant problem, then, concerns the discrimination between interpretations that are enactive and true and interpretations that are enactive and false.[13] The theory I have offered is a theory of enactivity, and thus amounts to an application of the methodology of

---

[12] See G. Seaborn Jones, "Some Philosophical Implications of Psycho Analysis" (Ph.D. thesis, University of London). Seaborn Jones was discussing the idea I put forward in J. O. Wisdom, "Psycho-analytic Technology," *Br. J. Phil. Sci.* VII (1956), but his point holds equally of the further development given above.

[13] The case of non-enactive interpretations has little interest, though there is a point worth noting. Suppose such an interpretation is true (it is perfectly possible to give a patient true interpretations that have absolutely no effect, as those learning to be psychotherapists know only too well), but the analyst could not discover this at the time because of its lack of enactivity. Years later in the treatment of the patient the analyst might discover that his earlier useless interpretation had been in fact true. But this would probably depend on being able to test enactive interpretations. The likelihood is that it will be easier to test for their truth those interpretations that are enactive rather than those that have no effect.

refutability to purposive action. (Psycho-analysts are vitally concerned with enactivity: it bears on what they call "technique.") Our problem now is to find a way of telling whether an enactive interpretation is true or false.

PROPOSED SOLUTION

What would be the situation in which an interpretation would be false even though enactive?

To consider this we revert to the view I have already presented about the structure of an interpretation. It consists of (i) a hypothesis about the motives contained in the patient's associations; and (ii) a hypothesis about the defence he uses to disguise these motives. The interpretation is false if either of these is false. Now it is certainly false if the patient's response has a structure that has to be interpreted differently. But could it be false even if the interpretation does fit the motive of the response? What this comes to is the question: could the patient somehow (i) preserve the same motive in his response and yet (ii) concoct a defence in the form expected by the analyst that would not give a true picture of the workings of his mind? If this is possible, we should have an interpretation that was false but ostensibly enactive.

This would be so if the patient had learnt from past experience to preserve the motive in his response and what sort of defence should be shown by it.[14] Here, I think, we have a statement of what the theory of the suggestion-effect, as it might be called, amounts to. It is worth stating, not only for its own sake and for the clarity gained, but also because it derives part of its power from remaining unarticulated.

An articulated theory is more or less immune to criticism. But now that we have a possible theory of the suggestion-effect before us, we can at once see an irreparable defect in it. The ordinary idea of suggestion, rooted in the context of hypnosis, is that the hypnotist tells a subject what to think and he thinks it, what to feel and he feels

---

[14] A remote alternative would be if the patient had learnt to read the analyst's mind, i.e., what response the analyst expected. In this case the charge of suggestion would presuppose clairvoyance on the part of nearly all patients—an assumption that those who have levelled the charge of suggestion would be unwilling to make.

it, what to do, and he does it. Here the idea is in part the same: namely that the patient shall produce in his response the motive interpreted (suggested?) by the analyst. But it is in part very different: namely that the patient shall produce in his response a form of defence that is *not* suggested.

Could a patient, however, learn from past experience to preserve the motive in his response and learn what sort of defence should be shown by it? Even if such a feat were possible, it could not happen *early* in the treatment.

For example, there is on record an interpretation given to a schizophrenic patient within the first minutes of the first analytic session, which produced relief in him and a response of personal contact (recognizably similar to the response of a stranger, say, if you happen to mention a mutual friend, as contrasted, say, with a reference to the weather). The interpretation was enactive; and clearly so, because no other way has ever been found of making contact with psychotics.

After all, then, there is quite a simple answer to the question of suggestion. It consists of two points: (i) the theory of corroboration of an interpretation involves a predictable type of defence in a patient's response, which is not suggested; and (ii) the type of defence could not have been learnt in the early weeks of treatment. This answer implies that psycho-analytic interpretation does not, from its intrinsic nature, operate by suggestion.

THE FINAL TEST

We can, therefore, test a clinical interpretation by the method described earlier in this paper, provided we also ensure in the way now described that no suggestion-effect is present, so that the interpretation is refutable.

Freud's Psychology of Language

JOHN C. MARSHALL

INTRODUCTION

It is now generally recognized that Freud's early neurological studies are both intrinsically important and in many respects crucial to a full understanding of his psychoanalytic works (Pribram, 1962; Wollheim, 1971).* The link between these two phases of Freud's work is provided by his deep and lasting interest in the psychology of language. Accordingly, I shall begin by describing briefly the context to Freud's investigations in the neuropsychology of language; this section will thus form a background to the discussion of Freud's original contributions to the discipline and their eventual transformation into the framework of psychoanalysis.

THE STATE OF THE ART

The correlation between head-injuries and disorders of language has always fascinated physicians. Clinical observations of language-impairment by Sumerian, Egyptian and Graeco-Roman scholars are among the earliest extant medical documents. Most of the major varieties of impairment that are currently recognized were astutely described between the Renaissance and the end of the eighteenth century (Benton and Joynt, 1960) and led to the first two systematic attempts at an explanation of the relationship between brain-structure and language-function; modern theorization begins with Gesner (1770) and Gall (1810).

The models for Gesner and Gall's interpretations were provided by Anglo-French associationism and Herder's organic metaphors, respectively.

The association philosophy, particularly in the form expounded by Hartley (1749), encouraged scholars to interpret disorders of cognitive functioning as failures of connection between the components of a vast associative machine. Hartley, with a little help

* A list of references other than works of Freud appears at the end of this article; see pp. 363–65.

from Newton's *Opticks,* provided the speculative neurology for this enterprise: "The doctrine of *vibrations* may appear at first sight to have no connection with that of *association;* however, if these doctrines be found in fact to contain the laws of the bodily and mental powers respectively, they must be related to each other, since the body and mind are. One may expect that vibrations should infer association as their effect, and association points to vibrations as its cause."

Prior to Gesner (1770), acquired disorders of speech had often been regarded as resulting from paralysis of the tongue or as one aspect of a generalized memory-loss. Gesner, however, paid particular attention to cases in which "semantic paraphasia" was an outstanding symptom—a patient would involuntarily say "Good morning" in the evening, and "Good evening" in the morning. Concerning such a case Gesner writes: "Thus in a quite special sense he seems to have lost complete control of his tongue." He notes that in patients whose speech consists in the main of incomprehensible jargon, some meaningful expressions may remain; these expressions will be highly familiar words, common phrases and expletives. In cases of severe expressive disorder, Gesner notes that comprehension of language may be relatively well preserved: "Therefore, I see only a forgetting of speech when [the patient] says meaningful words which do not correspond to his ideas or when he utters meaningless sounds that perhaps suggest to us a remote and often incomprehensible similarity to the correct words or give us a false impression of his thoughts." Likewise, he remarks that when comprehension is impaired the deficit is disproportionately severe for abstract concepts: Therefore ". . . just as some verbal powers become weakened without injury to others, memory also can be specifically impaired to a greater or lesser degree with respect to only certain classes of ideas."

Gesner, then, stressed the orderly linguistic nature of language-breakdown; but because "systemic" concepts were not available to him he could not make much sense of these regularities in terms of formal mechanism: "The vessels of the brain are surely not arranged in accordance with categories of . . . ideas and therefore it is incomprehensible that these categories should correspond to areas of destruction." Nonetheless, Gesner and his contemporaries laid the foundations for an associationist neuropsychology. Crichton (1789) is quite explicit. Concerning expressive disorders, he writes:

". . . this very singular defect of memory ought rather to be considered as a defect of that principle, by which ideas, and their proper expressions, are associated, than memory." Yet in spite of Hartley's original work and Mendelssohn's (1783) attempt, albeit with an inadequate formalism, to quantify the degree of association between internal states and their motor expression, the theory of dysphasia remained in a fairly primitive state for a century.

The second strand in eighteenth- and early nineteenth-century interpretations of language, sprang from quite different roots. German Romanticism from Herder to Von Humboldt conceived of psychological, sociological and political structure in terms of organic metaphors. Opposing what they regarded as the crude mechanical and "sensational" notions of the *philosophes,* such scholars took the growth of a plant or an embryo as their general model of mental capacity in man and animal. Notions of development and ramification from within, determined by innate dynamic principles, formed an essential part of "an ideology of cultural crisis" (Anderson, 1941).

Within such a tradition it was reasonable to think of form and function as intimately connected. As Herder (1772) writes in his *Origin of Language:* "The plucked chord performs its natural duty: it sounds!" In a later work, the *Ideen* (1784), he suggests that the "psychophysiological path of comparison" should be the basic methodological tool in investigations of human psychology. It was Herder's writings which convinced Gall that he should study comparative anatomy, and which determined the mode of explanation he sought —correlations between development of psychological functions and the growth of the nervous organs serving those faculties (Temkin, 1953; Lesky, 1967). In his first book, Gall (1791) notes: "Most philosophers it is true, find it ridiculous that the various psychic talents and concepts should be thought to have their seat in different parts of the brain. But if this is ridiculous, then it is ridiculous also that the different senses are located in different parts of the body, that our several parts feel in different ways . . . for sight and hearing are just as much psychic talents as are the different kinds of ideas."

As a schoolboy, Gall had observed that those of his classmates who were particularly good at learning verbal material by heart had large, protruding eyes; accordingly he placed the faculty of verbal memory in the frontal lobes. Later, Gall was to find "confirmation" for this notion when he studied a man injured in a fencing accident.

The point of the foil had penetrated the left frontal lobe; although the patient could recognize people and behave appropriately towards them, he could not recall their names.

The neurophysiological community as a whole was not overly enthusiastic about Gall's methods and theory (see Young, 1970), yet aphasiologists continued to report cases consistent with Gall's localization (Bouilland, 1825; Andral, 1834). Finally, in a long series of publications between 1861 and 1866, Paul Broca convinced most workers that expressive (motor) aphasia was primarily associated with lesions to the anterior portions of the left hemisphere (see Huard, 1960).

Given that differential impairment of different aspects of linguistic skill was well established, it now became possible to seek, and find, anatomical locales for subcomponents of the language faculty other than Broca's "seat of *articulate* language." More importantly, in order to avoid postulation of faculties *ad nauseam,* it was necessary to combine into one theoretical framework Gesner's associationism and Gall's emphasis upon anatomy. This step was taken by a number of neurologists (see Wernicke, 1874, and Lichtheim, 1885, for discussion and references), who were later to be referred to (contemptuously) as "the diagram makers" by Head (1926). Their intention was to explain the varieties of aphasia by invoking localized centres of different types linked in specified ways by association tracts. The magnitude of the "diagram makers' " achievement lay in the fact that they formalized their theories by finite-state flow charts; a particular diagram would thus generate, without benefit of intuition, a typology of the aphasias through injury to postulated centres and disconnections between them. It was realized that such a notation could, in principle, "explain" any constellation of symptoms by the expedient of proliferating centres and connections. Accordingly, it was argued that postulation of a centre was only justified if it enabled one "to represent the causation of other *derangements of speech*" (Broadbent, 1878) than the one which initially prompted it; a "simplicity criterion" was hinted at so that "the better theory" was the one which generated all the observed symptom-complexes (and no nonobserved symptom-complexes) by the smaller number of centres and pathways (Bastian, 1897).

Although these centres were regarded as innately given by the biological constitution of *homo sapiens,* notions of plasticity were not disregarded. Broca held the *innate* pre-eminence of the left hemisphere (in the majority of the population) responsible both for the fact that most people are right-handed, and for the fact that left-hemisphere lesions are correlated with aphasia. The notion of "innate" was conceived, however, in terms of inborn predispositions which could be strengthened, modified and perhaps changed by experience during certain critical periods. Broca thus guessed that if the left hemisphere was injured at birth, or shortly thereafter, normal language development, mediated by the right hemisphere, need not be precluded. (Freud, 1897a, was to vindicate this speculation in his studies of infantile hemiplegia.) The observed varieties of traumatic dyslexia were related to the patient's educational level and the method by which he had been taught to read (Wernicke, 1874; Elder, 1900).

Individual differences held considerable fascination for Charcot, as they had for Gall. Thus Charcot (1883) suggested that the "imaginal type" of a subject might be related to the patterns of deficit observed after head-injury; he thus argued that in word-retrieval different subjects may rely to a greater or lesser degree upon visual, acoustic or motor strategies. Injury to a particular lobe of the brain would selectively disrupt performance to the extent that the lesion corresponded with the subject's preferred retrieval-strategy. In part, Charcot adopted this idea in order to reconcile apparent counter examples with a strict localization theory of language-functions. One of his star pupils, Freud, was, however, to propose dispensing with the entire framework.

NEUROLINGUISTIC INQUIRIES

Apart from "technical" problems (that is, problems which could, in principle, be resolved *within* the diagram makers' paradigm), conceptual lacunae quickly came to light. The paradigm provided few (or no) suggestions concerning the internal structure of the postulated "centres" and the nature of the coding principles whereby they were interconnected; no serious notion of "computation" was available. One consequence was that the relationship between mind and body (or mind and brain) remained as mysterious as ever. What could it mean to "localize" a psychological faculty *in* an anatomical area? In spite of the fact that he maintained an agnostic position on this question, Gall had been thrown out of Austria by the Viennese priesthood for the crime of materialism. To no avail he defended himself: "When I say that the exercise of our moral and intellectual faculties depends upon material conditions, I do not mean to imply that our faculties are a product of the organism; this would be confounding *conditions* with *efficient causes.*"

Wernicke (1874), although subtitling his monograph "A Psychological Study on an Anatomical Basis," felt decidedly unhappy about localizing entire faculties. In explicit opposition to Gall, he reverts to the position that Kant (1798) argued for: ". . . only the most elementary psychic functions can be assigned to specific areas of the cerebral cortex. Everything beyond these elementary functions, such as the linking of different sense impressions to form a concept, thought, and consciousness, is a function of the fibre tracts that connect different cortical regions with each other . . ."

Even this weakening of the doctrine would not satisfy Freud: "But does one not in principle make the same mistake irrespective of whether one tries to localize a complicated concept, a whole mental faculty or a psychic element? Is it justified to immerse a nerve fibre, which over the whole length of its course has been only a physiological structure subject to physiological modifications, with its end in the psyche and furnish this end with an idea or memory? Now that 'will' and 'intelligence', etc., have been recognized as psychological technical terms referring to very complicated physiological states, can one be quite sure that the 'simple sensory impression' be anything but another such technical term?" (1891b).

In this passage we can see Freud taking up a correspondence or "two language" account of the relationship of mind to brain. He continues to discuss the cause-effect "chain of physiological events in the nervous system" and notes that "a mental phenomenon corresponds to each part of the chain, or to several parts." But the point has been made more strongly by the stress that Freud lays upon the "technical term" status of "will," "intelligence" and "sensory impression," etc. For Freud, however (as indeed for Gall, who wished to "put an end to the high-handed generalizations of the philosophers"), the issue concerns not the philosophical merits (or otherwise) of this position but the leverage it provided for constructing a "Psychology for Neurologists." A central concept of this enterprise was the notion of "levels of representation."

While working with Charcot at the Salpetriere Freud's attention had been drawn to the differences between hysterical and organic paralyses, and between hysterical and organic aphasias. For example, "The [hysterical] aphasic utters not a word, whereas the organic aphasic almost always retains a few words, 'yes' or 'no', a swear-word, etc." (1893c, I, 164). Likewise, it is possible for hysteria to "create total aphasia (motor and sensory) for a particular language without in the slightest interfering with the faculty of understanding and articulating another." In other words, the hysteric behaves as if he has not read the clinical literature on aphasia from Gesner onwards.

Similar points can be made with respect to paralyses. For example, ". . . the hysteric drags the leg like an inert mass instead of performing a circumduction with the hip as does the ordinary hemiplegic." The hysteric does not "know" that in organic hemiplegia "the proximal portion of the limb is always to some extent exempt." More generally, hysterical paralysis is "characterized by *precise limitation* and *excessive intensity* . . ." whereas in "organic cerebral paralysis . . . it is regularly found *that these two characteristics are not associated with each other.*" Freud sums up: ". . . Hysteria behaves as though anatomy did not exist or as though it had no knowledge of it."

In thinking about paralyses, Freud found the first two points that he was to extrapolate to a theory of the brain. Clinicians and anatomists prior to Freud distinguished two major types of organic paralysis, periphero-spinal and cerebral paralysis, the first being a paralysis *"détaillée,"* the second a paralysis *"en masse."* In the first case, "Each element in the periphery corresponds to an element in the grey matter of the cord, which as M. Charcot has said, is its nervous termination; the periphery is, so to say, projected upon the grey matter of the cord, point by point and element by element" (1893c, I, 161). Accordingly, Freud calls this a *projection* paralysis. But the mapping from the spinal cord to the cerebral cortex is no longer one-to-one. Peripheral elements are typically represented in the cortex in a many-to-one relationship; and it may even be the case sometimes that "one element on the periphery may correspond to several spino-cortical conductive fibres." Thus Freud proposes the term *representation* paralysis for the effects of cerebral injury. Given the explicitness of this terminology, it is now a (relatively) short leap to suggest that there may be many different cortical representations for the "same" function. Freud broaches this possibility in Letter 52 to Fliess: ". . . As you know, I am working on the assumption that our psychical mechanism has come into being by a process of stratification: the material present in the form of memory-traces being subjected from time to time to a re-arrangement in accordance with fresh circumstances—to a re-transcription. Thus what is essentially new about my theory is the thesis that memory is present not once but several times over, that it is laid down in various species of indications."

In published form, this approach is first worked out in the monograph on aphasia. Freud characterizes the relationship of fibre tracts (from the periphery) to the cortex in the following terms: "They contain the body periphery in the same way as—to borrow an example from the subject with which we are concerned here—a poem contains the alphabet, i.e., in a completely different arrangement serving other purposes, in manifold association of the individual elements, whereby some may be represented several times, others not at all" (1891b).

Consideration of language above all disposes one to this way of looking at neuropsychology. That the structure of language must be described on several, interrelated levels—phonologic, syntactic, semantic, etc.—and that these levels may be selectively impaired by brain-injury, leads naturally to interpreting other functions in an analogous fashion. Freud is now in a position to propose a radical alternative to the diagram makers' paradigm.

He does not, of course, deny that injury to different parts of the brain is made manifest in different patterns of psychological impairment. Rather Freud attempts to spell out the implications of Hughlings Jackson's remark (1874) that "to locate the damage which destroys speech and to locate speech are two different things." For Freud, "the appearance of centres" results from the anatomical fact that "the cortical fields of the optic, auditory and motor cranial nerves" are to be found in circumscribed areas of the brain. The "so-called centres" are sited in close proximity to these cortical fields: "Broca's area is immediately adjacent to the centres of the bulbar motor nerves. Wernicke's area is situated in a region which also contains the acoustic termination . . . the visual speech centre borders on those parts of the occipital lobe in which we know the optic nerve to terminate." Freud returns to the associationist paradigm: "The speech area of the cortex is seen rather as a continuous region of the cortex inserted between the motor fields of the cortex and those of the optic and auditory nerves—a region within which all communication and association subserving speech function takes place. The so-called speech centres revealed by the pathology of the brain correspond merely to the corners of this field of speech; they are not distinguished functionally from the interior regions; it is only on account of their position in relation to the contiguous cortical centres that they produce more obvious signs when they become disordered" (1897b, III, 240). The speech centres, then, "may claim a pathological but no special physiological significance" (1891b).

Having rejected topographical in favour of functional modes of explanation, Freud must now confront Gesner's dilemma directly. If localized subcomponents of the language faculty are an anatomical artifact, how are we to explain the systematic nature of aphasic breakdown? The dominating passions of Freud's life—to introduce *quantitative* considerations into neuropsychology, and to interpret the relationship between the normal and the pathological—here come to his aid.

Freud notes that aphasic errors and word-finding difficulties are not characteristic solely of aphasics: ". . . the paraphasia observed in aphasic patients does not differ from the incorrect use and distortion of words which the healthy person may observe in himself in states of fatigue or divided attention or under the influence of disturbing affects, the kind of thing that frequently happens to our lecturers and causes the listener painful embarrassment" (1891b). Dissociation of different levels of linguistic performance may also occur in the normal subject: "When I read proofs with the intention of paying special attention to the letters and other symbols, the meaning of what I am reading escapes me to such a degree that I require a second perusal for the purpose of correcting the style. If, on the other hand, I read a novel, which holds my interest, I overlook all misprints and it may happen that I retain nothing of the names of the persons figuring in the book except for some meaningless feature, or perhaps the recollection that they were long or short, and that they contained an unusual letter such as x or z."

Such a variety of dissociation is only possible in complex behaviour whose psychological structure must be explicated by multi-level descriptions: "The speech apparatus is . . . exceptional, in having at its disposal such a wealth of symptoms that it may be expected to betray, by the type and manner of the disturbance of function, not only the site but also the nature of the lesion." For twenty years, linguists had been stressing that the direction of the asphasiologists' efforts was misguided. Chaim Steinthal (1871) argued strongly that the emphasis on discovering the location of the speech centre had led to a lamentable neglect of straightforward, detailed observations of the varieties of linguistic impairment: "The clinical descriptions," he concluded, "are much too incomplete and are inaccurately recorded. Our physicians have as yet no clear concept of what the function of language is." It is sad that then, as in later times, linguists showed little inclination to collect and analyse their own data in this area. The current trend, in which this does happen, is of exceeding recent origin (cf. Blumstein, 1970; Whitaker, 1969, 1972). Nevertheless, Steinthal's influence was considerable in determining the philosophy of science adopted by later psycholinguists: "Psychology is the most necessary pre-requisite for a physiology of the brain, and it will also vouchsafe a rational psychiatry." (It is interesting to note that in 1930 Lashley found it desirable to repeat this message: "Psychology today is a more fundamental science than neurophysiology. By this I mean the latter offers few principles from which we may predict or define the normal organization of behaviour, whereas the study of psychological processes furnishes a mass of factual material to which the laws of neural action in behaviour must conform.")

Freud had clearly taken Steinthal's critique to heart. He refers approvingly to the elaboration of this position that had been undertaken by the great "neo-grammarian" linguist Berthold Delbrück. The *Jung-Grammatiker* regarded themselves as the intellectual heirs of Von Humboldt and Steinthal in that they continued the "psychologisation" of linguistics begun by those scholars. Brugmann's inaugural lecture at Freiburg (1885) pays homage to both Humboldt and Steinthal. Concerning the latter, Brugmann remarks that had the older generation understood what Steinthal was trying to do, a change in basic linguistic methodology would have resulted. For the neo-grammarians, the point of Steinthal's paradigm was, of course, that psychological laws provide an explanation for the dynamic processes of language change. These psychological factors were held to include memory-limitations, consistent slips of the tongue and analogical formations, determined by the strength and form of associative connections. The role played by the child in language-change was crucial; first-language acquisition was a process regarded as especially susceptible to (mistaken) analogy formation over the simplified, internalized grammars which characterize the early stages of language-learning. Associative errors were so highly prized for the insight they provided into possible mechanisms that the neo-grammarians occasionally felt constrained to redress the balance; "Are these aberrations, substitutions, and analogies the only processes in the psyche of the speaker? Does not the regular cultivation of the linguistic estate belong to the psyche as well? . . . I am not aware of any psychologist who considers only dreams, the intoxicated state, or delirium as the sole object of his science. Are we to regard lapses in speech as a higher grade of psychological process than speaking?" (Curtius, 1885).

Historically, then, Freud falls into place as the first neo-grammarian neurolinguist.

Freud follows Delbrück (1886) in distinguishing different linguistic varieties of paraphasia, including semantic substitution (where the patient says, for example, "Potsdam" for "Berlin"), and phonological confusion (where the patient may say "Campher" for "Pamphlet"). He notes that fusions may occur; the patient produces *"Vutter"* for *"Mutter"* and *"Vater."* In another type of paraphasia, specific lexical items will be replaced by more general (superordinate) terms. Function words and non-specific phrases may be relatively well preserved in patients who show perseveration and other "impoverishment in nouns, adjectives and verbs." "It is tempting," Freud remarks, "to differentiate between various types of paraphasia according to the part of the speech apparatus at which the mistake took place."

The diagram makers had attempted to interpret such symptoms by invoking rather vague notions about "minimal damage" to a centre, or "reduced excitability" of a centre. (These ideas are quite similar to Charcot's concept of a "dynamic, or functional, lesion" which was held to be the cause of hysterical symptoms.) Freud realized that *the form of representation* of language in the brain must be such that local lesions can disturb the functioning of a linguistically well-defined subset of structures. He agrees with the diagram makers that "partial loss can always be shown to be the expression of a general lowering of the functional activity of that centre." But, he continues: "It is not . . . a matter of course that the speech centres should behave in this way; their reactions to damage suggest a certain concept regarding their organization."

The hierarchical structure of linguistic descriptions of the adult's language provides part of that organization; the successive developmental stages of the acquisition-process result in further constraints. The entire system interlocks, with different modalities (acoustic, kinaesthetic, etc.) providing a different representation of the conceptual structure: "The safeguards of our speech against breakdown thus appear over-determined, and it can easily stand the loss of one or the other element." However, when serious damage is involved, the behavioural consequences will not be due solely to the local destruction but also to "the disturbing effect" of a lesion "on a much larger number of nervous units than those immediately involved." Impairment to a functional subsystem can thus result from local damage. In the monograph, Freud does not get very far with actually specifying a mechanism which would have the required properties. He does, however, take up a quantitative proposal by Grashey (1885) in which a whole complex of symptoms is explained by invoking one factor—a specific impairment in short-term memory (or "the duration of percepts") which would result in failures at other processing levels due to decay of the primary percept before further codings had taken place. As Freud points out, this explanation was not entirely satisfactory with regard to the particular case that Grashey investigated; nonetheless, the notion that there may be "cases of aphasia in which no localized lesion needed to be assumed and the symptoms of which could be attributed to an alteration of a physiological constant in the speech apparatus" is a powerful and potentially valuable concept.

It is clear that Freud's account of the aphasias lacks the formal elegance and beauty of the diagram makers' theorization. This is hardly surprising; he tried to interpret the microstructure of neurolinguistics in detailed terms that the diagram makers never dared attempt. In the concluding paragraphs of the monograph, Freud sums up, with absolute honesty, the virtues and limitations of his achievement: "I am well aware that the considerations set out in this book must leave a feeling of dissatisfaction in the reader's mind. I have endeavoured to demolish a convenient and attractive theory of the aphasias, and having succeeded in this, I have been able to put in its place something less obvious and less complete. I only hope that the theory I have proposed will do more justice to the facts and will expose the real difficulties better than the one I have rejected. It is with a clear exposition of the problems that the elucidation of a scientific subject begins."

Towards a General Theory

Freud was to make just one further attempt at producing a formal neuropsychology—the *Project*. Here he develops the notions of "contact-barriers" (later to be called "synapses"), quantitative thresholds, and excitatory and inhibitory connections. In other people's hands, such ideas were to form the basis of nerve-net theory and lead eventually to the demonstration that anything computable could be computed by such networks. Freud does not attempt to work out a theory of aphasia in his new notations; rather, his attention had turned to the role that language plays in other processes, the relationship of language and memory, language and consciousness, language and emotion. He shows how the formalism *"affords a possibility of representing memory"*; how the symbolic value of an object may become divorced from the object, and how the affect which is appropriate to the symbolic level may appear, to the hysteric, to inhere to the object itself. Finally, Freud suggests that "conscious, observing thought" is made possible by "speech association" representations: ". . . indications of *speech-discharge* . . . put thought-processes on a level with perceptual processes, lend them reality and *make memory of them possible."*

While these ideas are the basis of Freud's psychoanalytic works, it remained for other scholars (e.g., Pick, 1913, 1931; Thiele, 1928) to develop the theory of aphasia from the point where Freud left off.

However, in constructing the foundations of psychoanalytic theory, Freud was forced yet again to expand the notion of psychological explanation. In the beautifully lucid paper on "The Unconscious" he writes: "I propose that, when we succeed in describing a mental process in all its aspects, dynamic, topographic and economic, we shall call this a *metapsychological* presentation" (1915e, XIV, 181). By "dynamic" Freud intends to stress the importance of the changing states and internal interactions of the organism, and to indicate that much of this change is motivated from within. Man, for Freud, is never the *passive* object of environmental forces. Despite his disclaimer—"Up till now, psychoanalysis differed from academic (descriptive) psychology mainly by reason of its dynamic conception of mental processes"—it is clear that Freud's thinking on this topic draws heavily on the Herbartian psychology. It was Herbart who first suggested replacing taxonomies of elementary psychological states—mental chemistry—by changing relationships between psychological representations of experience—mental mechanics. (Herbart conceived his theory as a refutation of Kant's arguments that psychology could never be a "real" science; see Mischel, 1967.)

The importance of economic variables follows automatically from the notion of mental mechanics: ". . . we try to follow out the fate of given volumes of excitation and to achieve, at least relatively, some assessment of it." But calling such "quantitative considerations" "economic" allows Freud the possibility of cutting himself free from purely Newtonian concepts of energy; the direct link with physiology can be broken. In the *Project,* the idea of force and its economics had to be related to "the conception of neuronal excitation as quantity in a state of flow." In "The Unconscious," Freud allows that mental energy may be characterized quantitatively without necessarily having to be cashed in terms of physics.

But if neuronal theory is to be temporarily abandoned an alternative notion of mechanism must be proposed. Accordingly, Freud changes the meaning of "topographic." Although "Research has afforded irrefutable proof that mental activity is bound up with the function of the brain as with that of no other organ" and although "unequal importance" attaches to "different parts of the brain," "Our mental topography has for the present nothing to do with anatomy; it is concerned not with anatomical locations, but with regions in the mental apparatus, irrespective of their possible situation in the body" (1915e, XIV, 175).

Freud moves toward what we would now call an "information-processing" paradigm (Farrell, 1972), and gives a very clear example of the type of question that can be asked within this framework:

"When a mental act (let us confine ourselves here to an act of ideation) is transferred from the system *Ucs* into the system *Cs* (or *Pcs*), are we to suppose that this transposition involves a fresh registration comparable to a second record of the idea in question, situated, moreover, in a fresh locality in the mind and side by side with which the original unconscious record continues to exist? Or are we rather to believe that the transformation consists in a change in the state of the idea, involving the same material and occurring in the same locality?"

It is obvious that one can sensibly pose this kind of question in functional psychology without commitment to the actual physical means of representing the process in the brain. The mechanism may, as Freud notes, involve the localization of unconscious processes in subcortical areas of the brain and conscious ones in cortical areas. But alternatively, it may involve sub-cellular chemical mechanisms within one area of the brain, or principles analogous to holography may be implicated.

Furthermore, it is clear that, irrespective of the *physical* mechanism involved, at least one of the hypotheses (dual representation, unconscious and conscious, at a point in time versus single representation, either unconscious or conscious) must be false. Freud's discussion of how one might attempt to falsify one of them makes one wonder if Popperian critics of psychoanalysis have ever read Freud.

Once Freud had ceased to be primarily a *neuro*psychologist, the nature of his interest in language changed. In *On Aphasia* the dominant question is "What is the *form* of representation of language in the brain?"; the taxonomy of impairment and the nature of errors provide evidence relevant to characterizing the *general type* of organism which can display such behaviour. In later works, similar parapraxes provide evidence about the particular state of an individual language-user. Schilder (1951), discussing differences between neurotic and aphasic slips of the tongue, writes: ". . . the organic disorder manifests itself in psychic contents which are of no importance for the individual whereas the neurotic and the schizophrenic disorders occur in those words which are of importance to the individual."

As a clinician, Freud was, of necessity, concerned with the personal "diagnostic" significance of an individual's mistakes and lapses. But, as a psychologist, he retained his interest in more general theoretical issues. On this level, the dominant question of the later works is "What types of psychopathological impairment become possible as a consequence of our being talking animals?" Language indeed raises us above the level of other animals—but it thereby makes ideologies available which are capable of degrading us to a comparable extent.

REFERENCES

E. N. Anderson, "German Romanticism as an Ideology of Cultural Crisis," *Journal of the History of Ideas* 2 (1941), pp. 301–17.
G. Andral, *Clinique Medicale* (Paris, 1834).

H. C. Bastian, "Some problems in connection with aphasia and other speech defects," *Lancet* 75 (1897), pp. 933–42.

A. L. Benton and R. J. Joynt, "Early descriptions of aphasia," *Archives of Neurology* 3 (1960), pp. 205–21.

S. E. Blumstein, "A phonological investigation of aphasic speech" (Ph.D. dissertation in linguistics, Harvard University, 1970).

J. B. Bouilland, "Recherches cliniques propres à démontrer que la perte de la parole correspond à la lesion des lobules antérieurs du cerveau," *Arch. Gen. de Médecine* 8 (1825), pp. 25–45.

W. B. Broadbent, "A case of peculiar affection of speech, with commentary," *Brain* 1 (1878), pp. 484–503.

K. Brugmann, *Zum Heutigen Stand der Sprachwissenschaft* (Strassburg, 1885).

J. M. Charcot, "Des variétés de l'aphasie," *Progress Med.* 11 (1883), pp. 487–88.

A. Crichton, *An Inquiry into the Nature and Origin of Mental Derangement, Comprehending a Concise System of the Physiology and Pathology of the Human Mind and a History of the Passions and their Effects.* (London, 1798).

G. Curtius, *Zur Kritik der neuesten Sprachforschung* (Leipzig, 1885).

B. Delbrück, "Amnestische Aphasie," *Jenaische Zeitschrift für Naturwissenschaft* 20 (1886), pp. 91–98.

W. Elder, "The clinical varieties of visual aphasia," *Edinburgh Medical Journal* 49 (1900), pp. 433–54.

B. A. Farrell, "Clothing the Freudian model in a fashionable dress," *The Monist* 56 (1972), pp. 343–60.

F. J. Gall, *Philosophisch-medicinische Untersuchungen über Natur und Kunst im kranken und gesunden Zustande des Menschen* (Vienna, 1791).

—— (and G. Spurzheim), *Anatomie et physiologie du system nerveux* (Paris, 1810–19).

J. A. P. Gesner, *Die Sprachamnesie* (Nordlingen, 1770).

H. Grashey, "Über Aphasie und ihre Beziehungen zur Wahrnehmung," *Archiv für Psychiatrie* 16 (1885), pp. 654–88.

D. Hartley, *Observations on Man* (London, 1749).

H. Head, *Aphasia and Kindred Disorders of Speech* (Cambridge, 1926).

J. G. Herder, *Abhandlung über den Ursprung der Sprache* (Berlin, 1772).

——, *Ideen zur Philosophie der Geschichte der Menschheit.* (Leipzig, 1784).

P. Huard, "Paul Broca (1824–1880)," *Revue d'Histoire des Sciences* 10 (1960), pp. 47–86.

J. H. Jackson, "On the nature and duality of the brain," *Medical Press and Circular* 1 (1874), pp. 19–41.

I. Kant, *Anthropologie in pragmatischer Hinsicht* (Königsberg, 1798).

K. S. Lashley, "Basic neural mechanisms in behaviour," *Psychological Review* 37 (1930), pp. 1–24.

E. Lesky, "Gall und Herder," *Clio Med.* 2 (1967), pp. 85–96.

L. Lichtheim, "On aphasia," *Brain* 7 (1885), pp. 433–84.

M. Mendelssohn, "Psychologische Betrachtungen auf Veranlassung einer von dem Herrn Oberkonsistorialrat Spalding an sich selbst gemachten Erfahrung," *Magazin fur Erfahrungsseelenkunde* 1 (1783), pp. 46–75.

T. Mischel, "Affective concepts in the psychology of J. F. Herbart," *Journal of the History of the Behavioural Sciences* 3 (1967), pp. 262–68.

A. Pick, *Die agrammatischen Sprachstörungen* (Berlin, 1913).

——, *Aphasie* (Berlin, 1931).

K. H. Pribram, "The Neuropsychology of Sigmund Freud," in *Experimental Foundations of Clinical Psychology,* ed. A. J. Bachrach (New York, 1962).

P. Schilder, *Brain and Personality* (New York, 1951).

C. Steinthal, *Einleitung in die Psychologie und Sprachwissenschaft* (Berlin, 1871).

O. Temkin, "Remarks on the Neurology of Gall and Spurzheim," in *Science, Medicine and History,* ed. E. A. Underwood (London, 1953).

R. Thiele, *Aphasie, Apraxie, Agnosie* (Berlin, 1928).

C. Wernicke, *Der aphasische Symptomenkomplex* (Breslau, 1874).

H. A. Whitaker, "On the Representation of Language in the Human Brain," (Ph.D. dissertation in Linguistics, University of California, Los Angeles, 1969).

——, "Unsolicited nominalizations by aphasics: The plausibility of the lexicalist model," *Linguistics* 78 (1972), pp. 62–71.

Richard Wollheim, *Freud* (London, 1971).

R. M. Young, *Mind, Brain and Adaptation in the Nineteenth Century* (Oxford, 1970).

Genetic Explanation in *Totem and Taboo**

JEROME NEU

"One day the brothers who had been driven out came together, killed and devoured their father and so made an end of the patriarchal horde" (1912–13, XIII, 141). The "one day" of this sentence is not the "once upon a time" of fairy tales; it introduces what is meant to be the description of an actual event. It is meant to be a part of a genetic explanation of totemic and later religions, of their associated taboos and rituals, and, indeed, of a good deal more: and the form of the explanation would seem to require the truth of the description.

A genetic explanation explains by showing an event or state of affairs to be the result of prior events or states of affairs. It is obvious that not every list of events in chronological order will constitute a genetic explanation. They must form a "developmental sequence." "Each stage must be shown to 'lead to' the next, and thus to be linked to its successor by virtue of some general principles which make the occurrence of the latter at least reasonably probable, given the former" (Hempel; see also Nagel). Or, at least, the former must be shown to be in some way a "necessary" condition of the latter (i.e., make the latter at least *possible*). So there must be selection among events, states of affairs, and conditions to find those which form a genuine series. The criterion of relevance here is causal; that is, there must be general principles asserting relations of dependence between succeeding elements in a genetic explanation. (Even if one wishes to contrast the roles of "causes" and "reasons" in historical accounts, one is obliged to show reason-giving relevance.) Thus, in addition to his historical narrative, Freud must provide plausible connecting general principles if his account is to have

* The initial version of this paper was written while a Special Student at Harvard University and a Guest Student at the Boston Psychoanalytic Institute, with support from the Danforth Foundation. I am indebted to these institutions, and (especially) to Rogers Albritton, Shelly Errington, Robert Meister, and Richard Wollheim for helpful discussions.

All references to the *Project* and the correspondence with Fliess are to the *Origins of Psychoanalysis,* ed. Marie Bonaparte, Anna Freud, Ernst Kris (Imàgo, London, and Basic Bks., New York, 1954). They are indicated by a bare page reference. For references to works by authors other than Freud, see list at end of article, pp. 392–93.

any force as an explanation. It may well be that some at least of the claimed historical events can be dispensed with, and that what is of value in the account resides in its general conditions and principles.

PHANTASY AND REALITY

Freud anticipates the objection that his initial events, particularly the slaying of the primal father, did not occur. He disarms it by suggesting that they need not have. Phantasy would do as well as reality.

The parallel here is with Freud's rejection (in 1897) of his earlier "seduction" theory. That theory had been part of a broader theory of the sexual aetiology and "choice" of neurosis. According to it hysteria was produced by the passive seduction by an adult (usually the father) of a child before age eight; a variant "active" sexual experience led to obsessional neurosis. The earlier events acted through the mediation of memories, and Freud made efforts to explain how memories from a "pre-sexual" period could become active and traumatic at the time of post-pubertal hysteria. Eventually he was forced to abandon this whole attempt to preserve the innocence of childhood. In a letter to Fliess (September 21, 1897) he announced that "I no longer believe in my *neurotica*" (p. 215). The childhood seductions had always been implausible (especially in the numbers required), and became more implausible as Freud's own father seemed implicated by the neuroses of his sisters. Many factors contributed to their rejection, but most significant from our point of view was

> the definite realization that there is no "indication of reality" in the unconscious, so that it is impossible to distinguish between truth and emotionally-charged fiction. (p. 216)

It is then in a similar spirit that, at the end of *Totem and Taboo*, Freud claims that: "What lie behind the sense of guilt of neurotics are always *psychical* realities and never *factual* ones" (1912–13, XIII, 159). And, especially in light of the over-valuation of their psychical acts, or "omnipotence of thoughts," it is natural to ask, with Freud: "May not the same have been true of primitive men?" Freud's own answer is that

> the mere hostile *impulse* against the father, the mere existence of a wishful *phantasy* of killing and devouring him, would have been enough to produce the moral reaction that created totemism and

taboo. . . . No damage would thus be done to the causal chain stretching from the beginning to the present day, for psychical reality would be strong enough to bear the weight of these consequences. (1912–13, XIII, 159–60)

Effects must have actual causes, but impulses and phantasies can be as actual as external events: to explain why they should have equal causal efficacy, however, requires rather more than this.[1]

In rejecting the "seduction" theory Freud had raised a further question, which also has analogue for the thesis of *Totem and Taboo*, and that is whether it is necessary that the phantasy should occur in childhood: "It again seems arguable that it is later experiences which give rise to phantasies which throw back to childhood . . ." (p. 216). Now, the possibility of projection backwards in time is surely as open in the case of society as in the case of the individual. Might it not be, in other words, that history was not so much the memory of (collective) phantasy but rather the (collective) phantasy of memory?

However, if we leave aside questions about the force and dating of phantasies, there is a disanalogy between the issue of historical truth in the "seduction" theory and the problem that arises in connection with the primal horde. In the case of the individual, the patient supplies the description of the originating event, psychoanalytic insight comes into play in providing the connections between the originating event and its consequences, and cure (the removal of symptoms) is taken as strong evidence for the truth of the historical account. In the case of the primal horde, psychoanalytic hypotheses derived from individual cases are used *both* to connect events with consequences *and* to make plausible the description and actual occurrence of the events (or phantasies). At the same time, no disappearance of symptoms (e.g., religion) is to be expected with the revelation of their sources in the prehistory of society; or if such disappearance occurs, the connection between it and the account will have to be more complex than in the case of the individual. We should not, however, over-emphasize the severity of this disanalogy. In many individual cases one has to depend on reconstructions and

---

[1] I think it can be shown how and why the substitution of wish and impulse for external event should be sufficient to bear the explanatory weight; but this is a theme I explore elsewhere: "Phantasy and Memory: The Aetiological Role of Thoughts According to Freud," *International Journal of Psycho-Analysis* 54 (1973).

no direct "memory" is achieved (1937d, XXIII, 265–66; 1918b, XVII, 50–53). Also, "cure" is not the only or even perhaps the most important form of confirmation for psychoanalytic hypotheses and interpretations. It was one of the forms of evidence that originally convinced Freud of the truth of the "seduction" theory (1896a, III, 151–53; 1896c, III, 206; cf. 1895d, II, 6–7, 14, 17), but he came to reject that theory. In general, the mechanism of "cure" is very complex and the recovery of unconscious memories (or "insight") is not enough for the removal of symptoms (consider the importance attached to abreaction, transference, and "timing" interpretations); and the evidence of "cure" is in general of dubious value in establishing aetiology or causation: a therapeutic technique may simply introduce countervailing factors (and so alleviate symptoms) rather than remove exciting causes. (Hence, for example, the physical treatment of ulcers does not prove that ulcers are purely organic in origin.) The main excitement of Freud's theory in *Totem and Taboo* is in his discussion of the relations among infant, neurotic, and primitive; his exhibition of a parallelism between individual and mass psychology, between ontogeny and phylogeny (development of the individual and of the species). But it is precisely this that is the source of further (perhaps more significant) disanalogies in evidential status.

The problem which the "seduction" theory attempted to resolve is one in individual psychopathology, the aetiology of an individual neurosis rather than a social institution. The originating event, whether an event in the real world or the world of phantasy, is an event in individual history, moreover in the history of the individual who suffers, and he is alive both to remember the event and to experience the suffering. In the case of society, Freud seems to depend on a discredited Lamarckianism (or cross-generation "collective mind") to explain how "the sense of guilt for an action has persisted for many thousands of years and has remained operative in generations which can have had no knowledge of that action" (1912–13, XIII, 158). But the issue is not just the persistence of a (generally unconscious) "sense of guilt," for what is also necessary is to show that it, the guilt behind currently existing institutions, is connected with a primal event (or phantasy) which is its object. And for this purpose the postulation of the inheritance of acquired characteristics seems not only implausible but unnecessarily cumbrous. For if impulse and wish are the source of original guilt, and impulse and wish arise anew in every generation, why should not guilt too arise anew without being "transmitted" in any sense? But perhaps Freud wishes to deny that impulse and wish do *simply* arise anew.

Freud continues: "I have supposed that an emotional process, such as might have developed in generations of sons who were ill-treated by their father, has extended to new generations which were exempt from such treatment for the very reason that their father had been eliminated" (1912–13, XIII, 158). What is the mechanism of this *extension?* The question here becomes the source of Oedipal feelings. Would they arise in a fraternal as well as a patriarchal society? If so, would they arise out of biological instinct, or social organization and frustration of instinct, or would they be the legacy of prehistoric passions and crimes? We shall return to these issues shortly. We should note that transmission via "tradition" is not an alternative for Freud, he (usually) treats "tradition" as the "historical content of the mass unconscious," the *inherited* memory-traces of a civilization (Rieff, p. 30; see also 1939a, XXIII, 99–102).

The societal level of the phenomena introduces another complication. If plausibility is gained by substituting impulse or phantasy for actual killing, plausibility is lost because the phenomena to be explained are societal and so require the multiplication of any remaining doubts about individual cases. As Freud says in *Moses and Monotheism,* "An essential part of the construction is the hypothesis that the events . . . occurred to all primitive men—that is, to all our ancestors. The story is told in an enormously condensed form, as though it had happened on a single occasion, while in fact it covered thousands of years and was repeated countless times during that long period" (1939a, XXIII, 81). So we shall have to consider the universality as well as the source of the impulses to which he appeals.

However, in the end Freud, having argued that the events cited in his hypothesis need not have occurred, insists that in point of fact they did (1912–13, XIII, 161; see also Fox, pp. 168–69). A parallel here would be with Freud's vacillation in the "Wolf Man" case, where the seeming acceptance of an interpretation of the "primal scene" involving displacement and retrospective phantasy is then followed by an insistence on the reality (at least phylogenetic) of such a scene (1918b, XVII, 57–60, 95–97). (Both of these vacillations occur in the context of disputes with Jung.) Freud marshals a great deal of evidence for his construction of primaeval history,[2] summarized in *Moses and Monotheism* (1939a, XXIII, 84) under the headings of attested history (totemism and male confederacies), surviving replicas (Christian Communion for old totem meal), popular legends and fairy tales, and the mental life of children (animal phobias). Such support is in fact largely irrelevant to differentiating between a scheme representing reality and one representing phantasy. It is, however, important in relation to the *content* of the construction (whichever it represents). But it is all questionable in detail. For example, the anthropologist A. L. Kroeber reports that "Robertson Smith's allegation that blood sacrifice is central in ancient cults holds chiefly or only for the Mediterranoid cultures of a certain period . . . It does not apply to regions outside the sphere of affection by these cultures" (Kroeber, 1920, p. 302; but cf. Feldman). Then, for every bit of evidence from myths of father-castration, one must account for the alternative themes of fratricide and son-murder in myths (Rieff, p. 42). Finally, in Freud's account of totemism, the totem is supposed to be a displacement for the primal father. But observation shows that the relation between clan members and their totem animal is not in all cases one of identification with a forefather or ancestor (Lévi-Strauss, 1963). This is unlike the case of Little Hans' animal phobia, where the fact that he identifies horses with his father can be seen from his play, from correspondences between features of the horses he fears and his father's moustache and glasses, and other indications (1909b, X). "Displaced fear," like all claims about displacement, requires a background of continuity against which a change in object can be seen as "displacement." Such claims must depend on the details of each case.

THE OEDIPAL COMPLEX

Kroeber, in a later review (1939), suggests that Freud's thesis should be viewed as a timeless psychological explanation mistakenly treated as an historical explanation, and that stripped of its claim to historical truth it can be reduced to

> the proposition that certain psychic processes tend always to be operative and to find expression in widespread human institutions.

[2] On the general issue, see 1937d, XXIII.

JEROME NEU

Among these processes would be the incest drive and incest repression, filial ambivalence, and the like; in short, if one likes, the kernel of the Oedipus situation. (Kroeber, 1939, p. 307)

I think this is correct, but stating just what is right in Freud's approach and how it is right requires some sorting out. We must get clear on what Freud sets out to explain and how (or whether) he explains it. If the originating events occur in phantasy rather than external reality, is there any need or reason to assume they are ancient historical phantasies rather than current sustaining phantasies? What are the sources of the phantasies, and are the relevant impulses and wishes universal?

Certainly the most important general explanatory principles in Freud's account, whether viewed historically or as an account of the deeper psychological structures producing and sustaining more visible social institutions, are provided by the Oedipus complex. Indeed, Freud claims "that the beginnings of religion, morals, society and art converge in the Oedipus complex" (1912–13, XIII, 156). To provide an explanation, however, it must exist, and exist everywhere those institutions it is thought to explain exist. Malinowski (1927) seemed to challenge just this assumption. His study of the matrilineal and patrilocal[3] Trobriand Islanders claims that they have no concept of biological paternity. The mother's brother is the authority figure, and there is a strong taboo against sexual relations between brother and sister. Ambivalence centers on the mother's brother and sister's son relation, and relations between children and their mother's husband (i.e., biological father) are quite genial and friendly. So the Oedipus complex as formulated by Freud—lust for the (biological) mother and hatred of the (biological) father—appears as "only one among a series of possible 'nuclear complexes,' each of which patterns primary family affects in a way characteristic of the culture in which it occurs" (Parsons, p. 278). Ernest Jones tried to maintain the dependence of social relations on biological kinship by arguing that the seeming (i.e., conscious) biological ignorance of the Trobrianders, and even their matrilineal social organization, can be ex-

[3] Kinship, inheritance, and allegiance are through mother and her clan, home is house and village of mother's husband. Actually, the Trobrianders are, strictly speaking, "avunculocal" because at eight or nine the male child moves to the village of his uncle (mother's brother), where his inheritance is located, and remains there when married. But the Oedipal period (age four to five) is spent in the father's village.

plained as a form of denial or defence against the classical Oedipal feelings (i.e., "to deflect the hatred towards his father felt by the growing boy") (Jones, 1925, p. 120).

What is the upshot of this 1920's debate? Several issues must be separated, and I will touch on only some of them. If Jones is arguing that each individual Trobriander must experience hatred of his biological father and lust for his mother, but then invariably displaces these onto the maternal uncle and sister,[4] he seems straightforwardly wrong. There seems to be no evidence for such an early constellation of feelings. As Malinowski put it:

> I have always understood that a complex is an actual configuration of attitudes and sentiments partly overt, partly repressed, but actually existing in the unconscious. . . . If, however, as Dr. Jones seems fully to admit, the attitudes typical of the Oedipus complex cannot be found either in the conscious or unconscious; if, as has been proved, there are no traces of it either in Trobriand folk-lore or in dreams and visions, or in any other symptoms; if in all these manifestations we find instead the other complex—where is then the repressed Oedipus complex to be found? Is there a sub-unconscious below the actual unconscious . . . ? (Malinowski, p. 144)

Jones cannot claim that matrilineal descent, ignorance of paternal role, totemic system, and taboos provide the needed manifestations: for those are the things he wants to explain by reference to the classical complex, and what is to connect them (as defences) with otherwise unmanifested Oedipal feelings rather than a different set of otherwise unmanifested feelings? (But cf. Róheim.) If, however, Jones's argument is that the classical complex is the primal complex of the society (not the individual), and has been displaced in the course of history by the Trobriand complex, the issues deepen. First, if we accept that the notion of "displacement" is clear on the level of instinct theory and individual psychology (though, so far as identification of instincts is through their objects, the notion is not clear), it calls for explication when applied to society. In what sense, for example, is an individual member of society's instinct or feeling "displaced" when it has never (in his lifetime) had a different object; and if reference to periods before his life is to be brought in, how are instincts and feelings belonging to others to be related to his instincts and feelings? Secondly, Jones, by limiting the classical complex to

4 This is how I think Anne Parsons reads him.

primordial society, would seem to have admitted the dependence of
the form of the complex upon the form of society: in the case of the
original complex, dependence on the patriarchal horde.[5] This being
so, he cannot claim that the children of a fraternal society (after the
elimination of the father-tyrant) have an Oedipal complex in relation to fathers, and it is difficult to see how he can maintain that they
have one in relation to the totem as *father*-substitute. On this interpretation, can he maintain his position on the source and nature
of the nuclear complex? What is his position? Essential to Jones's
claim is priority of the Oedipus complex to society. But is this right?

We should first disentangle Jones's position from two apparent
difficulties. On the interpretation now being considered, the classical
Oedipus complex need not be universal. Jones can accept its present
non-universality, as he does on this interpretation, so long as he can
argue (as Freud does) that matrilineal society and its associated
nuclear complex are later developments.[6] And (this is the second
apparent difficulty) neither Freud nor Jones is committed to treating
the primordial crime as the origin of the Oedipus complex—indeed,
the opposite is true. Malinowski (pp. 148, 163, 167) makes the
mistaken interpretation. But it is clear that the complex is supposed
to predate society and, of course, the crime—in fact, it helps explain
the crime and the subsequent guilt. But is the Oedipus complex prior
to all society? If the primal crime is not its source, what is? Here
Jones and Malinowski do seem genuinely to differ. Jones's central
concern seems to have been infantile sexuality and the Oedipus
complex as its essential form. This he took to be a matter of biology, instinct, and invariable developmental stages. Malinowski
(pp. 244–49) denied infantile sexuality, but his main point was that
laws of kinship and incest taboos vary from society to society and

---

[5] Jones denies that the horde exhibits either mother-right or patriarchy ("as
we nowadays conceive it in its monogamic form"), thereby hoping to sidestep
the objection that mother-right was most probably the primal ordering of society (Jones, p. 130). Mother-right and taboo and the totemic system would be
alternative modes of defence against Oedipal tendencies. (See Fox, pp. 166,
170–71.)

[6] Parsons (p. 280) writes ". . . concerning the question of whether matrilineal social organization can be seen as a defense against oedipal affects, it
seems difficult now to see how a complex social pattern could be based on the
'denial' of an affect which occurs in the individual." But I think Jones could
reasonably argue that it can be so based so long as the account is historical,
i.e., so long as it is dead individuals who have arranged society to defend
against their (and their descendants') affects.

cannot be derived directly from the biological facts of mating and reproduction (which are presumably invariable).

Anne Parsons tries to divide the debate by dividing the Oedipus complex into two components: one of instinct and phantasy which can be regarded as a matter of invariant developmental phases; and another of identification and object choice dependent on social structure (Parsons, p. 282). Certainly instinct theory allows for variation or displacement of objects. This is the point behind Kroeber's claim that

> Malinowski had really vindicated the mechanism of the Oedipus relation. He showed that the mechanism remained operative even in a changed family situation; a minor modification of it, in its direction, conforming to the change in given condition. (Kroeber, 1939, p. 308)

But can biological instinct be the sole and sufficient ground of affect and phantasy? And are instinct and phantasy independent of identification and object choice in the way Parsons' reconciliation seems to imply?[7] It is difficult to see how jealousy could be based purely on instinct, without reference to social relations and beliefs, for how does it obtain its object and what makes it "jealousy"? A Trobriand boy's hostility to his maternal uncle, unlike an (unrealized) hostility to his father, cannot be based on *straightforward* sexual jealousy, for the maternal uncle most emphatically does not have sexual relations with the mother. Even if based on "sexual instinct," the hostility must be mediated by (socially conditioned) beliefs. It is no help to suggest that the boy makes a mistake, that he is jealous of the uncle because he mistakenly thinks he sleeps with the mother, that perhaps the child is as ignorant of parental intercourse as he is of the male parent's genetic role. Admittedly, the Trobriand conjugal bed is a rigidly masked reality (Malinowski, pp. 106–7), but no more so than the Viennese bed of Freud's time. In addition, the child is sexually well informed and it is unlikely that he is not aware that his parents sleep together (one must remember the Trobrianders are patrilocal,

7 The implication is odder given Parsons' recognition of the cultural shaping of phantasy and symbolism, a recognition which appears implicitly and then explicitly in her reference to Rapaport: "according to whom it is the fact of delay in drive expression which gives rise to the symbol, [as contrasted with] at least one facet of Jones's (1912) summary of the psychoanalytic theory of symbolism according to which there are biologically given types of primary symbolic content." [Parsons, p. 287]

and the mother's brother might live quite far away). Even if the child were wrong, it would be his *beliefs* and not his biology that directed his jealousy (though now the jealousy would be more clearly "sexual"). Jones's defence seems to depend on a paternal trauma (the biological father's sexual relations with the mother), a postulation in accordance with a trauma theory that should be rejected with the early "seduction" theory (Parsons, pp. 283–85). If impulse and wish and their representatives in phantasy are what matter, it is irrelevant whether the father or uncle actually has sexual relations with the mother. The maternal uncle is the significant authority figure in the child's life, and importantly, in the mother's as well. Anne Parsons speculates that the boy may "become aware of the strong affective importance which the brother has for his mother [authority figure and a primary object in her phantasy life]; and when his jealousy and anger are awakened, he deals with them by identification. The mother's brother then becomes the primary rival" (Parsons, p. 286). Even Jones, in the context of explaining avunculate organization (in light of brother-sister taboo and likely repressed incestuous tendencies), suggests "that the uncle, being the unconscious lover of the mother, is therefore the imaginary father of her children, and logically wields the *potestas* over them" (Jones, p. 127). This may be the boy's phantasy as well as, in an extended sense, the society's; and in his case the phantasy is a result of societal organization and derivative *beliefs*. Society affects feelings rather than simply arranging different defences (matriarchy, totemism . . .) against (biologically) *given* feelings. The (male) Oedipus complex as lust for the (biological) mother and hatred of the (biological) father is too narrowly conceived. The Oedipal complex clearly needs broader statement if it is to capture the nature of nuclear complexes in general. One such statement is suggested by Fenichel:

> The human infant is biologically more helpless than other mammalian children. He needs care and love. Therefore, he will always ask for love from the nursing and protecting adults around him, and develop hate and jealousy of persons who take this love away from him. (Fenichel, p. 97)

Here the "instinctively" given human potentialities are derived, as they must be, from the nature of human childhood: the biological *and* social context of human development. Perhaps when this is done it can provide, as Kroeber suggests, an explanation of other pervasive features of society, such as incest taboos.

Given a broader sense, the Oedipal complex is indeed universal. But it is not clear that this makes it any more plausible to regard the Trobriand nuclear complex as a defensive transformation of a primordial constellation. What makes one version of the complex a *defence* against another? What shows the classical Oedipal complex to have been (in all societies) the earliest form? Even if some one version of the complex was originally universal, it presumably shifted with changes in family structure, and these changes (presumably) have varying origins and explanations. "If the institution of the family were to change, the pattern of the Oedipus complex would necessarily change also. . . . The problem of the origin of the Oedipus complex is thus reduced to the problem of the origin of the family, an interesting and still unsolved chapter . . ." (Fenichel, p. 97). Róheim, however, thinks he has an argument for the biological origin and necessity of the classical Oedipal family, and so for the classical Oedipal nuclear complex (1950a, esp. pp. 202–19). I take the argument to be roughly as follows: Men necessarily cleave to their wives as substitutes for their mothers, and they do so because infantile dependency is not only prolonged in humans but also is never completely overcome. Róheim argues that this is a *biological* condition on the basis of "Bolk's views on the retarded evolution or foetalization of mankind." I find this argument bizarre. It returns us to our first interpretation of Jones, and, in fact, Róheim goes to great effort and length to show that the Oedipus complex is universal by finding myths (etc.) he can interpret as manifestations of unconscious Oedipal feelings. But I wish to focus on the argument above. The alleged biological necessity is not a necessity, it is not even a fact. Men do *not* in all societies (do they in ours?) cleave to a single wife in marriage and child-raising, and where they do cleave it is not clear that the wife is *always* a "substitute mother" in the relevant sense. The relevant sense requires, I think, that the wife fulfill the same dependency needs in the same way as the mother. (Again, "displacement," here as elsewhere, requires a background of continuity against which a change in object can be seen as "displacement.") Róheim is as aware of the variations as anyone; but if he wishes to treat them as superficial defences against unconscious feelings he must meet all the difficulties we have raised, including those about the notion of "defensive transformation" (and perhaps Parsons'—see note 6). The evidence, in any case, overwhelmingly favors the view that families meet a variety of needs in a variety of ways, and nuclear emotional constellations vary with their structure (Lévi-Strauss, 1960). But we still have not come to the most bizarre feature of the argument. Even if Róheim's claims about cleaving were facts, they would not be explained by or follow from the evolutionary characteristics of human or non-human organs and organisms. The alleged connection with Bolk's views escapes me. There is nothing offered to connect them with psychological attitudes or Oedipal emotions. I have been wanting to emphasize in relation to those feelings (what Róheim neglects) the importance of thoughts and beliefs (and so society) in shaping them. These thoughts (which must be allowed to include unconscious thoughts) also place constraints on the interpretation of myths: we must beware of using Róheim's (or any other outsider's) free associations in interpreting their meaning in their culture. (Compare the interpretation of dreams, where it is the dreamer's associations that count.) In any case, I conclude that the continuation of infantile characteristics is not a biological fact on a level with (the fact Fenichel focusses on) the prolonged nature of mammalian infantile helplessness and dependence. (I should also note that it is not entirely clear that Róheim *really* means that family structure and nuclear emotions are *biologically* determined. He speaks of the father as the person the child "sees most frequently and who serves as an ego-ideal" and says "it makes absolutely no difference whether this 'father' is the real progenitor or not. The same is valid for the mother concept" [p. 204, n. 100]. He also speaks of the father as "the intervening stranger" [p. 214].)

Other problems connected with the universality of the Oedipus complex (e.g., the development of women and the claims of instinct theory) appear different in the perspective of a broadened conception of the complex. They seem more issues of infantile dependence than infantile sexuality. Or rather, we can begin to see the importance of issues of dependence in understanding the nature of "infantile sexuality." We should also note that our understanding of the Oedipal complex needs broadening along another dimension. Given the importance of beliefs (conscious and unconscious), and given the extraordinary sexual theories of children (1908c, IX), it would be remarkable if Oedipal sexual desires took the forms of normal adult sexuality (e.g., desire for genital union—few four-year-olds can conceive of such union, let alone conceive of it as desirable). The sexual relations desired in Oedipal contexts must be understood more broadly, which should not surprise us, for it was Freud who taught us how extensive the concept of "sexuality" actually is.

EXPLAINING TOTEMISM

If, however, we continue to suppose (with Freud) that there is a universal nuclear complex *and* that the classical Oedipal complex was its primary form, would we not then have to expect that totemism would be universal (at least as a stage in the history of every society, and so in every existing "primitive" society)? The answer is *No*. *No*, because genetic explanations typically supply only necessary conditions (and those of a special sort), not sufficient ones (Gallie). Other factors will determine whether defences against the Oedipal complex will appear, and whether they will take the form of totemism. The problem is complicated because it is questionable whether existing "primitive" societies represent early stages of all societies. It is even questionable whether there is a unified phenomenon characterizable as "totemism" to be explained. The various elements of clan division, exogamy, taboo, identification with animals, and religious ritual are by no means always connected or even present in a given culture. (See Lévi-Strauss, 1963, and Fox, pp. 163, 171f.) In any case, there is no reason to suppose that the classical Oedipus complex is prior to society, or that it was at the beginning or at any other time universal. I think we must now revise Freud's hypothesis about totemism, so that totemism (whatever it is) is seen as a defence against the nuclear complex (whatever form it takes) rather than always the classical Oedipus complex.

Can we learn nothing about the source and function of "totemism" from the distribution of "totemism" (giving it some fixed sense) among primitive societies? In connection with *Totem and Taboo*, John Whiting suggests "that the mother-child dyad may have to take its place along with the oedipal triad as an important determinant of personality development" (Whiting, p. 154). There are many grounds for believing this to be true, but Whiting's own argument based on the distribution of totemism (the sense of which he leaves unspecified—so his statistical categories may conceal important differences) is not compelling. He found that more societies (in his small sample) with mother-child households than with nuclear (i.e., husband-wife-child) households have totemism. If totemism is (Freud's hypothesis) a defence against a wish to kill and eat fathers, the family conditions in the different societies would have led one to expect the opposite result. Whiting proposes that one can explain the surprising presence of totemism in the mother-child household societies if it really represents mother-son conflict (after weaning, etc.) rather than father-son rivalry. He says that

> in the mother-child household, it is the son who has exclusive possession of the mother. Under these circumstances the rivalry should originate from the father's jealousy of the son. Luckily, however, since the mother-child household seldom occurs except in societies with polygyny, he has another wife to turn to for love and comfort. (Whiting, p. 153)

So Whiting does not deny that if the father had occasion to feel jealous, rivalry would result, he argues merely that the presence of other wives luckily prevents such jealousy from arising. But since when has the presence of alternative satisfactions precluded jealousy? (And the other wives are more than likely also to have sons.) Secondly, the disproportional absence of totemism in nuclear household societies shows nothing until we are told something about alternative defences. The claim that totemism is a defence against certain feelings does not preclude the possibility of other defences, and their presence may explain the absence of totemism. In any case, broadening the notion of the Oedipal complex will necessarily broaden the range of feelings totemism may be regarded as a defence against, and we should be prepared to discover that the nuclear complex is sometimes essentially dyadic.

This discussion, of course, applies only to totemism as live ritual or practice rather than mechanical inheritance created in response to now dead feelings. So in a Trobriand-type society totemism would be a defence against present hostility to uncle, not against ancient hostility to father made unnecessary by avunculate organization. (There can be too many defences.) But again here, we must explain how ritual defends against feelings, which is easier perhaps than explaining how one set of feelings defends against another (as on the cross-generational reaction-formation reading of Jones). And here we are dealing with an ontogenetic rather than phylogenetic explanation. Instead of fragmenting the explanation across history so that the sons atone for, or defend themselves against what the fathers did or wished, we are interpreting Freud as explaining surface social structures in terms of underlying social and psychological structures. If we are to accept Freud's claim that only "psychical reality," impulse and wish, is essential to his account, then we should require that each generation develops afresh the feelings that sustain its institutions. Without live conflict, ritual tends to die. Where a ritual is maintained, but the feelings which sustained it have changed, the meaning of the ritual has been transformed.

We must also recognize, however, that feelings develop in the context of given institutions. It is conceivable that totemic prohibitions produce the feelings they are supposed to "defend" against. (Desiring the forbidden fruit because forbidden.)[8] This would be rather like Radcliffe-Brown's suggestion that ritual magic may produce anxieties instead of being a way of coping with risks (Lévi-Strauss, 1963, pp. 67–68). Thus Lévi-Strauss argues ". . . it is not present emotions, felt at gatherings and ceremonies, which engender or perpetuate the rites, but ritual activity which arouses the emotions" (Lévi-Strauss, 1963, p. 71). One should say something about "displaced" emotions (rituals and any attendant emotions may be directed onto substitute objects), about originating feelings which need not be felt on the occasion of the rituals derived from them, and about the

---

[8] In Freud's account, the pattern of totemic prohibitions is the pattern of Oedipal desires. There is no point in prohibiting what people do not desire. As Frazer puts it, "The law only forbids men to do what their instincts incline them to do; what nature itself prohibits and punishes, it would be superfluous for the law to prohibit and punish" (quoted in 1912–13, XIII, 123). Though established prohibitions may call up or maintain desires that would otherwise not be present, one cannot explain the origin or establishment of prohibitions without reference to prior feelings and desires. Freud also provides, incidentally, certain important correctives to narrow utilitarian theories of punishment. He notices that a real danger in allowing crime to go unpunished is imitation (not based merely on calculation that "one can get away with it"), and that many forms of punishment allow a surreptitious imitation:

. . . What is in question is fear of an infectious example, of the temptation to imitate—that is, of the contagious character of taboo. If one person succeeds in gratifying the repressed desire, the same desire is bound to be kindled in all the other members of the community. In order to keep the temptation down, the envied transgressor must be deprived of the fruit of his enterprise; and the punishment will not infrequently give those who carry it out an opportunity of committing the same outrage under colour of an act of expiation. (1912–13, XIII, 71–72; see also Roazen, p. 135 f.)

importance of thoughts and beliefs in the nature of emotions. But I will confine myself here to pointing out that the suggestion is difficult to maintain in relation to totemism, where ritual may explain manifest feelings towards the totem animal, but it is less obvious how it would explain unconscious feelings towards significant people. Further, if feelings are the effect rather than the cause of institutions, how could certain feelings ever be absent (given the institution), how could they change (or how could the "same" practices have different meaning in different societies), and how would rituals ever be born or ever die (as they undoubtedly occasionally do)?

The situation is, of course, more complex than this suggests. Feelings sustain ritual, and ritual sustains and shapes feelings. Feelings necessarily involve beliefs (i.e., we identify feelings through beliefs) which are in turn influenced by social structure: as we have seen, relations of dependence can lead to a constellation of feelings and associated institutions, and relations of dependence are a matter of both biology and social organization. The interplay is complex, but I think we can understand how Freud leaves us with a "deep" explanation (of social structures in terms of underlying psychological structures) even after we have rejected the explanation (which he also provides) which gets its "depth" from the history of the race.[9]

EXPLAINING SOCIETY AND MORALITY

Malinowski makes the charge that Freud "tries to explain the origins of culture by a process which implies the previous existence of culture and hence involves a circular argument" (Malinowski, p. 153). Initially, this charge is based on Freud's reference to "some advance in culture, like the use of a new weapon" in his description of the primal crime. The reference is readily eliminable (or the "new weapon" may just be the sons' penises, their sexuality); the charge, however, has a more substantial basis. As Malinowski points out, without the prior existence of culture, "the sons could not have instituted sacraments, established laws and handed on customs" (Malinowski, p. 155). That is, the guilt of the sons and their "de-

[9] It is also possible, though I think in some ways less fruitful, to regard and interpret *Totem and Taboo* as poetry rather than explanation. See N. O. Brown's archetypal dialectic of fathers and sons (Brown, chap. 1).

ferred obedience" could not be institutionalized, as in the totemic taboos ("They revoked their deed by forbidding the killing of the totem, the substitute for their father; and they renounced its fruits by resigning their claims to the women who had now been set free" [1912–13, XIII, 143]), without prior institutions.

> . . . we are asked to believe that the totemic crime produces remorse which is expressed in the sacrament of endo-cannibalistic totemic feast, and in the institution of sexual taboo. This implies that the parricidal sons had a conscience. But conscience is a most unnatural mental trait imposed upon man by culture. It also implies that they had the possibilities of legislating, of establishing moral values, religious ceremonies and social bonds. All of which again it is impossible to assume or imagine, for the simple reason that *ex hypothesi* the events are happening in pre-cultural milieu, and culture, we must remember, cannot be created in one moment and by one act. (Malinowski, p. 165)

Conscience is not the important point. Ambivalence (i.e., a countervailing attachment to the murdered and hated father) would presumably be sufficient to produce the needed remorse (1930a, XXI, 132). Malinowski's assumption of the impossibility of instinctual conflict in pre-human and in pre-cultural states (Malinowski, pp. 163–64), besides being wildly implausible, is also not to the point.

The substantial difficulty to which Malinowski alludes can be brought out by looking at the standard criticism of social contract theories of the state. Social contracts, even hypothetical contracts, cannot explain the origin of obligation because they presuppose a prior obligation to obey contracts, and are therefore circular. One does not need a social structure in order for it to become *imprudent* to commit a certain act, but one is necessary if there is to be an *obligation* not to commit it. The father presumably prohibited murder by his strength. The combined strength of the sons does not make totemic murder any more of a "crime," it can only establish a prohibition of the same kind as existed in the patriarchal world. The situation is not improved by interpreting Freud's hypothesis as myth or "Just-So Story" (1921c, XVIII, 122). Social contract theories are generally interpreted as myths or logical fictions having explanatory value (Roazen, p. 136), but remain vitiated by their circularity. Freud's social contract theory labors under the additional difficulty that it requires at least some psychical reality: the "contract" is not binding on later generations unless they inherit the guilt that led to it.

Explaining Morality and Guilt

What of guilt? Freud thinks his hypothesis of the primal crime can explain the origin of guilt. In a way, Malinowski was not entirely wrong in thinking the killing of the primal father the "origin" of the Oedipal complex—it is the origin of the *internalization* of prohibitions (previously maintained by father) against Oedipal wishes (the wishes, of course, do *not* start with the crime, they are what lead to it). What was there before there was guilt? There was remorse. "Remorse" is "reserved for the reaction after an act of aggression has actually been carried out" (1930a, XXI, 137). This reaction is a fear of loss of love from an external authority. It is the view of the external authority and the individual's dependence on that authority that make any particular action "aggressive" or "bad" (1930a, XXI, 124–25). And so we now come back to the question, What difference does the doing of the primal deed make? It creates the super-ego and so "guilt" in its wider sense:

> the institution of the internal authority, the super-ego, altered the situation radically. Before this, the sense of guilt coincided with remorse. . . . After this, owing to the omniscience of the super-ego, the difference between an aggression intended and an aggression carried out lost its force. (1930a, XXI, 137)

But for this to be plausible, surely an actual event, not just the phantasy of an event, is required. Impulse and wish would not be enough to create guilt originally, for they could not (by definition) be sufficient to produce remorse. But is remorse necessary? Must remorse for an actual crime be an essential step in super-ego formation?

I would like to suggest a possible explanation of why Freud should (here) think so: in mourning an actual loss is suffered and the lost object is internalized. This is the pattern of identification and introjection first expounded by Freud in "Mourning and Melancholia" (1917e, XIV). He elsewhere asks, "Is it quite certain that identification presupposes that object-cathexis has been given up? Can there be no identification while the object is retained?" (1921c, XVIII, 114). Freud raises this "delicate" question only to leave it, but we can tackle at least one aspect of it. First, one must distinguish withdrawal of cathexis from destruction of the object (whether or not cathexis is necessarily withdrawn in identification). Now, what is internalized is never an actual external object, it is a psychical representation of that object, and so it is not a condition of the existence of an object in me that it cease to exist in the external world (I do not have literally to swallow it in order to incorporate it).[10] There is no reason why fear of loss should not be enough to lead to identification and introjection, and so super-ego formation. And one need not suffer actual loss (or total loss) to fear loss; one need only be dependent (and, perhaps, aware of that dependence) (1926d, XX). And dependence is the condition of all humans in childhood. Hence we can see that the biological origin of guilt is connected with the biological aspect of the Oedipus complex, but it need not involve heredity or an historical tragedy. Freud is wrong to insist that "we cannot get away from the assumption that man's sense of guilt springs from the Oedipus complex and was acquired at the killing of the father by the brothers banded together" (1930a, XXI, 131). Freud explains that the super-ego is heir to the Oedipus complex (1923b, XIX, 36; and 1933a); but we have seen that neither need be a (biological) inheritance from earlier generations.[11]

Freud occasionally suggests an alternative biological account of the origin of guilt, or at least "shame." Shame is one of the triad of repressive forces "disgust, shame and morality" said to be organic, due to the proximity of the sexual and excremental organs (pp. 147–48). But why should there be disgust at *those* organs? (p. 192). And Freud realized even as he proposed the theory (in 1896) that sex is sometimes pleasurable (p. 148). The geography of the body, even supplemented by speculations about smell (1930a, XXI, 99, n.,

[10] In *Totem and Taboo,* the sons kill the primal father, and "Cannibal savages as they were, it goes without saying that they devoured their victim as well as killing him. . . . in the act of devouring him they accomplished their identification with him . . ." (1912–13, XIII, p. 142).

[11] There is another possible explanation for why Freud should think an actual crime an essential step in super-ego formation, i.e., why dependence and ambivalence should not be enough. As Melanie Klein puts it, "It seems probable that depressive anxiety, guilt and the reparative tendency are only experienced when feelings of love for the object predominate over destructive impulses" (Klein, p. 285). So ambivalence requires a certain balance to be effective in producing remorse and guilt, and Freud *may* believe that balance can be achieved only after the deed: "After their hatred had been satisfied by their act of aggression, their love came to the fore in their remorse for the deed" (1930a, XXI, 132; cf. 1912–13, XIII, 143, n. 1).

Some analysts, including Klein, argue that guilt develops earlier (oral or anal stage) than the Oedipal stage.

106, n.), is not enough to explain repression. Interestingly, in his *Three Essays on the Theory of Sexuality*, Freud treats shame as "organically determined and fixed by heredity" (1905d, VII, 177), but also as having a cultural source in the history of the race:

> . . . these forces which act like dams upon sexual development—disgust, shame and morality—must also be regarded as historical precipitates of the external inhibitions to which the sexual instinct has been subjected during the psychogenesis of the human race. We can observe the way in which, in the development of individuals, they arise at the appropriate moment, as though spontaneously, when upbringing and external influence give the signal. (1905d, VII, 162, n. 2)

Thus, oddly, an instinct is born. Freud does not think it odd: ". . . we must not exaggerate the difference between inherited and acquired characters into an antithesis; what was acquired by our forefathers certainly forms an important part of what we inherit" (1937c, XXIII, 240). I want to agree that the contrast between instinctual motivations and social influences (especially in producing repression) cannot be taken as clear and absolute (this was a main point in our discussion of the universality of the Oedipus complex), but I wish to maintain a narrower conception of "instinct" and a more complex notion of its interaction with culture and environment than Freud's unacceptable Lamarckianism allows.

Certainly we inherit much from our forefathers, but it need not come through our genes. Freud appeals to Lamarckianism to hold the historical steps of his account together. This would be unobjectionable if Lamarckianism were true, but since it is not, other mechanisms must be appealed to. And once they are brought in, they make the historical conjecture itself otiose (even if, by chance, true). Freud himself has illuminated many of the mechanisms of transmission. For example, it is the parent's super-ego, rather than the parent, that gets internalized (in either case it is, of course, the psychical representation that gets internalized):

> As a rule parents and authorities analogous to them follow the precepts of their own super-egos in educating children. . . . They have forgotten the difficulties of their own childhood and they are glad to be able now to identify themselves fully with their own parents who in the past laid such severe restrictions upon them. Thus a child's super-ego is in fact constructed on the model not of its parents

but of its parents' super-ego; the contents which fill it are the same and it becomes the vehicle of tradition and of all the time-resisting judgements of value which have propagated themselves in this manner from generation to generation. . . . The past, the tradition of the race and of the people, lives on in the ideologies of the super-ego, and yields only slowly to the influences of the present and to new changes . . . (1933a, XXII, 67)

And the strength of the super-ego is due to various complex mechanisms. It is reinforced when aggression is projected onto an external authority figure and then internalized with it, or when aggression meets a solid wall of acceptance and is turned inward (that is, in the face of parental love and kindness, the child feels himself that much worse). As Melanie Klein emphasized, "the severity of the super-ego which a child develops in no way corresponds to the severity of treatment which he has himself met with" (1930a, XXI, 130). Guilt is a force of repression, but is itself reinforced by repression. Dependence leads to ambivalence about aggressive feelings (whether these are primary or the result of instinctual renunciation imposed from without), and with the creation of the super-ego by identification with the unattackable authority, "every piece of aggression whose satisfaction the subject gives up is taken over by the super-ego and increases the latter's aggressiveness (against the ego)" (1930a, XXI, 129).

In the pre-super-ego world restricted to "remorse,"[12] what made an act "bad" was conflict with the interests and wishes of some external authority on whom the individual was dependent. (So *anything* could be the object of remorse.) With the super-ego there is now an internal authority. But it is not clear that that is the step that produces morality and civilization. Morality depends more on the character and source of the principles involved than their location. As we have seen, the totemic taboos, created by the institution of society, do not make the acts they prohibit in any stronger sense "crimes." The prohibitions are backed by the combined strength of the brothers, but though greater it is not different from the strength of the primal father. In the early stages,

. . . the sense of guilt is clearly only a fear of loss of love, "social" anxiety. In small children it can never be anything else, but in many adults, too, it has only changed to the extent that the place of the

---

[12] It is worth noting that though this is the world of the very young child, it is not necessarily the world of the primitive.

father or the two parents is taken by the larger human community. Consequently, such people habitually allow themselves to do any bad thing which promises them enjoyment, so long as they are sure that the authority will not know anything about it or cannot blame them for it; they are afraid only of being found out. . . . A great change takes place only when the authority is internalized through the establishment of a super-ego. The phenomena of conscience then reach a higher stage. Actually, it is not until now that we should speak of conscience or a sense of guilt. (1930a, XXI, 125)

Internalized, the prohibitions form part of the shared super-ego. Each now fears the loss of the other's love, not only because of deeds but also because of desires ("since nothing can be hidden from the super-ego, not even thoughts"). But Freud can go no further in explaining guilt as a reaction to the transgression of moral principles than he can in explaining the "moral" character of totemic principles. It is not (simply) a matter of democratic strength. Even of democratic strength internalized.[13]

JUSTIFYING GUILT

Feelings of guilt, in the strict sense, are not detachable from acknowledged moral wrongs. One may be guiltless and still feel guilty, but this is because we (sometimes and for some purposes) blur the difference between action and intention. Given a strong enough super-ego, we can sin in thought alone and feel guilty for it. But sometimes we have not sinned even in thought, we just think we have, and then our guilt may be neurotic. Whether guilt in a particular case *is* "neurotic" will depend on the particular explanation of our mistake; guilt may be exaggerated or otherwise unjustified without being neurotic.[14] This can happen in a variety of ways, that

[13] Another way of putting it is to say that Freud contributes to our understanding of authority guilt and association guilt, but not principle guilt. What gets left out are the important connections of guilt as a moral feeling with moral concepts and principles (and beliefs about them). See John Rawls's (1963) valuable discussion.

[14] In explaining a neurotic symptom psychoanalytically we show it to be a *neurotic* symptom; i.e., if its explanation were purely physiological (for example) it would not be "neurotic." What sort of explanation is possible (available) determines what the thing to be explained is. The character of the thing to be explained is not "given" independently of the possibilities of explanation (the explanation we offer).

is, we can make a variety of mistakes. We may believe we have committed a heinous wrong, but in fact have *done* nothing. More interestingly, what we in fact did or wanted to do may not really be wrong. What is regarded as wrong varies from culture to culture. "Since the sense of guilt depends on the internalization of social values and ideals it is impossible to assess whether someone has a moral or neurotic sense of guilt unless one is familiar with the culture in which he lives and understands every nuance of its system of values" (Rycroft, p. 40). But one may wish to argue that an entire culture is "neurotic," that its system of values is itself "wrong." To sustain such a claim would require very general discussion of "humanity," "rationality," and moral concepts and principles. Freud does not need to justify totemic guilt in order to explain it. As we have seen, however, he has not shown that the guilt he explains is "moral" or "principle" guilt. It is also worth emphasizing that he has not explained it away, i.e., it may be the case both that totemic guilt is moral *and* that his explanation is true (as far as it goes). Further, we can see that though the guilt that sustains totemic prohibitions against killing and incest may be justifiable (certainly guilt is *appropriate* given the prohibitions, i.e., it is not neurotic within the society), it is not justified *by* Freud's explanation of its source. Can unjustified (e.g., inherited, defensive . . .) guilt itself justify later actions and restrictions on action? Having raised the question, I will note only that the suffering created by such guilt is real enough, and the fear of such suffering is real too. These could become the justification for action; but often the action should be treatment of the guilt (attacking the mistakes) rather than avoidance by compliance. And though guilt (whatever its source) may be a factor to weigh in, it does not follow that guilt is a cost we can never afford to bear. (See Mead, and Rycroft, p. 44.)

A genetic explanation is sometimes the only "justification" that can be given (we often excuse ourselves by presenting the steps that led us to do what we did), but to explain is not to justify. Freud was in general aware of this.[15] Still, one would like to know why Freud

---

[15] In the case of the "Rat Man," Freud reports: ". . . I pointed out to him that he ought logically to consider himself in no way responsible for any of these traits in his character; for all of these reprehensible impulses originated from his infancy, and were only derivatives of his infantile character surviving in his unconscious; and he must know that moral responsibility could not be applied to children. . . . I only produced these arguments so as once more to

felt he had reached the "origin" of a phenomenon only when he could trace it back to a "father," and why it was only after the death of his own father that he could trace his own origins (in his self-analysis). Erik Erikson speaks of the "originology" of psychoanalysis:

> In its determination to be sparing with teleological assumption, psychoanalysis has gone to the opposite extreme and developed a kind of *originology* . . . I mean by it a habit of thinking which reduces every human situation to an analogy with an earlier one, and most of all to that earliest, simplest and most infantile precursor which is assumed to be its "origin." . . . In exclusively studying what is repetition and regression and perseveration in human life, we have learned more about the infantile in the adult than was ever before known. We have thus prepared an ethical reorientation in human life which centers on the preservation of those early energies which man, in the very service of his higher values, is apt to suppress, exploit or waste. In each treatment, and in all our applications, this reorientation governs our conscious intentions. . . .
> . . . we were dismayed when we saw our purpose of enlightenment perverted into a widespread fatalism, according to which man is nothing but a multiplication of his parents' faults and an accumulation of his own earlier selves. We must grudgingly admit that even as we were trying to devise, with scientific determinism, a therapy for the few, we were led to promote an ethical disease among the many. (Erikson, pp. 18–19)

OEDIPAL EXPLANATION

Finally, Lévi-Strauss raises a question, not about the justification provided by genetic explanation, but about its possibility (at least where it refers, as Freud's does, to recurring feelings):

> Contrary to what Freud maintained, social constraints, whether positive or negative, cannot be explained, either in their origin or in their persistence, as the effects of impulses or emotions which appear again and again, with the same characteristics and during the course of centuries and millennia, in different individuals. For if the recurrence of the sentiments explained the persistence of customs, the origin of the customs ought to coincide with the origin

---

demonstrate to myself their inefficacy. I cannot understand how other psychotherapists can assert that they successfully combat neuroses with such weapons as these" (1909d, X, 185 and 185, n. 2).

of the appearance of the sentiments . . . (Lévi-Strauss, 1963, pp. 69–70)

First, it is not clear that this applies to Freud's account at all. The parricidal (or Oedipal) impulse is meant to be a recurring feature of human life; but "guilt" is supposed to be something new in the world: it does not (according to Freud's account) become a recurring sentiment until after the primal crime. And totemism is the result of inclination to parricide *plus* guilt arising out of ambivalence after the deed. So, in Freud's story, the customs do seem to appear with the origin of the (or an) explaining sentiment. Still, it must be admitted that it is not clear that one needs the sort of internalization involved in guilt in order to have totemism (Steiner, p. 26). Why should ambivalence and remorse not be enough to lead to the social contract (even if it is maintained by external authorities)? And, of course, we have seen that it should be possible to dispense with Freud's historical claims in accounting for guilt and totemism. Secondly, on a more abstract level, the origin of the impulse need not be, as Lévi-Strauss seems to assume, the simultaneous origin of all its effects. A recurrent impulse can explain the origin or at least persistence of a custom, while of course something else must explain the earlier non-existence of the custom (despite the presence of the impulse). (Cf. Freud on "Tubercle bacillus" [1896c, I, 209].) Again we must note that genetic explanations are not (usually) the presentation of sufficient conditions. More often they reveal which disjunct (not itself necessary) of a disjunctively necessary set of conditions actually operated (Gallie). Sometimes (depending on the setting of the problem) they specify a condition (not itself necessary) which is an instance, i.e., fits, a general description (not disjunctive) of what is a necessary condition (e.g., a reason may be specified which was "the very compelling reason" which must have operated). What counts as an explanation depends on what you need and want to know.

Admittedly, an impulse cannot be *the* cause of a custom which did not begin when the impulse began: something else, or the removal of something else, must explain why the custom appeared when it did and not before. (See note 11 on need for deed.) But this does not preclude the impulse explaining the persistence of the custom, or even figuring as *a* cause in the explanation of its origin. One cannot explain everything at once.

REFERENCES

Brown, Norman O. *Love's Body* (Vintage, New York, 1966).

Erikson, Erik H. *Young Man Luther* (Norton Lib., New York, 1962).

Feldman, Sandor S. "Notes on the 'Primal Horde,' " in *Psychoanalysis and the Social Sciences,* Vol. I, ed. Géza Róheim (Int. Univs. Press, New York, 1947), pp. 171–93.

Fenichel, Otto. *The Psychoanalytic Theory of Neurosis* (Norton, New York, 1945).

Fox, Robin. "*Totem and Taboo* Reconsidered," in *The Structural Study of Myth and Totemism,* ed. Edmund Leach (Tavistock Publications, London, 1967), pp. 161–78.

Gallie, W. B. "Explanations in History and the Genetic Sciences," in *Theories of History,* ed. Patrick Gardiner (Free Press, New York, 1959), pp. 386–402.

Hempel, C. G. *Aspects of Scientific Explanation* (Free Press, New York, 1965), pp. 447–53.

Jones, Ernest. "Mother-Right and the Sexual Ignorance of Savages," *International Journal of Psycho-Analysis* 6 (1925), pp. 109–30.

Klein, Melanie. "On the Theory of Anxiety and Guilt," in *Developments in Psycho-Analysis,* ed. Joan Riviere (Hogarth, London, 1952), pp. 271–91.

Kroeber, A. L. "*Totem and Taboo:* An Ethnologic Psychoanalysis" (1920), in *The Nature of Culture* (Univ. of Chicago Press, Chicago, 1952), pp. 301–5.

———. "*Totem and Taboo* in Retrospect" (1939), in ibid., pp. 306–9.

Lévi-Strauss, Claude. "The Family," in *Man, Culture and Society,* ed. Henry L. Shapiro (Oxford Univ. Press, New York, 1960), pp. 261–85.

———. *Totemism* (Beacon Press, Boston, 1963).

Malinowski, Bronislaw. *Sex and Repression in Savage Society* (Kegan Paul, Trench, Truebner & Co., London, 1927).

Mead, Margaret. "Some Anthropological Considerations Concerning Guilt," in *Feelings and Emotions* (the Mooseheart Symposium), ed. Martin Reymert (McGraw, New York, 1950), pp. 362–73.

Nagel, Ernest. *The Structure of Science* (Harcourt, New York, 1961), pp. 25, 564–68.

Parsons, Anne. "Is the Oedipus Complex Universal? The Jones-Malinowski Debate Revisited and a South Italian Nuclear Complex," in *The Psychoanalytic Study of Society,* Vol. III, ed. Warner Muensterberger and Sidney Axelrod (Int. Univs. Press, New York, 1964), pp. 278–328.

Rawls, John. "The Sense of Justice," *Philosophical Review* 72 (1963), pp. 281–305; and (revised) chap. 8 in *A Theory of Justice* (Harvard Univ. Press, Cambridge, Mass., 1971).

Rieff, Philip. "The Meaning of History and Religion in Freud's Thought," in *Psychoanalysis and History,* ed. Bruce Mazlish (Prentice-Hall, Englewood Cliffs, 1963), pp. 23–44.

Roazen, Paul. *Freud: Political and Social Thought* (Hogarth, London, 1969).

Róheim, Géza. "Oedipus Complex, Magic and Culture," in *Psychoanalysis and the Social Sciences,* Vol. II, ed. Géza Róheim (Int. Univs. Press, New York, 1950a), pp. 173–228.

———. *Psychoanalysis and Anthropology* (Int. Univs. Press, New York, 1950b).

Rycroft, Charles. *Anxiety and Neurosis* (Allen Lane the Penguin Press, London, 1968).

Steiner, Franz. *Taboo* (Penguin, Baltimore, 1957).

Whiting, John. "*Totem and Taboo*—A Re-evaluation," in *Psychoanalysis and Human Values,* ed. Jules Masserman (Grune, New York, 1960), pp. 150–54.

WORKS OF FREUD CITED

1891b	*On Aphasia*
1892–93b	"A Case of Successful Treatment by Hypnotism"
1893a	(with J. Breuer) "On the Psychical Mechanism of Hysterical Phenomena: Preliminary Communication"
1893c	"Some Points for a Comparative Study of Organic and Hysterical Motor Paralysis"
1893f	"Charcot"
1893h	"On the Psychical Mechanism of Hysterical Phenomena"
1894a	"The Neuro-Psychoses of Defence"
1895d	(with J. Breuer) *Studies on Hysteria*
1896a	"Heredity and the Aetiology of the Neuroses"
1896b	"Further Remarks on the Neuro-Psychoses of Defence"
1896c	"The Aetiology of Hysteria"
1897a	*Die infantile Cerebrallähmuny*
1897b	*Abstracts of the Scientific Writings of Dr. Sigmund Freud*
1900a	*The Interpretation of Dreams*
1901a	*On Dreams*
1901b	*The Psychopathology of Everyday Life*
1905d	*Three Essays on the Theory of Sexuality*
1905e [1901]	"Fragment of an Analysis of a Case of Hysteria"
1906a	"My Views on the Part Played by Sexuality in the Aetiology of the Neuroses"
1906c	"Psycho-analysis and the Establishment of Facts in Legal Proceedings"
1907c	"The Sexual Enlightenment of Children"

1908b	"Character and Anal Erotism"
1908c	"On the Sexual Theories of Children"
1908d	" 'Civilized' Sexual Morality and Modern Nervous Illness"
1908e	"Creative Writers and Day-Dreaming"
1909b	"Analysis of a Phobia in a Five-Year-Old Boy"
1909d	"Notes upon a Case of Obsessional Neurosis"
1910a	*Five Lectures on Psycho-Analysis*
1910c	*Leonardo da Vinci and a Memory of his Childhood*
1910i	"The Psycho-Analytic View of Psychogenic Disturbance"
1911b	"Formulations on the Two Principles of Mental Functioning"
1911c	"Psychoanalytic Notes on an Autobiographical Account of a Case of Paranoia (Dementia Paranoides)"
1912c	"Types of Onset of Neurosis"
1912d	"On the Universal Tendency to Debasement in the Sphere of Love"
1912g	"A Note on the Unconscious in Psycho-Analysis"
1912–13	*Totem and Taboo*
1913j	"The Claims of Psycho-Analysis to Scientific Interest"
1914c	"On Narcissism: an Introduction"
1914d	"On the History of the Psycho-Analytic Movement"
1914e	"The Representation in a Dream of a 'Great Achievement' "
1915a	"Observations on Transference-Love (Further Recommendation on the Technique of Psycho-Analysis)"
1915c	"Instincts and their Vicissitudes"
1915d	"Repression"
1915e	"The Unconscious"

1916–17   *Introductory Lectures on Psycho-Analysis*

1917a   "A Difficulty in the Path of Psycho-Analysis"

1917c   "On Transformation of Instinct as Exemplified in Anal Erotism"

1917d   "A Metapsychological Supplement to the Theory of Dreams"

1917e [1915]   "Mourning and Melancholia"

1918b [1914]   "From the History of an Infantile Neurosis"

1919a   "Lines of Advance in Psycho-Analytic Therapy"

1920a   "Psychogenesis of a Case of Female Homosexuality"

1920g   *Beyond the Pleasure Principle*

1921c   *Group Psychology and the Analysis of the Ego*

1922b   "Some Neurotic Mechanisms in Jealousy, Paranoia and Homosexuality"

1923a   Two Encyclopaedia Articles

1923b   *The Ego and the Id*

1924b   "Neurosis and Psychosis"

1924c   "The Economic Problem of Masochism"

1924e   "The Loss of Reality in Neurosis and Psychosis"

1925a   "A Note upon the 'Mystic Writing Pad' "

1925d [1924]   *An Autobiographical Study*

1925i   "Some Additional Notes upon Dream-Interpretation as a Whole"

1925j   "Some Psychological Consequences of the Anatomical Distinction between the Sexes"

1926d   *Inhibitions, Symptoms and Anxiety*

1926e   *The Question of Lay Analysis*

1926f   "Psycho-Analysis": an article in the *Encyclopaedia Britannica*

1927c   *The Future of an Illusion*

1928b   "Dostoievsky and Parricide"

1930a   *Civilization and Its Discontents*

1931a   "Libidinal Types"

1933a   *New Introductory Lectures on Psychoanalysis*

1937c   "Analysis Terminable and Interminable"

1937d   "Constructions in Analysis"

1939a [1937–39]   *Moses and Monotheism*

1940a [1938]   *An Outline of Psychoanalysis*

1940b [1938]   "Some Elementary Lessons in Psychoanalysis"

1940d [1892]   "On the Theory of Hysterical Attacks"

1940e [1938]   "Splitting of the Ego in the Process of Defence"

1950a [1887–1902]   *The Origins of Psychoanalysis* (including "A Project for a Scientific Psychology")

BIBLIOGRAPHY

ALEXANDER, Peter, and MACINTYRE, Alasdair. "Cause and Cure in Psychotherapy," *Proc. Arist. Soc. Supp.* 29 (1955), pp. 25–58.

BERGMANN, G. "Psychoanalysis and Experimental Psychology," *Mind* 52 (1943), pp. 352–70.

CIOFFI, Frank. "Wittgenstein's Freud" in *Studies in the Philosophy of Wittgenstein,* ed. Peter Winch (Routledge, London, 1969).

———. "Freud and the Idea of a Pseudo-Science" in *Explanation in the Behavioural Sciences,* ed. Robert Borger and Frank Cioffi (Cambridge, Cambridge, 1970).

———. Review Discussion of Richard Wollheim, *Freud,* in *Inquiry* 15 (1972), pp. 171–86.

COLBY, K. M. *Energy and Structure in Psychoanalysis* (Ronald, New York, 1955).

DILMAN, I. "The Unconscious," *Mind* 68 (1959), pp. 446–73.

ELLIS, Albert. "An Operational Reformulation of Some of the Basic Principles of Psychoanalysis," in *Minnesota Studies in the Philosophy of Science,* Vol. I, ed. Herbert Feigl and Michael Scriven (Univ. of Minn. Press, Minneapolis, 1956).

EZRIEL, H. "Experimentation within the Psycho-analytic Session," *Br. J. Phil. Sci.* VII (1956–57), pp. 29–48.

FARRELL, B. A. "Can Psychoanalysis Be Refuted?," *Inquiry* 4 (1961), pp. 16–36.

———. "Introduction," in S. Freud, *Leonardo,* trans. A. Tyson, (Penguin, Harmondsworth, Middlesex, 1963), pp. 11–91.

———. "The Status of Psychoanalytic Theory," *Inquiry* 7 (1964), pp. 104–23.

———. Comment on Frank Cioffi's "Freud and the Idea of a Pseudo-Science" in *Explanation in the Behavioural Sciences,* ed. Robert Borger and Frank Cioffi (Cambridge, Cambridge, 1970).

———. "The Validity of Psychotherapy," *Inquiry* 15 (1972), pp. 146–70.

——, WISDOM, J. O., TURQUET, P. M. "The Criteria for a Psychoanalytic Interpretation," *Proc. Arist. Soc. Supp.* 36 (1962), pp. 77–144.

FINGARETTE, Herbert. "'Unconscious Behavior' and Allied Concepts: A New Approach to their Empirical Interpretation," *J. Phil.* 47 (1950), pp. 509–20.

——. "Psychoanalytic Perspectives on Moral Guilt and Responsibility," *Phil. Phenomenol. Res.* 16 (1955–56), pp. 18–36.

——. *Self-Deception* (Routledge, London, 1969).

FLEW, Antony. "Psycho-Analytic Explanation," *Analysis* 10 (1949–50), pp. 8–15. Reprinted in *Philosophy and Analysis,* ed. Margaret Macdonald (Blackwell, Oxford, 1954).

——. "Motives and the Unconscious," in *Minnesota Studies in the Philosophy of Science,* Vol. I, ed. Herbert Feigl and Michael Scriven (Univ. of Minn. Press, Minneapolis, 1956).

FRENKEL-BRUNSWIK, E. "Psychoanalysis and the Unity of Science," *Proc. Amer. Acad. Arts Scien.* 80 (1954), pp. 271–350.

GLOVER, Jonathan. "Freud, Morality and Responsibility," in *Freud: the Man, His World, His Influence,* ed. Jonathan Miller (Weidenfeld, London, 1972).

GOLDMAN, Alvin I. *A Theory of Human Action* (Prentice-Hall, Englewood Cliffs, N.J., 1970).

HARTMANN, Heinz. *Essays on Ego-Psychology* (Hogarth, London, 1964).

———, KRIS, Ernst, and LOEWENSTEIN, Rudolph M. *Papers on Psychoanalytic Psychology* (Int. Univs. Press, New York, 1964).

HILGARD, Ernest R. "The Scientific Status of Psychoanalysis," in *Logic, Methodology and Philosophy of Science:* Proceedings of the 1960 International Congress, eds. E. Nagel, P. Suppes, and A. Tarski (Stanford Univ. Press, 1962), pp. 375–90.

HOOK, Sidney (ed.) *Psychoanalysis, Scientific Method and Philosophy* (N.Y. Univ. Press, New York, 1959).

HUTTEN, E. H. "On Explanation in Psychology and in Physics," *Br. J. Phil. Sci.* VII (1956–57), pp. 73–85.

JONES, David H. "Freud's Theory of Moral Conscience," *Philosophy* 41, no. 155 (January 1966), pp. 34–57.

JONES, G. Seaborn. *Treatment or Torture* (Tavistock Publications, London, 1968).

KRIS, Ernst. "Psychoanalytic Propositions," in *Psychological Theory*, ed. M. H. Marx (Macmillan, New York, 1951), pp. 322–51.

LACAN, Jacques. *The Language of the Self*, trans. and ed. Anthony Wilden (Johns Hopkins Press, Baltimore, 1968).

MACINTYRE, Alasdair. *The Unconscious* (Routledge, London, 1958).

MADISON, P. *Freud's Concept of Repression and Defense, Its Theoretical and Observational Language* (Univ. of Minn. Press, Minneapolis, 1961).

MARTIN, Michael. "Mr. Farrell and the Refutability of Psychoanalysis," *Inquiry* 7 (1964), pp. 80–98.

——, MARGOLIN, Sydney G., CHRISTIANSEN, Björn. "The Scientific Status of Psychoanalytic Clinical Evidence," *Inquiry* 7 (1964), pp. 13–79.

MILES, T. R. *Eliminating the Unconscious* (Pergamon, London, 1966).

MISCHEL, Theodore. "Psychology and Explanations of Human Behaviour," *Phil. Phenomenol. Res.* 23 (1962–63), pp. 578–94.

——. "Understanding Neurotic Behavior: from 'Mechanism' to 'Intentionality,'" in *Understanding Other Persons*, ed. T. Mischel (Blackwell, Oxford, 1973).

MORRIS, Herbert. "Guilt and Punishment," *The Personalist* 52, no. 2 (Spring 1971), pp. 305–21.

——. "Guilt and Suffering," *Philosophy East and West* 21, no. 4 (October 1971), pp. 419–34.

PETERS, R. S. "Cause, Cure and Motive," *Analysis* 10 (1949–50), pp. 103–9. Reprinted in *Philosophy and Analysis*, ed. Margaret Macdonald (Blackwell, Oxford, 1954).

——. "Freud's Theory," *Br. J. Phil. Sci.* 7 (1956–57), pp. 4–12.

——. *The Concept of Motivation* (Routledge, London, 1958).

PODRO, Michael. "Art and Freud's Displacement of Aesthetics," in *Freud: the Man, His World, His Influence*, ed. Jonathan Miller (Weidenfeld, London, 1972).

PRIBRAM, Karl. "The Neuropsychology of Sigmund Freud," in *Experimental Foundations of Clinical Psychology*, ed. Arthur J. Bachrach (Basic Bks., New York, 1962).

PUMPIAN-MINDLIN, E., ed. *Psycho-Analysis as Science* (Basic Bks., New York, 1952).

RAPAPORT, David. *The Collected Papers,* ed. M. M. Gill (Basic Bks., New York, 1967).

——. *The Structure of Psychoanalytic Theory: a Systematizing Attempt* (Int. Univs. Press, New York, 1960).

RICOEUR, Paul. *Freud and Philosophy: an Essay in Interpretation,* trans. David Savage (Yale Univ. Press, New Haven, 1970).

RIEFF, Philip. "Freudian Ethics and the Idea of Reason," *Ethics* 67 (1956–57), pp. 169–83.

——. *Freud: The Mind of the Moralist* (Gollancz, London, 1959).

ROAZEN, Paul. *Freud: Political and Social Thought* (Hogarth Press, London, 1969).

RUSSELL, Bertrand. *The Analysis of Mind* (G. Allen, London, 1921).

RYCROFT, Charles, ed. *Psychoanalysis Observed* (Constable, London, 1966).

SCRIVEN, Michael. "The Frontiers of Psychology: Psychoanalysis and Parapsychology," in *Frontiers of Science and Philosophy,* ed. Robert G. Colodny (G. Allen, London, 1964).

SHERWOOD, Michael. *The Logic of Explanation in Psychoanalysis* (Academic Press, New York and London, 1969).

SHOPE, Robert K. "The Psychoanalytic Theories of Wish-Fulfilment and Meaning," *Inquiry* 10 (1967), pp. 421–28.

——. "Freud on Conscious and Unconscious Intentions," *Inquiry* 13 (1970), pp. 149–59.

——. "Dispositional Treatment of Psychoanalytic Motivational Terms," *J. Phil.,* LXVII (1970), pp. 195–208.

——. "Physical and Psychic Energy," *Philosophy of Science,* 38 (1971), pp. 1–11.

SIEGLER, Frederick A. "Unconscious Intentions," *Inquiry* 10 (1967), pp. 251–67.

SKINNER, B. F. "Critique of Psychoanalytic Concepts and Theories," in *Minnesota Studies in the Philosophy of Science,* Vol. I, ed. Herbert Feigl and Michael Scriven (Univ. of Minn. Press, Minneapolis, 1956).

SMYTHIES, J. R. (with COPPEN, A. and KREITMAN, N.). *Biological Psychiatry: A Review of Recent Advances* (Heinemann, London, 1968).

SPECTOR, Jack J. *The Aesthetics of Freud* (Allen Lane, London, 1972).

STARKE, J. G. *The Validity of Psycho-Analysis* (Angus, Sydney, 1973).

TOULMIN, Stephen. "The Logical Status of Psycho-Analysis," *Analysis* 9 (1948–49), pp. 23–29. Reprinted in *Philosophy and Analysis,* ed. Margaret Macdonald (Blackwell, Oxford, 1954).

WALKER, N. "Freud and Homeostasis," *Br. J. Phil. Sci.* 7 (1956–57), pp. 61–72.

WILDEN, Anthony. *System and Structure* (Tavistock Publications, London, 1972).

WISDOM, J. O. "Psycho-analytic Technology," *Br. J. Phil. Sci.* 7 (1956–57), pp. 13–28.

——. "A Methodological Approach to the Problem of Hysteria," *Int. J. Psycho-Anal.* 42 (1961), Part III, pp. 224–37.

——. "Comparison and Development of the Psycho-analytical Theories of Melancholia," *Int. J. Psycho-Anal.,* 43 (1962), Parts II–III, pp. 113–32.

——. "A Methodological Approach to the Problem of Obsessional Neurosis," *Br. J. of Med. Psychology* 34 (1964), pp. 111–22.

——. "What is the Explanatory Theory of Obsessional Neurosis?", *Br. J. of Med. Psychology* 39 (1966), pp. 335–48.

——. "Freud and Melanie Klein: Psychology, Ontology, and Weltanschauung," in *Psychoanalysis and Philosophy,* ed. Charles Hanley and Morris Lazerowitz (Int. Univs. Press, New York, 1970).

WOLLHEIM, Richard. "The Mind and the Mind's Image of Itself," *Int. J. Psycho-Anal.* 50 (1969), pp. 209–20. Reprinted in Richard Wollheim, *On Art and the Mind* (Allen Lane, London, 1973).

——. "Freud and the Understanding of Art," *Br. J. Aesthetics* 10 (1970), pp. 211–24. Reprinted as above.

——. *Sigmund Freud* (Collins, London, and Viking, New York, 1971).

CONTRIBUTORS

PETER ALEXANDER is Professor of Philosophy at Bristol University. He is the author of *Sensationalism and Scientific Explanation* and *Introduction to Logic*.

MARGARET BODEN teaches philosophy and psychology at the University of Sussex. She is the author of *Purposive Explanation in Psychology*.

HERBERT FINGARETTE is Professor of Philosophy in the University of California, Santa Barbara. He has written on the philosophy of mind and the philosophy of law. He is the author of *The Self in Transformation; On Responsibility; Self-Deception;* and *The Meaning of Criminal Insanity*.

CLARK GLYMOUR teaches philosophy at Princeton University. His principal interests lie in the philosophy of science.

STUART HAMPSHIRE is Warden of Wadham College, Oxford. He has taught philosophy at London, Oxford and Princeton. He is the author of *Spinoza; Thought and Action; Freedom of the Individual; Freedom of Mind;* and *Modern Writers and Other Essays*.

JOHN C. MARSHALL works at the Medical Research Council's Speech and Communication Unit at the University of Edinburgh. His work is principally in psycho-linguistics. He is a joint editor of *Language: Selected Readings*.

THEODORE MISCHEL is Professor of Philosophy at the State University of New York at Binghamton. He is the editor of *Human Action* and *Cognitive Development and Epistemology*.

THOMAS NAGEL teaches philosophy at Princeton University. He has written in the philosophy of mind and on moral and social philosophy. He is the author of *The Possibility of Altruism*.

JEROME NEU teaches philosophy at the University of California, Santa Cruz.

BRIAN O'SHAUGHNESSY teaches philosophy at Bedford College London. He has written widely in the philosophy of mind.

DAVID PEARS is Research Student at Christ Church Oxford. He has held visiting professorships at various American universities. He is the author of *Bertrand Russell and the British Tradition in Philosophy; Wittgenstein; What is Knowledge?;* and is the editor of a collection of essays on Hume.

DAVID SACHS is Professor of Philosophy at Johns Hopkins University, Baltimore. He has written articles on the interpretation of Greek philosophy. He has published verse in various magazines.

WESLEY SALMON is Professor of Philosophy at the University of Arizona. His interests lie in induction and the philosophy of science. He is the author of *Logic; The Foundations of Scientific Inference;* and *Statistical Explanation and Statistical Relevance.* He edited *Zeno's Paradoxes.*

JEAN-PAUL SARTRE first introduced Husserl to France and his early books on the imagination were of a strongly phenomenological character. His most notable philosophical works are *Being and Nothingness* and *Critique of Dialectical Reason.* In his later writings he has been heavily influenced by Marxism. He has also written novels, plays and literary criticism, including studies of Baudelaire, Genet and Flaubert.

ROBERT C. SOLOMON teaches philosophy at the University of Texas in Austin. He is the author of *From Rationalism to Existentialism: The Existentialists and their Nineteenth Century Backgrounds.* He is the editor of *Phenomenology and Existentialism* and the volume on Nietzsche in this series.

RONALD DE SOUSA teaches philosophy at Toronto University. He has written articles on epistemology, philosophical logic and the philosophy of mind.

IRVING THALBERG is Professor of Philosophy at the University of Illinois at Chicago Circle. He has written a number of articles on the philosophy of mind, and is the author of *Enigmas of Agency.*

FREDRIC WEISS teaches philosophy and political economy at Ramapo College, New Jersey.

J. O. WISDOM is now Professor of Philosophy at York University, Toronto, having taught for many years at the London School of Economics. He has written extensively on scientific method and the methodology of psycho-analysis. He is the author of *Foundations of Inference in Natural Science* and *The Unconscious Origin of Berkeley's Philosophy*.

LUDWIG WITTGENSTEIN was born in Vienna in 1889 and died in Cambridge in 1951. He wrote the *Tractatus Logic-Philosophicus*. His posthumous publications include *Philosophical Investigations; The Blue and Brown Books; Remarks on the Foundations of Mathematics;* and *On Certainty*. His influence on the philosophy of the twentieth century has been understandably vast.

RICHARD WOLLHEIM is Grote Professor of Philosophy of Mind and Logic at University College London. He is the author of *F. H. Bradley; Art and its Objects; Freud; On Art and the Mind;* and a novel, *A Family Romance*.

INDEX